THE GOOD NANNY GUIDE

The Good Nanny Guide is written by two mothers with more than thirty years of hiring and firing nannies, mother's helps, maternity nurses and au pairs between them. They have drawn on the experience of hundreds of employers, nannies, training colleges and agencies to produce a unique reference book which aims principally to give parents comprehensive information about, and the confidence to cope with, the business of employing someone to care for their child in their own home.

Charlotte Breese and Hilaire Gomer met in the maternity ward of the West London Hospital when each was having her first child. Now they have nine between them. They have experienced just about every form of child care. Charlotte Breese has employed living-in NNEB-trained nannies, maternity nurses and temporary nannies. Hilaire Gomer has hired daily and living-in nannies, mother's helps, au pairs and childminders.

Charlotte Breese worked as a publisher's editor and helped to pioneer the market for information books on the Middle East. Hilaire Gomer is a freelance journalist who has worked for numerous national newspapers.

THE
GOOD NANNY GUIDE

The Complete Handbook on Nannies, Au Pairs, Mother's Helps, Day Nurseries and Childminders

CHARLOTTE BREESE AND HILAIRE GOMER

VERMILION
LONDON

For Olivia and in memory of Georgia

First published by Century Hutchinson Limited in 1988

This edition published in 1997 by Vermilion
an imprint of Ebury Press
Random House, 20 Vauxhall Bridge Road
London SW1V 2SA

Random House Australia (Pty) Limited
20 Alfred Street, Milsons Point, Sydney,
New South Wales 2061, Australia

Random House New Zealand Limited
18 Poland Road, Glenfield, Auckland 10, New Zealand

Random House South Africa (Pty) Ltd
Endulini, 5a Jubilee Road, Parktown 2193, South Africa

Random House UK Limited Reg. No. 954009

Catalogue record for this book is available from
the British Library.

ISBN 0 09 181551 7

Printed and bound in Great Britain by
Mackays of Chatham plc, Chatham, Kent

Papers used by Ebury Press are natural recyclable products
made from wood grown in sustainable forests.

Contents

Acknowledgements

We are indebted to all the following employers for filling in a detailed questionnaire well:

Serena Ballin, Nicky Baring, Claudia Bartosik, Kipper Bosanquet, Judith Becher, Imogen Mary Birch-Reynardson, Judi Bodenham, Sarah Bolton, Victoria Borwick, Charlotte Burnaby-Atkins, Carolyn Chambers, Renu Chopra, Sarah Cottenham, Ros Caldecott, Caroline Davidson, Sarah Douglas-Pennant, Juliet Dunn, Elinor Elliott, Patricia Elliott, Damaris Fletcher, Susie Green-Armytage, Mary Hall, Siri Harris, Rachel James, Kay King, Lucy Le Fanu, Jean Letts, Penny Lucy, Philippa Lloyd, Loraine Melville, Victoria Moger, Cheryl Mowinckel, Emma Mumtaz, Bunny Murray-Willis, Katie Neilson, Jane Nerizzano, Kathy Pflaum, Fiona Peel, Laura Pym, Phyllis Rennell, Tish Seligman, Caroline Serocold, Gill Smith, Elodie Stanley, Davina Thackara, Mary-Rose Thompson, Anne Tickell, Sarah Tillie, David Toms, Bridgett Walters, Rebecca Willer, Cherry Williams, Sarah Williams, Victoria Wilson, Suzanne Woloczynska, Bobby Wylie.

A few of those listed below are nannies, but to all those nannies who returned questionnaires anonymously as we requested, very many thanks. Others to whom we are grateful for research, help or information include:

Deborah Bedford, Cecily Breese, Jean Richardson, Deirdre Davis, Dawn Watts, Jennifer Ellard, Mary Padfield, Jenny Curtis, Stephen Patrick, Tessa McCormack, Nanny Jones, Patsy Smith, Betty Parsons, Christine Hill, Lizzie Heskett, Polly Woodman, Fayleen Mun-Gavin, Denny Chambers, Helena Buxton, Caroline Dawnay, Louise Davis, Mary McRae, Pamela Townsend, Camilla Harford, Peter Johnson, Peter Breese, Bert Myrin, James Odgers, Hilary Clarke, Angela Hovey, Sally Ann Lloyd, Sheila Bellamy, Jeanne Magagna, Hugh Thompson, Judith Hackman, Kelly Meighen,

Dick Odgers, Jilly Norris, Linda Layton, Nicki Sievwright, Jessica Johnson, Barbara Nicholls, Jane Ingham, Clare Bryne, Morwenna Haig, Karen Smelt, Winifred Symonds, Julie Rhodes, Angela Orssich, Gail Seaton, Kathrin Ahrens, Nathalie Phillimore, Clare Odgers, Sabrina Duppel, Victoria Russell, Rick Pflaum, Nick Whitmey, Robert Sutton, Melissa Perkins, Jackie Baxendale, Susan Hay, Mrs Baxter, Radina Batica, Julia Bates, Clare Asquith, Jane Ingham, Nina Prentice, Ann Biddescombe, Caroline Alcock, Mrs Wasmuth of the Pre-Select Agency, Solihull, Ann Bristow of the Kensington Tax Office, Sue Owen of the NCMA, Peter Moss of the Thomas Coram Research Institute and Lucy Daniels of the Working Mothers' Association.

Special thanks to John Gomer and Peter Borrett for all their work on the word processor. Also to Sarah Wallace and Sarah Riddell of Century and Sarah Sutton of Vermilion for their efficiency and kindness.

Preface

A book about nannies is a book about people, as well as many issues which are not at first sight anything to do with the subject. The aspects that a nanny touches on in her employer's life are limitless – all human life is there.

The effect of a nanny on the household is deep. Children make parents emotional and this colours the climate of their dealings with whoever is in their house looking after their children for them – be it nanny, mother's help or au pair. The book discusses questions of personalities, background, taste, morals, manners, standards, class, child abuse, maternity, child psychology, state-funded child care, childminders, day nurseries, sex, work-place crèches, handicapped children, holidays and travel, the Inland Revenue, suing, nannies' residential colleges, idealism, discipline, training, the role of parents and child-rearing philosophies.

When the two authors started having children there was no book that could give them a few clues about the pros and cons of childminders, the art of living with a residential nanny or an au pair, the advantages of daily nannies and whether maternity nurses were worth the cost. They had to learn from more experienced mothers, and through trial and error. They have refined their interviewing techniques and become better at dealing with nanny problems over the years. Day nurseries were not an option in those days, as they are for many parents today.

Throughout the book the authors have used 'he' almost always when referring to children. This was done purely because most child carers are women, so using 'he' limited the potential confusion of too many 'shes' in the text.

Chapter 1

Definitions

History does not relate quite when the word 'nanny' joined the English language. Even the *Complete Oxford Dictionary* has little to say about it or its derivation.

The appellation 'nurse' was used as early as the fifteenth century to refer to a woman who looked after children. Nurse itself sprang from 'wet nurse', a woman who was hired to suckle a child – a 'nursling'. She did this for various reasons, including the death of the child's mother in childbirth or, if she survived, because of her vanity. Bonding was not even thought of. Americans still call breast feeding 'nursing' – an example of archaic English surviving elsewhere.

The comic nurse in Shakespeare's *Romeo and Juliet* started her stay at the Capulets as the heroine's wet nurse. By the eighteenth century some wet nurses had metamorphosed into nurses, having stayed on after a child had been weaned – they were then aptly named 'dry nurses'. The first reference that Jonathan Gathorne-Hardy could find in his book *The Rise and Fall of the British Nanny*, published in 1972, was in a letter in 1711 from Lady Mary Wortley Montagu to her nurse calling her 'Dear Nanny'. By the next century the job of a nursery nurse was established. Every good home had one. By the early twentieth century the word 'nanny' had become common parlance, though nurse, 'nursie' and 'nana' remained current up to the Second World War. Nursery nurses were in demand during the war, running government nurseries so that mothers could contribute to the war effort.

Nanny is an odd word. We talk about nanny goats – the female of the billy goat, and there may be some link between the wet nurse as suckler and goats who were milked. 'Nan' and 'nanny' are diminutives for granny, apparently originally popular in Wales and the Midlands, and 'nan' has survived among the working class today. In the past nannies took on the surname of their employers sometimes, and thus became known as 'Nanny Caldecott', for example. Some research seeks to prove a connection between 'nanny' and the christian name Anne, as it was a nickname for Anne. It is just possible there is a link between granny and nanny and St Anne – she was the mother of the Virgin Mary and therefore a granny.

Why Do You Employ Other People to Care for Your Children?

It is not just the people who can afford it who want to employ someone to care for their children some of the time. Some feel that child care is a never-ending task which no one has found a way of mechanizing. Other women would love to have some help with their children, but feel it is a luxury they can't justify unless they have a job.

Today mothers admit more openly than they did in the past the desperation and claustrophobia they can feel after days and weeks of looking after their offspring single-handed. Once it was the norm up and down the land for mothers to grin and bear the relentless demands of whining voices and clutching hands. They would not have found a sympathetic ear for their grumbles. After all, caring for kids and keeping the home fires burning had been a woman's lot since the cavemen.

Mothers give the following reasons for employing carers for their offspring:

I need another pair of hands. I don't want all three dragged everywhere each time one of them is collected from somewhere.

To keep my independence and to stop me going potty.

I have to be able to work away from home at any time. I couldn't be with children 24 hours a day.

I like to have some energy left for my husband at the end of the day. This way I can work part-time and enjoy my children.

Business entertaining is part of my life and so I have to have someone to dilute my other responsibilities.

I would be an appalling mother if I had to be with the kids all day.

I'm 41 and run my own business. I find babies exhausting and restricting.

To try to ensure that the kids have a cheerful person with them most of the time. She is also good back-up if I'm ill so that the children's routines can go on. This is very important to me.

Freedom to do other things rather than just be a mother.

The Nanny Explosion

It was natural for Jonathan Gathorne-Hardy in his book *The Rise and Fall of the British Nanny* to write about what he thought was the last gasps of a dying breed. Ironically, just as the ink had dried, the dinosaur, as in Jan Pienkowski's *Meg's Eggs*, began to uncurl.

The main reason behind the rising demand for nannies and every kind of child care is the fact that more women work than ever before.

The latest UK General Household Survey figures emphasize to what extent Britain is now a two-wage economy and how most mothers with dependent children do some sort of work and need child care.

The percentage of married couples with dependent children who work either full- or part-time inches upwards with every survey, and now stands at 62 per cent. Also, more and more women with dependent children, regardless of marital status, work either full- or part-time: standing at 60 per cent compared with 51 per cent 10 years ago. 'Economically active' single mothers now total 30 per cent compared with 20 per cent 10 years ago. Nearly 50 per cent of women with their youngest child aged 0–4 years now work full- or part-time compared with just 30 per cent a decade ago.

Whereas in the 1980s the parents of children under five who both worked full-time were a pioneer group and too small to be more than 'interesting' for national statistical purposes, in the 1990s, as the percentages creep up, home-owning (double mortgage and therefore double income) families, particularly in cities and towns, have become the norm and have contributed significantly to the rise of nannies being a linchpin in a modern lifestyle. Whereas in the 1980s it was a joke that 'upwardly mobile urban professional' couples (Yuppies), started out as Dinkies (double income, no kids), and then turned into Tinkies (two incomes, nannies and kids) in the 1990s, everyone's doing it.

People used to think that the upwardly mobile who hired help for their children were wealthy city slickers. Some of them are, but there are hundreds of thousands of 'normal' middle-income couples all over the country who can afford a resident nanny, mother's help or au pair in their four-bedroomed semi-detached. Today people whose parents wouldn't have dreamt of, let alone have been able to afford, living-in help for their children, are doing just that, and they are not just the professional class, they include middle management, secretaries and administrators. Lack of space makes countless families hire daily nannies or they take the child to the nearest day nursery or childminder.

Twenty years ago, feminism helped to turn around women's, and the media's, attitude to the female's role in society. The introduction of statutory maternity leave, pay and allowance in the 1970s made it easier for many women to return to work after having their first baby. It is now the norm for women to work, married or not, and it isn't entirely acceptable any more for a woman to sign off when she starts a family. Being 'just a housewife and mother' is no longer fashionable; today a woman is defined by her work. Flexi-time mums say incredulously of the full-time mother with school-age children, 'What does she *do* all day?'

Women who do not need to work are choosing to do so. Their mothers actually gained social status by giving up work to have children. The arrangement was considered fine by both husband and wife. In fact it was only the wives of poor men who had to work. The poor still work and never feel a guilty pang – they don't have the option.

At 35 a woman used to be described as an 'elderly primagravida' (first-time mother). But now first-time mothers in their 40s abound – famous ones include Ursula Andress (she was 43) and British actress Patricia Hodge (42 for her first, 45 for her second). More women continue to bear children into their late 40s these days – Lady Annabel Goldsmith was 46 when she had her last and Britt Ekland was a similar age. At Queen Charlotte's Hospital in London they report, 'The expression "primagravida" is obsolete. We see 40-plus expectant mothers every day.'

Medical advances in obstetrics, ultrasound and amniocentesis, as well as better nutrition, increase the chances of the survival of the foetus. So more women feel it is safe to postpone child-bearing until their middle and late 30s and even well into their 40s, and these women are even less likely to stop work than those in their 20s. One study backs up the truism that the more a woman has worked the more likely she is to have 'work-committed attitudes'.

As well as all the sociological changes that have occurred, there has been a big emphasis also on pregnancy, birth and children. The media, the manufacturers and the advertisers have joined the bandwagon. The post-war baby-boom generation – the young of the 1960s – are now parents in their 40s and 50s with money to spend on their children. At last there are changing rooms in motorway cafés and crèches at airports. There are American-style restaurants that provide high chairs and menus for the under-fives. There are Alton Towers, Thorpe Park, Legoland in Windsor,

EuroDisney near Paris, plus Eureka and the new children's museum in Halifax.

There has been the growth of the National Childbirth Trust (NCT), followed by the Maternity Alliance and the Parents at Work Association. Not to mention the proliferation of child care and birth gurus like Sheila Kitzinger, Le Boyer, Gordon Bourne, Hugh Jolly, Penelope Leach and Miriam Stoppard. The royals, headed by Princess Diana's progeny, helped to fuel the fashion.

A working woman today, married or single, doesn't want to be saddled with children too soon. If at all possible she likes to get the mortgage payments underway and kit out a home. This is all made so much easier by a double income. If she lives with someone, she and her partner want to enjoy what two incomes bring them – sunny holidays, a bigger, nicer home, a better car, even two cars, at least for a while. Many enjoy two incomes so much that they don't want to suffer a drop in lifestyle when they do have children, and the wife returns to work as soon as it is feasible.

If a woman has a professional training – and more and more have – she can pursue a career and have a family as well. She may be fortunate enough to earn a big enough salary to afford an NNEB nanny and go back to work straight away, or alternatively, she may prefer to take her child to a day nursery when he is several months old. Even if a mother isn't earning a great deal, using a day nursery or a childminder can make returning to work economic sense.

More women are divorced and find themselves the major breadwinner for the first time. More divorced men now get custody of the children and need child care. There are more single parents who have to work, too. Some mothers work because they don't wish to rely on social security benefits. Others work and still have need of state benefits and rent rebates.

How Many Nannies, Mother's Helps and Au Pairs Are There Out There?

According to the General Household Survey, 64 per cent of families where the mother works all or some of the time uses one or several forms of child care. As has always been the case, 36 per cent of families resort to family and friends to look after their children under five. But a growing number – now 38 per cent of families – use childminders and nannies (annoyingly lumped together by the Survey), rather than relations. An increasing number – now up to 11 per cent – choose private day nurseries. Happily for 29 per cent of families, who have children of the appropriate age, they can use nursery schools, pre-prep, and primary schools.

There are 110,000 registered childminders but no formal statistics for the thousands of women, girls (and a handful of boys) who look after children in the children's own home, but the numbers are rising.

There is a plethora of various nursery nurse and child care courses involved in the care of children up to and including the age of seven (see Chapter 7). The most famous of these is the two year Diploma in Nursery Nursing (NNEB), organised by the Council for Awards in Child Care & Education (CACHE). About half the annual 10,000 NNEB graduates, along with around 10,000 graduates of other child care courses, go into nannying in private homes as opposed to working in local authority and private day nurseries. Let us assume that these nannies stick it for about five years on average. This means there is a total of around 70,000 nannies with varying degrees of qualification in circulation in any one year.

There are absolutely no figures on British and foreign mother's helps (that includes Australians and New Zealanders and EU girls); there may be as many as 30,000 in any one year. Nicholas Coleridge guesstimated in *The Spectator* that 'there are now 400,000 full-time or part-time nannies in Britain, only half of them British, the rest predominantly Australians, Filipinos, New Zealanders and Irish. The total nanny economy, much of it black, is worth, about £40 billion a year, comparable with the North Sea oil industry.' All those figures strike us as much exaggerated.

We do know that 12,000 Western Europeans living outside the EU and the European Economic Area enter this country under the au pair arrangement (see Chapter 8). If that number is multiplied by 10 to account for the undocumented number of EU girls who can work in the country at anything they please, but choose to work as au pairs, then the grand total for 'in-home child carers' as the Americans put it, could be somewhere between 150,000 and 200,000.

Three Types of Mother with Dependent Children

Full-time working mothers

Most working couples would prefer some flexibility in their working hours to allow them to spend more time with their children. In practice, to compete in a conventional job you must keep conventional hours. If you do this, you have to delegate the greater part of your child's upbringing to a hired hand. After aeons of the caveman approach, it is not surprising that the modern career woman feels guilty about this abdication of her role as mother. It doesn't half hurt. The anomaly of this arrangement is that if she pays a lot for substitute attention and security, she feels less guilty.

Part-time working mothers

Another group of women challenge the dilemma by working part-time. This enables them to satisfy feelings of responsibility and duty to their children as well as achieving something for themselves. They lose the kudos of a career, but feel that this halfway house has much to recommend it.

Full-time mothers

A third group do not have the problem. They toil not, neither do they spin full- or part-time – at least not gainfully. Some of them, however, may not *necessarily* spend more time with their children than the other types, though it is fair to say that most do.

Full-time mothers may be excellent organizers. Some see themselves as 'be-ers' rather than 'do-ers' – they may enjoy exhibitions, squash, home-making, hunting, shopping, socializing, cooking, entertaining, charity work and fund raising, interior decoration and travelling. Usually they are married to men on comfortable incomes or they live on a generous divorce settlement. Some are the wives of busy men who need a consort. Husbands who are diplomats, MPs, businessmen who have to entertain clients, farmers or men in the Services tend to share their jobs with their wives.

Many members of all these groups of mothers have one common denominator – they employ nannies, mother's helps or au pairs. For a vast variety of reasons they want some time, space and/or peace, and they have decided to buy it.

It doesn't matter into which category you fit; it is a shock at some point to every new mother to find that a child is there to stay and cannot be left at all. You cannot go out alone to shop; you can't pop out to the letterbox without it becoming an expedition; you and your partner can't go out without arranging for someone to babysit. A Moses basket at supper with friends is feasible for a few months only. Any sort of peaceful, uninterrupted work is out of the window until you have found care for the baby.

The Working Parent's Problems

It is plausible to argue that the less time a mother spends with her child, the less time she wants to do so. Unless a working mother is determined to know her child well at all costs and squeezes in time in the morning and/or evening most of the working week, the symbiotic pleasures of parenthood may not be as strong. Some contend that if you are unpractised at something you get less pleasure from it, though it may be questionable to align raising a child with the obvious analogy of playing the piano.

Combining children and full-time work is not easy, and requires a great deal of discipline and stamina. A strategy used by those who want to achieve a guilt-free trip to work in the morning is to hand over the child to the chosen carer as soon as is decently possible after the birth. The agencies report that the shortest period is two weeks, though six weeks is a popular cut-off point. All the mothers say, 'I fed him myself.' Career women make a point of breast feeding to help to bond – just like the books tell them.

If you escape your baby's charms – and Mother Nature arms the Cupid fearsomely – by the time he is two years old, you've done it. You are over the maternal hump and the chances are that your armour is impenetrable. Happily, in no time he is off to nursery school, so he wouldn't have had any need of you for half the day anyway, and full-time school is on the horizon.

Women are prepared to risk feeling guilty now and possibly regretting their behaviour much later when their children have grown up and moved away. They believe that it is possible to have it all – and it is. Many people manage to combine a career and children. They don't always do it without a hitch, but they do it well enough to make the envious world gasp.

More and more working mothers believe firmly that it is the *quality* rather than the *quantity* of time spent with their children which is the most important thing for both them and the child.

Absentee Parenthood

For some employers the nanny is a commodity. She provides a service just like the car cleaner, the carpet-cleaning company, the home-delivery butcher and fishmonger, the interior decorator, the window box gardener, the visiting valet or the silk flower arranger.

Employers shell out for their window cleaners and house painters but many skimp on child care. Uncharacteristic bargain hunters proudly announce that they've found an inexperienced mother's help to look after their three children 'for a lot less than an NNEB', before dashing out to work or to do the bulk buy. It can be concluded that the quality of child care is not as visible (if at all) to other people. Young children are not regarded as objects of conspicuous spending by these parents. Thus their care doesn't receive the same attention and financial outlay as things that friends and neighbours will register, like the new kitchen floor or the better car.

The children of absentee parents are not processed in quite the same way as the house, the car and the garden, but their children's caretaker has as much control as she did in the golden age of the nanny. She has total responsibility for them for all or most of the week, and a few employers can't face the weekend without support.

Nannies are more likely to receive less enthusiastic and relevant comment and appreciation for their work with children from this type of employer. The more they do, they find, the more they are asked to do. 'It's give, give, give, with this lot. If you didn't love their children you wouldn't stay a minute,' says one nanny resignedly.

Nannies do like sole charge. But they don't generally approve of working women, unless the nanny becomes the mainstay of a lone parent. Most nannies' mothers didn't work and many say they won't when *they* have young children. More than that, they do not approve of families where young children are seen and not heard, and where the parents do not spend much time with their offspring.

Employers have to watch to see that their nannies cope well with being with children all the time. One nanny writes, 'I sometimes feel like a single mother. I feel trapped. I wish I had more money and more time to myself. It's a great job for a couple of years but no lifelong career.'

One nanny who is effectively a surrogate mother says: 'If the parents are away from home for long periods the children rely on me for love, security and comfort. Children always behave differently with their mothers, testing their love and pushing them to the limit. The parents don't seem to realize that the child needs *their* attention as well as mine. I find myself taking complete responsibility for the children's emotional welfare, especially if the parents abandon their responsibilities.'

To wind up the contentious theme of absentee parenting, one Hampstead author says: 'Motherhood has had a bum rap of late. Women don't want to consider how much power they have handed over by not being around that much while their children grow up. Children are little vessels into which any amount of good or bad may be poured and stored. If you put in crap, that's what you'll get.'

'Why do mothers not realize that children are part of them? They will also become partly like those who take care of them. How can they fail to?' says Jeanne Magagna, child psychotherapist at the Tavistock Clinic.

The Hangover from the Old Guard and the Modern Nanny

There are two main misconceptions about nannies. The first is rooted in the real-life memories of a tiny minority whose families were cherished by devoted women sequestered on the top floor. Many of these memories have found their way into literature (Evelyn Waugh, Nancy Mitford, M. J. Farrell, A. A. Milne, etc.). Many people have heard about Winston Churchill's adored nanny, Mrs Everest.

The famous royal nannies were Clara Knight, the Queen Mum's and then her daughter's nanny, and Mabel 'Mambo' Anderson, nanny to the Queen's children, who was later re-enlisted to cope with Peter Phillips. Then the mould was broken by Nanny Barnes, nanny to the little princes at Kensington Palace. Although, like other royal nannies in the past, she had no formal training, Barbara Barnes hit the headlines when she left the job before Prince William had reached the age of five. The media reckoned that she went because there were classic nanny employer/employee problems.

The other fantasy version is to be found in stage, screen and literature. Julie Andrews reinforced the image twice – as a singing and dancing mother's help/governess in *The Sound of Music* and, of course, as Mary Poppins. In *Peter Pan* a Dulux dog was anthropomorphized into 'Nana' , who cared for the children and was more aware of danger than crusty Mr Darling, their father.

Nanny was presented as a cosy omniscient, as familiar as a piece of nursery furniture, in the world of A. A. Milne's books about his son Christopher Robin. Wendy Craig, who played the nanny in the TV series *Nanny*, whose career spanned the post-war period until about now, presented a more realistic picture of nannying. As did Rachel Billington, one of the many children of the Earl of Longford, writing in the *Daily Telegraph* about the family's notorious nanny who gave 'little whiffs of gas to quieten her over-energetic charges'. In a panic, her mother had appealed to her father about what they should do. He replied, 'We must watch and pray; you watch and I'll pray.'

Some parents find boyfriend trouble too threatening. A magistrate mother says: 'Our Norlander's boyfriend was over six foot and built like a barn door. He had tattoos in unexpected places and several convictions for GBH. As he muscled his way through the narrow passage of our Chelsea house, he snarled, "Where's yer toilet missus?" He and the nanny spent a lot of time in the bathroom together and intimidating and uninhibited noises would echo around the house. In the end she had to go, though the children loved her.'

Many parents avoid 'it' by employing older women. There are few on offer and even fewer are clones of the old school. As the divorce statistics rise, so there may be more mature nannies joining the market who have brought up their own children and need a new direction. This has been the pattern in America. In Saudi Arabia, nannies over 30 are considered the best bet.

Employers blank out of their minds that 'nursery duties' of yore were much more limited than today. An old-fashioned nanny did not clean, cook, shop, pay the milkman or answer the door. She did have specific skills, at which her successors rarely excel, like smocking, darning, knitting and sewing for her charges. She was completely reliable because she had nothing else but the children to occupy her. It was a vocation. Her employer gave her a secure home for ever. She experienced life through the comings and goings of her adopted family. Her fulfilment came from her great pleasure in her charges' development over the years and from the way everyone relied on her. She was the linchpin, the only person who knew where the mothballs were kept and she provided the shoulder to cry on for every member of the family she served.

Nothing could be more of a contrast to the modern nanny. She is probably the life support system to working parents. She may have most evenings free and may live elsewhere. She may spend her weekends as she chooses and may well not accompany the family on holiday. She is unlikely to stay longer than two years at the most. Today, nannies want a change and move on. One mother, brainwashed by fond memories of the old guard, says bitterly, 'She just treats your child as a job and is as fickle as the office junior.' She may leave after six weeks if her employers don't know how to treat her.

Historically, nannies and parents were on the same side. Today, too often nannies and parents are at loggerheads. The profession is full of prejudice and there is little balance between two extreme views. Employment agencies, training colleges, unions, employers and employees pick sides and stick to them. One faction holds that nannies do too much for too little without enough appreciation from snooty, divorcing, demanding, mean employers. The other bunch insist that nannies don't know the meaning of work nowadays and they are sex-crazed and over-paid, while bullied employers bend over backwards in vain to please these unreliable little minxes.

This polarization is unhelpful and unprogressive. The Them and Us syndrome is always good for a grumble on both sides whether it involves age, social class, educational background, north and south, town and country, money, privilege, holidays, sex as usual, appearance, tastes, opinions, phobias, role of parents, or myriad other minor clashes. Any or all of them can have the effect of chalk grating across a blackboard. Part of the point of this book is to enable employers to spot looming difficulties and deal with them amicably.

The current heyday of nannies is likened by some agencies to the golden days of the secretary in the mid 1960s to the early 1970s – the good ones were in short supply and everyone wanted them so they were paid a packet. There are plenty of nannies available, but now there is a chronic shortage of *good* ones; too many fussy employers are chasing too few effective nannies (particularly the case in London). The result is that nannies' wages are beginning to look quite competitive with 'ordinary' jobs for the first time. Many argue that the calibre of nannies has dropped as salaries have risen. Employers complain: 'When I put an ad in *The Lady*, I am lucky if I come up with a single, remotely worthwhile applicant'.

Unemployment has helped to bridge the gap between supply and demand for mother's helps at least. Girls from the north particularly are encouraged by their parents to travel south and seek work as mother's helps. Many agencies make monthly recruiting visits to Leeds, Manchester, Solihull, Walsall, Nottingham, Rotherham and points north. Girls of 16 and 17, most with little or no specific training in child care, work for a whole range of employers, many on small and medium incomes, once again concentrated in London and the Home Counties. Many of the jobs are not well paid and involve much responsibility and long hours while parents are away at work.

The green baize door has gone, but parents still have to maintain the relationship of employer and employee with their nanny, mother's help or au pair, and it is intrinsically uncomfortable. Lack of space and mutual claustrophobia are peripheral to a central dilemma – that of master and servant.

A servant is defined in the Oxford Dictionary as 'a person who has undertaken, usually in return for stipulated pay, to carry out the orders of an individual . . . especially one who lives in house of master or mistress receiving board and lodging and wages and performing domestic duties'.

At the heart of the matter is the fact that a nanny's status remains low compared with what her peers do. This stems from her willingness to live, in effect, at the beck and call of others. She has given up part of her freedom and has joined one of the few jobs left that is closest to unwaged labour. Nannying, like housekeeping or being a butler, is an anachronism. But it is a popular choice for many today because there *are* major compensations, particularly for an 18-year-old when other work can be hard to come by.

The British are as embarrassed by employing domestic help as they are about death. In the late twentieth century it is not socially acceptable to describe a nanny as a servant. A nanny 'helps out', she is 'part of a team', and sometimes a 'real friend'. This is the very most a nanny is prepared to be – her training, her mother and her peers tell her, and rightly, that she's not there to serve a family, and that she should beware of being treated like a servant. Nannies were never described as being 'in service' in the past, but they knew their place. Luckily, the whole master/servant relationship was easier then because the nanny had her own separate accommodation on the nursery floor. This was her domain, shared with the children; parents and other staff visited.

Today's almost extinct substitute for the harmonious set-up of bygone days is the daffy, socialite mum who is delighted to see the children in their dressing gowns briefly before she goes out again. She may employ an excellent trained nanny who runs her nursery floor impeccably. They don't meet much and they coexist happily and separately.

The reality of most people's domestic arrangements is comparatively chaotic. There is not room to swing a cat, the parents are devoted to their kids and want them there most of the time. The nanny copes well, but far from infallibly in a maelstrom of unsynchronized plans. The smallness of most homes means that all personal details are everybody's business.

There are still vestiges of an old-style approach to a nanny being a loved and trusted servant in the house and this may verge on straightforward snobbishness. One nanny says that she was upset to be asked to eat in the kitchen rather than joining the adults for dinner when they were spending the weekend away. 'It's very hard when you are a member of the family at home'. This can be described as a kind of imagined snobbery, but it does illustrate how quick to take offence some people may be.

Colonial types, like the Canadians, are aghast at the inherent snobbery which abounds in everyday life in the UK. They are detached and are thus mostly amused by their employers' embarrassing views. One New Zealander says: 'I can talk to my employers easily, but there is a basic distinction about what we think is important in life. Bluntly, I am not such a snob as they are. But I suppose I accept the differences here and my status in their house.' An Australian says: 'A lot of my employers' friends give the impression that they cannot be bothered to talk to you or even say the pleasantries to you, let alone treat you on equal terms.'

Some employers appear to be inverted snobs. They are embarrassed that they have a nanny: 'Believe it or not, we have a nanny' or, even more uneasily low profile, they talk about 'someone to help out with the kids a bit' when they have a full-time trained nanny. Quite rightly, nannies themselves dislike being explained away, so if an employer is sensitive to the stigma of not doing all the child rearing single-handedly and being able to afford proper help with it, she should not belittle the nanny's role to acquaintances in front of her. Trained nannies don't like being described as 'help' and mother's helps badly want the appellation 'nanny'.

There are nanny pecking orders which are as confusing to the uninitiated as a knees-up in a masons' lodge, but vary considerably depending on the location. Roughly, it goes something like this: nannies trained in residential colleges mostly have friends trained similarly and tend to come from more middle-class backgrounds. Other trained nannies stick together quite a bit, a few experienced mother's helps may join the clan as honorary members. The au pairs mostly spend time with other au pairs or foreign friends; unless they have good English they won't stand a chance with the NNEBs and even with the ordinary mother's helps. As usual, the Antipodeans and North Americans are different and, because they are not easily pigeon-holed by their peers, get on with all strata.

One nanny sums it up:

> You have to learn to live with lots of people being a nanny and living in. You have to get used to their little habits, their personalities, fit into their lifestyles and be flexible. You have to learn to respect other people's homes and not abuse certain comforts, perks and privileges.

They must learn to treat you as a nanny, as an equal, not a low servant. You have to learn to get on with each other and have a happy relationship.

A Nanny's Job Description

A nanny's or mother's help's job is to make sure that the children in her care are nourished emotionally, physically and intellectually. The crucial point is that she's required to do all this to someone else's specification. Her way is only as good if it is the same way as her employer's.

Nannies have to be flexible because there is no right and wrong in child care; hundreds of families do things quite differently. This is one reason why employers say they like young nannies – either so that they can boss them around without encountering too much resistance or/and because the girl has just left home and she will be more used to restrictions. One common misapprehension among nannies is that they will be their own boss as a nanny.

A sensible nanny realizes that her job is like many other jobs, albeit with a number of important differences. Long hours, babysitting and some weekend work, even when employers give ample warning of their own plans, will play havoc with a girl's 'normal' social life. It is also tough to live and work with people who are not family or contemporaries, and to have to adapt to their way of life – their diet, plumbing, budget, manners, habits, smells, affectations and worse intimacies. Most employers have not experienced live-in help before, so they probably will not have practised the little rituals of politeness and respect which decreases everyone's sense of trespass.

People agree that good nannies display: enjoyment of children, kindness, discretion, willingness, patience, stamina, unflappability, stability, efficiency, flexibility.

There is a general trend for some qualified and unqualified nannies to underestimate how necessary it is to be organized to survive the day satisfactorily, from everyone's point of view. The employer's dream nanny is aware of the benefits of 'time and motion'. She plans for the next day, checks that things work and where they can be found. Employers complain again and again that their nanny cannot, or will not, adopt a reliable routine. The trouble is that the minutiae of the job are petty and it is troublesome to get every detail exactly as someone else likes, particularly if they are being petty too.

It takes all sorts to make a nanny and all sorts to hire them. One woman's nanny can be another woman's nightmare. Both sides need self-control, discipline and the will to make the affair long-lasting, which is what it is all about. Given the artificial nature of the relationship, it is vital that the employer *likes* the nanny she chooses.

Why do nannies want to look after children?

> Most of the time children are fun to be with and life is never predictable.

> It's what I enjoy doing and feel that I am good at.

> I enjoy seeing a child develop and have pleasure in playing a part in his growing up.

> I honestly just love children. I love their company. I also feel that it's the best experience that anyone can have who wants to bring up three children as I do eventually.

> I prefer working in a home rather than in a day nursery because I'm not very outgoing and do the job best with a one-to-one relationship.

An experienced trained nanny comments:

> I love working with them and find it a rewarding and fulfilling career. Nannies nowadays do an important job and most of them realize that it is a job, not an excuse to stay at home and be a slug and do nothing all day but watch TV. The general opinion of nannying is that it's a cushy option and that it's not really working at all.

A good nanny treats nannying as a career if she does it for at least five years. Mrs Louise Davis, principal of the Norland College says, 'It's not a job with a career ladder. There is not much difference between two and 10 years' experience in terms of pay and appreciation of the years dedicated to children'. There is slightly greater scope for promotion for NNEB graduates who decide to work in day nurseries and nursery schools rather than become nannies. NNEBs find it frustrating that they are not supposed to 'teach' the under-fives in nursery schools, that's the province of the teachers.

Most nannies and mother's helps genuinely want to work with children. A few want to leave home, go to a city, travel abroad, be part of a lifestyle that they will probably never be able to afford and get off the dole. The second-rate reason why too many girls go into nannying is that they can't think of anything else to do. Sadly, even some NNEBs do the training without feeling strongly about it either way and when they reach the job stage they can *still* take it or leave it.

The Elusive Professional

'It is a weird job for a young girl nowadays when you stop to think about it. Living in someone else's house and abiding by all their rules is so unlike the way of the world now,' muses one employer.

Theoretically, training and experience will have moulded a nanny into a professional. As a professional she will be able to handle the restrictions and acknowledge employers' rights if she is resident in their home. In practice, will she remember to be 'professional' when it does not suit her? It takes maturity, discipline and a sense of honour to do as you said you would when there is no one there to see. No one but the children that is, and they won't tell or know the difference. There are some nannies who can hold their heads high from start to finish of their nanny careers in ethical terms. Some nannies behave professionally, but many do not know what the word means.

Trained nannies may never have heard the word 'professional' in two years of college. Untrained nannies, mother's helps and au pairs may never have considered the concept. Professionals do not sit on their boyfriends' knee while on duty; they do not take the easy way out with their tasks – for example, giving the children excessive sweets, TV or soporific cough medicine – wilfully disobeying instructions. They do not spend hours having long-distance telephone conversations with parents and friends, and their boss has a right to know what they are doing and where for every moment that he is paying her. Nannies mean well, but many of them don't do their job professionally, trained or not.

Another big problem that employers find difficulty in coming to terms with is that live-in child carers are not hired primarily for themselves but for the services they provide. However much an employer may feel that it is essential that she employ a nanny, she still may dread the whole business. Many employers resent sharing their private space with the hired help and may find the commitment it takes fairly demanding.

Throughout this book we encourage employers to behave like professionals towards their nannies. What do we mean by this? To inform ourselves and to produce a consensus about the best way to be a good employer of whomever cares for the children, we have gathered advice from employers, employment agencies, nanny unions, nannies, mother's helps, au pairs, training college tutors and their principals. By the end of the book, faithful readers will know what is expected of the employer who is professional.

One mother who had au pairs and mother's helps for her first family, treated herself to a nanny for the only child of her second marriage. Her nanny stayed nearly three years. 'When I recruited her replacement when my daughter was three, I realized that I just didn't have what it takes any more. The older children were all at school, Elspeth was at nursery school. When the new nanny from Wakefield got homesick, I decided I'd rather manage without any so-called help ever again'. This is typical employer burn-out.

Another example of an employer cracking under the strain is when a mother felt she must leave her job and return to either full-time or part-time motherhood because she couldn't take her nanny's unreliability any more. This mother was too worried to work effectively. Nanny fatigue finally took its toll.

Oddly enough, it may take an emotional hiccough or drama – divorce, illness, redundancy, another baby, a death – to cause a mother to reconsider. If for whatever reason she feels vulnerable, it is probable that she will feel the need to be closer to her child than before.

One type of nanny that employers quickly tire of is the one who starts to identify with them and their lifestyle too much. Tell-tale signs of this emerge when she asks questions like, 'Where did you get your new dress?' and 'What did it cost?' She tells you that she, too, would like to have people in to dinner and will you be out next Tuesday? She soon needs time off to get her hair done and iron her dress and she makes you feel like Cinderella's stepmother if you demur. Nannies employed by Sloane Rangers may start wearing puffa jackets, Barbours and pearls. She can direct the builders as well as you can, and she knows exactly where to find them in your address book. A bit spooky.

It is a rare nanny who can maintain the balance so that you all stay friends over a long time. 'After three years she still calls me Mrs Braithwaite and never oversteps the line. When she leaves at Christmas, I shall miss her. I rely on her as I would a friend and even as a sister'.

High Turnover

When women have a high turnover of nannies in a short time, they worry that it reflects badly on them. They're right: it does. Consistency of care should be the prime objective of every employer – you don't need more than elementary psychology to know that children can display disturbed and even neurotic behaviour if they feel insecure. It is far from ideal if the person who is closest to them for most of the time, changes frequently.

A high turnover can mean that the employer is deliberately, though unconsciously, selecting an inappropriate nanny because she does not want to relinquish the maternal reins. The hiring and falling out go on indefinitely. Other employers may not interview perceptively and form an inaccurate picture of the girl's character. They may pretend the job is something it isn't and are found out within days; they may have delusions about themselves and the sort of people they want to live with, or they may be impossibly exacting. It is unlikely that an employer is jinxed time and time again.

Some employers have no idea what a nanny ought to do. Their nannies continue to leave in droves when they've been ordered to clear up the dog mess and the employers still wonder why. It reflects well on the nannies that these employers are often dazzlingly rich and offer fat whacks and juicy perks, but they desert them notwithstanding.

A Final Word

Much of the angst generated by the employer and her nanny or mother's help is self-inflicted. Some people become a little unbalanced about the whole gamut of problems they feel the nanny is creating for their perfect family.

Both employers and child care employees have to hold tight to an optimistic and positive approach to their life together.

The Breese/Gomer line is that employers should: think and talk about it; set up good pay and conditions; work out their rules; interview exhaustively; grill referees; give the employee clear instructions; avoid asking for favours; and not stand for any nonsense.

Try to make your children's welfare come first and insist that the nanny does so too. If a nanny convinces you that she puts their needs before her own convenience and that she enjoys being with them, you will find yourself liking, respecting and trusting her.

Read on. This book tries to tell you how to achieve all this – and heaven too . . .

Chapter 2

House Rules
and the Big Four

House Rules

If guests and fish are supposed to stink after three days, how is a family to put up with living with someone who is staying indefinitely? The need for House Rules is clear to the experienced employer, the residential training colleges and the employment agencies. House Rules may vary greatly, but everyone agrees that the wise employer will have decided on their consistency before even interviewing a nanny. Rules can always be relaxed but it causes problems when they are made up as the occasion arises. Do discuss the broad principles with your husband and/or anyone else who may be affected.

To make your lives together work, it is essential that you think through as precisely as possible what your views are on the following: smoking, drinking and drunkenness, boyfriends and curfew, what you are called, how the nanny is to use the car if at all, where in the house the nanny may or may not go and what she may or may not use without asking, when and how often she may use the phone, who may or may not stay, and for how long, how much time you intend to spend in her company, and the need for confidentiality on both sides.

House Rules do not cover 'Sackable Offences', though you need to be even clearer about these, and have thought about them properly before interviewing. Turn to page 41 for a discussion of Sackable Offences. Having said that, a House Rule, if ignored repeatedly and after warnings, can often turn into a 'Sackable Offence'.

Many new employers will wonder justifiably why it all has to be so complicated and regimented. In the 1990s a proportion of employing mums have a 1960s-style liberalism towards other people's ideas and habits. Almost all employers start out that way; many have the sense to do a swift volte-face and metamorphose into House Rules devotees after the first few months of employment. Some exchange written contracts with their nanny. Information about these is detailed in Chapter 17.

What should she call you?

Most employers prefer to be called by their first names, as is the norm for a boss and his/her secretary and in most jobs. One mother says: 'It's impossible to live with someone so intimately and not think it absurd to be called anything but your first name.' Others make the distinction according to the employee's age; some like to change tack after a few months, and some say that it depends on the girl herself and her attitude. One mother argued for first names on the grounds that remarriage meant that her name kept changing, which made everyone giggle.

Some employers confuse formality (i.e. Mrs) with respect, believing that 'some barriers must remain up if you don't wish to breed contempt'. Finally, one experienced employer who has tried it both ways says: 'It doesn't matter really. The relationship either works or it doesn't.'

There is a small number who like 'Mrs X'. Actually, if she is called Mrs Higginbottom the nanny will probably come to the usual cosy compromise and call her Mrs H. Significantly, most of these employers have living-in nannies and they give a number of cogent reasons for their choice:

I'm too informal and it reminds us who is boss.

It creates an air of authority.

They're young enough to be my daughters, what do they call their parents' friends anyway?

I was taught by my first nanny who said she much preferred it, because when there are problems or disagreements it makes the situation clearer.

When in doubt nannies use 'you', as do au pairs. A few call their employer 'mummy' which takes a bit of getting used to; one titled employer claims she prefers it to all the other misnomers.

One old-style agency deplores the use of first names, while another states that the use of Mrs distances the employer from the nanny to the nanny's advantage – like a uniform, it protects the nanny from being put upon and from too much over-familiarity.

Whatever you feel about this, one employer suggests that the nanny addresses her employers' friends and family formally until they invite her to call them by their first names.

Confidentiality

The Federation of Recruitment and Employment Services (FRES – see page 311) model contract of employment states that 'it is a condition of employment that now and at all times in the future you keep secret the affairs and concerns of the household and its transactions and business.'

It's not just the royals, rock stars and Hollywood who care about their privacy. There are instances when the nanny's discretion can matter very much to you, particularly if you are nearing the divorce courts, are rich, political or important in public life. Your child could be an abduction target or the press could be riveted by titbits about your private world.

Anne Diamond, a TV presenter, won an injunction granted over the telephone from the judge's home to stop the presses and silence her former nanny. It was granted on the basis that the nanny as an employee owed the couple a duty not to reveal confidential information acquired during the course of her job.

Even if an employer is not obviously vulnerable, it is sensible to mention to your nanny that you do not like her to gossip about your family and friends to anyone. Of course, if she is human she is bound to chat about her job, but she should be made aware that it is unprofessional and potentially trouble making. The onus is on the employer to be discreet; blackmail could be a temptation to a nanny scorned, or in the very rare circumstances when an employer hires a complete nutter.

The nanny's dress on duty

Fewer and fewer employers like their nanny to wear a uniform; most feel that it is too formal and ostentatious. There are a number of employers who keep a nanny and her uniform to some extent as a status symbol. This keeping up with the Jones's syndrome is prevalent but rarely so unsubtle. It is illustrated by one principal of a private training college who remarked that, 'One of my girls worked for a family who made her wear uniform when the children were visiting their paternal grandparents. They were a bit more upper crust than the other set.'

Not surprisingly, the big residential training colleges are proud of the identity that their uniform gives them, and the girls are encouraged to wear it if that suits the employer. One Norlander reacts against the whole idea of wearing her uniform. She feels that it is uncomfortable, over-formal, and anyway she 'wouldn't want to work for anyone who was more interested in me as an obvious status symbol than in their children's happiness'.

A graduate of an NNEB college doesn't have an official uniform like those of the private colleges, but sometimes an NNEB creates her own version and prefers to wear it. The advantage of a uniform (and like the image-conscious NNEB mentioned above, it is easy to buy an adaptation) is that there is no risk of her wearing what an employer might consider to be unsuitable clothes. It is not chic to wear an apron, but many nannies wash their clothes constantly (which is expensive) as a result of wearing trendy numbers which the baby wrecks with sick and dribble. Smart clothes may inhibit the nanny from initiating any sort of mucky play like making mud pies or pretending to be a snake along the floor.

Another and less obvious plus about the uniform for the nanny is that when she is out of uniform, she is visibly not on duty. This reminds everyone that she has working and non-working hours which should not be so 'flexible' (a favourite word of employers) that she never has a moment to relax and be off-duty.

Wearing a uniform does not guarantee a smart appearance. One mother says that one of her nannies looked so scruffy in uniform that she suggested that she wore her own clothes – the result was a great improvement. It would be politic to ask the nanny how she feels about her uniform, particularly if you are in two minds about imposing it. Remember that many girls enjoy putting together outfits and accessories and having to don a uniform every morning if she yearns to sport an emerald track suit, with big white earrings and white sneakers, might not be the best way of keeping morale high.

Don't forget that a uniform can be an added expense. It is reasonable that an employer pay for or contribute towards replacing a worn-out uniform as well as footing any dry cleaning bills that are necessary. Some employers give their nannies a uniform allowance. Some generous ones give them a clothing allowance.

Most nannies feel more comfortable in mufti, but that makes it the employer's job to comment on its practicality if necessary. Do so straight away. It will continue to annoy you but be harder to bring up later. One mother couldn't abide her nanny sitting down to lunch al fresco in her pink bikini and requested that she dress for meals, please.

Footwear is often a problem. Several mothers raise the vexed question of pink fluffy slippers with high heels. Not so much the slippers, but the fact that some nannies and mother's helps like to wear them all day around the house. High heels are ruinous to wood floors or lino and are dangerous up and down the stairs when carrying a baby or child. They also discourage the girl from running with or after the children. In an emergency a nanny moves quicker in flat shoes. There is a lot of bending and stretching when looking after children, so trousers or jeans are sensible.

Smoking

Ninety-nine per cent of employers prefer non-smokers. A growing proportion are militant about it and will sack a nanny who lies about her habit. Some are more lenient and ban it while the nanny is on duty and a few, some of whom may themselves be smokers, just don't mind. Some employers insist that smoking only occurs outside the house; others let the nanny smoke in her own bedroom. One realistic working mother says that she has to 'leave it to the nanny's discretion, but hoped that she didn't'. Several nannies told us that they were well aware that their employers disapproved but didn't want to bring up the subject.

All the residential training colleges have strict non-smoking policies and Princess Christian College guarantees adherence to its rule because it has smoke detectors. This attitude provides an excellent example and good training for nannies who are highly unlikely to be able to smoke at the home of their employers.

All the agencies report that employers are becoming increasingly mindful of the health and fire hazard caused by smokers, so that almost no one wants to employ a nanny who smokes, any more than one who can't drive. Nannies are well aware of the current trends, but can't, as Louise Davis of Norland College sagely comments, 'give it up the week before taking a job'. Never trust a self-confessed 'social smoker' not to be a pack-a-day girl on the quiet.

If you run a smoke-free household, don't forget to remind her that you won't like her friends smoking either. Any new mother has only to imagine her reaction to the sight of an eight-month-old baby reflectively chewing a fag end left around by his nanny, as one employer reports, to understand why this subject causes feelings to run high. Another thing to remember, if your nanny is allowed to smoke in the house (one employer allows her nanny to smoke only in the garden), is to ban her smoking when she is ironing. One mother was so cross when a large stack of freshly laundered clothes stank of tobacco that she insisted that it all be washed again.

It is not part of a caring professional nanny's image to smoke. It would be helpful if the NNEB and other courses spelled this out to trainees. Apart from the fire and health dangers, a committed smoker needs a cigarette as often as she can make time for one. This does not bode well for her charges and their schedules. Shortness of temper and of breath, and dealing with nicotine craving are far from ideal for a nanny.

Drinking and drunkenness

Like all good things, a bit of drinking is fine so long as it is not overdone. One employer sums it up succinctly with, 'I don't mind as long as they don't get pissed.' Most people agree that nannies should not drink while on duty and shouldn't drink their employer's liquor unless it is offered. Some employers go so far as to prime the nanny straight away that, when she is offered a drink by anyone when she is on duty she should not accept more than one glass. Many employers, however, offer the nanny a drink at the end of a hard day and exchange news and views over it.

Drunk nannies are a rarity and there seem to be few instances of hangovers, falling up the stairs at night, or passing out on the bathroom floor at 4 am. These real reported examples are probably exceptions. Beware Australians and New Zealanders; they receive a dishonourable mention here.

It is not sensible to give your nanny or babysitter a bottle of wine before exiting in your glad rags. Having drunk half a bottle, could she get three children out of a burning house? One of the principals of the private colleges reminds us: 'Young girls in London for the first time, and not used to drinking, do get drunk.'

Tell your nanny if you allow her to use your car that she may not drink and drive whether on or off duty. Regardless of any moral view, it invalidates the insurance if she is involved in an accident.

Just as you would rather be oblivious to any effects of drink on your nanny or mother's help, similarly she shouldn't have to cope with drunk employers.

Where and what is out of bounds

Almost all employers' stated aim is to make their house the nanny's home. However, when they think about what this actually means in terms of loss of privacy and peace, their list of exceptions is lengthy. Here is a characteristic response: 'Absolutely their home, but they must ask to use the phone, there won't be any dinner party invitations, and our working lunches don't include her.'

Another conflict arises, frequently and justly pointed out by nannies, that although most employers are glad to have a nanny on call at any time, many of them resent their physical presence when off duty and don't want to meet them around the house. Unless you are lucky enough to be able to offer her 'a separate flat in the nursery wing' (a stately home/green baize door option), it is unkind to make her unwelcome. Hope to heaven that her training college will have mentioned the employers' need for time alone in the evening, and that it won't be necessary to lecture her about the strains on a modern marriage.

Anyone who employs a trained nanny or even an English-speaking mother's help need feel no guilt about telling her to amuse herself after work. It is less easy to take this line with au pairs; part of the deal is that they need to practise their latest English word on you and they are meant to be part of the family (see Chapter 8).

The majority of nannies eat at the same time as the children and therefore leave you and the kitchen free to entertain your spouse in the evening. A few nannies take a tray to their room, some are 'always out when we are in' or 'are anywhere but where we are'. One mother disingenuously comments 'she has always been part of the family, but she prefers meals on her own'.

Some employers are not particularly privacy conscious; others quite enjoy a bit of companionship. A third group are the sort who live up a long drive in the country and are happy to have the nanny around a lot of the time. The nanny, of course, may have her own plans.

Most employers are agreed that their bedroom, their own bathroom if they have one, and the living/drawing/sitting room are out of bounds to the nanny, especially in the evenings when most employers like to be alone together. It all depends how much space you have. Obviously it is unfair on the nanny to be confined after work entirely to an 8-foot-square bedroom and a galley kitchen. If you have lots of room(s) she won't feel deprived, and you needn't feel mean if she has a large comfortable room to herself (see Chapter 5).

Other no-go rooms in some families include the study, the dining room, the husband's dressing room, the cellar and the attic. Most employers are quite relaxed about the nanny using a particular room for a bona fide purpose, like, for example, an au pair asking to use the piano in the sitting room.

Possessions can cause problems. Employers want to believe themselves to be sharing, caring and generous with their goods and chattels, but mostly they find it easier to be generous with their cash. It is sensible to tell your nanny not to borrow or use anything without asking. What is *anything* ? Tell her exactly what you are sensitive about, be it your food processor, sewing machine or stereo equipment. You are entitled to be irritated if having pointed out the no-go areas of the house, the nanny uses any objects found in them. As one mother put it, 'I respect their belongings and would like them to respect mine.'

To summarize, the employer's home is not the nanny's home and however much you may want her to feel 'at home' for your own purposes, don't get confused and give the nanny inconsistent signals. Clear messages from the start about the way you want to live in your home should help reduce future friction. Both parties need to learn respect for each other's 'space' and to nurture a mutual, and entirely healthy, desire to be apart some of the time under the same roof.

The telephone

Even the most open-handed of employers grumble ferociously about their nannies' abuse of the telephone. What is most upsetting is that an employer has to recognize that she is virtually impotent. One working mother speaks for thousands when she says: 'The telephone is always a headache. I get very cross inside, but do nothing about it except complain to my husband, who says "do something".'

To the question 'How much do you use your employers' phone?' the stock response from nannies is 'not a lot'. Very few choose not to use the phone often, but this is such a common understatement as to be a misapprehension by the nanny, rather than a conscious rip-off. Most have never seen, let alone paid, a telephone bill and their hurt innocence, when first confronted with the beast by an irate employer, is legendary.

This is one area in which the employer may feel quite free to act as if she were the nanny's parent. Do not feel inhibited to say 'Please Jenny, get off the phone' after 20 minutes long-distance off duty, or after three minutes mid-morning with two children round her feet who might be otherwise entertained. A neat way out of such crass confrontation is to say quietly 'I must ring my mother now, I'm afraid.'

The received wisdom on this issue is that employers request that nannies ask before making long-distance calls, and are otherwise free to make local calls when and as much as they wish, although there is usually an embarrassed mumble about off-peak times. Remember to mention to any Canadian, Australian or New Zealand mother's help that you will log her overseas calls when they appear on your itemized phone bill. Also remind her that local phone calls do cost money in this country (unlike in her own).

An employer expects her nanny to make arrangements to meet other nannies and children, to check times of engagements and to organize her own social life. These conversations should be short and to the point; most employers resent anyone gassing about the joys of the night before on the morning after. As one mother says, 'I always recommend off-peak times, but I am out most mornings and she starts phoning as soon as I've left. I sometimes can't get through for hours.'

What do you do about a phonaholic? Mercifully British Telecom's itemized phone bills have taken much of the friction out of the issue. The nanny can be shown her long-distance, lengthy calls and their cost. Some employers will pay a percentage of her calls, others deduct from her wages each quarter. Even with itemized phone bills there are always the local calls which add up alarmingly with a phonaholic. At the first sign of uncontrolled chit-chat, show her the last phone bill and say that it is not expected to double in the next quarter. When it does, show her the new bill, jump up and down if it is your style, and threaten to make her pay the difference next time.

Phonaholics have friends with the same problem and they all do it all the time – even at midnight and at 6 pm, when little children are bound to be in the bath. When you answer a phone call from the mother's help's best mate at an inconvenient hour, say 'Can you ring back later please' or even, cheekily like one exasperated mother, 'She does work you know.' Apart from crises, tell your nanny you don't expect her friends to ring after, say, 10 pm.

One employer's wheeze is to give the nanny her own phone and pay the rental. Another's is to install a 'tell cost' machine which will make it clear how much she is spending. *In extremis* and Getty style, either have a pay phone or add a locking device. The latter seems over the top, not least because the nanny might need to dial 999.

Naturally enough, nannies need to be in touch with their families and this should be encouraged. One employer deals with this by inviting the nanny to ring home once a week from wherever she is (her job takes her abroad frequently), and she never fails to remind her. If you don't offer her a specific time to ring home each week, she may, as another mother reports, take the intitiative and enjoy a lengthy talk every time her employers go out in the evening.

In fairness to nannies, it is silly to pretend they are unique as employees in ignoring the ethics of the whole thing. As anyone who has ever worked in an office knows, one of the accepted perks of the job is ringing long distance when in the mood. This awareness is summed up by a nanny, 'Yes, I use the phone a lot, but I'm not supposed to.' Employers often don't set the best example, by gossiping to girlfriends at peak times. Mobile and car phones are becoming more and more common, and if the office pays the bill, employers do not seem in the least restrained.

Use of car

These days employers need nannies, mother's helps and often au pairs too, to drive, and the agencies and training colleges do all they can to encourage a girl to acquire a driving licence. Some employers generously help finance driving lessons – this is genuinely altruistic because the chances are that she won't have become a competent enough driver during her stay with them to be able to help out on the school run and the like.

Use of a car has become an expected perk of nannying and it is not uncommon for employers to provide a car exclusively for her use. Most people now let the nanny use the car or the second car if there is one, when they don't need it. It is expected that she ask before driving away and always give her employer priority and reasonable notice.

She must be insured to drive the car, and it can be an added expense for the employer, and especially punishing if she is under 25 and with no 'no claims discount' (see Chapter 8). Tell your nanny the terms of her cover (comprehensive, third party) and explain any excess clauses, i.e. that the insured, not the insurance company, has to pay the first £50 or £100 or whatever of any claim. Remind her that often it is best that a car owner doesn't claim on insurance for a minor bash, in order to protect his no claims discount, but the car still needs to be fixed and the bill paid.

Again, employers often don't set a good example by being much too casual about damage done to a company car. Keep quiet about the fact that the car is company-owned, if it is. The perks of your job are not her business. Cynically, in the knowledge that young nannies are accident prone, they are frequently allocated the company car to reduce the repair bills that come out of the employer's own pocket.

Some mothers have a blanket rule that their nanny never drives the children for safety reasons and peace of mind. Others make quite sure that the carer is a competent driver before letting her take the children out in the car. Any sensible parent lectures her on the absolute necessity of child safety belts, and of course her own. A nanny failing to put on a child's seat belt is negligent and is asking for the sack.

Petrol can be a perk, though most employers ask the nanny to refill the petrol tank after her private use. Employers don't usually expect her to contribute to any of the running costs but may restrict how far she may travel in the car. One employer, for example, doesn't mind her nanny using it in and around London, but objects to a long trek home to Cornwall every other weekend because of the wear and tear on the vehicle. Mention this early on, as undoubtedly the girl will soon figure out that using the car is much cheaper than even her Rail Card to get home.

Incidentally, another and less obvious reason for the nanny's preference for using your car for the trip home is that it is a tangible sign to her family and friends that she has a real job in which she is valued. For any young person a car is a symbol of status and independence, and it doesn't do the employer any harm that the nanny is bucked up by being allowed to use the car and show it off at home. In central London, where there is a nanny to every square yard, there is an overt one-upmanship about what make of car different nannies drive – the Mercedes, the Porsche and the convertible Golf GTI versus the Fiesta, the Renault and the Montego Estate.

Accidents *do* happen, and often to nannies. Many recently qualified nanny drivers still have very little experience of driving, particularly in big cities or abroad. Employers are amazingly long-suffering about 'nanny's little prangs'. They often excuse her, saying: 'It wasn't really her fault', though one says ruefully: 'Our experience hasn't been great so far; three dented cars and one write-off.'

If the school run dominates your life, au pairs are not ideal as they are used to driving on the other side of the road. The household bike is often on offer to take them to classes, though there is the safety angle to consider. Think of your explanation to her Barcelonan mama when she is strapped up in the local hospital.

Spell out to the au pair how often and how quickly bikes get stolen, particularly in a city. Tell her about the padlock, fixing to the railings, *never* leaving it unpadlocked in the street and even then not for long or overnight. If it isn't insured, warn her that if it is lost, damaged or stolen she will have to fork out for its replacement cost, if that is what you have decided. Given this litany she may well decide not to bother and that will cut out probable future irritation.

Some employers are keen that the nanny use the car at night as a protection against assault or mugging. Many recognize that employers are far from delighted to pay up for accidents incurred when off duty. One drawback of being 'good about the car' is that you may soon see it bulging with giggling nannies who can't quite remember where they live, all yelling instructions in your nanny's ear. You are the only one in the street to have provided a taxi service for other nannies and there could well be a crash round the corner.

When the inevitable happens, her fault or not, you have to deal with her shock, injury, and possibly other people's. There is also the embarrassment of her having to tell you and you having to be decent about it, not to mention possible loss of the no claims discount or an unwanted repair bill. There seem to be few circumstances in which an employer can assume a combination of a nanny and wheels which will not be time- and cash-consuming.

May they stay?

If an enlightened employer is keen to have a long-stay happy nanny, allowing her to have friends to stay is a perk to offer which shouldn't cost much or cause trouble as long as you lay down a few guidelines. A nanny's parents may be glad to spend a weekend in the house if you are away, so that they can have a look at the way their daughter lives and spend some time with her. It is nice for her to feel that she can play hostess to them and to her friends too.

Most employers restrict a nanny's overnight visitors to 'great girlfriends whom we know' and 'members of her family'. Some girls prefer visitors to descend only when the family is away, no doubt realizing that it is a worry for employers to leave a nanny behind alone in a house at weekends with or without the children (especially if she is young and in a big city for the first time).

A few nannies think it best that visitors are only invited when the employers are in residence. Employers are unanimous in discouraging weekday overnight visitors; requiring proper notice of anyone's arrival; and making it clear that any stay should be limited to a night or two only. They also evince a definite preference for female visitors.

'It's all right in principle if it suits us'; 'if they ask me and it isn't a man', and 'as long as we don't become a doss-house for all sorts' are characteristic caveats. An experienced mother is precise: 'With permission, as long as we and they know them well i.e. that the friend won't be casing the joint, drink all the booze or be a nuisance to us in any way.' Another adds: 'No to the friends she might have met the week before.'

Letting the nanny have a friend or her mother to stay can suit everyone. Parents treating themselves to a weekend away from the children tend to feel more confident if the nanny has her mother with her.

The issue is different, as always, with au pairs and foreign mother's helps because they don't usually have any kith and kin in the country. But beware of being kind and letting her friends transform your home into the local YWCA. The travelling friends of Antipodeans are magnetic when it comes to spare beds.

Inviting people to sleep over, as the North Americans have it, is a fun thing to do, if you have the space and it's no trouble because you won't be there and you trust the nanny with the house in your absence. Score high by being the first to raise the topic. A convertible sofa in her bedroom is particularly appreciated. Try to emulate one mother who writes 'I know her friends, like them and welcome them. If the nanny sticks to our rules then they can all have a good time.'

Curfew

With a responsible nanny who has a professional attitude to her job, the need to give instruction about when she is expected to be home at night does not arise. It has been mentioned before that it is not a good idea to make up rules as you go along and it is especially hard when you are already cross and/or disappointed with a nanny's behaviour. Be realistic every time. It is much easier to relax the rule when you are entirely satisfied that the nanny has boundless energy and good humour in the early morning which is sustained throughout the fun-filled day. Many mothers are sure that their nanny or mother's help can cope after a night out and don't have a curfew.

In contrast, some employers are adamant about a strict curfew. They like to lock up; they have sensitive ears and don't want to hear her footsteps up the stairs when they are trying to go to sleep, or hear the sound of her ablutions in the bathroom. Above all, a few of them actually worry until they know their nanny is safely tucked up in bed. This feeling is more prevalent when she is still in her teens and is with a London family. The same concern is more common with young au pairs and mother's helps from abroad. One advantage of insisting that an au pair or nanny is back by midnight is that the employer doesn't have to lie awake debating whether it is time to start ringing police stations and hospitals at 3 am when there is still no sound of creeping footsteps.

Mrs Davis of Norland says that employers must not forget that their nannies are young with lots of energy. This is a timely reminder to those former Yuppies who assume bedtime after the News at Ten has become the norm.

One delightful curfew story tells of the couple who returned after a night out to see their Dutch au pair Saskia all dressed up for a night on the town. Often her night began when they returned home. She used to go to the West End and have a whale of a time. They were surprised by this strange social life, but as she was excellent at her job and never showed a sign of fatigue after returning at 6 am from her outings, they let her carry on.

An incidental bonus of a curfew is that it renders your nanny just about ineligible to babysit for other people and get exhausted that way. Employers who hire babysitters, especially if those babysitters are also other people's living-in nannies, might think about being conscientious and returning at the agreed time. Don't take advantage of the fact that the babysitter is never going to say to you: 'Please be back on time, I need to get up early.'

Imposing a curfew assumes that the nanny is working the next day. It could be some time between 11 pm and 1 am. Most employers lift the curfew if she isn't on duty in the morning. Many allow, nay encourage, the nanny to stay out all night when she is off so long as as they know in advance. Others are not so keen and allow the carer to stay out the night for a specific reason like a friend's all-night birthday party. Many employers insist that she telephones if she is going to be exceptionally late or, if there is a curfew and she is not going to be back in time, that she ring and explain why.

The trouble with instituting a strict rule about when to be in at night, is that the employer must enforce it if it is ignored, if he is to retain credibility about the rule and about all the house rules. An employer who says 'Be sure to be back by midnight' is wasting everybody's time if a new nanny comes in even ten minutes late, and he or his wife does not mention this fact and ask her why? If he isn't strict about the curfew the nanny will quite understandably feel that it doesn't mean anything.

One college principal says: 'A nanny must not put her needs and social life before children and family.' Every employer and good nanny will agree.

Boyfriends

To misquote Dorothy Parker, it could be said that if all the nannies in Kensington were laid end to end, no one would be the least surprised.

A mother and her three-year-old daughter were walking in an idyllic Dorset valley one weekend, having just admired the farm animals. Reflectively the little girl remarked: 'Billy the bull, mum, what's he doing?' 'Making babies, darling.' They walked on. 'Is that what Kathy and Abdul were doing yesterday afternoon?' In this way one mother discovered how her child was entertained while she was at work. On Monday evening the mother tackled the nanny and her boyfriend together. Abdul saw the point and agreed not to cross the threshold unless the mother was there. He was soon bored with the nanny who then attempted suicide while left in sole charge.

This may sound an incredible story. It did happen. It points up only a few of the myriad problems associated with allowing the nanny's boyfriends into your home. It also illuminates the fact that a sensible, trained nanny (which this one was) may turn into an unrecognizable, love-lorn wreck within weeks, once smitten. There are countless examples of this sort of thing occurring.

Some employers may imagine that their youth was spent in gentle romantic pursuit of the opposite sex and, whatever else, it certainly took longer to score in those days. Today the pace can be quicker and plenty of pre-marital sex is the norm. AIDS may slow down the process somewhat, but don't be shocked if your young nanny or mother's help assumes the whole business of sex to be a matter of fact.

It is hard for an employer to deal with this area successfully. There is no other subject which exercises both employers' and nannies' tongues more energetically than what to do about boyfriends and sex. The truth is as one nanny puts it: 'If you are residential you really can't have an affair; men and nannying just don't mix.'

The most important piece of advice to a new employer from a mass of experienced ones is: 'Don't agonize over it. There is no solution that will suit everybody. But remind yourself, "He who pays the piper calls the tune".'

Experienced nannies are well aware that this subject is the bitterest pill of a live-in job. It's the main reason that they become daily nannies if they can. It's also the main reason why employers would prefer a daily nanny, if money and highly organized routines presented no problems.

It is hard for nannies not to feel that a ban on boyfriends in the house smacks of a hangover from *Upstairs Downstairs* when 'followers' were shown the door. Several comment that they don't understand why their employers are prepared to trust them with their children, but don't trust them not to choose a boyfriend who joins his girlfriend while babysitting, has a plate of baked beans, nicks the silver and heads for Rio.

There are a few nannies pro the boyfriend ban: 'It is difficult. Never have a boyfriend in the house, then there are no problems and employers don't have to worry that the kids are neglected as they would if the boyfriend stayed the night.'

A Norlander with years of residential experience says, 'I think it's a bit of give and take on both sides. Obviously discretion is the keynote. No one has ever given me rules exactly, but employers are within their rights to lay down a few guidelines.' Another says, 'My boyfriend, now husband, was welcome at all times. It's the same as living at home, you don't have as much privacy as you would like. Yes they can make rules, it's their house, and they are concerned for your welfare.'

Employers relate a wealth of horror stories from their friends and relations and often from their own experience too. The most common rules are 'no men in the house at all'; 'no men in the house unless we are there and then out by midnight and never upstairs'; 'no men ever in the house while on duty' and variations on that theme. Obviously a sane employer will relax the rules for a steady boyfriend – but this is where we meet a problem of definition.

Many employers report that their nannies become affianced surprisingly often. One nanny divulged over the cornflakes that she 'got engaged last night and it didn't half hurt'. Just as 'engagements' are not always what they seem, so also the 'steadiness' of a boyfriend can be called into question. Out once with a guy and he's a boyfriend, twice and it's 'steady'. Some mothers reckon the boyfriend a feature of the household after a couple of months; others think this is an absurdly short time and don't acknowledge anything less than six months' courtship.

If an employer has to consider the vexed question at all, she would prefer a long-standing stable relationship which was in place when she hired the nanny. This assumes that the first passion is spent and that he lives nearby (vital), preferably with his own roof. It can be disastrous to hire a nanny who has a serious boyfriend living far away. The most caring employer will probably fail to settle the lovesick girl, or the faithless man will drop her within weeks for a local lass and you will have to pick up the pieces.

A Wiltshire mother remembers, 'When one of our nannies discovered the opposite sex, it blew her mind. When out of love she was moody and when in love she could think of nothing else. The children were forever being taken to wherever her current beau was employed in the village.' To say that the reason for this restriction is that the nanny may not be paying your child adequate attention is superfluous; it can be dangerous too.

One working mother was told by a neighbour that she had passed her nanny embracing a man on a seat at the Round Pond in Kensington Gardens. Before her very eyes the little boy she was meant to be looking after fell into the water. The nanny hadn't mentioned it to the mother, and had threatened the boy with a beating if he did.

There is no other job which permits an employee to sit on her boyfriend's knee half the afternoon and get paid for it (apart from the notorious casting director's suite and the same sort of boss's secretary). Don't stand any nonsense on this one. Boyfriends are not allowed to accompany nannies in or out of the house while they are on duty.

Back to babysitting. If you have a daily nanny or mother's help and you get her to do occasional overtime, which means babysitting, she may not want to come unless her boyfriend is in tow, which is why she 'lives out'. A babysitter may feel the same way. It is very common in North America for the devoted couple to arrive together. Many British parents buy this line and let the boyfriend come too, because they are between a rock and a hard place and know they have no option. The employer of a live-in nanny does not have this problem, but even so many are generous and feel that babysitting is not 'on duty' in the strict sense and, feeling guilty about being a curb on young love, invite the boyfriend to sit in too.

Nine times out of ten this is fine. The tenth time is graphically described by many employers. 'Imagine my fury when I discovered Sandra with her policeman boyfriend snogging on our drawing room sofa while the kids went unpotted.' There are other things nannies are reluctant to do in front of their admirers, especially being covered in sick by a teething baby, or feeding a bawling infant who refuses to burp quickly. Just like the Billy the Bull story, no one wants their nosey eight-year-old snooping round the door and witnessing a torrid scene.

Such behaviour is unprofessional in the extreme. One employment agent says, 'If she leaves the door open so she can hear the children, it's fine if her boyfriend is there while she's babysitting.' This is irresponsible advice to a new mother. When you know your nanny very well and her boyfriend is someone you like and trust then maybe it's OK, but only then can you decide.

The fear that boyfriends may burgle is not a fantasy that employers dream up to spoil nannies' fun. Any nanny talking to a strange man about a weekend away with her employers or their plans to take her on holiday puts the household at risk. Copying a key takes seconds. And you haven't yet invited them past the front door. Tell your carer that careless talk costs money. Some readers may think that this sort of detail is a bit paranoid, but in cities the crime rate is rising and who wants to be part of the statistics?

It isn't the case that most employers mistrust their nannies, but they cannot be expected automatically to like and trust her friends until they know them. One agent with 25 years' experience, who describes herself as a dinosaur on matters moral, says:

> If the boyfriend is allowed in the house, then he must only be entertained in the sitting room or nursery and must leave at a proper time. The nanny may not do as she wishes in someone else's house. I may be very old hat, but that girl should not be in a residential job. Employers are cowardly and don't want to deal directly and correctly with their nannies, because they don't want to have to sack them with all the ensuing fuss and bother. They ought to be clear and say "the human race must go on but not in my house".

How can you avoid the boyfriend problem? Some nannies are cosy, homely and not particularly keen on going out or acquiring a boyfriend. They may also be less than lovely and may often be overweight. It is cynical and rather unkind to bank on your nanny limiting her life to your children – a prisoner of her spotty face and lack of discipline with the doughnuts – or to hire her with this ulterior motive. Many employers choose nannies and mother's helps whom, they hope, will not attract boyfriends, and, even better from their perspective, won't have any social life.

Some employers rejoice in the fact that their nanny's idea of a good day off is to be huddled in bed with a box of Milk Tray and the fourth Mills and Boon of the week.

Sex and nannies

Oddly enough, the subject of lesbians hardly emerged in all our research, although a few mothers had vague indications of this proclivity, having observed a few rather unbalanced same sex relationships. One funny story starts off with a family and some friends having a drink in the garden one summer evening and hearing titters from the au pair's bedroom. A pair of frilly knickers floated down into the delphiniums nearby. Suspicions were confirmed, the employer had noted no boyfriend and a butch girlfriend. Nothing was mentioned and the au pair's leanings presented no problem.

There have been many cases of nannies' and mother's helps' pregnancies and abortions reported to us by employers. Sometimes the nanny is too scared to tell her parents and the employer feels responsible for arranging the abortion (sometimes paying for it too), and dealing with guilt and possible other side effects. The way to avoid all these hassles is to talk about it and point your nanny in the direction of the nearest family planning clinic.

Working parents were astonished recently when their nanny confronted them with the words, 'I've liked your baby so much, I want one for myself, so now I'm five months' pregnant; will it be OK if I go on working for you?' They weren't convinced that she would have the same stamina or time to do her job properly, so they had to tell her to leave.

A few employers do keep nannies and even au pairs on throughout their pregnancy. Sometimes they marry their boyfriends, or go home. Rarely, they remain nannies in the household and look after theirs and yours together. At this point an employer has not only adopted a parental, but also a grandparental role, and one can only wish them luck: no job description can be this flexible.

Sex and employers

The classic story of the husband getting off with the Scandinavian au pair sounds rather dated, possibly because real life is rarely that straightforward. For example, a nanny and her employer were having an affair and the employer's wife announced that she was expecting another baby. The nanny gave in her notice at once, outraged that her lover had been two-timing her so flagrantly. The agency to which the nanny returned for tea and sympathy was furious with her, quite rightly, for her lack of professionalism.

Male employers with a dim recollection of Tom Jones and Fanny Hill who entertain the fantasy of a modern nanny wilting with desire while he exercises his *droit de seigneur* are out of time and out of luck. Wives are beadier than ever, and some recognizing their dear husband's little ways, tell the agencies not to send pretty nannies. Jamie Turner of the eponymous agency, says of his Australians and New Zealanders, 'Occasionally girls are too good-looking, which poses a threat to the exhausted mum of three who is not feeling her best. She can't cope with some sensational bit of crumpet driving the old man crazy.'

Unless employers and their friends are being super discreet, the instances of male employers jumping into bed with the nanny are too few to focus on for long. However there are many instances of territorial and macho display; nannies have myriad recollections of peacock behaviour.

Apparently, husbands walk into the nanny's bathroom, bedroom and lavatory much too often to be so amnesiac. They walk around the home intimidating all viewers with their dazzling boxer shorts and hairy pot bellies. 'Short towelling dressing gowns open to the navel are offputting at breakfast', and, 'he gets undressed anywhere except his own bedroom' wail two nannies. This can verge on harassment, although it does seem almost unconscious and nannies are very forgiving: 'I just laugh', they say.

Rarely, infatuation may strike the nanny, too. One father went upstairs to get a suitcase and was amazed to find in a cupboard a shrine to himself. His photograph was mounted and surrounded with lipstick kisses and buttercups, Indian beads and burnt joss sticks. He beat a hasty retreat and guess what happened? As usual, nothing.

Nannies sometimes date employers' friends and relations. This can be tricky. Tread warily. As several report, she may end up as your sister-in-law. Discourage weekend guests from corridor-creeping; the unfairest part of this is that the lustful guest departs and most employers feel they have to sack the nanny for lack of discretion on Monday morning. If there are signs of vital business clients or your husband's boss murmuring to the nanny, take urgent action and explain why her intimate relationship with either would be considered a Bad Thing.

One erstwhile head of CACHE mentions employers' double standards. He says, 'Why shouldn't a nanny have a boyfriend in the house when her employer may be having an affair?'

It is a fact of nannying that an employer can say 'do what I say and not what I do' and mean it. Living in makes a nanny privy to secrets that no one else is in a position to comment on. It is not logical for a nanny to think she can do what you do. You pay her and your private behaviour is not intended as a model for hers. Having established this as a point of principle for any residential staff, it is obviously far from ideal for a nanny to be forced to observe her employers behaving like alley cats. Don't expect respect. Do-as-you-would-be-done-by is the good rule in all personal dealings and a nanny may leave if your standards are too different from those you insist she live by.

Nannies can be bricks – and even mortar – in a crumbling marriage when it is essential that she doesn't let on that she knows anything about what is going on, turns a deaf ear to all rows and shields the children from the fall-out. 'Practising for a play again, dears' is the line when the parents are shouting at each other. One nanny tells us that she is staying on in the job after five years there already, and by giving evidence in court she hopes to ensure that the mother isn't granted custody of her charges. It is unfair of employers to put pressure on a nanny to stay for the sake of the children in these sad circumstances, and most nannies and mother's helps are well advised not to become involved.

Honesty

Apart from any moral view, it is not practical to keep someone in the house who tells lies or steals money or valuables. Some employers are apparently so desperate to keep a 'good' nanny, that they turn a blind eye to the disappearance of the odd fiver, and ignore a bit of glossing over the exact facts of the case whenever she is discovered to be in the wrong.

Experienced employers will know the thin end of the wedge. Honesty has to be a House Rule for the protection of your children. If a nanny can lie, fib, prevaricate, cheat or fudge about little things, even by omission, you do not know exactly what is going on. This is your right as an employer.

Once a nanny has forfeited your trust you have to be on the look-out until some time has passed and you're sure it was uncharacteristic and is unlikely to recur. Some parents can't cope with the insidious erosion of trust or the stress of the anticipation of the next time, and consider it a sackable offence. One mum says, 'It can be the most dangerous thing there is if you don't know exactly how and why a toddler hurt himself. How is a doctor to produce a diagnosis?'

Some people think it anachronistic and even pious to insist on the whole truth. Qualities such as integrity, honesty, honour, courage (much needed for owning up) and loyalty are essential for all jobs like nannying that involve much discretion and responsibility for other people's possessions, including the most important, their children. They are never out of date and employers should prize them above any other consideration. They are just as vital as professional competence. A nanny should say what she does and do what she says.

Sackable offences

Employers and their partners will have to be clear before they hire a nanny precisely what 'beyond the pale' means in their household. In other words, what a nanny could get up to for which you would sack her at once. It is only fair that she should be quite clear if certain behaviour, in or out of your house while in your employ, will mean summary dismissal. Also, it makes things easier for you. One clear example of summary dismissal is provided by one employer who, having refused permission for any boyfriend to go into the house, returned after an evening out to find her nanny and a man in the employer's bed. She was told to pack her bags and she left that night.

It is difficult to pontificate on what constitutes a Sackable Offence Situation (SOS) for different families. Employers sack nannies for many reasons. A specimen statement of employment produced by FRES mentions 'theft and drunkenness as examples of reasons which might give rise to summary dismissal'. It also lists as reasons which might give rise for the need for disciplinary measures:

a causing a disruptive influence in the household
b job incompetence
c unsatisfactory standards of dress or appearance
d conduct during or outside working hours prejudicial to the interest or reputation of the employer
e unreliability in time keeping or attendance
f failure to comply with instructions and procedure

Employers report that the following Sackable Offence Situations have provided grounds for dismissal if, having been warned, a nanny does nothing to correct them: dirtiness, unkindness to children, theft, dishonesty, smelliness, smacking, general bad temper, moodiness, rudeness, neglect of children, swearing, sulking, boyfriends overnight, men in beds or anywhere *in flagrante*, getting off with the husband, drunkenness, insincerity, favouritism, irresponsibility, loose behaviour, arrogance, being a know-all, insolence, pregnancy, sluttishness, slovenliness, overfamiliarity, hypochondria, unpunctuality, idleness, selfishness and shopping for herself on duty.

If you need to take disciplinary action, they suggest that the procedure might be: first – oral warning; second – written warning; third – dismissal.'

Pick your own, and be reassured that if you see any signs of the above, you are not alone. One father summed up many an employer's SOS as 'theft and fornication on the premises'.

The Big Four: Pay, Time Off, Holidays and Perks

The price of nannies continues to rise. As there are too few trained and experienced nannies for too many jobs, so they are earning the most they ever have in real terms.

Each proven rung up the nanny career ladder will add to the cost. So, you get what you pay for – the well-worn cliché that if you pay peanuts you get monkeys is indubitably the case in the nanny market. An untrained 18-year-old mother's help will expect not less than £90 net in the late 1990s in London, a bit less than that in the country.

The new NNEB nanny will cost more – £120 net plus all found is the bottom line for London, a bit less elsewhere. Experienced (i.e. around two years in a job or two) NNEBs earn between £120 and £200, occasionally more in London. Nannies with less well known qualifications are a little cheaper.

If you are taking a girl from one of the residential fee-paying colleges (see Chapter 7) – expect to pay more. A Norland probationer commands a minimum of £140 gross a week, but when fully fledged after her nine-month probationary period with your family, it goes up. An experienced nanny from any of the above colleges (and experience means more than two years) earns in the range of £180 to £250 net all found. The upper end of the scale is most often afforded by working parents, though these nannies can earn double this figure in North America or the Middle East.

Daily nannies are expensive and you will have to spend extra on babysitters or pay the daily nanny more to babysit occasionally, if you can persuade her to do so. A daily nanny will cost you roughly £5 an hour per day for about 10 hours every weekday. Daily nannies are usually trained and experienced, but there seems to be less variation in earnings. In a city a babysitter will cost you about £3–4 an hour and a lift or a taxi home.

Obvious and hidden costs of live-in help

- Employer's National Insurance contributions; pay rises; bonuses; overtime pay
- Extra help when she is away
- Employer's presents and treats for the nanny
- Time spent recruiting and cost of advertising and/or agency fees and organizing her tax and National Insurance payments or paying an accountant to do it
- Lighting and heating her bedroom
- Hot water for washing, bathing and laundry
- Electricity – elsewhere for her use. TV, radio/cassette, sewing machine, the hairdryer, etc.
- All her food and drink
- The telephone
- Use of vehicle(s) – wear and tear, possible extra insurance, cost of accidents, possible cost of losing employer's no claims bonus
- General wear and tear on the employer's home and probable need for redecoration in the nanny's bedroom and bathroom – carpets, chairs, tables (effects of cigarette burns, nail varnish and coffee spills), sheets, towels, etc.

There is a premium for hiring a temporary nanny, reflected in the fee to the agency for finding her and the transient nature of her stay with you.

Part-time nannies are usually also mature and their rates are to be compared with those of the daily nanny.

The whole aim of sharing a nanny is to reduce the cost. The family with whom she lives and boards usually contribute less to her wages than the family whose child she also cares for. For example, an experienced NNEB might expect £150 upwards for looking after two children from separate families. The host family might expect to pay £60 to £65 of this figure.

There are three sorts of mother's helps; the untrained English girl, the Australian or New Zealander and other girls from overseas whose mother tongue is not English. Mother's helps are employed to do the housework as well as to look after the children, although the Australians and New Zealanders go mostly to households where a cleaner is also employed. The minimum wage for full-time foreign and British girls is £80 per week in London, the younger English girl (about 16 to 18) will make just about exactly this, but the older and more experienced girl may make as much as a new NNEB, at which point she graduates from the kitchen floor and is called a nanny.

Australians and New Zealanders don't care much what they do, but must be paid a good whack, i.e. £130 plus a week net.

Foreign au pairs are the most exploited of this group of child carers. They can be paid as little as £30 per week for well over the Home Office guideline of 30 hours a week. In London, the going rate is around £45 a week; the au pair plus arrangement means that she works longer hours and is paid more.

Childminders are paid between £80 to £120 a week gross, and more in London. The hours are similar to those worked by a daily nanny, to fit in with office hours.

One employer comments, 'You start by paying as low as you dare and you raise it by a few pounds every four to six months'. A second says, 'A decent wage pays dividends in terms of results: quality of child care, loyalty, and length of stay.' Another has a strict 'invest in the best' policy which she reckons is particularly vital morally to the working mother. 'The difference between a fairly ordinary nanny/mother's help and a really reliable nanny who can safely be left on her own and let me live a trouble-free life is the price of a good meal each week.' Yet another says smugly, 'She is expensive and worth every penny.'

Be honest from the start about the nature of your own finances and only hire a nanny whom you can afford comfortably. This is sensible because otherwise you will resent the drain on the family purse and this will become obvious to the nanny, whose perks won't measure up against those of her friends, and she will leave you sooner rather than later.

It is short-sighted to pay below the going rate. This is less easy to do, of course, with a trained nanny or in London where there are plenty of comparisons nearby. Having discovered the extent of the discrepancy between her meagre pittance and her contemporaries' fat pay packets, she will either ask you for a rise, or just leave.

It is easier to get away with paying a mother's help and particularly a foreign mother's help less than what is currently accepted in the area. The scope for paying au pairs way below what is acceptable even for so-called 'pocket money' is even greater. It is disgraceful how many people take advantage of a girl who isn't staying long in this country, and has no means of knowing what is reasonable. Even if she does realize she is being genuinely exploited, she is probably returning to the fatherland shortly and won't confront her employer.

Salary rises

There are lots of reasons for raising your nanny's salary, none better than another, but the good rule is to do it as often and as generously as you can afford. Some people say raise it every six months. In the 1990s this means around £10 a week rise a year. The important thing is to have a 'carrot ahead always' says one mum, so that a wonderful nanny will stay that little bit longer. Also keep a weather eye on other local nannies' pay and rises, and try to be sure you are slightly ahead of the street.

Employers link their nanny's pay to the inflation rate, another gives them a rise for 'extra experience' as often as she remembers. One working mother gave her nanny a pay rise when she received one herself. By contrast another says flatly, 'I give a rise when I'm asked for one.'

Any nanny will anticipate a salary rise linked to the arrival of a new baby and her increased responsibilities and probably increased hours too.

Bonuses are a way of giving your nanny a pat on the back. Christmas and Easter are good opportunities and a bit of extra cash for her holiday in Switzerland or wherever is a nice thought. Some employers go so far as to discuss a bonus scheme in the interview; others prefer it to be a spontaneous gesture of appreciation for a job well done.

Time on and time off

A nanny's hours on duty are very long compared with those of an ordinary job. In effect, many nannies spend most of their week on 24-hour duty. Some nannies point to the fireman analogy, meaning that a nanny may be asleep but at any minute is required to leap into her boots and sort out a night-time crisis, just like a member of the fire brigade. But this argument ignores the reality that a nanny who is expected to be on 24-hour call five days a week is not likely to be *en poste* for the next. Why should she stay with such treatment? In all our research, it is clear that the aim of most parents is to keep the nanny happy, well rested and content with the job, so that she will stay for as long as possible. In fact, nearly all employers reckon it is their job to deal with their children at night.

Asking nannies to do more hours than were discussed and agreed at the interview is, nevertheless, a common transgression by employers and one which causes a lot of resentment. You must be clear exactly what you want your nanny to do from the beginning. If you are a working mother who may occasionally be caught in a 6 pm conference, don't say that you will always be home by 6.30 pm. It raises expectations and is disappointing. Warn her by phone the moment you know it is going to happen, avoid doing it often and grovel if you have messed up her evening rendezvous. It is a form of blackmail to behave unreliably with a nanny's time off, because obviously she cannot leave the baby alone in the house. In an office job, she would be able to clock off on time.

If you are a busy working mother who cannot guarantee to be back when scheduled all the time, spell it out to her at the beginning that it will be that sort of job, and you will be wise to pay her over the odds for inconveniencing her. This is the way people think in London where there are lots of well-paid jobs and too few nannies. Exploitation will occur more where nannies are isolated and jobs scarce. Relocation presents a great problem to many nannies, which is a pity for them.

One employer's neat ploy is to tell the nanny that she is to 'keep the children's hours', but in reality this is from 7 am to 7 pm in most households. Obviously au pairs are different (see Chapter 8). Baby-sitting comes with the job. It may be a 12-hour a day job, but most nannies tell us that they have quite a lot of time off during the day when their charges are asleep or at school. Some employers suggest a quiet time for all after lunch so that the nanny can have a break.

There are many different formulae for giving nannies time off. A nanny graduates to all weekends off as soon as she can swing it. Nannies who are in sole charge during the week expect all weekends off and mostly get them. Most nannies work a five-day week. This trend is supported by the rising numbers of working mothers who want to look after their children themselves at weekends.

Those that want more help at weekends pay a lot extra and then, unless they employ a separate weekend nanny, have to make alternative weekday arrangements so nannies don't collapse with sleep deprivation. Here are some examples of overtime arrangements:

- two weekends off a month and two extra days off;
- one weekend working a month and a day a week off;
- half a day a week off and every weekend;
- one and a half days off a week and a whole weekend off once a month.

If you have a chance, be generous with extra time off. Do not impinge on the nanny's free time at all. If she is in the house on her day off, it is not good enough to say, 'Can you keep an eye on the baby who's asleep upstairs while I pop to the shops?' Remind everyone in the house when it is her day off and, if she is sleeping in, to be quiet.

It depends a lot on the atmosphere of the relationship, but, unless you are quite relaxed when your nanny is around, it is not unreasonable to expect her either to stay in her room or to leave the house on days off. You cannot be expected to have to hoover around her and you won't enjoy her watching how ineptly you deal with the chores. Long weekends, i.e. starting on Friday lunchtime right through to late Sunday or crack of dawn on Monday, are a treat for everyone on occasion. Splitting a day off mid-week into two is, incidentally, a bonus for the employer and sometimes agreeable to nannies too. Be flexible with reasonable notice about her granny's 50th wedding anniversary, and swap days off if requested.

Holidays

Holidays should be paid. The range is from two (mean) to four (generous) weeks. Bank Holidays often are not honoured but either they should be, or they should be made up in some way. Some employers save on the expense of holidays by offering, say, three weeks' paid and one or two weeks' unpaid.

Often foreign mother's helps and au pairs don't seem to merit holidays, paid or unpaid. This is partly because they are usually here for a finite stay, ranging from six to nine months on the whole (see Chapter 8). The English have a tendency to insist that being abroad makes every day a holiday, and because the foreign girls, unlike the outspoken Australians and New Zealanders, don't demand it, they miss out. If the latter work for a year they should get at least two weeks' paid leave.

Perks

Bonuses are a perk. Experienced nannies say that in their first job or maybe two, they focussed on salary to the exclusion of other factors like perks and the employer's personality, but that the quality of their lives became increasingly important to them. In other words, the nicer the accommodation – spacious, gracious, warm, comfortable – the nicer the food – varied, exotic and generously available – the nicer the holidays – hot sun, well staffed hotels, general luxury and impressive postcards to send home – the better. And that is just the beginning.

A rich employer who is happy with her nanny may be an endless source of bounty. It is not just the Middle Eastern employer who can lavish presents and treats on an employee. All our researches have shown that English employers can be extremely generous and inventively so, though a few have no conscience. One London agency says, 'They promise a girl perks in lieu of better pay and then the perks never materialize.'

Some examples of a worthwhile perk are totally self-contained and well-decorated accommodation with a separate entrance and telephone line; a smart car for the nanny's exclusive use and petrol, service, insurance all paid; the employer may make available her hairdresser, dressmaker, masseuse, exercise class, manicurist free of charge to her nanny.

There are also recreational facilities like the tennis court, the indoor and/or outdoor swimming pools, horses, jacuzzis, saunas, helicopters, yachts, and even complete gymnasiums.

Holidays and travelling generally can provide well-known inducements to a nanny to stay that extra summer or year. In fact, some employers are amusingly cynical about the way in which they oh-so-casually mention that the toddlers are going on safari in the autumn, though they engineer the conversation to coincide with the first signs of discontent during the previous winter.

Sensible tactics also comprise the inclusion of the nanny where practicable in any treats and luxuries. Simultaneously, the employer must remain aware of how an expensive lifestyle may transform the nanny from a simple, appreciative, willing young girl into a spoiled, idle creature who complains of the service on the Air Canada flight.

Less exotic and more affordable nanny entertainment can be provided by tickets to pop concerts, musicals and the ballet. Fund them to take the children skating, up the river, and to the local Disney offering. Extra time off is always popular.

Most employers report themselves embarrassed by their nanny's largesse towards them and their children on birthdays, at Christmas and on such unlikely festivals as Father's Day. One way of repaying their kindness is to give them carefully chosen special presents at Christmas and on their birthday. Remind whoever is travelling abroad to include a token for the nanny in their baggage when they return.

Chapter 3

Pick Your Own

It might seem patronizing to try to generalize about the character of the nanny. Nannies were simply women, and as various as that: there were witty nannies, devious nannies, murderess nannies, and lesbian nannies (rare), drunk nannies and scholar nannies . . . all occupations that demand particular qualities or impose special conditions inevitably tend to make those that practise them resemble each other in certain respects or attract people with the qualities required by the conditions. This is particularly true of vocations – that is, occupations to which people feel called because of some special skill or need, occupations which frequently demand sacrifices they are willing to make to fulfil that need or use that skill.

Jonathan Gathorne-Hardy,
The Rise and Fall of the British Nanny

The Ideal Nanny

The question of whether an ideal nanny exists is confidently answered by many employers who can't speak highly enough of a present incumbent. In fact, it may be observed that celebrities, from Mick Jagger to Esther Rantzen, given the chance to talk about their private lives, all take the opportunity to give their nannies a puff – a good insurance policy for a warm greeting on returning from work.

It is surprising, given how much time this book spends discussing the problems of the nanny/employer relationship and its pitfalls, how often both parties like each other and get on famously. Everybody's human and, regrettably, nannies are no exception. Even an ace has her weak points. It all depends how much you trust, depend on and genuinely like your nanny as to whether you focus on her minor faults and they drive you mad, or whether you choose to ignore them almost entirely because she's so great in virtually every other way.

Diana Forney (NNEB, NN, RSH, consultant to the nanny profession in America) commented aptly on this subject in the *National Nanny Newsletter*:

> A good nanny has a stable and happy disposition coupled with a good sense of humour. She is not subject to intense and obvious mood swings or bouts of unpredictable behaviour. For this reason most successful nannies have already passed through the teenage years. She has a good sense of herself, likes herself and knows how to take care of her own needs without requiring guidance or constant direction from the outside, since nanny work is frequently isolated and can be quite lonely. She needs to be trained and alert enough to recognize the value of good nutrition and exercise to maintain good health. She needs to be independent enough to be able to make friends and find entertainment outside the household in which she is working. To this end she needs hobbies and interests outside of child care work. She has resolved her relationships with her own family in such a way that she can work professionally in another family without involving her past experiences and relationships in ways that may not be healthy. That is to say that she knows what the role of nanny is and should be, and she is not seesawing back and forth between playing the role of another child in the family or competing with the mother for her position.
>
> The successful nanny is also the realistic nanny. She is the one who is working in this profession because she likes the work not because she craves the money or power of association with wealth. She knows that the work is difficult and at times tedious in whatever circumstances . . . those nanny applicants who perceive their work as a casual job are certain to be disappointed (as are their families).
>
> It needs to be noted that the successful nanny is a person who has a strong sense of ethics and responsibility coupled with integrity and honesty. She is kind but firm with the children in her charge and is honest and respectful of the privacy of the household in which she is working. . . .
>
> Finally the nanny must be wise enough to negotiate the business aspects of her professional work, i.e. understand the contracts and deductions and wage issues and be assertive enough to discuss and resolve disputes as they arise in the job. Absolutely every job has some elements of personality conflict which will emerge. It cannot be helped when one is working so closely in a household. The successful nanny is the one who can discuss conflict without ruffling feathers unnecessarily. She can assert her own needs while respecting the other point of view. She operates as a professional from her knowledge and intellect, not from emotion or instinct.

It might be helpful to read the following comments before discussing what type of nanny you want to live with. A top ten of qualities employers most prize in their nannies is listed below in the order in which they were most frequently mentioned:

cheerful
clean and neat
humorous
flexible
punctual
polite
reliable
fun
child-loving
honest

They also like them to be: enthusiastic, affable, wholesome, attractive, creative, friendly, hygienic, sympathetic, generous, loyal, dedicated, immaculate, reliable, kind, strict, affectionate, observant, trustworthy, conscientious, caring, warm-hearted, even-tempered, unflappable, tidy, stable, tough but tender, resilient, imaginative, calm, easy, firm, organized, professional, unmoody, hard-working, intelligent, quick off the mark, efficient, nimble, considerate, funny, tolerant, pleasant, patient, healthy, unselfish, out-going, serene, robust, good-natured, educated (both well and highly), well-groomed, middle class, smiley, gentle, unobtrusive, tender, sensitive, consistent, charming, inventive, practical, keen to learn, cuddly, safety-conscious, engaging, adaptable, perceptive, jolly, resourceful, down-to-earth, enterprising, easy-going, imaginative, persevering, unflurried, direct, straightforward, demonstrative, ingenious, aware and instinctive, loving, sensible, mature, presentable, lively, industrious, energetic, competent and happy.

They don't want much do they?

One sage old mum puts her finger on some of the best nanny attributes with this definition:

> A good nanny knows she has to win the child's affection and respect before she can tell him to stop picking his nose. Our best nanny said she hated putting the children to bed because she wanted to go on playing with them. Once that level is reached there is never any problem with discipline.

Another comments that the 'ideal' type of nanny you want and/or find changes as the children grow older. The loving, warm person who cuddled the baby may not be the best companion to kick a football with five years later.

Perhaps the most telling commentary on a nanny's role was provided by the employers' remarks about their own needs:

Attractive in an unchallenging way, friendly and polite.

Kept me in good order so I never took her for granted.

Always has a sweet smile especially at breakfast.

Sensitive to our set-up.

Has a quiet voice.

Likes music and sings to the children while they bath.

Cooks easily and efficiently.

Organizes toys and clothes well.

Has plenty of ideas for amusing kids.

Keeps the place in order seemingly effortlessly.

Is always learning.

Is quick to learn a good routine and not thrown by the odd exception or diversion.

Never cuts corners.

Nothing is too much trouble.

She mucks in with anything.

Is a ray of sunshine.

Doesn't do the job by the book.

All this sounds more like applying for a new wife by mail order than an employer paying someone to be capable and pleasant. It is essentially an entirely personal choice.

Nannies were less voluble about their ideal employers, but because they all said the same thing, their top ten list of 'requirements' created itself:

easy-going

down-to-earth

kind

friendly

appreciative

humorous

fun

fair

reasonable

ordinary

The amusing aspect is that the only two adjectives in common on the two lists are 'fun' and 'humorous', so if employers think they can't grin and bear it they had better start trying. Nannies pray that you will laugh like a drain when they have flooded the bathroom. 'Laughing it off' and 'luckily she saw the funny side' are common pronouncements, which will make any experienced employer grind her teeth.

Readers will quickly get the picture from the following comments that how employers behave towards a nanny matters crucially. There is only one, a mother's help, who says, 'They must be courteous and reasonable but I need not like them.' All the others say:

Extremely important that I like my employer.

Looks at me as an equal.

A bad relationship causes a bad atmosphere and is sensed by the kids.

My employers are great people and I respect them.

Somebody friendly, which matters a lot if you live in.

A relationship with an employer is like one with a friend or a guardian and is bound to go up and down. Your overall feeling must be liking them.

I like a boss who doesn't become too friendly and nosey.

You'd better like her. Your employer is your charge's most treasured possession.

Different Options

Your choice is limited straight away by what is available, where you are, whether you are at home or out at work – full-time or part-time, how much money you have, how big your home is and whether you can stand the idea of sharing it with a stranger. Just as important are the matters of whether you feel you *want* help with your children and can reconcile it with your image of yourself – will it embarrass you to be an employer?

On offer throughout the country, although the choice may be limited if you live somewhere remote, are the following options for child care: a living-in full-time nanny, a living-in part-time nanny, a living-in full-time mother's help, a living-in part-time mother's help (probably shared), an au pair, a part-time daily nanny, a full-time daily nanny, a temporary nanny, a maternity nurse, a private or state day nursery, nursery schools, crèches at work, child-minders and babysitters.

First it is necessary to decide whether you want your child looked after in your home or elsewhere. If the former, you then have to decide whether you want the carer to live with you or to come to the house every day – a live-in or daily nanny?

Many employers feel that it is unquestionably best that a child is looked after in his own home surrounded by his possessions, that he nap in his own bed, play in his own garden and have his own friends to tea. They also reckon they have more control of what their child gets up to during the day if the carer comes to the house.

Others feel less strongly about it and say that they like their child being with other children while they are out at work and provided the children have plenty of space and light and food, taking the child out of his own environment is fine. The alternatives to your own home are childminders and nurseries.

Childminders and day nurseries

This book is principally concerned with in-home care and its stresses and pleasures for the employer, but this option is restricted to a tiny percentage. Almost all children of working parents are looked after by members of the family (at home) and by child minders (elsewhere). A smaller minority still attend state day nurseries. In practice, this is more of an option that it used to be. Due to the decline in the number of council-run nurseries over the last 20 years it is difficult for a family without major problems, like poor housing or very little money, to secure a place for their child. In most areas local authorities have more involvement with community day nurseries.

Private day nurseries are another matter. Good for big city life, they are usually of a high standard and staffed by trained nursery nurses.

Workplace crèches are mostly cheaper if subsidized and the facilities are also good. Everyone wants more of these – there are far too few at present.

Live-in or live-out?

Now we come to the advantages and disadvantages of daily and residential in-home care, i.e. daily and living-in nannies and mother's helps. Let's start with all the cons of living-in help.

Live-in nannies need more food, light, heat and hot water, and use of the telephone and car than daily nannies. In addition they use washing and drying machines, dishwashers, heated rollers and hair driers, their own TV and a whole host of other appliances on occasion. They take up space which would possibly otherwise be let or used for something else. In other words, residential nannies are the most obviously expensive options on offer, though it may seem that a daily one costs as much when it's time to pay her. Their salaries take a sizeable chunk out of an employer's post-tax salary.

Deprivation of privacy makes some employers decide they prefer daily help. Some mothers don't react well to the close relationship that a nanny may develop with their child or do not want to make the effort that it takes to live alongside someone else. Most employers feel responsible for their live-in nanny, but this weighs on them. Some others dislike the usurpation of their role in the home: 'It doesn't feel as though we live there when we get back after a day's work. Depending on the nanny it either looks like a dentist's waiting room or a tip.' There is a major problem when either live-in or live-out nannies or mother's helps fall ill, go on holiday or leave without notice, i.e. there is no built-in back-up system, as in a day nursery with several staff.

Other possible disadvantages of the live-in help include her personal habits, her manners, her friends and, above all, her boyfriends. All these things will impinge on you and your family and can be ignored if the nanny leaves at 6 pm. A live-in nanny needs more appreciation, not just for the job she does, but also for herself as a person. The turnover of live-in nannies can be for all these reasons higher than with daily nannies; it is a bigger strain for everyone.

Neither live-in nor live-out nannies do any housework apart from the children's rooms, washing and ironing their clothes, tidying toys and preparing and clearing up their meals. A live-in nanny will also clean her own room and her own and the children's bathroom.

The pros of live-in help include flexibility, 'You don't get that rushed feeling in the morning or the frantic after-work dash', paid-up babysitting and tailor-made attention for your children. Many parents are grateful for the fact that their children come to trust and love another adult who is a constant in their lives. The hassles of snow, rain, transport strikes, traffic hold-ups and just being unpunctual (and using most of the latter as excuses) are blissfully irrelevant.

Two major pluses of a live-in nanny are that the employer can get herself up and organized for the day without having to wake, dress and feed the children breakfast as well. At the other end of the day she and her husband can go out without having struggled through mass bath time, safe in the knowledge that if a child wakes up, he will be tended to by his nanny who will have the advantage of knowing what sort of day the child had, and why he might be upset.

All the expense and fuss of organizing babysitters (see Chapter 8) argues for the live-in nanny. Using a daily nanny will certainly ration your nights out and she will charge extra as well.

Daily nannies

Daily nannies receive the biggest pay cheques of the entire group. If a nanny counts up all the perks of a residential post, she is quids in; but, and it is a big but, as the nanny gets older she values her freedom above cash in hand and perks. After a few years it is a normal progression in the nanny world to choose daily work. It follows that daily nannies are also more mature in every sense. They are mostly trained and experienced, and are wiser and more careful. They know what they are doing and what they want to do with any luck, though a few get unhappier with every year that they don't have a husband and their own babies.

What is wonderful about daily nannies is that they are not homesick and their relationship with their employer is less close in ways which cause friction. Some mothers report that they feel much more grateful and affectionate towards a daily nanny – familiarity sometimes breeds a certain wariness. It is also good that children are less able to play mother and nanny off against one another and 'know where they are' with whomever is around.

Some people will pay the earth not to have living-in help. Whether the mother works or not, some families mind less about the hassles of babysitting arrangements than keeping their home their castle. Their dislike of the living-in nanny and all the repercussions is so great that they would rather have a lodger in the spare room who babysits at night and have a daily nanny. 'We found this the best solution and we've tried every permutation. Our expectations of nannies who lived with us had become so low that we abandoned them,' as one mother relates.

For many people who don't go away for weekends often, a nanny's constant presence off-duty can be a severe strain. 'It isn't that we make love on the shagpile in the living room or wash up Friday night's supper on Sunday night – but if we ever wanted to we could, without fussing about what a nanny will think. The solution is have a daily nanny.'

The biggest gripe about a daily nanny is that she may not be able to arrive punctually every morning unless she lives very close to the job. Transport hold-ups and deep snow, even if they delay her as little as five times a year, can be too many times to live through if the mother is a doctor on call or a barrister due in court in thirty minutes. The daily nanny must have a telephone. If she is ill, she must inform her employer as soon as possible – a temperature at 7 am should mean a call at 7.05 am to give you a chance to replace her and/or reorganize the schedule.

Not hearing much about her personal life and problems can turn into a problem. Few employers know when a daily nanny goes to bed at night, if she is experimenting with cocaine or whether her boyfriend beats her. Her lifestyle, unbeknown to you, may have an impact on your children. Try to talk to her about herself and her life when opportunities present themselves.

The other obvious difficulty is the babysitting. One of the main reasons that she is a daily nanny is that she wants her evenings to herself. Even if she agrees to a couple of nights a week babysitting in her contract, don't expect her to like it. Many employers say it makes waves to insist and they resort to babysitters.

Employers comment:

> It's impossible to have a daily nanny in the country.

> An advantage of a daily is that they are not hanging about in the evening; this can be a bit of a problem with a live-in. Ironically, one who definitely doesn't hang about in the evening is also a problem.

> Dailies are useless when I need them most: before breakfast, at bath time and for babysitting.

> Your house is your own to row in, to undress in, to swear in, to scratch in, to drink in, that's why I don't live in a commune. Having a nanny from 8 to 6 is bad enough: no nannies after dusk, they turn into werewolves.

> It is much easier to choose a daily nanny than the live-in kind. I have had wonderful daily nannies that I could never have lived with.

Nanny sharing

One way of making daily and living-in nannies cheaper is to set up a share arrangement, ideally with a friend or neighbour. This is an increasingly popular solution for part- and full-time working mothers because of the crippling expense of your own nanny. There are several ways of doing it. You can halve the week between two families, or halve the days, or the nanny can live with

one family and care for both families' children at the other home.
Both families share the expenses and, although the nanny herself
(whether live-in or daily) is paid a bit more for the extra responsibilities and work, it is a lot cheaper *per capita*.

A few very capable nannies say that they earn most by giving five
different families a day a week or variations on this theme, partly
for the money and partly for the interest. An enterprising nanny
may advertise on local newsagents' notice boards and organize
this gruelling regime herself; alternatively mothers can get together
and work it out. A few agencies are happy to co-operate.

Nanny sharing is a happy option for families who wish to keep
a long-staying nanny; they can arrange that she is kept busy out of
the house looking after other people's children a couple of days a
week in their home and defray the costs of her salary, as well as
caring for the host family's children after school. It can also be a
boon if two families have only one child each. Some think it a plus
if they are much the same age; others think that a gap avoids the
problems of looking after 'twins'.

There are built-in problems to the nanny share. It is essential to
like and respect the people with whom you share a nanny and,
some swear, they have to know them very well. However hard two
families try to be fair, someone always thinks they are losing out
and that their children are getting a rawer deal. If something
straightforward, like a car pool, or something intimate but short-
term, like a shared family holiday, can cause stress, the scope for
trouble with a nanny share is great.

Discipline, theories about diet, potty training and manners are
examples of child-rearing issues which some employers feel
strongly about and others don't – the twain should never meet in a
nanny share. One mother who wasn't that twitched about healthy
food says: 'I was a little impatient of the endless supplies of dried
apricots and sugar-free low-fat this and that I was expected to provide for their child – it pushed up my grocery bill something
chronic.'

One of the families sharing the nanny may upset the applecart
within months: they don't get on with the nanny/can't stand
you/think your child an unruly vandal/move house/dad is made
redundant/have quads/or the other mum decides to become a
full-time mum, so the nanny share has to be redesigned. Time and
time again with childminders, day nurseries and shared nannies,
mothers finally get fed up with the complications and hire someone for their exclusive use.

Temporary nannies

Some nannies make temporary nannying their life. They like the high rate of pay, comparative lack of friction with employers and the detachment from their charges that a nomadic life ensures. They look on temp work as a busy efficient job. The good ones tend to have had lots of experience, they may be 25 or 26 at least. Many of them share flats where they return between jobs. They are used to sole charge and well qualified to have it. They are the crack troops, the Flying Squad, who expect to sweep in and take over with the minimum of explanation and hand-holding. See Agencies (Chapter 18) for those that specialize in temp work; this is an area when a steady relationship with an agency pays dividends. For an old and valued client a good agency will find a good match within hours.

People employ temps when their usual child care arrangements break down. They need a temp when they take holidays, because mum is sick of mumming and wants a holiday, but with the children, or when her usual nanny is taking her holiday elsewhere simultaneously, or when there is a family holiday and mum wants help. Temps are also sought when the nanny is ill or something pressing has happened back home.

It is an expensive way to buy your way out of a crisis. It can also present a new set of problems rather than provide solutions. Coping with a stranger at short notice may prove an organizational and emotional strain. Do not skimp on references just because you are in a hurry. Rely on word of mouth or a reputable agency. One agency says her temps 'are stunners, the best of the lot. They are adaptable, flexible, have few hang-ups and don't bore for Britain about their boyfriend problems.' One temp with years of experience says, 'It's much harder work but it suits me. I love it. If there are problems with the family, I can say to myself in two weeks I'll be gone.'

Mother's helps

Mother's helps are a cheaper version of nannies. They are not trained, they do housework, and some of them graduate to being called a nanny after several years' experience. Then they stop doing housework and get paid the same as a trained nanny. People increasingly like age and experience better than training and no or little experience. It is a common misapprehension of new mothers that new NNEB-trained nannies are ready for sole charge posts.

Many employers want cheap help, and don't want someone who knows her rights. As one mother puts it: 'An untrained nanny doesn't carry a red book.' There is much less opportunity to exploit a trained nanny and a good thing too.

Many mothers feel that aptitude has nothing to do with training and they value common sense and integrity alongside age and experience. As Robin Rice says in *The American Nanny*, 'Intelligent, sincere, child loving candidates are rare enough without demanding training.' Another reason why employers like mother's helps is because there are lots of them about and they are easy to replace. One mother who could well afford a Norlander much prefers to train her own 18-year-olds and pay them generously if they listen hard and do the job well – her way. One of the things that experienced employers can't stand is being dictated to by a nanny who thinks she knows it all when she has just qualified.

For further discussion of mother's helps, including Australians and New Zealanders, see Chapter 8.

Au pairs

Au pairs are another form of part-time nanny, shared with their language courses. They are very good value, young, inexperienced with children, want to spend time *en famille*, often have poor English and don't stay much longer than about six months on average. See Chapter 8.

Having reviewed all the choices, work out with your spouse exactly what you think will suit you best and plumb the depths of your pocket. Afford as much as you can; try and treat hiring a nanny like buying a car – people always spend a bit more on that special trim or extra feature – but don't overdo it or you'll end up resenting the weekly drain on the family coffers more than appreciating the smoother ride. The cliché that 'You get what you pay for,' is so relevant to the nanny world.

You Know What You Like

Once you've decided what sort of child care you need, and for how many hours a day, and how much time you expect to spend with the nanny or mother's help, then it is time to examine and analyse your own preferences and prejudices. Be dead honest and insist your husband is too; consider your children's apparent likes and dislikes. Consciously dredge up your unspoken biases: you don't have to reveal them to anyone; just be aware that they inform your thinking more than you usually want to admit.

The ways in which people confess to prejudging the issue tell us a lot about employers. Employers do not want: militants (we think this means left-wing), fanatics of any kind, particularly in the time-honoured battlegrounds of health, religion and politics (in fact anyone who bangs on about anything often), gossips or 'thickies'. One is exhaustive in her dislikes: 'won't have starchy, snobbish, uniformed racists.'

Employers can't tolerate nannies who are: chippy (this makes them most uncomfortable), bossy (too much competition), over-confident, self-conscious and shy, apathetic, humourless, trendy and punky, dreary, phony or fantasizing. Many of them complain of unattractive accents and vocal pitch, summarized by: 'I couldn't employ a Cockney/Northern/Irish/South African/Antipodean/ refained taipe, however marvellous they were with the babies.'

Geography

One mother says that she 'can't stand sulky, stuffy, Southern, stuck-up types whom you know will not be loyal to one'. She likes girls from the North, particularly from Yorkshire. It must be said at once that if an employer has had a successful nanny from one place, she will tend to imagine that everybody from there will make ideal nannies for their family. In fairness to them, such silliness does often seem to unearth a string of good girls who are compatible. Perhaps if the employer is prejudiced in favour of a girl from a particular geographic area, expectations are self-fulfilled, rather as your stars come true.

Many others say that the Australians and New Zealanders are terrific – 'hard working, fun, adaptable, enjoy the outdoors; they generally muck in and don't faint at the sight of a scrubbing brush.' One might suggest that for some people familiarity breeds contempt and they prefer anyone with a different outlook – a Close Encounter in fact. Maybe this is what many an effete Londoner imagines he discovers in the hardy, down-to-earth, no-nonsense girl from the Borders. Others claim to find them incomprehensible and untameable and, worst of all, they find they get homesick. Often they don't stay long with the Sassenachs.

Every would-be green welly, easily recognized by the brace of black labradors crammed in the back of the school run Range

Rover in Clapham, insists that his nanny is born and bred in the country. They have a rose-spectacled view of apple-cheeked wholesomeness in these girls. It usually escapes their notice that nannies can become bright-lights-big-city as fast and as completely as though born within the sound of Bow Bells. Their ideal is to net a girl who will be as much at home at the muddy point-to-point near the renovated weekend cottage just outside beautiful downtown Newbury, as she will in the Smallbone swagged, dragged and gagged interiors of Wandsworth. 'You don't want a townie,' they all chorus.

The real thing want 'someone who will treat the farm as an adventure playground rather than a prison from the razzle dazzle'. Several mothers complain that 'English country girls are spoiled by their mums and are lazier and chippier than any foreigner' and 'within days they can't stand staying with granny away from the discos'.

Background

'Background' consists of another set of prejudices about the nanny's or mother's help's family which is supposed to provide you with further comforting indicators. 'A happy background is vital' – so many mothers say this that it's hard to imagine any nanny being foolish enough to reveal the mildest dislike of a sibling or letting on that she has lived away from home since she was 17. Unfortunately most employers are right to suspect that a nanny will treat children as she was treated herself as a child, but you would have to be psychic to know the details in advance.

No employer wants to be bothered with 'anything complicated' for choice, and the preference is unanimous for a nicely brought up girl with nothing less than perfect manners. When people ask nannies 'What do your parents do?' they hope to find that mum is a housewife and devoted to her brood and with high hopes for them. Ideally, dad is a policeman or something vocational, or anything self-starting, a volunteer at the local youth club and a pillar of the community. Employers hope to ascertain that the nanny's background is 'legal, decent, honest and truthful' and also confident, motivated, and well ordered.

As for the nanny's own achievements to date, employers are delighted to hear about the Guides, the Duke of Edinburgh's Award, the church choir, the school swimming team, and anything that sounds healthy, active and therefore laudable (all very Edwardian – a combination of cold baths and the team spirit).

Physical appearance

Prejudices about how and whether a nanny or mother's help looks the part professionally are personal in the extreme, to the point of offensiveness. Employers are outspoken in their dislike of bad skin, spots and greasy unkempt hair (especially teased peroxide spikes or coxcombs). Untidy, torn or dirty clothes in emerald and orange are too eye-catching for safety. Tights or stockings should be neat and unexceptionable and shoes should gleam dully. No diamanté bows, chains or studs anywhere about her person. Finger nails bitten to the quick or talons like Cruella de Vil are not popular. Anything else unhygienic is frowned upon too – bad teeth and breath are taboo. Slouching and slack posture receive minus points. Employers feel nervy about anyone larded in make-up.

Fat is a feminist issue but not in the world of nannies. The archetypes of Posy Simmonds and her ilk, for all their stated enlightenment, don't want a fat, ugly nanny in the house any more than anyone else does. The Sloane types are more likely to be sympathetic and associate bulk with comfort, succour and affection.

'Hugely fat and therefore hugely lazy', as one mother said dismissively as an unjust generalization, though even fat nanny employers admit that the long haul up the London staircase and the daily dash to the ducks look like a big effort and resembles a Babar illustration too much for complacency. No one minds an unlovely face much, as long as it is creased with smiles and comes with a warm personality.

Colour

There are a few black nannies working in the UK now and a few Asians as well. The agencies report that sadly there is still resistance to employing a black nanny, and, where the chance comes up more often, a mother's help of a different colour from the employer. As has already been discussed, most employers want to hire nannies who look and behave as much like themselves as possible; it makes sense (unattractive though it is) that they should feel the need to be as consistent in this area as in the others.

It is hard to put much faith in some employers' assurances that they would naturally *like* to hire a black nanny, if they have never done so. The unavoidable claustrophobia of a residential job may make someone of a different colour that much harder to relate to. 'There are enough imponderables', said one mother hopelessly, 'without a multi-racial challenge.'

A black nanny who works in Fulham tells us that she has always insisted that she wears a uniform when she goes out with her white charges. Other blacks are insulting if they assume the babies are hers.

It is telling that the Race Relations Act Section 4 allows discrimination within a private household where a private employer can discriminate on grounds of race.

One family, who had been brought up in South Africa, employed a member of the Xhosa tribe for ten years in the depths of the English countryside. She weighed more than 20 stone, could balance a tray on her bottom and carried the entire family's laundry on her head. Foreign diplomats import every nationality as child carers; it seems that everyone likes what they know best.

Health

Most employers do not ponder the vital areas of health and a positive attitude to illness. Thanks to the AIDS spectre this subject is more to the forefront now than before. Most employers would not altruistically take on a nanny who is disabled, or has a history of mental instability, is epileptic or suffers from diabetes or dismenorrhoea (painful periods). If you are to be spared, you must be prepared to ask these questions.

Male nannies

An increasing number of employers consider hiring a male nanny; and particularly as a daily nanny. Australian and New Zealand males are the popular pioneers here. Correspondents who thought they might hire a man tended to have sons and plenty of space:

> He could kick a football with our lads.

> Specially useful during the holidays and cricket season.

> Daily would be best. I don't want to meet a man when I'm in my dressing gown late at night, both of us competing for the teething baby.

In the US the expression 'mannies' has been coined or – by one family who always had them for summer holidays – 'nanny men'.

There are a few male NNEBs, most of whom go into state nursery jobs. One who qualified from Brixton College says he enjoys being a novelty factor and 'children often show a preference for me rather than other members of staff, which can be a bit embarrassing'. He is adamant that he would not want to be a private nanny which he considers 'the least stimulating experience'.

There is not much tried and tested experience to draw on from which anyone might make special exceptions or rules for male nannies. One thing is sure, as usual – if employers want what they know, they won't choose this route to hassle-free child care. A husband's reaction is generally negative in dealing with another male in the house to whom he is not related. The Naked Ape is notoriously territorial. Most women are still too modest to be relaxed with a male employee, especially when it comes to under-wear mix-ups and communal washing facilities.

AIDS is mentioned straight away by employers when quizzed on the male nanny option. This is too devastating a question to bring up during an interview with a male nanny for most parents, but it is clearly not one to be avoided. Any employer will want to know why the man wishes to be a nanny and be entirely satisfied that his needs from the job are normal. Employers may also be con-cerned that they expose their little children to homosexuality: this may be stupid, but it exists as a fine example of knee-jerk prejudice.

One employer says, 'It would be fine as long as he was comfort-able in this position.' Some mothers feel that 'the need for a female lap' is important and so will not employ a man. Another echoes, 'Girls are better with little girls.' The last word goes to four-year-old Harry: 'Good idea, we could hit each other.' His sister said she'd be too shy and her mother sides with her.

Age

As one sensible mother comments, 'Maturity varies tremendously' and another agrees, 'If older meant more mature then I like them older. But it's not usually the case.'

The current career pattern for a professional nanny may be out-lined as follows. Unless she attends residential college she is qual-ified at 18. She may spend two years working alongside a mother in the country (probably near her home). Then she may move to London and work with two children and a baby (a more demand-ing job) with a part-time working mother. Her third job may be res-idential still, but plenty of sole charge is considered to be promotion and she may stay for two years. After this she could well take a post abroad for a while and then return to live in a flat with friends and be a daily or temporary nanny.

Most stop being nannies at about 25 when either they help run a nursery school or day nursery or take other child-related jobs, or they get married. There is, as Angela Hovey of Occasional and Per-manent Nannies agency points out, a difference between a 'career' and a 'life nanny'. The latter are the traditional sort who find the constant care and cherishing of other people's children sufficiently fulfilling to continue as a nanny indefinitely. They should have a conservation order on them because they are so rare, but not quite extinct.

The favourite age range is 18–23. Many prefer 24-year-olds but 'I always end up with the green 18-year-olds. They should pay me for what I teach them after years of indoctrinating new nannies', is a common gripe from experienced employers. For this reason many will consider anyone up to 45 'and possibly older if she had been living in a family for years'. Another section positively avoid the older nanny: 'In the winter they sit at the Albert Memorial gossiping and they move like transhumant goats to the bandstand in the summer. Awful old black crows.' Another observes uncharitably and accurately that 'they are a dying breed'.

The super-responsible and highly paid jobs, involving weeks of sole charge and/or extensive travel and a life shared with security guards and kidnap risks, go to more mature nannies of 35-plus with a proven and impeccable track record. Most ordinary families have no need for such a paragon.

Age can have its drawbacks. A mature nanny is more likely to be 'right', i.e. to know how to handle a tricky child after years of experience and may insist that things are done her way. She may also be that irritating type that knows that there is a 'right' way to do things and makes sure that everyone knows when 'standards' slip. She may also reminisce *ad nauseam* about the well-ordered lives of her erstwhile employers in comparison with the chaos around her now. No one likes a nanny lording it over them. In fact most mothers know that they want to be boss. As one mother put it, 'She needs to be younger than I am.'

It may also occur to the sensitive mama that nannies of a certain age may much regret not having had their own babies. Menopausal problems can be just as hard and more embarrassing to deal with than the teenage kind.

As a generalization, it is true that 18-year-olds are more likely to cause difficulties than 23-year-olds. They are mostly away from home for the first time, they are likely to be man-mad, they may resent any sign that you are protective towards them, and they may not have enough confidence or experience yet to take criticism gracefully. They have a great deal to learn still and leaving them in sole charge ('even of your cat', as one agent says nastily) is asking for trouble. If it passes you by, it will be due to sheer good luck, not good judgement (see Chapter 6).

Where To Find Her

> But if it were me . . . well, I should get somebody to put in the morning paper the news that Jane and Michael and John and Barbara Banks (to say nothing of their Mother) require the best possible Nannie at the lowest possible wage and at once. Then I should wait and watch for the Nannies to queue up outside the front gate . . .
>
> P. L. Travers,
> *Mary Poppins*

That was in 1934 and a lot has changed. The art of selling your family as attractive bait and hooking a good one who doesn't have to be thrown back instantly, either to grow up a bit more or because she was an odd fish, is damned hard work. The ones that got away may sound fun in the telling, but are very wearing for all concerned at the time.

People will do anything to get a good nanny. The reckless will risk losing old friends by trying to poach a desirable one. More likely, the present employer won't know the predator at all and her nanny will be approached at the One O'Clock Club or clinic. Even then she'll be lucky to learn about it at all and only if the nanny decides to reject the overture . . . this time.

'Word of mouth' is an oft-quoted source. Its great advantage is that it doesn't cost a bean and reduces the time taken up by interviews. Don't let the fact that the 'mouth' belongs to a great friend inhibit you from ploughing through your usual question-and-answer session with the available nanny. Tell everyone you meet that you are looking for a nanny or any other type of carer and ask them how they found theirs.

Hiring daughters of friends or friends of friends can be risky. One mother remembers taking on a Sloane mother's help, the daughter of friends of her parents back home in Northumbria. She found the arrangement a little awkward. 'We found ourselves eating with her every evening and I became embarrassed about giving instructions.'

It is far from ideal for the nanny whose parents are friends of her employers. One such got so fed up of the covert pincer movement to exploit her and clip her wings that she left the job and the country simultaneously when the joint pressure became too great. 'Whenever I did something wrong my Mum and Dad were told by my employers at once and they gave me a rocket too. I never got a pay rise and my parents were unsympathetic. It was a bad idea from the start.'

If you fancy the top brass, apply direct to the private college registries (see Useful Addresses). Several recommended telephoning or writing to their local training colleges, or to any that they have heard are particularly good. For details see Chapter 7.

Agencies cost money. They may save time, however, and be conscientious enough to save you hours of interviewing by phone and in person. Their experience may guide your decision. How do you choose an agency and how do you know if it is any good? See Agencies, Chapter 18.

Advertising

Employers' favourite organ in which to place an ad for a nanny, mother's help, au pair or any kind of help for their children, whether full-time, part-time, shared, live-in, or live-out, is *The Lady*.

It is a fuddy-duddy, rag-bag of articles on anything from the Aland Islands (between Finland and Sweden, we note with interest) to 'Score with Scones' (how do you do that?). The magazine has a faded, missionary/Simla/Miss Marple nostalgic feel. It is hard to pigeon-hole its market, so it is the more surprising that its fame has travelled from Calgary to Canberra with stop-offs at Lisbon, Stuttgart and Malmö. It sells 69,000 copies each week but claims a readership of 300,000. Every would-be nanny and trembling employer from Truro to Uist via The Wirral buys it from their local newsagent.

Its copy is wedged between two wadges of 'hotels, guest houses and board accommodation', 'activity and interest holidays', and 'houses and flats to be let'. The vital part is billed as 'Domestic Situations Vacant in the British Isles' (Cooks, Housekeepers, Mother's Helps, Nannies), followed by a brief 'Situations Wanted'. The last is always worth checking out and do this well ahead of time, as the advertisers are often living abroad and often give addresses and box numbers rather than telephone numbers.

The Lady's publication day is officially Thursday, but it's available by lunchtime on Wednesday in the London area. 'Prepaid classified advertisements' instructions appear near its end. It is good value for a short ad. It won't take instructions on the telephone. The most vital bit of the small print is to send your ad *to arrive no later than the first post on the Wednesday of the week before you wish the ad to appear*. Don't forget that Bank Holidays cause chaos and mean that your ad must arrive even sooner; check exactly when if you need to cut it fine and always allow for the vagaries of the post.

One mother cursed when she chose to use a box number

because she was in a hurry to get someone and giving her phone number would have speeded the process. Most employers reckon that box numbers, like being ex-directory, are more of a nuisance than an advantage, and having one costs more. A few employers with time on their hands like box numbers because they prefer communicating by letter rather than by phone.

A few use *Nursery World* because this is the magazine of the trained, career nanny; it is quite pointless to advertise for any other type in it.

A growing number cling to *The Times* in the rather quirky belief that their sort of nanny will see it there. The funny thing is that sometimes they do. London dwellers may chance their arm with the London *Evening Standard*. It's impossible to predict what sort of response you will get, if any. It is not a net for trained nannies but it can be worthwhile for au pairs and mother's helps. The trawl will probably produce some highly unsuitable applicants. Its greatest advantage is that it is cheap and quick, and you know fast – within 24 hours of placing the ad – whether it is going to produce anyone remotely possible. The downside is that it is here today and gone tomorrow, unlike a periodical like *The Lady*, which has a shelf life of about three weeks and also gets passed around the nanny network.

One mother always scans the CGA magazine (the Country Gentleman's Association) where nice gels' 'member's daughter' adverts appear as they fill their time between school and university looking after kids, dogs etc.

If you specifically want Australians and New Zealanders, advertise in the London give-away magazines LAM and TNT and put a card in New Zealand and Australia Houses. Also consider putting cards in shops or anywhere else with a high concentration of them, such as the ski shops in Kensington High Street or the travel agencies in Earl's Court. For further information on how and where to find them see Agencies, Chapter 18.

Advertising in local newspapers either in London or in the country may produce a good NNEB candidate, or a mother's help whose parents live near you and this may be a big plus. If you are a Roman Catholic, or think that they have indubitably more moral strictures placed on them by being so and you want to cash in on it, go for the Catholic press. Employers report success with cards in newsagents, laundromats, clinics, surgeries, church newsletters, grocery shops, chemists, sports and leisure centres, second-hand children's clothes shops and schools. For advice on au pair hunting, see Chapter 8.

One word of caution – if you advertise locally there is a good chance that you will attract someone else's nanny away from an existing job. Fair game you may say, you didn't make the contact initially. But you still have to live in the neighbourhood having effectively pinched another woman's child carer. And your children may be at school with her old charges. Anyone who has a good nanny lives in fear that she will be headhunted, like Aunt Dahlia's chef Anatole in the Wodehouse stories. Just weigh up the sensitivities involved and decide if you will deal with them with equanimity. One mum says:

> I moved from London to Wiltshire and our ad offered a cottage and more money than was usual down there, as I later discovered to my embarrassment. A local girl applied and I took her on, but had unwittingly poached her from a woman who had four haemophiliac children who attended the same school as we then did. She never spoke to me and many of her friends were hostile too. I certainly wished I'd advertised further afield.

Writing an advertisement

Employers are as opinionated as ever about the compilation of an arresting and effective ad. In summary, they belong to two groups: those who rabbit on fulsomely about their darlings and comfy houses, and those who despise the gush and keep it short and plain. The latter is cheaper. It is not necessarily better; it must depend on the personality of the nanny reading it and on how she feels that day as to whether she wants to wallow in the details or likes the brisk, no-nonsense approach. One mother's help tells us that she always goes for the warm-sounding advertisements, which give the names of the children. She also likes big ads on the simple grounds that the family is more likely to be well-off and pay generously; there must be many nannies and mother's helps who think the same way.

Some mothers swear by the upfront approach. They are happy to spend the extra, even splashing out on the semi-display kind because they think it's advantageous that the nanny conjures up a partial picure of the type of family she may join straight away. At one end of the scale the revelation on the facing page may meet your eyes.

Presumptuously, we can learn a lot from this slightly altered real-life example of an unusually up-market ad. Only Princess Michael rivalled this style and level of expenditure in *The Lady*.

It is amusing to note that even Lady Paddington doesn't have high expectations of the duration of her nanny's stay. It depends

Lady Paddington needs a very kind,
reliable, trained or experienced

NANNY

(21 years +) from May

To be lovingly responsible for Harry (7), Charlotte (2), and to take charge of a new baby expected in the summer when our maternity nurse leaves in October.

Louise (11) is at boarding school and Emily (10) will be separately organized.

Large, very comfortable London home. Some weekends and holidays in lovely country house in Suffolk. Above average salary for the right applicant. Time off excellent. Other help in the house in every respect. Non-smoker, animal-lover preferred. Car driver and good references essential. Applicants must be looking for a permanent position (one year minimum) as continuity of loving care especially for little Charlotte is a priority.

Please apply with references and telephone number to:
The Countess of Paddington,
29 Arundel Gardens,
London W8

on your view, but what else *could* she offer? It seems a short time for any job, let alone one in which the applicant is probably a top-rank career nanny.

By contrast, one experienced au pair procurer always spends her pittance on the lowest possible deal in *The Lady* thus:

AU PAIR: non-smoking, good English, for two tinies. 0171 937 3276

She says that this weeds out the foreign girls who speak no English and is designed to gather potential interviewees who will learn more by telephone. She does admit that a detailed ad would lessen the amount of time needed to sift the applicants on the phone. Employers of au pairs write much shorter ads anyway, because the job is part-time, short-lived and training or experience is not expected, though they are usually longer than the above.

Employers recommend that if you have a difficult or unusual family set-up, like a one-parent family, or a disturbed/handicapped/or fostered child, you are advised to be open about it in the ad. It is better to attract a nanny who quite likes the idea than one who is put off on arrival for interview.

If you like lists of qualities in your advertisement, take your pick from the Ideal Nanny definitions listed on page 51. Otherwise it is pragmatic to mention any perks that will catch the jaded job hunter's glance, like foreign travel and holidays, weekend houses, own car and separate accommodation. It is stupid to be flashy in ads as elsewhere, so don't try to impress.

It is noticeable that people don't stipulate the salary, or mention the Big Four (see Chapter 2) except with carefully considered adjectival vagueness. For example: 'good' as in 'good salary to the right person'; 'flexible but generous time off'; 'ample holidays'. Understandably, employers prefer to spell out the terms and conditions of the job once they have had a look at the applicant. This lack of specifics has a purpose. It enables the employer to be flexible, particularly about pay if she chooses, at the interview. If a smashing NNEB walks in whom you know is a bit above your price range, then it is still possible to offer her £10 per week more than you originally intended to pay to secure her.

The best months to advertise for nannies are December (employees like to make a move in the New Year) and June (to catch the new NNEBs or school leavers for the early Autumn). Au pairs are best recruited in the summer for September; this is the most likely time to achieve a year-long stay; January is the other time to do it. In general, avoid March, April, November and December for an immediate start.

The depressing story from many employers is that however widely their net is cast, even with money no object, sometimes they are just plain unlucky and they don't even interview a single good candidate. One mother says that after a semi-display effort in *The Lady* she received 'fifty replies on the phone and ended up with only five hopefuls, two of whom didn't appear and one of whom turned out to be the best ever. A damned close-run thing.'

Suppose your ad has flopped. What next? The interview processes and the 10-day time lag in *The Lady*'s schedule have rendered you desperate. Some experienced employers anticipate this and book the ad to appear in two consecutive weeks. You must cancel fast for a refund, but if you hope not to be knocking on the agencies' doors, which is going to cost a great deal more, a consecutive ad is a sensible precaution.

If this procedure fills you with gloom and nausea, particularly if you have spoken to 60 nannies and mother's helps and seen six, all of whom were mediocre, reconsider the agency option.

Insist to yourself that you *will* find the right person for your family. It is so easy to feel demoralized, but that won't find a nanny. Brace yourself, drop your shoulders and start again.

Chapter 4
Interviewing

By Telephone

Telephone interviewing is time-consuming, hard work and can be confusing, particularly if your desire for an au pair outstrips your knowledge of her language or if a nanny's broad Yorkshire might as well be Swahili to your cleaning lady who answers the phone for you if you are out.

An advertisement in a magazine or newspaper elicits a great deal of telephone interviewing. The only way to avoid this is to give a Box Number inviting candidates to write with their details first. One mother asks them to write the moment they put the receiver down. If there is plenty of time before the job starts, a written application can work well, but there is then the big risk that many nannies, mother's helps and au pairs rightly reckon that they are worse on paper than in person and can get a job with someone else much more easily and quickly – by telephone.

Some mothers are impressed by a clear and neatly written letter and feel that the fact that the girl *has* been bothered to put biro to paper is a mark in her favour. Often the girl who turns up does reflect the orderliness of her letter, but not always. One employer reflects drily that, 'It was one of my major misconceptions at the beginning that anyone could write a decent letter. Six years as an employer has taught me that my best nannies have all been 'awful spellers' or appallingly illiterate by my standards. Now I couldn't give a fig how they spell banana on a shopping list. I'm just pathetically grateful that they are buying them.' Nevertheless, asking for a written CV is one way of cutting down on applicants, if you have a huge response, and it may also provide clues to personality.

You will also have to interview on the telephone if you decide to use an agency. The employer is usually given the name, phone number and details of a suitable girl or vice versa, but in either

About the applicant

- What is her full name?
- What is her telephone number? (Get this down immediately; it's surprisingly easy to forget about it entirely.)
- Does she smoke?
- How old is she?
- Where is she living now?
- When can she start? (This often does cut down applicants. It's amazing how many insist on starting tomorrow or not for at least a couple of months.)
- How much experience has she had with children? How old were the children and how long did she work in each job?
- Has she any qualifications? NNEB or equivalent, CSEs, GCSEs, Os and As?
- Can she drive?
- Has she organized references for herself? Could she please bring them with her to the interview? (No references, no interview.) It depends on her experience, but she should have at least three (one personal and two professional as a minimum) if she is experienced.

case, the telephone provides your first contact. Some agencies will ask you to fill in a questionnaire and will have given the applicant a similar one which you will have read; this will cut out some of the questions. A quick chat with the agency about CVs and other details that you may receive should weed out some obvious duds.

It is a sensible idea to cancel outings in the evenings and plans to go away for weekends during the interview period, unless you mention your intended absence in the advert.

Before the phone starts ringing, remember to consult your spouse about whether he intends to appear at the interviews and find out if he will be available during the allotted time span. Don't stray from the phone for long for at least three days after the publication which carries your ad hits the streets.

If you go out, try to arrange that the present nanny takes down the relevant details and give her the basic telephone interview equipment (see below). If she is capable, get her to arrange the interview schedule. Incumbent nannies can be excellent telephone interviewers and, if they sound positive about the job, will also give your lovely family the thumbs-up.

About your family

- Tell her about the size of your family, the ages and sexes of the children; mention twins or children with special needs if you have them
- Describe the type of accommodation you live in and will provide for her
- Be honest about communications – buses and trains – particularly if you live in the country. Tell her if a car is provided for her use
- Give her a brief job description making it extremely clear what type of help you want. (Employers/employees are too often vague about what exactly an au pair or mother's help is expected to do.)
- Tell her if you have a cleaner (a big plus).
- Tell her where you live and how to get there. Offer her travel expenses if you have decided to pay them
- Mention pay (see below), holidays etc, particularly if attractive
- Remind her to bring not less than three references

Decide what you want to do about paying or contributing to the applicants' travel expenses – trains, tubes and maybe a taxi. Make it clear whether you are or are not prepared to reimburse them. Agencies press their clients to pay them. Some mothers think it the done thing; others think the applicants can perfectly well arrange other interviews on the same day and shell out themselves, as indeed they would have to do for most other jobs.

Telephone interviews should be kept fairly short – especially if you have invited applicants to reverse the charges in the advert. Write down a list of major questions and keep it by the phone. Also have ready your Filofax or a large sheet of thick paper or card (it doesn't slip so easily while writing with one hand) for names and details and find two biros that work. Leave them by the phone. The whole business is fraught enough as you juggle a baby, a phone and a burning saucepan not to want to worsen the experience by failing to find something with which to write.

Attempting to memorize some half-heard mumbles about Hull Tech, while the 'beep, beep, beep' goes is no fun. A frazzled mother can't think when a nanny rings her from a call box. Take down her number at once and ring her back straight away.

If you have more than one telephone, ideally try to keep this equipment safely by one of them all the time, and use only that phone in that room for all incoming calls for the duration.

Many employers hire mother's helps and au pairs over the phone without a personal interview, because they have no choice; the girl lives too far away, i.e. abroad. Many agency au pairs or mother's helps have to be taken 'blind'. This does increase the risk of landing a no-hoper, but it is often successful. It is always best to set aside the time to see anyone who is going to look after your children and/or live in/work by day in your home. Even if you hire a temporary nanny for the weekend, and in whatever crisis, don't rely totally on an agency's assessment of personality.

Many employers reveal the Big Four (see Chapter 2) over the phone. Others feel strongly that applicants should turn up for an interview and find out about the family before enquiring what they are to be paid. The other considerations that make up the package – perks like holidays abroad, her own wheels or flat, a swimming pool, or a charming, amusing and entirely delightful family (harder to sell this one) – should count for something. They make an average salary bearable.

Obviously, from the girl's point of view, she doesn't want to travel miles and go through the whole interview only to be told that she will be offered less or the same as she is paid at present. Incidentally, several nannies told us that they went to interviews having been attracted by a big salary advertised in *The Lady*, only to find that the employer never had any intention of paying that amount and had just used it as a ploy.

It is best to ascertain what the nanny is earning currently over the telephone, then she has to hope that you won't be a goof and offer her half that sum.

It is comforting that the principal of one college advises her students to: 'Go for the job you think you'll be happiest in. Money is important, but use of car, if you think you'll be well fed, your own bathroom and TV and travelling are all to be borne in mind. You must be happy or there's no point in any of it.'

Some parents spend some time on the telephone interviews and then say to the girl that they *may* ring back in a matter of hours to invite her to come for an interview. This gives the employer a chance to put the phone down and write detailed comments of her impressions of the applicant. Was she articulate? Friendly and easy to talk to? Did she sound doubtful about anything? Was she enthusiastic? Did her description of her previous experience make it sound ideal/OK/barely adequate/grisly? Do you care if you never speak to her again?

This may sound like mind-reading being passed off as intuition to someone who is not used to using the telephone as a means of screening people professionally. Many agencies place great store by these skills and some are extraordinarily perceptive after years of experience. Don't mistrust a funny feeling; if something niggles nastily, take note and mull it over during the day.

Another little-used technique is to encourage the nanny to ponder what you have told her about the family and job and to call again if she would like to come for an interview. Unlucky   for some, this seems extremely cocky to many employers whose instinct is to haul in all comers. If she does ring back, it means she is keen and it also avoids wasting time arranging inter-   views with nannies who may not bother to show up (quite common).

A nanny may not come because she has already found another job and doesn't make the effort to inform you, but, as often as not, she has not liked the sound of the job. It may well be that she only took down your address and laborious directions because she couldn't think of a way of telling you that it all sounded hellish and was unable to bring the conversation to a close.

Another tip to avoid wasting time is to ask the nannies nicely to ring you if they find another job or if anything crops up to prevent them from coming. Explain humbly that you have a few things that you could be getting on with instead of waiting for her non-appearance. Often they will respond to your plea.

Never pursue someone who doesn't ring back and never hanker after those who don't turn up. Apart from the bracing spilt milk clichés, you may console yourself with the thought that they have a lot to learn and mercifully will not now have a chance of doing so at your expense.

When setting a time and day for the interview, be explicit about directions and give her the approximate time the journey should take. Punctuality gains marks, so help her achieve it.

Eyeball to Eyeball

The principal points which the parent must investigate for herself . . . have reference to the *moral qualifications* of the applicant: and if there is found to be any defect here, however healthy or otherwise desirable, her services ought to be declined. Temperance, cleanliness, a character for good conduct, fondness for children and aptness for their management are among the most important requisites. An amiable disposition and cheerful temper are also very desirable. It is unnecessary to allude to other qualities which a woman who is sought as a nurse should possess; they will naturally suggest themselves to any thoughtful mind.

Bull's *Hints to Mothers*, 1851

The employer hopes to discover much in a short time during an interview, but she must concentrate on organizing the data so that she is able to answer two crucial questions by the end of it.

Do I think this nanny/mother's help/au pair will be good at this job?

Do I like her enough to have her come and live (or be around the house a great deal – as in the case of a daily nanny) with us?

Many employers confess to being 'more nervous than the nanny' when they dealt with their first batch of interviewees, even though some had been quite relaxed about hiring and firing in offices for years. Comfortingly, most think that they learnt the ropes fast and that the experience of having talked to many applicants gives them the confidence to know what they want, judge it expertly and not settle for anyone who doesn't match up to their criteria. A few are still far from satisfied with their interview technique and dread it.

Everyone agrees that it is unlike an ordinary interview. It is just as well to treat it that way because your decision will make an impact on every important aspect of your life.

Some people say that their husbands like to interview nannies with them. If so, organize the double act so that you don't confuse the nanny by constant disagreement, hysterical giggles, quizzical looks or other distracting behaviour. Incidentally, some nannies say that two people make an interview more intimidating. Decide if you prefer to interview together, one after the other, or let him second-guess your choice of brilliant finalists.

Choose somewhere comfortable to sit where you and the interviewee can both see each other clearly. Silence the phone, try to organize things so that the children are occupied elsewhere and you will not be interrupted. Now concentrate on the substance of the interview, relax, and be prepared to give the candidate your undivided attention.

An employer might think it safe to assume that all the obvious duds and kooks have been eliminated by careful telephone interviewing and that she is now going to view a parade of suitable candidates. You may be in for a shock. A 'good telephone manner' is a most deceptive tool.

If you don't like the look of the girl, can't understand a word she says or can see only dimly what looks like a nightclub hostess slumped on your sofa wreathed in Turkish cigarette smoke . . .*cut the interview short.* You will save both her and yourself time, trouble and further embarrassment if you firmly and politely show her the door.

Some mothers and nannies claim to hate a 'formal' interview and 'despise a bombardment of questions'. Although techniques of interviewing differ widely and you will need to vary the questions to suit individual applicants, the fact remains that you will kick yourself later if you don't cover essential ground. Your job is metaphorically to spin an impenetrable web in which bad nannies may entrap themselves across your front door, thus effectively denying a bad carer access to your children. It is best to be able to assure yourself that you have performed this task conscientiously. Since this is your only chance to grill an applicant (preferably subtly performed – she should not be aware of the heat), and to exchange a great deal of information, many questions and answers are inevitable.

Say to the nanny that you will tell her exactly what the job entails – warts and all. This is a better line than giving a misleading, or false, picture as too many employers do. Say that the interview will be direct and personal because both of you have to discover crucial details about the other and make judgements and decisions quickly.

Ask her

Training   Is she trained (cooking, home economics diplomas), to do the job? Ask to see a photocopy of her certificate(s). What other exams has she taken? Where did she train and what did she think of her training? (See Chapter 7)

Experience   How many jobs has she had? With how many children? What were their ages and sexes? How much sole charge has she had? Why is she a nanny? How long did each job last? Where were the jobs and why did she leave them? Which previous job did she enjoy least and why?

References   (she should have brought them with her). Were there any jobs from which she was not given a reference? If so, why? Has she shown you what her tutor said about her if she did the NNEB or other training? Will she mind if you talk to her mother? (Obviously this would seem a peculiar request if you are interviewing someone mature, but with a young girl many employers mention how frank mothers can be about their daughters. Others go further and insist that a good mother equals a good nanny, especially they say, if she has only just left home.)

Her home and background Where does she live? What exams has she taken? What are her parents' jobs? How do they feel about her coming to live where you live? How does she get on with them? (Big red flashing lights if she says she hasn't seen her mum since she was 16; it is important that she has a home to return to in various circumstances, not least illness.) Will she be homesick if she lives a long way from her? Has she got brothers and sisters? What are their jobs? Are they a close family?

All this aims to give you a reassuring picture of a happy, disciplined and stable background: if divorce, remarriage or recent deaths emerge, it is a good idea to ask searching questions and satisfy yourself that the nanny has come to terms with the event. Most employers insist that their nannies come from a stable home environment.

Boyfriends Does she have a boyfriend or fiancé? How will he fit into her life in your home? When will she expect to see him? Does he welcome the idea of her taking the job?

About herself Does she smoke? Does she drive? When did she pass her test? Has she driven in other jobs? Does she have a clean licence? Has she got her own bike/car/moped?

Does she practise a religion? What are her hobbies? How does she spend her free time?

Does she know the area where you live? If going to a city, i.e. London, for the first time, does she have friends or relations there? If she doesn't, how will she make friends? Does she like the countryside? Is she knowledgeable about it? Does she enjoy walking or playing on a beach (or whatever you need her to enjoy while on duty)?

Would she say she was quick, patient, resourceful, efficient or any other qualities which you consider essential for the job? (Many interviewees say yes to everything but it can be instructive to see how she handles the query.) Is there any one thing about her which might cause you trouble if you employed her?

Her health Is she generally fit and healthy? Has she had any recurring illnesses? Dismenorrhoea (painful periods)? Any major operations? Has she suffered from depression or any other mental illness? What about diabetes? Migraines? Epilepsy? (All these questions are vital if she will have sole charge and/or the employer works full time away from home.)

Think about asking whether she has ever had an AIDS test. No nanny or mother's help who thinks she may have AIDS should work with other people's children.

Many employers will be just too embarrassed to ask such a thing at an interview. But bear in mind that girls in their late teens and twenties, particularly if they were brought up in a city (Glasgow? Liverpool?), who may have had several boyfriends and/or are at all promiscuous are capable, in theory, of contracting AIDS. Obviously if any member of *your* immediate family has AIDS you must tell her about it. (It is possible that in the future AIDS Test Cards may have to be carried by everyone to prove to people that they were cleared at their last test.)

Hobbies   Does she like taking exercise? Does she need a lot of sleep? Does she enjoy swimming, cycling, or whatever your children most enjoy?

The children   Does she know how to entertain children? Playdough, endless reading, colouring, painting? Puzzles and creative and educational toys? Can she sing or play a musical instrument?

Sole charge   Does she insist on 'sole charge'? (no good if you are around during the day). Does she like the responsibility it entails? Is she alert to potential dangers to children in the home and elsewhere? Try a couple of quick questions about how she would deal with a common emergency, e.g. a child choking or a fat fire in the kitchen. These should be answered swiftly and confidently.

Her future   What are her ambitions? What does she see herself doing in five years' time?

The next part of the interview is the best opportunity you will ever have to be opinionated – so make the most of it. At this point you have to decide whether or not you can cope with self-revelation. You should outline *all* your House Rules (having checked through the list in Chapter 2) and reveal all or some of the eccentricities of your better half, adored offspring and cherished home.

Tell her

Her routine   Tell her everything you can about a typical day's chores and responsibilities. Working mothers must discuss the 'sole charge' issue and watch out for nannies and mother's helps who seem too keen to be left alone with the children. One in 1,000 may be a nut; a greater proportion may be lazy and prefer not to look after the children as you would wish in your absence.

Mention the need for a generally helpful attitude, and that she will be expected to muck in with busy family life to which everyone has to contribute as the occasion arises. If she is trained, discover whether she will ever wash your tea cups or post a letter for you. Explain that you have no intention of exploiting her and you understand her job description, but you will take it to heart if she is stand-offish and waits for the butler – that's you – to do things that aren't strictly her job. Many nannies are rigid about their duties and if you want adaptability, better say so now.

Your children   What are her views on discipline? Explain if you don't want the children to be smacked or shouted at. Do you mind how much TV they watch? Tell her everything you can about your children – their personalities, school routines, hobbies, friendships, likes and dislikes, any illnesses or other problems (grommets? speech therapy?) and what you want her to do with and for them. Try a couple of 'what if?' questions about how she would envisage occupying them and 10 visiting children on the third rainy day on holiday in Gairloch.

Animals   If you have animals, however big or small, and you will want the nanny to feed or care for them at all, tell her precisely the extent of her involvement. Is it mucking out a pony after breakfast or shoving the budgie a cuttlefish once a month? Don't be too astonished if she raises her eyebrows and claims she is allergic to all furry creatures. Seriously, better check.

House Rules   There are many petty preferences and rules, i.e. use of phone, washing etc that are best left to the first week of employment (see Chapter 5), but now you have to deal with those abrasive and revealing areas we call the House Rules (back to Chapter 2). Be explicit and explain why you think they are necessary.

The applicant must understand that you feel *very* strongly about a few items. It is fatal to be wishy-washy – decide what you like and dislike and lay it on the line. Remember the hundreds of nannies who complain they were never told any of the rules at the interview and would never have taken the job if they had been. Better now than in a month or so.

Just to remind you briefly of the subjects that you should cover, here is the list: boyfriends, late nights, smoking, eating habits, friends to stay, dress on duty, confidentiality, out of bounds.

You and your partner's life   If your family follows a religion, tell her. Mention any religious rituals observed by the family. Describe your own close relatives, particularly if they live with you or come and stay for protracted periods. Talk about your husband's job and travel schedules if relevant, and your own. How much time do you spend with the children and in the house? Mention any plans for the future or changes in your lives which you can foresee and which will affect her job. Moving house? New schools for the children? New baby planned? Getting divorced?

Your neighbourhood   Outline the transport facilities, amenities, parks, swimming pools, shops, classes and anything else which might be appealing. Tell her about the existence of other nannies in the area and how you will make arrangements for her to meet them.

The Big Four   (see Chapter 2) – the nuts and bolts of the job that she certainly will want to hear all about: pay, time off, holidays and perks.

Ask her how much she is expecting to earn or has been earning – she may think of a number and double it, but you are stuck with her base line – and then tell her by how much you will increase it. However good you reckon your package to be, there's not much chance that most nannies will take a penny less than they got last week. So when she announces it was £100, there's not much mileage in saying 'Come, take fifty,' like the Mayor of Hamelin and reminding her of a chance to see the Matterhorn.

Explain your tax and National Insurance and sick pay arrangements (see Chapter 17) and any special bonuses.

Tell her how many days off she will have a week. How many nights, on average, she will be expected to babysit. What her working hours are. Explain any overtime terms – cash and/or time off in lieu. Do you expect her to get up at night for the children? How much paid and unpaid holiday will she have and when may she take it?

Mention the car and foreign travel. Think up anything else that your nanny-hiring neighbour doesn't offer or hasn't got – a jacuzzi, you will pay for her to learn to drive or learn to play the piano, you are a Cordon Bleu, your brother has a power boat, your father-in-law is good for Wimbledon, opera and theatre tickets, the holiday shack in the Bahamas/Hayling Island/Lake District or anything else you can flash in front of her eyes as long as she will genuinely benefit from it.

Some mothers think it is daft to chat intimately at an interview about exactly what you want in a nanny; they prefer to let the nanny pick up their preferences and dislikes once installed. Actually most nannies say that they are pleased to get as much information from a future employer as they can. The more open you are about yourself, the better she will be able to judge whether her behaviour and attitudes will blend with your own. Be as direct as you like.

First tell her of anything you can't stand, i.e. stealing, swearing, lying (in every form from fudging to bare-faced). Integrity and saying what you mean, and vice versa, is crucial in a nanny. Being unkind to the children, racist views, untidiness, unpunctuality or anything that has driven you mad or you have come across in previous nannies may be mentioned. Of course she is not about to reveal herself as a kleptomaniac, but she'll either empathize with you for bringing up such concepts, may look as if she does, demur or not react at all. Watch like a hawk.

Then you could talk about what you hope she is and will be: affectionate, observant, adventurous, patient, communicative, fun, sensitive to you and your husband's privacy, appreciative of the children, imaginative about entertaining them and aware of safety hazards. She should be able to cope calmly in crises, be reliable and responsible with other people's children when they visit, and able to fit in easily with your family and friends.

Speak of your need for consideration and honesty on both sides as problems arise and assure her of your concern and interest in her happiness in the job and well-being generally. She must feel that she can bring up difficulties with you, and that you will make time to listen and discuss things. 'The more you give, the more you will get' is the cliché that fits the bill. Don't be embarrassed to use it if you can guarantee that you are a good employer.

Either you have chatted your way through and round some of these suggestions and she has interrupted you constantly or intermittently in her queries, or you should invite her to ask you any questions. A good, professional nanny will have prepared several.

Remember, all the time another process has been going on: the nanny or mother's help has been assessing you. She wants to be sure that you have enough money to pay her promptly and cheerfully and the intention and capability of raising her salary.

She also needs to check out the family and its attitude to having a nanny. One way she can do this is by talking to the present incumbent. This should be encouraged because it is advantageous to you too, unless you have fallen out with her. The departing nanny can be a great help in judging a contemporary and a potential successor. The cleaning lady, your mother, a neighbour or any old friend might be persuaded to appear to give her the once-over and/or provide another point of reference.

The applicant has a right to ask your nanny any questions about the personalities of members of the family, how everyone treats the children, whether she has been paid reliably, and if she has experienced any serious problems during her stay. A residential nanny must assure herself as best she may that the people she is going to be living with will be reasonable and considerate. There can't be a better endorsement of your family and lifestyle than from the current nanny. One nanny writes: 'Their previous nanny had stayed three and a half years and recommended the job; it counted for a lot.'

Show her

You will score points if you can show her written notes from previous nannies giving *you* a good reference as an employer – at least give her the phone numbers of old trusties, so that she can hear about you for herself. Incidentally, if you have had any or many failures, tell her now before she discovers the skeletons in your cupboard for herself.

Either you or the present nanny can now take her on a tour of the house or flat and point out the best features of the bedroom and bathroom she will use. It's time to introduce her to the children, if they haven't already found you. One agent never interviews girls in an office. She doesn't feel that there is much point since she can't see how they react to children. She suggests that it is a good idea to try to leave the visiting nanny alone with one or more of your offspring. Make an excuse to go, and take this opportunity to scrutinize her references. Leave the door ajar and come back quietly, so you can get a glimpse of how she is getting on. If she is on her knees playing dominoes and helping the youngest cheat to win, that's good news. If she has made up her face again and is staring blankly out of the window while the children are jumping on the chairs, she has just lost the job.

Ask her again if she has any questions. If she seems to be a winner, don't risk losing her to the next interviewer; be definite and enthusiastic and tell her that, subject to having checked out her references, you will ring her at a certain time (preferably within 24 hours or you may lose her) and offer her the job. Unless you feel very positive about her and want to capture her without fail, don't raise her hopes. Say you have 'three or four others to see', but that you will ring her as soon as you can.

Time to Reflect

When she has left, it is good to remind yourself on paper about her responses and reactions. You may ponder some of the following: Was she confident? What was her chief facial expression during the interview? Was she fun for the children to meet? Was she well turned out? Did she seem 'together'? Was she punctual? Did she whinge about the journey? What questions did she ask first (pity if she dwelt on money and time off)? Was she easy to chat to? What was she enthusiastic about? Did you like her voice and laugh? If you have steep stairs, did she bound up them effortlessly or sound like she was on the verge of collapse? Did she talk too much and have a lot of strongly held opinions? Do you feel worn out by an hour in her company? Would her appearance (height/size/spots/breath/moustache/choice of clothes) depress you day after day?

Recapture your reactions to her. Several mothers warn that ignoring hunches, gut reactions or their intuition may result in self-recrimination later as just the problems they had sensed at that first meeting materialized. Don't worry about being irrational or seemingly absurd; if anything bothered you about her, don't push it aside.

The vital thing is for the interviewer to be sure that her abiding impression is of having just met someone whom she likes, can respect, trust and talk to easily – in short, a nanny with whom she can live and who will put the children's needs before her own. You need to think that she will be capable of loving them and liking you back.

Chase Those Refs

Checking a nanny's and a mother's help's references are vital. Doing the checking thoroughly is a nuisance and time-consuming, particularly if the referee doesn't answer the telephone and/or is not particularly helpful when you do get through to her.

References are not easy to write. Nor are they easy to read. First impressions can often mislead and confirm the employer's rose-tinted view of her chosen girl. However heart-warming a nanny's references are, there should be at least three of them. Preferably *all* of them should show that she has finished each job and been given a reference – check at least two of them.

One employer was delighted with a nanny's references which one Kensington agency said they had checked out thoroughly when they read them to her over the phone. Several weeks later the employer and nanny were at loggerheads and the employer burst out in exasperation, 'Heaven alone knows why you had such brilliant references from your last job.' 'They weren't,' muttered the nanny, 'the agency said it was best to leave out the last sentence.' After close questioning, the nanny revealed that the last sentence had read, 'She can be short-tempered and aggressive and is sometimes unable to cope.' The moral is obvious – *always* check yourself.

Checking references of nannies whether trained or experienced or both is essential and fairly straightforward. What does take an effort is getting a young British mother's help to organize references, even if she can't produce something related to child care. It is even harder to get references for a foreign mother's help, let alone an au pair. Try to insist on references whenever you can, even if you are only hiring a short-stay au pair or temporary nanny.

It is an indication of how few employers value references, let alone care about checking them, that so many EEC nationals or Australians who have worked on and off as mother's helps for several families have just one or even no references to show for their experience. Many foreign mother's helps or au pairs who have worked for a British family often haven't known that they ought to ask for a reference before leaving. Their employers have not volunteered one.

Checking references

- Insist on at least two or three references and ensure that you see the originals
- Ask to see a training certificate if the nanny is qualified Ask for her tutor's name and telephone number
- Require details of every gap in her CV
- Remember that a reference from hotel work is not such a good guarantee of honesty as one from work in a private home
- You should be offered a reference for each job she has had. If not, investigate
- Character references for first-time employees are much better than nothing
- Don't automatically assume that if she was sacked in a previous job that it was her fault

The trouble is that the prospective employer doesn't know if the referenceless girl is just foolish and/or inexperienced or whether she deliberately didn't ask for a reference because it would not have been a good one. Any employer will wonder if the girl is pretending that she doesn't know about the importance of references.

Whatever she says, call her bluff and insist on procuring former employers' telephone numbers. If an agency is supplying the foreign girl then it should have taken up references responsibly. Some agents are extremely lazy about making a girl provide references and they rarely check them, particularly if the referees live in the girl's own country. A young, traditional type of au pair who comes straight over from her motherland to stay with a family should be able to send references or at worst, bring them with her.

The trouble with written references is that they can be faked. Sometimes this is obvious, like when, as one mother describes, 'Her one reference was in an uneducated hand; an unlikely looking piece of paper which had something unconvincing scrawled on it.' Just occasionally a checked reference is also a fake. A few nannies will go so far as to get their girlfriends to do a little act for them pretending to be Mrs Bloggs, her last employer. The sinister part is that if a nanny will go this far, she may have done it often and the whole sting may be thoroughly convincing. Like a Hitchcock film, the nutter doesn't look nutty, in fact the kleptomaniac, child abuser or thief takes pains to look extra 'normal' and appealing.

Some employers tend to dismiss the likelihood of them landing a fruitcake, and say that 'hiring a nanny is all about trust anyway and it's silly to be paranoid.' Some go so far as not to put much store by written references or indeed verbal ones, because of the possibility of forgery. Others mistrust them because of notorious fudging on the part of former bosses who are too chicken to say that the nanny was just average. As one mother says, 'I tend to go on a gut feeling that the one I choose will work, and so far that has stood me in good stead.'

Like burglars, the tiny fraction of criminals who are masquerading as nannies (and they do exist), are probably amazed about how easily they con their victims and think what a gullible lot they are. Many employers can't believe that the psychopath nanny can breathe the air of their friendly suburb.

When this book first went to press an eye-catching case was current among employment agencies. A girl, let's call her Melody Scott, looking like a mouse and 'plain and accommodating' in a brown overcoat was wooed by every agent that interviewed her.

She had wonderful references for the last four years which agents checked, but there were none for the previous four years when her boss had died, she said.

It emerged that she had been in Holloway prison and the judge had acquitted her of stealing jewels once. He wouldn't convict because of her plausible story and appearance. He felt that she was being set up by her employers. In Melody's next job she was caught stealing and was sent to prison. One leading agency placed her with an American family.

Another agency found out that Melody was working again and tipped off the agency which had placed her. The second agency, after some disgraceful deliberation and delay, rang the American employer. She said they were delighted with the nanny but had just sacked the cleaner of five years' standing for stealing designer jumpers and money. The employer refused to believe the agents' information, but agreed eventually to take Melody's spectacles off and check to see whether there was a scar across the bridge of her nose, which the convicted criminal had. Sure enough, there was the scar. She was sacked and blacklisted by the agencies, but is thought to have got another nanny job through *The Lady* recently. She and others like her are at large.

The case of one untrained mother's help who had one reasonable reference, but not a great deal of experience, was even more serious. She seemed pleasant and capable. Her employer became suspicious when after a few weeks she kept noticing bruises on the inside of her seven month old son's thighs. The mother's help owned up and admitted that she had done it. She had been pinching and bruising him hard and regularly when he grizzled. She got the sack of course.

She may never get another child care job again; even if she does she may never abuse a child again, but she very well might. She may be mentally ill and in need of psychiatric help. Unfortunately the employer did not tell the police nor did she get in touch with, or go and see, the girl's parents. Will her next employer have the sense to check whatever references she offers? She may lie and say that she hasn't worked before as a mother's help; if so will the interviewer ask for a reference from her doctor, priest or teacher? These may not reveal that she abuses children but it might give some clue.

One more time . . . the moral is *always* check references. At the very least if your nanny does something appalling, at least you can console yourself that you made every effort to check that she was bona fide.

Making the phone call to the referee

Try to get through to the relevant person direct. Do not leave a message saying who you are and why you called. The idea is to winkle out of the referee an unpremeditated comment on the nanny in question.

If you get a cold response, or a sighed 'I've just written her the reference', be charming and apologize for taking up her time. Introduce the conversation with something like, 'Just ringing to check that you didn't have a gun to your head', or 'It's so important that I get the right girl, can you answer a few questions?'

Reassure her that what she says to you will be in complete confidence and that the nanny concerned need never know which referees you contacted. If the referee isn't voluble and forthcoming try to enlist her sympathy. Say that it is vital that you don't make a mistake and if she has any doubts about the trustworthiness or integrity of the girl, could she please be completely open? On occasion you may get a complete unbuttoning beginning with, 'I always loathed her, I'm so glad you rang . . .'

It is important to have an idea of the needs and lifestyle of the woman to whom you are talking. Her expectations of her nanny or mother's help may be different from yours. For example, she may want a high level of hygiene in her home but she may not be interested in whether the nanny enjoys playing with the children. You may live in a scruffy house, but can't bear the sight of a nanny not messing about with paint and board games with your children.

The first thing you want to do is to check to see if the interviewee's story and reference match what her former employer actually says. Remember the written reference may be a fake. Ask her how long the nanny worked for her and how much she was paid. Ask about her duties. What did the family like best about her? What was her biggest drawback? Ask the employer what qualities the nanny has which make her a good nanny. Could she become a better nanny? Ask whether the girl was sensitive, discreet, quiet or noisy. Ask about her friends, particularly boyfriends, and whether the employer had a curfew and did that work? Ask whether she was the gregarious type and always out of the house when off duty or did she like to curl up on her bed to read or watch telly? A crucial question *never* to forget to ask is 'Would you hire her again? And if not, why not?'

Ask how many days was she off sick? Was she healthy on the whole? Did she have any health problems that might affect her work? Did she ask for more than a reasonable time off to visit the dentist and doctor? Was she a good time keeper?

All health and punctuality questions are vitally important for the daily nanny or mother's help. If a nanny lives with a family it is a lot harder for her to reckon that a cold can keep her in bed. A daily nanny just has to get her boyfriend to ring up and say sorry, she is unwell this morning. She may be ill, she may be under the weather but capable of going to work, or she may just feel like a day off.

Make it clear that you want to hear about the applicant's good and bad points as perceived by her former boss. This will give you a clearer idea of the girl's personality. What irked her previous boss may not be the thing that would get on your nerves, but it may and whatever it is, it is all useful information. A referee may say, 'Well, don't expect her to do any of the washing up that isn't the children's!' or 'She is a sweet girl but you do have to spoonfeed a bit, memory like a sieve.' Weigh and measure these types of comment and decide if you are that bothered about small things, as long as she is competent, honest and nice to have around.

Listen intently to your interlocutress's voice and its tone. This can give so much more away than anything she might write in a reference. Many employers will not willingly volunteer disparaging comments about their former nannies. A change in tone, anxiety and hesitation on the line can all be clues that she is holding something back. Ruthless employers say baldly, 'I sense you hesitate – was there anything about Sheila's behaviour that makes you do this?'

Another common characteristic is for the former employer, anxious not to let the girl down, to harp on her good points. For example, a former employer might say, 'She was good with our two boys; very sweet with them . . . they liked her a lot.' At this point you must ask, 'Did you and your husband like her?'

A mother living in Harrow, used to interviewing professionally, drew up an impressive list of statements which she sends to former employers to react to before hiring mother's helps for her child. Referees are asked to mark their responses according to an ingenious scale split into four. Here are a selection of her statements put in question form:

- Did she have strong views on many general issues which she expressed in forthright tones?
- Was she emotionally stable?
- Was she very untidy and disorganized?

- Was she imaginative with the children and did she show lots of initiative?
- Was she passive with a tendency to sit and do nothing unless told otherwise?
- Did she know about nutritious food and was she able to cook it?
- Did she adore the children, love them spontaneously or was being a nanny just a job for her?
- Did she play with the children or were they often bored because she didn't?
- Did she have an excellent idea of good educative play and spend a lot of time doing this?
- Did she ever let you down?
- Did she have no sense of discipline and let the children do as they wanted or was she a strict disciplinarian?

Put your best effort into reference checking. Rely on your judgement as you may, remember that it's the nanny's last hurdle – but your last line of defence.

Decision Time

Once you have checked her references, and talked to her mother, your nanny, your spouse or any other relevant person, ring the applicant as fast as you can to say yes or no and hear her decision. If you have decided against her, do the decent thing and don't leave her up in the air – ring and say no. Feeble excuses include 'I have taken someone with more experience/someone less experienced and therefore cheaper' or just say that you were spoilt for choice and it had been a hard one and that's that. Wish her luck and try to reassure her that she was a strong candidate, if she was. Don't squirm any longer, hang up.

If she cuts in with 'Sorry, I have just accepted another job', control yourself while on the line. Don't bite the flex and shriek four-letter insults. Once you have put the phone down, have a primal scream. It is surprising, given your brief acquaintance, how disappointing it can be when your ideal, or even best-of-the bunch, nanny tells you this. In a strange way it is difficult not to take her rejection personally. However, thrust aside these useless thoughts and console yourself that it may be for the best – she wasn't *perfect* after all.

If the next best was good enough, telephone her. Otherwise you may have your second classified advertisement in *The Lady* to fall back on, or you may have to re-advertise. This will take time to organize and produce results, so at this point it might be prudent to start ringing the agencies (see Chapter 18). You may be lucky and nannies may ring up as much as two to three weeks after the advertisement appeared, but don't rely on this. Get weaving. Ring friends or friends of friends for any 'leftover' applicants to their ads.

At this point panic may set in, especially for working mothers due back in harness in two weeks' time. As mentioned earlier, try to leave months rather than weeks for the nanny search, so if the first ad fails to draw anyone good or the first choice fails there is time to find another girl.

If the nanny accepts the job, it is a good idea to write to her stating the exact date when she is due to start work and a convenient estimated time of arrival. Confirm the terms of the employment – pay, holidays, the contract if there is to be one, sick pay and notice – and explain any trial or overlapping period with the existing nanny.

Some mothers think that it is a good idea to have a new nanny come and work for a day, a weekend, a week or even two to see if they like each other. One mother says, 'It is good psychologically for the carer. She feels you are giving her a chance to assess the family properly. One did back out after a day. At least she did it then.'

If the employer wants to see more of a nanny in advance of a firm commitment, the weekend option may be worth considering. It may be expensive, but in the country particularly it can be helpful. Other employers say to the nanny, mother's help or au pair that she will be 'on trial' for two weeks, a month, even three months.

Suggest arrangements for how her luggage is to arrive at your home if she won't be bringing it all with her, and say you will meet her at the rail or coach station if that is the plan. Say an extra prayer that night, there's many a slip . . .

Chapter 5
The First Week

From the moment your first nanny or mother's help arrives you cannot hope to live as before, unless you live in a huge house or are blessed with a separate nanny wing or flat. Even then having a living-in nanny touches on every part of life. This is not surprising, but it is less of a shock if you think a bit about how both of you will live together before she arrives.

The trouble is that initially, and possibly indefinitely, you may feel that you don't want a stranger living with you and the family, but you have decided you need her. This is the crux of all difficulties between nannies and employers. Some nannies are not suited to residential posts and some employers find the whole business of having a living-in nanny more stressful than others.

It also helps if you and your partner are good at leading a communal life and can curb emotions of most kinds in public. A nanny does not expect to be belted into a front seat at the amateur dramatics that are your private life. There is no need to metamorphose overnight into a nagging prude, and the idea of living *pour encourager les autres* is dated, off-putting and smacks of *Upstairs Downstairs*. However, experienced employers report unanimously that a bit of dignity, distance and discretion is the only way to achieve long-term employer/nanny mutual respect. Experienced nannies concur. They don't like witnessing drunken scenes, or listening to tearful stories and personal revelations. You'll regret them as well.

It won't be a surprise to hear that setting such a marvellous example is a helluva strain. If royal employers long to have scrambled eggs in front of the telly in their dressing gowns, so the rest of us, who aren't used to the endless discipline of hot and cold running servants around us, look forward to the nanny's holidays when we can jump in the bath with the children.

Employers claim they talk easily to their nanny, as do nannies. Topics of conversation most often include: anything to do with the children, the house, the nanny's family, the employer's family, friends, neighbours, what's in the news, on TV, on at the local, and the like. Employers say that they do not talk about family finances, personal relationships and family tensions, nor do they gossip about friends, husband's or wife's job, or colleagues. Employers do not want to turn into an Auntie Marje in constant discussions of the nanny's boyfriends and social life. The best sort of nanny does not want to work for employers who live vicariously or are 'too nosey and too matey'.

Louise Davis of Norland recommends to her students and to employers that they 'should remember that neither of you are your normal selves during the initial period'. Be in no doubt that it is not going to be easy, prepare yourself and your partner for a different way of living at best and, at worst, a rough ride.

It will have a great effect on your child or children too, naturally enough, and the only person who can shoehorn this stranger into their lives successfully is you. If you are going back to work for the first time and leaving an older child, take him to your office and show him what you will be up to each day. With younger children give the nanny every aid and advantage in the first week. Send her off on favourite expeditions and give the children plenty of time with both of you around so that they can see that you are relaxed and confident in the new nanny's company.

Nannies, mother's helps and au pairs do not just arrive with their baggage; they also bring their opinions, habits, manners and little ways which can change you from the cool rational executive you hope you are into a paranoid, scratchy fish-wife. The nanny also has to cope with all your prejudices, foibles and petty rules. She is likely to be a lot younger than you, perhaps living away from home for the first time, and may find your home as alien as a crash-landing on Mars.

Be aware of the possible differences in your upbringing and experience. Focus on the variations of background, family life and education. For example, she might not yet have prepared an avocado, she may never have been abroad, she may not have heard of Beatrix Potter and you will have to show her how to open a bank account in the morning.

All this can be hard to deal with and many employers and nannies find these differences embarrassing. You may find that you are much more entrenched in the way you do things than you thought. The way you speak, the way you eat, the way you dress and how you expect the nanny to do those things with and for your children may be important to you. Spell out your preferences precisely and in detail; she cannot be expected to be psychic.

Experienced employers all mention the initial strain of dealing with these personal items but they get better at speaking plainly about 'areas of friction', as we call them. Start off with realistic expectations of the nanny, considering her age and experience. Assume she knows little about the art of living in someone else's house.

Recognize resentment and envy; your nanny may feel both. It is crude to leave estate agents' blurbs about six-figure houses which you covet on the breakfast table and simultaneously ask her to try not to drink too much of the fresh orange juice. This is a serious point. You may take your microwave, video, expensive holidays and jewellery as a matter of course, but to her it may be testing to live alongside this wealth and luxury, which can be flaunted objectionably. Her mum isn't so lucky and works just as hard or harder, with much less tangible result.

Even if your new nanny has lived with a family, it may have had a quite different lifestyle from your own. Some people think that having a nanny who is 'experienced' will shortcut the process of 'house-training' her. To some extent this is true, but one man's meat is another woman's poison – and we don't recognize this simple fact often enough. There is not a *right* way of doing almost anything, just millions of personal preferences.

An aspect that must be tackled, and is related to class-ridden mores, is the subject of manners. The Pre-Select Staff Agency nanny information sheet sums it up: 'Manners maketh Man and young ladies into well-respected employees.' You may insist that you are a liberal, easy-going employer, but how well would you react to having breakfast with a tousle-haired, evil-smelling nanny reaching across your husband for the Weetabix with a grimy, scarlet-painted hand? Just one of those unlovely traits can make a brave employer quake at the prospect of an inevitable 'talk'.

Some nannies don't realize that unchecked B.O. is for some employers not only unappealing but inappropriate to her role and girls have been sacked for not responding to tactful hints. One mother tried to tell her nanny what her best friend obviously had not dared. The girl took it like a lamb, so the employer crowed to her husband of her successful diplomacy. Within hours the nanny had left, and the employer found a note in the waste paper basket saying 'The bitch said I stank.' Perhaps this is a good enough illustration of just how upsetting the manners issue can be for both sides.

If you believe, like the classic old nanny, that 'manners are caught not taught' then watch to see that your nanny is aware of her manners in front of the children. Pray heaven you got this part right at the interview stage and it won't be necessary to deal with this now: you will know within hours. Things she needs to watch out for in your children's behaviour, if you care, include: farting, coughing, sneezing, sniffing, yawning, burping, elbows on the table, saying 'excuse me' at the appropriate times, and of course constant reminders to say 'please' and 'thank you'.

'Verbal class distinction by now should be antique'? Apparently not, though it isn't a subject many people enjoy tackling, though it may bother, nay obsess, them.

In her book *Class*, Jilly Cooper has some apt comments on this touchy area.

> The nanny/employer relationship is interesting because it is one of the few occasions when the classes meet head on, not just during the day, as people do in offices, but at all times, and the nanny has to adjust to a completely different lifestyle . . . Samantha Upward's au pair comes in very red in the face, saying 'Zacharias refused to say "Pardon".' Whereupon Samantha goes even redder and stands on one leg saying 'Well actually we always say "What", don't know why.'

One mother resorts to saying to her nannies that in the south it is more usual to say 'loo' than 'toilet'. Another explains that it helps the child to hear just the one word – hers – when he is being potty trained. Perhaps, if you care about these things, it is best to say 'I prefer x to y' with no further explanation. One confusion which can need clearing up is when the nanny refers to Granny as 'nanny' or 'nan'. Other words that grate include such old chestnuts as: lunch/dinner, pudding/sweet/afters, tummy/belly, bottom/bum.

There are also a whole range of grammatical grouses and other misuse of words like boring, dirty and ignorant. There are a few nice malapropisms like, 'It's six of one and a dozen of the other if you ask me,' and a few nannies drive their employers barmy by their oft-repeated aphorisms, for example, 'Once funny, twice silly and three times naughty.'

Some nannies have very strong regional accents and the children and employers may genuinely have difficulty understanding her. 'It was agonizing,' says one mother, 'she said please may I have a *something*? She said it eight times before I twigged – by which time we were both puce and she was close to tears and I was desperately trying to make her see the funny side – but I challenge any southerner to interpret the word "cup" as it sounds in broad Yorkshire without some practice.'

Another miscellaneous point to raise is that of babysitting for other people, or indeed her acceptance of any kind of extra work while you are paying her wage. Many nannies babysit for other families to supplement their salary. What is wrong with that? Most employers of live-in nannies find that it is impractical and exasperating in practice. Their friends and neighbours keep the nanny babysitting until 2 or 3 am and she is worn out and bad-tempered the next day. Say no and avoid having to backtrack later. You have no reason to feel guilty about this if you are paying her generously.

It is kind to think hard in advance, or from previous experience if you've done it before, about the things that irritate you. For example: loud music, dregs of petrol left in a shared car, your husband's mayonnaise disappearing in the midnight binge, her underwear left in the bathroom. Tell her about these things straight away. It will be tougher to mention them three weeks after she has arrived, and you'll kick yourself for your silence.

When she has discovered you are irrational and impossible to please, sweeten the pill by suggesting that once a week you sit down together (at a set time and on a definite day, so that it is not skipped) to have a News and Views session. This may not be your style, but, an American import, it is recommended by Louise Davis of Norland as a safety valve for both parties. Communication is the most common word that both nannies and employers use to capture the essence of a successful partnership. All lines of communication should always be kept open. Neither should sulk, the children hate it, and as one mother says: 'There is nothing more awful than a frost in the house. 'Nannies mustn't think that the News and Views session means that they can't make complaints or ask questions between sessions.

Tell the nanny what you hold dear – be it the cashmere sweater or the dinner service, the mangled silver spoon given by a doting godfather and gobbled by the waste disposal or the coffee rings on the oak dining table. These disasters happened simply because employers have failed to instruct properly and/or been too silly or lazy enough to allow the nanny to handle their precious possessions, most of which are outside her domain. It is all too easy to allocate blame and turn the nanny into a scapegoat for numerous little details for which employers should take responsibility themselves.

Do beg her to ask you about anything that she does not understand fully. It may be about child safety, emergency drill, sorting the washing, using the iron, about the food processor, sewing machine etc. And tell her what exactly is out of bounds to her, so that neither of you have unpleasant surprises and respect each other's privacy – another plank of a good partnership.

Our correspondents list the following items that their nannies may not use: their clothes and personal belongings, make-up, scent, jewellery. Some nannies do take and use these things without permission. Coincidentally, these are all good presents for nannies. First-time employers may be surprised to learn that the vast majority of employers report little or no dishonesty on the part of their nannies (this is confirmed by the agencies) – it is quite rare and almost all the instances we have unearthed have been cases of kleptomania. Casual thieving is far from the norm.

Jobs for the Employer

If you have a written contract or work agreement with your nanny (see Chapter 17) your first duty is to ensure that you both sign it and keep your separate copies safely.

If you have not employed a nanny before, try to make her room as hospitable, practical, spacious and pretty as possible. A basin is an advantage. Lots of cupboard, drawer and storage space will help her to keep it tidy. There should be enough good light, at least one comfortable armchair, a table and desk to write at, a bed you would be happy to sleep in, a washable bedspread, a television, and as large a pinboard as you can fix to the wall. The idea is to make it as much like a bed-sitting room as possible, so it is also a good plan to provide a few mugs, an electric kettle and perhaps a toaster too.

Employers should never forget that the nanny's bedroom is a symbol of her independence, privacy and her own and possibly only little world in your house. Ideally, you should allow her to do what she wants with it. It is significant and encouraging when the nanny makes the room reflect her own personality, draping it with scarves and posters from floor to ceiling. This is a sign that she is settling in. Don't ruin this good feeling by being possessive about the colour co-ordinated Laura Ashley.

Always knock on her bedroom door (and hope she follows your example) before entering, ask her permission if you need to go into her room for any reason. Try to treat it as a foreign embassy in your country – inconvenient on occasion, but sacrosanct and not subject to local law.

Remember to tell your children that they may not wander in and out of the nanny's room; entrance is by invitation only. The door must be capable of being properly shut, even locked. This is also to protect children from her pills, potions and make-up. Remind her to be conscious of how inquisitive and foolish toddlers can be.

Miss McRae, erstwhile principal of Princess Christian comments, 'I expect to be able to knock and walk in, as I would for a daughter.' Slovenliness, squalor, including unwashed dishes, coffee cups, left-over food, unmade bed, airlessness and smelliness need not be tolerated. 'Don't forget she is not in a flat doing her own thing,' says an experienced agent. It is not reasonable that someone in your employ should rejoice in a pig-sty – and it's not most people's image of the ideal child carer.

If you are a seasoned employer, you should dust the highest shelves, muck out the cupboards and remove all traces of the former occupant, redecorating as necessary. If the result is gloomy and barracks-like, you did it wrong. Start again and think as for a daughter. The nanny has to spend a lot of time there and you want her to be happy in it and proud to show it to her friends and family. It is advantageous to you in the long run to ensure that her room is demonstrably nicer than those of her contemporaries who are daily nannies living in flats, otherwise she'll wonder what she's missing. Understandably.

It is a nice gesture to equip her with a pair of bright trainers and wellington boots, if she has none. Make sure that she has a watch which works and also an alarm clock. She may have to be lent or given effective waterproof clothing; this is specially your responsibility if you hire her for a city job which involves visits to the country. Fill up and organize the sewing basket and show her the nail scissors, sellotape for mending books, glue for fixing toys and shoe polish.

Even an experienced residential nanny may feel homesick, if only in some cases for the familiarity of the last job. Tell her about the Under 24 Rail Card. Persuade her to be in touch with any friends in your area and suggest she rings home in off-peak hours at least twice a week in the first month. If you live in London, explain the underground and bus weekly pass schemes, buy her a bus guide and an A-Z. Extra efforts should be made for nannies and mother's helps in the deep country when public transport is minimal and nanny networks non-existent.

Don't leave your nanny too much by herself at first; invite her to accompany you occasionally, even when off duty, until she has made her own friends. Be overtly kind, friendly and appreciative. Introduce her to other nannies and show her the local clubs, exercise classes, sports centres, library, museums, theatres, cinemas and places of interest.

If you have recently moved house or if you are having your first baby you may not be plugged in to the nanny network in your area. You could ring several local nanny agencies and get them to give phone numbers of nearby nannies. Also, ring the nearest NCT group or the local private school and ask to put a flyer in their newsletter.

If your new nanny or mother's help has not lived in a big city before, it is important to talk to her about the dangers of urban life. In most areas it is not advisable to walk alone at night and public transport is no defence. Part of the reason that many employers impose a curfew on their young nannies is because they feel responsible to the nanny's parents and, if their daughter had not returned by 2 am, the employers think that they should call the police and hospital departments. In other words, they treat their nanny as they would their own teenage children when they behave unexpectedly.

Impress upon her that people are mugged even in 'smart' areas. Handbags are snatched or slit open. In discos they are stolen if put down on a table when dancing. Remind her never to put down the car and/or the house keys while she is out or, worse still, leave your address written down alongside them. She should not leave anything of value in the back of the car and ought to lock the passenger seat door as well as her own when she is driving around late at night. Nanny employers say that they have to have the locks changed or keys replaced because their nannies are ignorant or careless. One emphasizes: 'I had never come into contact with the police before I had nannies. They are always losing things in public places.'

Your nanny or mother's help may not have a bank or building society account. Encourage her to open both. Banks will issue her with a cheque card after three months. Spell out the necessity of keeping chequebooks and cheque cards separately.

It is advisable to register her with both a doctor and a dentist as soon as she arrives which will save time if she needs them in a hurry. Several employers pour themselves another gin and murmur the address of the local family planning clinic also. Some of the employment agencies run detailed medical checks on any nanny they send abroad. These, along with private security checks, may become the norm in the future, as they have in the USA.

Emergency Drill

A safety-conscious household will have, as a minimum precaution, two fire extinguishers, a first aid box, telephones and good neighbours. Introduce her to all of them. You should explain precisely what you want her to do in case of crisis in your absence.

If one of the children has a bad accident, she should not be afraid to call 999 immediately and ask for an ambulance. While waiting, she should consult the Red Cross book kept to hand and try to arrange for any other children to be looked after by a neighbour. It is better to call for an ambulance than to jump into the car with a sick or hurt child and get stuck in a traffic block while the child screams. If a fire breaks out which is more than a brief blaze, tell your nanny to leave the house with the children *at once*.

From the first day you relinquish direct responsibility for your children to anyone else (nannies, mother's helps, au pairs, babysitters, the cleaning lady, members of your family or friends), a list of emergency telephone numbers should be written out clearly by the phone. It should include both parents' work numbers, back-up local help (friends, neighbours, shop-keepers), other members of the family, doctor, schools and the address of the local hospital. Don't forget the plumber and electrician and someone who can service essential machines.

It is a good idea if the au pair writes down her parents' full address and telephone number, international code and all. Stick it up on the pinboard, rather than stuffing it in a drawer and searching for it frantically when fate does strike. This address is always useful after she has left anyway, so that her mail can be redirected.

If the girl encounters a burglar or intruder, she should not attempt to provoke or tackle him alone, but to do what he says if the children are around, then leave the premises as quickly as possible. She should be wary of approaches in the parks or streets, especially if the stranger seems unduly interested in her charges.

For a fuller discussion of safety in the house and with children generally, see Chapter 6. Several agencies and mothers comment, 'Too many nannies don't seem to realize that looking after children is literally a matter of life and death.' They feel that many NNEB colleges do not underline this or teach the necessity of safety measures.

Frequently your nanny will be responsible for locking up the house. Remind her to shut windows, doors, window locks, security locks as well as traditional locks and particularly garden doors. Most burglars try to break in during the day – when the nanny has taken the children out. Do not hide the door keys in super-obvious places. Explain the alarm system and if you have a number code for your door lock, make sure she takes a note of it and carries it everywhere. When she is inside the house, especially in cities, ask her to use the spy-hole if there is one, or leave the door on the chain and speak through the gap if she is in any doubt about the identity of the caller. If she is to be the last person in bed at night, or if she is looking after your children when you are away, make sure she knows about double-locking doors and putting the chain on too.

It is worth talking to her about the kinds of people who may call – Jehovah's witnesses, market researchers, freelance roof repairers, double-glazing salesmen, political canvassers, charity soap and duster sellers, hawkers and con men of all types – and that's before you start on the list of people who might be expected. The general rule may as well be – stop them in their tracks on the doorstep. On no account let them in. Don't give them a chance to practise their smooth patter; just instruct the nanny to say, 'My employer is out. I am afraid I am very busy.' Don't give a name or phone number. Forewarned is forearmed.

First Week Indoctrination

By the first week, you will have organized insurance to cover the nanny to drive the car and you should drive in it with her not only to familiarize her with its idiosyncrasies, but also to assure yourself that she is a competent driver. If she is coming to London or another city for the first time, do not let her drive the children until she knows the routes and basic skills of driving in heavy and competitive traffic. Safety belts for the children must be fitted on every trip however short. Don't allow her to drive other people's children without their express permission. One of the nastiest employers' stories concerned a nanny who took three children for a drive in the country in Wales. None of them was wearing a seat belt; they missed a hairpin bend, and went off the road and down a hill. The children were killed. The nanny survived. She was wearing a seat belt.

One way of alleviating the chore of having to show the carer the ropes and your every quirk in detail is to delegate it to the out-going nanny. There is good and bad in this. The advantages include consistency for the children; they can get used to the new nanny gradually if the nannies overlap for a week, rather than being left with a stranger. Working mothers don't have much option and probably have to leave the children with the new nanny, so it is a good idea for them to arrange an overlap. If you have a cleaning lady, get her also to tell the nanny what standards you expect her to live by in her room, the children's areas and the bathroom.

It is generous and sensible to give a party for the nanny who is leaving so that the new nanny can meet the local nannies and mother's helps. It also helps to combat homesickness; someone else has done the job, survived and even apparently enjoyed it. The disadvantage of overlap is that it will cost you two salaries for a week. The nannies may not like each other. The outgoing nanny may not brief the new one effectively and leave out some vital aspect about the emergency drill or locking up the house. She may infect her with her own bad habits or get jealous of the children's dawning affection for the new incumbent.

If you decide against the overlap procedure, then you, the employer, must be around constantly for the first week to explain how you want your children to be cared for and how the house is run. Some mothers also hand over a written routine either for the week or by the day, or both. Others have covered these details in a written contract or work agreement (see Chapter 17). Still others deal with everything verbally. You will have a crash course in getting acquainted while you show her everything and that's a good reason for doing a lot of the indoctrination yourself. It will also give you ample opportunity to observe.

Overlapping is not exclusive practice for trained nannies. It can be useful for British mother's helps and, if their English is good enough, why not foreign mother's helps and au pairs?

Housework and Chores

Trained nannies expect to clean and keep tidy their own, the children's rooms, bathroom(s), the playroom, and to clear up the kitchen thoroughly after use. Some nannies do not have to hoover or dust or do basic cleaning, as there is a cleaner. Our researches show that this is unusual; most employers who have both a nanny and a cleaning lady reckon that the latter is there for communal areas and for the employer's private rooms, *not* to nanny the nanny. An employer is not entitled to expect a trained nanny to do anything else in the way of housework. There may be leeway for negotiation for any other domestic chores which don't concern the children, but they are a matter for discussion.

Housework causes friction. Some au pairs rather enjoy housework e.g. hoovering and dusting and cleaning the kitchen thoroughly. Some much prefer it to looking after children. A number of au pairs have never done any housework. This is because they are upper class girls and their mothers employ cleaners and maids. It is fair to say that the vast majority are not keen. The result is that they don't do it well.

As with mother's helps of whatever nationality, an employer will get a better result from an au pair if she shares the chores. An au pair with more than one child can't be expected to do that much housework properly anyway, and it isn't good for the child to be trailing round after the dustpan all morning.

One mother solves the problem by allocating an hour on a Monday for the au pair to tidy, dust and hoover the children's room, her own and the communal bathroom. On Thursday she asks her to vacuum the stairs and hallway which takes about 20 minutes.

> I don't think even with two small children to look after this is asking too much. I make a point of asking her to do nothing else, unless for some reason she is childless occasionally.
>
> I do the rest of the house including the children's playroom. She can see me sweating over a hot hoover some days just as I pass her on the stairs on her vacuuming day. I will ask my children when they are teenagers to do the same, and most of my au pairs do that much adequately. Even then it is not a particularly thorough job, but they aren't experienced housemaids.

Remember during the first week to tell the girl *exactly* how to work all the machines. Many au pairs, for example, have not used a dishwasher, a washing machine or a British-style upright or cylinder cleaner before. Keep reminding yourself that her English is not good and speak clearly and simply. Be prepared to demonstrate and explain the workings of a machine several times. When in doubt au pairs tend to say 'yes' rather than 'Could you repeat that please?' Ask them specifically to say the latter as often as it occurs to them.

Every mother will tell a story about how the vacuum was broken by the au pair. Au pairs have a tendency not to empty the dust bag until the machine is so full it ceases to function properly. They let the brushes get so clogged with string and hair that they won't go round. They will run hoover quite blithely over glass, large pebbles, hair grips, playdough, plasticine. When you show them the hoover's broken black rubber band they look mildly surprised. They are insensitive to any machine's condition, so keep an eye on it. Unless it comes to a complete halt and, in the case of a hoover, the room is full of the smell of burning rubber, they will use it for weeks so stuffed up with bits that it picks up nothing.

All forms of help are potentially lethal with dirty washing. Au pairs, particularly from the poorer parts of Europe, may not have used a washing or drying machine before and if they have, probably not one as sophisticated. Every au pair and mother's help is likely to turn an entire wash either grey or pink at least once, just as their employer has done in the past.

Show her how the washing machine works and remind her that it is expensive to repair, and that she must be gentle with its knobs and knockers. Spell out the importance of sorting clothes into different fabric types and of separating *pale* from *dark* colours.

Wool is a major problem. She *may* be able to cope with a washable wool wash. Experiment with children's jumpers rather than your mohair creation strewn with rainbow-coloured blobs. Many mothers just don't risk it and do all wool themselves. The question to ask yourself is: 'Will I be utterly miserable if she shrinks my Aran sweater?' If so, then don't risk it, she may get it right twice, but sure as wool shrinks she'll get it wrong the third time.

Some girls are good at ironing but have an annoying habit of doing their own things first. Others take ages to get around to it, and seem to manage to leave the one shirt you would have liked to wear on the morrow unironed at the bottom of the basket *again*. It can be weeks before clothes reach the end of the washing/ drying/ironing process. Some employers insist that the ironing basket is emptied daily.

Many girls are frightful at ironing. If she is the sort who, far from dashing away with the smoothing iron, manages to create creases as opposed to ironing them out, you will find yourself at 10 o'clock at night doing it all again. Added to this, she may be careless and scorch viyella, silk and wool. If you have doubts about her skill, don't risk anything precious like a child's party frock or a white silk blouse.

Many nannies will make sure that you are not going to exploit them before offering to do extra jobs. If you make feeding the cat at 4pm feel like the thin end of the wedge, they have no reason to oblige you. Build a relationship first, don't take advantage of the nanny and gradually, if it is not enforced, a happy *modus vivendi* will emerge.

The Daily Routine

Other nanny chores include hairwashing, nail cutting, dusting, wiping paint surfaces (skirting boards and bookshelves), cleaning the bath and lavatory, keeping the children's books, toys and clothes in good repair, changing sheets and towels, packing suitcases when going away, shopping, cooking and organizing meals, washing and sterilizing baby's kit, whizzing baby's mush, organizing nappies, making sure that the children's clothes fit, mending, especially name tapes, letting in electricians, paying the milkman and taking accurate telephone messages.

A nanny's day

Imagine a family with three children and working parents. James is six, Emily is three and the baby is nine months.

07.30 On duty. Get children up, washed, help them get dressed. Draw curtains, pull back beds, open windows.

07.45 Breakfast. After breakfast, while children go to loo, clean teeth, brush hair, collect school things, clear up breakfast table and kitchen (wipe up bits from floor and high chair). Put on washing machine.

08.35 All in car to take James to school. Collect extra child for carpool. Drop James at school 08.55. Everyone back in the car again. Drop Emily at playgroup and return home.

09.30 Make beds, tidy and hoover rooms. Put baby to bed for her rest. Transfer washing to drier.

10.00 Ironing and prepare lunch.

11.30 Baby up, play and read.

12.15 Collect Emily from playgroup.

12.30 Lunch for baby, Emily and nanny.

13.30 Baby to rest. Read and play with Emily.

15.15 Pick up James. Take all three out to play.

16.30 Prepare tea.

17.00 Tea. Clear up tea. Children play and James does homework. Clear up toys and playroom.

18.00 Bath, clean teeth and then read until mother or father returns. Put out clothes for the morning. Set breakfast table. Sort out washing and put away.

19.00 Bed. Off duty.

Imagine you have to add to that James's gym classes, Emily's dancing class and the baby's monthly clinic visit. All three like to attend the duckling class at the local swimming pool and to visit the library. One may get ill and the other two may catch it. All three have birthdays which need celebrating and so do those of their friends. These same friends and others frequently come to play and for extra meals, as do grandparents, up from the country to shop. Halloween, Valentine's Day, Mother's Day, Easter and Christmas are all energetically celebrated by children. Some mothers need their nannies to buy clothes and fit shoes for their charges. They will also shop for playdough, stationery supplies and the odd toy. After all, James is learning his tables, Emily is trying to read and the baby wants to walk and talk. It is a hectic schedule.

If you are a working mother, your nanny cannot possibly do all this alone. If you are working part-time or not at all, you can make her life a lot simpler and gentler by being a chauffeur and a bulk shopper, and by taking the children independently to the relevant activity, so that James is not attending the baby's clinic and the baby isn't forced to enjoy watching the gym class.

Given this list, it's amazing that so many nannies think they prefer 'sole charge' (see Chapter 6). A nanny's duties are less onerous if there is only one or even two children to manage. Most employers tell us that they prefer to deal themselves with the children's educational and medical problems and contact with the school and hospital staff (homework and hearing tests). They prefer in the main to be responsible and responsive to their children's needs at night and make a big effort to be around after bath time to read, kiss, hug, sing or amuse.

It will take time for you to trust her, but you should try to take that leap in the dark as fast as you can manage it and give her clear indications that you are doing so. Opinion is divided as to what is best done about petty cash. Some employers insist that their nannies account for every penny, 'not least because it makes them *think* about the value of my money and not be too cavalier with it or think I am', and others say, 'Be sure to give her a big enough float to cover emergencies and don't insult her with accounting for it – surely if you trust her with your child you trust her with your money?' 'Er, sort of,' say a third group who start strictly and ease up when they get to know their nanny better.

Time-Keeping and Remembering

Time keeping, like a poor memory, can make employers twitch. Unless mentioned, the nanny may be quite oblivious to the agonies she is causing. The employer is tense, worried and, after a bit, pretty cross as she waits for her entire family to arrive home three-quarters of an hour after she had asked them to be back to go to the dentist. Try to avoid an outburst, but make it clear at the soonest quiet opportunity that it is not to happen again and explain your obsession. If routine rules your household, instruct the nanny to be ready ten minutes *before* a deadline rather than two minutes afterwards.

First check that she has a watch and an alarm clock and that both work. Buy both for her if necessary. Knots in handkerchiefs may not be enough. One employer of a scatty au pair, in desperation scrawled '12.30' in felt tip on the back of her hand. The girl was quite amazed but it worked a treat.

Planning Ahead

Most busy families have a large communal diary by the telephone in the kitchen where the nanny and the mother, and occasionally the father, write down appointments, lunches, teas and all comings and goings. Whoever logs their plans first gets priority, more or less. Just because you have a live-in nanny or mother's help who expects to babysit at your convenience, it is not fair to insist that she be infinitely flexible. She should not often have to change her plans to suit yours when you make them at the last minute. Many nannies complain, understandably, that they don't feel properly independent and can't make a solid plan with their boyfriend to meet because 'you never know when they are going to need you for babysitting'.

It is also important to be aware that Friday and Saturday nights are *the* night for nannies' socializing too, so don't always insist on them for yourself. Some nannies will only babysit two nights a week and will insist that this is written into their contract. If it is, you will either go out less, have to find an alternative babysitter or discover this limitation suits you fine.

Employers of trained live-in nannies need not feel inhibited about requesting babysitting, as required, within reason. With forward planning which is adhered to, it shouldn't be a great sacrifice for a nanny *sometimes* to have to babysit three or four times in one week. She can always invite her girlfriends or members of the family to visit when you are out (see the House Rules, Chapter 2).

Don't let the nanny become bored. 'The devil finds work for idle hands' will become evident if you do. Be generous with your praise, thanks, and just as important, apologies for any inconsiderate behaviour on your part.

Ensure that her life is interesting and varied. Try to include her in the odd treat or special weekend. Encourage her to learn a new skill – to take driving lessons, evening classes, swimming or exercise classes. Always enquire if she is looking down or peaky and show concern and interest in her well-being generally.

Off-Duty Activities

Many employers know surprisingly little about what their nannies do when off duty: out of house, out of mind. It is sensible to acquaint yourself with the whole nanny, not just the bit that works for you. Her hobbies and interests tell you about her health and current state of mind. If a nanny frequents the Hammersmith Palais nightly or is a born-again Buddhist in Battersea Park three nights a week, there is not a lot you can do about it, but it gives you a chance to prepare for problems. How the nanny spends her free time may have no connection with your family life, but it pays dividends to show interest. There is a bit of genuine altruism here, a desire to want her to have an enjoyable time, but there is self-protection too.

What do nannies, mother's helps and au pairs do when they are not on duty? Some say they like cooking, knitting, sewing, patchwork, embroidery, tapestry, practising music, reading, listening to tapes, resting, drawing, colouring, painting, dressmaking, writing letters, watching TV, having friends round to supper, giving a dinner party, and having a nice quiet night in.

Out of the house they like: walking, jogging, badminton, squash, exercise classes (aerobics, weight-lifting, dance), swimming, sightseeing, architecture, antiques, wine, photography, learning a new language, eating out, night classes, the cinema, concerts, pubs, sunbathing, theatre, nightclubs (London nannies go to the Hippodrome and Stringfellows), running local Brownies and Guides groups, going to young people's clubs and societies, gardening, skiing, shopping, and joining a friend who is babysitting in the evening.

On weekends off nannies may go to their parents' home, 'which I still regard as mine as opposed to my work home', says one reassuringly. Some stay with local friends or go and visit friends in other parts of the country and a few go and stay wherever their boyfriend happens to be. They also have their friends or relatives to stay in their employers' house when they are away.

There may be a complication here if an employer has not previously ascertained that the nanny has a family in this country with whom she is on speaking terms. One employer warns:

> I didn't think it was suitable to leave an 18 year-old alone in a very large London house over an entire weekend. She hadn't made any local friends because she had only just arrived and I thought it could be lonely and frightening for her. We couldn't take her with us to stay with friends. So I said, 'Why don't you go home?' She looked at me fiercely and said 'They don't want me there; this is my home now.' 'Fine,' I said out loud. 'Heck,' I said to myself, 'what happens if she's seriously ill? Is *everything* about her to be my responsibility from now on?'

A happy nanny has friends. She meets them at the park, at her exercise class, at playgroups, ballet classes, One-O'Clock Clubs and in local shops, churches and clinics – anywhere where there is a crowd or a queue or where people have time to talk.

Encouraging a nanny to be busy is part of a good employer's job. It is a relief to see a nanny organizing her time off purposefully and looking after her own social, emotional and physical needs. Employers always feel cheered when nannies take some exercise rather than hearing the perennial moan about 'running up and down stairs all day is enough exercise for me'.

Modern employers no longer expect much in the way of domestic skills. Gone are the days of the nanny who spent her free time knitting, sewing and making clothes for her charges and their dollies. Few employers get more than minimal mending: sewing on buttons and name tapes and repairing a hem is about the limit: even a zip can cause trouble.

If an employer finds that she has hired a quiet and/or anti-social nanny, she may feel guilty if the nanny doesn't go out much and seems incapable of making plans and initiating outings with friends. No employer wants her nanny to describe life with the family as 'lonely' as so many nannies do. Equally, an employer cannot be expected to do more than encourage the nanny to make friends and have fun and enjoy herself when not nannying.

Chapter 6
The Roles of a Nanny

This chapter concerns the subject of continuity of care. It is not helpful for a baby or young child to receive conflicting or contradictory messages. Mother and nanny need to discuss and decide on what their responses will be to given situations in advance.

Synchronizing reactions is not easy. Some obvious areas of difficulty can be illustrated in the following ideas: 'Eat up what you're given'; 'Because I said so'; 'It's better for the child to walk than to be carried'; 'It's rude to walk about with nothing on' and 'Crying exercises their lungs.' These areas, if dealt with inconsistently, can cause a child to be perplexed, frustrated and miserable.

Keep in the forefront of your mind that what matters is that nanny and mum should work as a team for the children's good. It is only when the team is working well together that a mother will relax, trust can grow and interference will not be necessary. Try to talk these things through and, if you find that the nanny is firmly but immutably disagreeing, then recognise that there is trouble ahead.

When is a Nanny not a Mother?

Employers have strong views on this subject. Many say that when they are around, the nanny is not a mother. A few expect their nanny to be mother-like when the mother isn't there. Some give more detailed comment:

When she doesn't remember details and can't plan ahead

At bedtime except very rarely

Also when the children are ill, or when they need congratulating when something good has happened

You need a mother rather than a nanny to scold and lecture seriously when a child is dishonest, cruel or manipulative

In most ways she isn't a mother: she can't deal with schools, teachers and reports, hospital and other tests and she can't be expected to cope with some crises alone.

At the age when the children themselves consider they have grown out of the nanny.

A nanny is never a mother. The relationship is quite distinct; children are always quite clear about the difference. The nanny is an additional relationship for the child, not instead of.

Although nannies are very involved with your children, the ultimate responsibility is never theirs. They go off duty.

At evening prayers.

What nannies say:

A mother doesn't have to be working not to see much of her children. I can't understand why they don't find a three-year-old good company some of the time. She prefers to go to the hairdressers, shop and have lunch with friends.

I can't understand why they had children when they can't be bothered with them.

I treat Jacob very much as if he was my son. I wouldn't treat my own children any different.

I'm going to leave this job so I cannot and should not become too emotionally involved.

You can never take the parents' place. You can't help loving them and getting close to them, maybe too close, but then you are the one bringing them up, almost.

I tell the children that I am not their mother and that I'm not one of the family. That's very important.

Nanny as Sole Charger

Sole charge is nanny jargon and most new mothers have no clue what it entails. Nannies cannot know in advance whether they are fitted for such responsibility, but ideally the wise employer will not give a sole charge post to any nanny who has not had at least two years' experience. The reliable employment agencies feel this strongly and refuse to let untried nannies take sole charge posts. If an employer is paying for an NNEB anyway, it is silly not to pay a bit extra for experience and avoid a new nanny's mistakes – she'll get her chance at sole charge when she has learned a bit in a supervised job.

'NNEBs too often have an inflated view of their own ability. They want a job without the mother around and insist on sole charge,' says a long-established nanny agent. 'I tell them that they are only 18 with no practical experience and that I would prefer them to work where there is a mother to alleviate the responsibility.' There is no doubt that part of the attraction of working alone is simply to do with a novice's wish to practise – and make mistakes – in private. Another agent reports that a father started working from home while writing a book and the nanny rang up to complain, 'He watches everything that goes on.' The agent responded, 'Is there anything he can't watch?'

This last point may well give working mothers cause for concern. Many confess to telephoning the nanny constantly to see how things are. They worry a great deal about what goes on in their absence, and have to fight back the fantasy (they hope) that their beloveds are sitting in a row in front of the telly Test Card munching liquorice allsorts.

The temptation for working mothers to trust the nanny to get on with the job responsibly and unsupervised is strong. This is how executive working mothers are treated by their superiors at work. Their bosses have complete trust in how they do their job and give them autonomy in their offices. So it suits them to treat the nanny with as much respect. Wonderful, but what if she abuses the mother's trust and how on earth *is* the working mum to know what's going on in her absence? The boss at work is at the most a floor or a lunch away; the absent mother has no opportunity of checking on her employee's ability to get on with the work in hand.

Many employers are wrong in thinking that they needn't worry about what the nanny or childminder does in their absence so long as their child can talk and tell them what happened that day.

Some children aged two or three are capable of saying, 'Joyce hurt me today on the leg' or 'Joyce was cross today', which provides a little information to go on. Other children may not even give this much away. It is probable that if a child has been pinched, slapped, shut in a cupboard or generally roughly treated that he won't mention it. They may not tell about less extreme but nonetheless undesirable events, for example: 'We watched telly all day. Joyce had a little sleep.' 'When we cry Joyce says shut up 'cos she's on the phone for ages.' 'We met Joyce's boyfriend in the park and we had three lollipops each.'

Hoping that you will hear about any oddity from the children's lips is vain. One member of Parents at Work (PAW) from Harrow tells of the time that she came home early on a hot day and the house was like an oven. There wasn't a single door or window open. The children and nanny were sweating in the playroom.

It emerged that her nanny's fear of creepy-crawlies was so strong that she hadn't let the children go out into their large pleasant garden for the nine months she had been in sole charge of them. They had been denied the paddling pool, sandpit and swing week after week throughout the summer. The nanny had always opened the windows and doors ten minutes before her employer's estimated time of arrival.

A working mother must rely entirely on the nanny to report humdrum happenings like whether the children painted, made paper hats, read the new library book, fell over in dancing or decided they liked spinach. She has to be trusted not to take the easy option with their nutrition, play, manners, nappies and in running the home.

How can a working mother prove to herself that her nanny is to be trusted? Shirley Conran in *Superwoman* writes:

> Check on your minder. There is no reason to trust her until she is proven trustworthy. If you can't hop home unexpectedly yourself, get someone else to do so. This sounds nasty but they're *your* children and you can't take risks. Also check carefully with other parents about your child-minder, playgroup or nursery school. *Never stop checking.*

One full-time working mother turned overnight into the part-time-from-home kind:

> I arrived back at lunchtime to pick up a file to find our new NNEB and another nanny with their feet up watching the TV in my sitting room with three under-twos on the floor behind the sofa. My daughter, aged 11 months, had a biro top in her mouth. There were no toys in the room, swilling potties graced a bookshelf and the room was full of cigarette smoke. I kept telling myself that I did not need to feel guilty, but *something* made me choose that day to walk in on that scene. And I am damn glad I did and I'm now around enough to ensure that all that will never happen again.

Working mothers have various tools at their disposal if they want to monitor the home front. They can ask the nanny to keep a log, diary or scrapbook of events. This can serve several purposes. It helps a mother and nanny communicate, allows working parents to keep in touch with the day's events and makes them feel more involved in their child's upbringing. It also provides details of developmental changes which the nanny observes in the children, i.e. little Johnny didn't hear the doorbell; Henrietta spoke her first sentence. This is not much to ask; a trained nanny will have done her 'observations' on her course and will probably enjoy doing them again.

Who can an employer co-opt for the job of checking up, if she is stuck in the office herself? A cleaning lady is an obvious answer, if you have one. Appoint her official spy and make time to hear her full report, maybe an evening call once a month. Don't ask her to mention just major problems; you want to hear *anything* of note. If she's not that sort of cleaning lady, what about a mother, a mother-in-law, a sister, neighbours, other local mums, the PAW or NCT network (see Useful Addresses). Arrange a secret rota, ideally at least one person to look in on different days and different times to give an independent report.

The temptation is to ease up after a month or so, but err on the side of caution. Keep going for longer than that and rely on your greatest friend to be a brick and go on calling. Nannies can change overnight with a new devastating experience – good or bad. Watch out for the new love. Vigilant mothers ask nursery school teachers to get in touch immediately if they feel at all concerned about the nanny's attitude to the child, her road safety drill or anything else. Local shopkeepers can also be a help in keeping an eye on comings and goings.

Make sure that the house diary is full of friend's and tradesmen's calls – the more your children are seen by third parties, the more you can relax. So arrange a couple of lunches and teas a week with other nannies and their charges, and/or with a friend who is at home. Local activities like swimming or gym are all to be encouraged. It is important to organize these yourself if your nanny is clearly not taking the initiative. It is a ghastly prospect at the end of a long day at a desk, but an outing a day keeps the guilt at bay.

If your nanny is the gregarious type, you can't relax either. You want to know exactly where she is taking the children; check it is not too ambitious a project – too far or for too long a time. Be sure to have met your nanny's best nanny friends, the ones with whom she is most likely to arrange outings. Prick up your ears if you gather that the children seem to spend the whole day out of the house, or for that matter in it with a permanent *ad hoc* crèche going on in the playroom and kitchen. Too much socializing with other nannies in the park isn't ideal. Many working mothers complain of too much nanny natter and not enough nanny and child playing/reading/painting.

Don't feel inhibited about banning other people's nannies whom you don't like or approve of when you are not in the house. Your nanny must accept your veto about where she goes and whom she sees while on duty. If she doesn't, then she shouldn't be working for you.

The working mother/nanny relationship is less stressful all round if the nanny doesn't live in. The simple fact that their paths barely cross makes friction minimal. But other problems are legion. One of them is when to talk; the baton is handed over from one bleary-eyed minder to the other at dawn and swapped again at dusk when both are even more weary. Who has the strength to care about the potty-training progress reports or what they had for tea today? Once a week both nanny and employer should get the log, sit down quietly and have a News and Views session.

Working mothers get frustrated by being unable to prevent nannies doing things their way, even when they know that their employer would disapprove. One working mother sums it up: 'I have always felt that my little prejudices – food, creative play and the like are treated very seriously when I am around, and are out the window when I am through the door. I fear that if you hand over your home to what is in effect a housewife, she feels entirely justified in doing things her way in her domain.'

Nannies like sole charge because it is more peaceful not to have another adult in the house. She can do the routine exactly how and when she likes. If a mother is not around to object, it is not surprising that she leaves the bits under the high chair till the end of the day rather than bother to clear up after each meal. No one interferes with her methods or second guesses her decisions. The children have no opportunity to ricochet from one adult to another – nanny is big boss.

Some mothers say that they would rather die than admit to their colleagues that having children entails responsibilities which may occasionally interfere with their job. At the moment many mothers simply lie about taking the day off saying they are ill, when in fact their nanny or childminder is under the weather and can't look after the children. This puts off the day when employers, whether a small company or a multi-national, accept that once in a while an employee who is also a father may have to be off from work to look after his child.

In Sweden someone who has to stay at home from work to tend to a sick child under 12 years of age receives an allowance for 60 days a year. Days are also allocated for short-term child care and to visit schools. Think Swedish; persuade your partner to take a day off; come home early to deal with an accident or chat up teachers – do it 50–50. Why should he always be indispensable? Until child care is genuinely shared between working parents, employers will look askance when, as usual, it is only their women staff that go home in a hurry.

Don't overload the nanny or expect too much in your absence. All standards will slip; she will become exhausted and be ratty with the children. An experienced nanny will say firmly that there is too much on the agenda and Maisie just won't be able to do dancing that day. An inexperienced nanny won't have the nerve to say 'no'. She will try to meet all the deadlines and she or one of the children may well end up having a mishap. If this happens it is mostly the employer's fault.

Each additional child is a complication to the sole charge nanny. Three children can easily feel like twice two. A few parents who insist on a Rolls-Royce childhood for their offspring, and intend to continue to work full-time themselves, hire another pair of hands (a mother's help, an au pair, a daily or part-time nanny), to back up the nanny and work under her direction.

When a mother is at home when the nanny is on duty, especially if she is not usually there, she can feel curiously displaced. One mother says that she found herself asking her nanny if she could join her for a walk with the baby? Other mothers say that they wouldn't dare upset a nanny's routine.

While it is a fault on the right side that employers should listen to their nannies' wishes and advice, it is mildly idiotic to defer to them on all subjects. Betty Parsons, much loved and now regrettably retired guru and ante-natal-instruction-expert, advises inimitably: 'Rule your own roost. Find someone who will adapt to your particular household. No child should be left *entirely* in a nanny's care. Bonding with parents is vital. The nanny must realize that the baby does not belong to her. Remember *you* must get her to do things *your* way for *your* child.'

It is important that a mother tries to resolve her attitudes and thoughts about why she is working and not choosing to look after her children herself at home. This is the subject of at least one other book, but suffice it to say that guilt is a pain in the neck for nannies to deal with and to have to make allowances for as well.

When working mothers hire a sole charge nanny, both employer and nanny should be aware that it is an *extremely* responsible job. As one agent put it, 'I screen out nannies who think they can whizz on a coffee round and stick junior in a bouncy chair.' The nanny programmes a child's development – introduces the child to solids, encourages him to look at books and crawl – major areas which should be taken seriously and monitored carefully by the mother.

Ignore the mothers who claim they have 'complete confidence' in their nanny. It is healthier to respect and like a nanny but remember she is human and fallible. Be vigilant and energetic and *humble* enough not to be complacent about your choice of nanny and the way the house is being run at the moment. It cannot be ideal.

Nanny as Shrink

A committed nanny will give a child her undivided attention some of the time. From this will grow that wordless communication which is instinctive between mother and child. Some mothers cannot cope with the intensity of this closeness; some revel in it. Some nannies do not want it; others think it is that getting inside children's skin which provides the intense challenge of the job. But it is this loving understanding, which gives the child the security that someone minds specially about him, that prepares him for complicated events like the dentist, first day at school and being nice to Grandpa who's a bit gaga these days.

One old nanny says, 'The motherly instinct is lacking in modern nannies. You have to work on the kids for a long time before you establish a real rapport. I make sure that I do as Mum would do in every way I can. So I have a lot of observing and listening to do in a new job.'

Jeanne Magagna, child psychotherapist at the Tavistock Clinic, says: 'I always ask the question – is the meeting between caretaker and child generating love or promulgating hate, promoting hope or sowing despair, containing pain or eliciting persecutory anxiety, fostering creative activity or creating confusion?'

If you watch a child with a good nanny, you will see how she feels things *with* him. A mother can't help doing so. If a child is secure in the knowledge that people notice and care and act on his behalf, he rates himself highly.

A nanny may have favourites or even a chemical reaction against one of the children. If the latter occurs the employer probably knew from the beginning that there was a mutual antipathy and hoped things would improve. They may not. Maybe the nanny picks on one child much too often and you are uneasy that she quite enjoys her power over him. It is just as unfair when she thinks one of them is more cuddly and says so. Coincidentally, the one she is likely to want to cuddle most is the baby and his siblings may like him less. This is unprofessional behaviour and potentially damaging. Either the pattern is changed or the nanny must go.

> One nanny played favourites. I had to talk to her and tell her to try and play fair as she bullied the less favourite and he knew it.

> Another nanny liked the child she had been with since he was a baby and she didn't have much sympathy for the older one.

> We had one nanny who was very fond of my elder son and found it difficult to love the baby. I fired her in the end.

Nanny as Safety Net

> You know, at least you ought to know,
> For I have often told you so,
> That children never are allowed
> To leave their Nurses in a crowd . . .
> And Always keep a-hold of Nurse
> For fear of finding something worse.
>
> Hilaire Belloc,
> *Jim*

On average, four children a day are killed in an accident in the UK. Accidents are the most common cause of death among toddlers and older children; the under-fours are especially at risk. Each year one child in six visits a hospital casualty department where one in every three patients is a child. One in every six children in hospital is there because of an accident. According to Department of Trade and Industry statistics, the home is as dangerous as the road.

Many nannies find it dreary that an employer wants a long discussion with them about safety. But mother's helps and au pairs may never have thought about any aspect of child safety, so it's the employer's job to educate them. Even if they are trained, they may have had very little practical experience of living with children. Apart from the lack of practice in spotting possible hazards for a one-year-old or a three-year-old, nannies cannot be expected to have the supposed maternal sixth sense. They have to learn it and preferably not by their mistakes with your children. Do not play down the subject; defer to the training enough to say briskly, 'I'm sure you know all this already, but I will feel better if you hear it from me too.'

Do not rely on the carer's instinct to know when a child is about to have an accident. Prepare his environment properly in both home and garden to avoid dangers. When he is at the park, in the street, in other people's houses, and on public transport she will have to be extra vigilant and become the child's ears and eyes. Many parents only become safety-conscious after a frightening accident involving a visit to the hospital's outpatients' department.

Accidents *can* be cut down if whoever is looking after the child is paying him full attention. Better safe than sorry. No parent should remain relaxed about a nanny who says, 'I hope you realize your son's accident-prone?' after the sixth visit to casualty when she and the boy are becoming a bit of a joke to the doctors. One baby's leg was broken when he fell from the changing table while his nanny was out of the room – the doctors did not call that baby 'accident-prone'.

Apart from trying to protect the children, every employer wants to save the whole family *and* the nanny from the awful repercussions of a serious accident. If it clearly could have been avoided had the nanny been paying attention, the loaded word 'negligence' rears its ugly head. (For a discussion about professional negligence, insurance and the law, see Chapter 17).

By the late 1990s there were several horrific stories of cruelty to children by nannies which had come to court. Perhaps the most infamous was that of Carol Withers, who was found guilty of grievous bodily harm to babies in her charge in two separate jobs (see Chapter 7). This and other cases have made many unwary employers much more strict, and this new trend of toughness with interviews and reference checks is echoed in agency procedures. One doctor employer, on being told by her nanny that the child in her care had a nasty bruise on his head, organized an immediate X-ray which revealed a fractured skull. The nanny said she had no idea how it had happened and was sacked at once. The employer felt that her nanny's ignorance of the incident made her no less responsible for it and just as guilty of negligence.

One mother had the experience of driving down the High Street of her local shopping area to see her nanny posting a letter on one side of the road and and her daughter beginning to climb out of her buggy on the other. Another mother threatened her nanny with the sack if she left the baby outside the shops again after two babies had been snatched in the same area in a month – she forgot again and was told to leave. Another had to go when a mother was told by a neighbour that her two-year-old twins had let each other out of their car seats, climbed out of the front door of the car, held hands, looked left and right and crossed the road to rejoin their nanny in the bank.

Tell your nanny or mother's help that there are *no* circumstances in which your children are to be left alone in public places. Explain why. A few examples to start you off – escalators to fall down, supermarket shelves stacked with heavy tins ready to tumble if the bottom one is shifted, strangers who may offer sweets or pretty puppies ('like this one in the car') and even dog mess in the park from which a child can contract a rare blood disorder called *toxicara canis* and become gradually blind. Do also ask your nanny specifically not to allow your children to pet strange animals, they may have fleas, bite or scratch.

A safe road crossing drill is vital. Nannies must always hold a child's hand. If the child is unreliable and impulsive and little, perhaps he should wear reins, but if this idea does not appeal it is essential that a nanny hold each child by the hand firmly. She should also teach them good habits of safety drill by setting them an example and be sure to use designated crossings and not jaywalk or push the buggy into the road from behind parked cars. Children shouldn't be allowed to hurtle along and then teeter on the edge of the pavement. Nannies should be aware of all this, but if they are young or have no experience of heavy traffic and city life, spell it out – and take them for a practice so that they can witness your responsible road drill and learn how serious you are about the whole routine.

The dangers in the country are often as great as in the town, though they can be different. For example, a weekending child can clamber on to a combine harvester, or wander down the middle of a lane thinking that just because he is in the country there probably won't be any cars and may be allowed to wobble about on the main road learning to ride a bike as the only tractor to pass that week swerves round the corner. He can be tempted by poisonous berries – e.g. yew and laburnum – or paddle in ponds, streams or bogs without being aware of the dangers.

The *First Aid Manual,* issued by the Red Cross, should be read, marked and learned by anyone responsible for children's lives. It is essential to know *exactly what* to do in cases of choking, suffocations, burns and scalds, poisoning, cuts and falls.

It is not possible here to cover all aspects of safety with children in the home. The most important point about talking to your nanny or mother's help about the whole subject is to ensure that she understands that prevention is best. Remind her to beware of, among other things, children:

- suffocating on plastic bags
- choking on peanuts
- grabbing at boiling saucepans
- playing with matches
- unlatching safety gates
- climbing on banisters
- exploring power sockets and frayed wires
- drowning, unattended, in two inches of water.

She should be aware that the nature of the danger constantly changes with growing children. With each stage of maturity one clutch of hazards recedes and another batch looms – the baby who was immobile yesterday can roll off a changing mat tomorrow and the crawling child can suddenly clamber up to things that were previously out of reach.

Nanny as Nurse

The nanny or mother's help should always tell you if she notices any symptoms of illness, particularly high temperatures or a child's behaviour which is out of the ordinary. If she cannot get in touch with you, she should ring the doctor or the local clinic for advice.

Princess Christian, patroness of the training college, inveighed against the 'mischief of soothing powders and syrups'. The use of the latter can be controversial, given that Phenergan and Benylin expectorant are sold without prescription. Some others prefer the dispensing of medicines to be their exclusive province. Occasionally there can be a mix-up and the child gets a double dose or none at all, so whatever you decide, be consistent and consult closely. Incidentally, remind your nanny about the contents of children's medicines; there are sugar-free options.

If you are around, take it in turns to nurse and entertain a sick child both by day and by night. The same rule applies for teething, colic and feeding babies in the middle of the night. Trained nannies certainly expect to do this as part of their routine, but if you aren't working long hours yourself, it is important that you relieve her, so that she can catch up on her sleep to do her daily job as well. Louise Davis of Norland recommends that 'three nights in a row are enough for any nanny without support'. Another principal warns that 'many employers don't realize that nannies need to recharge their batteries'.

Most parents sleep within earshot of their children and usually cope with a wakeful child. This is one reason for the parent to

bother to go personally to hear if anything is specifically wrong or
has upset the child during the day.

One employer says: 'Good nannies sleep like logs. If they are
unmoved by the racket during the day, it is no wonder that they are
unmovable at night. I used to think it was deliberate, but they are
just like my older children – they sleep like babies but my baby
doesn't.' Another says, 'He who hears first, deals.' Some reckon
that 'night duty is for parents'. This is definitely the case with au
pairs.

Nanny as Cook

It will be a bonus if your nanny or mother's help cooks well and
has heard of modern nutrition and diet. Trained nannies are meant
to have learned about food values, a balanced diet, and vitamins.
The chances of meeting a nanny who is fond of brown rice, pulses,
beansprouts, wholemeal bread and spaghetti, low fat milk,
polyunsaturates, steamed veg, fresh fruit and grilling rather than
frying are slim – and the nannies aren't.

Before you flounce in and throw a fit about the nanny's cooking
and choice of tins, frozen food and instant whips for the children,
remember that this is a very touchy area. You are criticizing her
mum's cooking, which may be pre-war in outlook and includes a
new-to-you recipe for cooking cabbage. Start with cold water, boil
for twenty minutes and serve straight from the hob in a slotted
spoon when it has sat in the water for another half an hour before
lunch. One raw carrot would be more nutritious. Raw is good for
you, and this is a positive plus for lazy nannies.

Keep a sense of proportion; it is not vital that every meal is
served and prepared as you would choose, but don't ignore its
content. A large majority of employers have the same criticisms to
make: more fresh food, inventiveness and use of recipes, less fat,
sugar, salt, cakes, biscuits, orange squash, chips, fish fingers,
sausages and tomato ketchup.

Employers often say that they greatly dislike their nannies
giving their children sweets as treats – not least because they feel
that this is the province of the parents. The nanny may not be using
sweets as a bribe (very naughty) but, even if she is just being generous, it's a good idea to persuade her that raisins or a big juicy red
apple can have the same effect. It helps if they lead the way.

Don't forget to remind nannies that children and especially
babies do not need added salt in their food. One mother tells us that

her baby was fed an Oxo cube a day by her NNEB-trained nanny and had to spend several weeks in hospital after severe dehydration.

Certain 'E' numbers and other additives have been definitely linked to allergies and problems such as hyperactivity, eczema and asthma. This is the worst aspect of having a nanny who is idle or unaware of healthy eating. One family is so against such additives as tartrazine (E102), sunset yellow (E110) and benzoic acid (E210) that they instruct their nanny to read every label on everything she buys. She has learnt to enjoy being a tartrazine-spotter, but she was always keen on the subject thanks to a good NNEB course.

Mothers often put aside enough food for the children's lunch from their cooking the night before because they know how hard it is to break habits of a lifetime. Almost all the mothers we consulted put themselves in charge of the weekly bulk shop so that they could monitor the intake. It is quite a good idea to decide together on weekly or daily menus, then an employer does not have to nag at every meal. If your nanny has never encountered this entire subject before, do not get cross if she thinks you are a bit barmy – recapture your own reactions to the first health food freak you met years ago.

You will need to agree about how much and what your children are to eat. Some people feel they would rather their children ate anything, rather than everyone having to suffer rows over muesli, greens and fruit. Some nannies are rigid about children finishing what is on their plates and can take punishment too far for wayward eaters. It is necessary to know the nanny's approach before leaving the children's meals to her. As Katharine Whitehorn writes in *How to Survive Children*, 'A food is not necessarily essential just because your child hates it.'

If you have a nanny who is too bullying about your children's eating habits, remind her that she is at least twenty years older than the miscreant and that it surely cannot be true that confrontation is the only way to get what you want from the under-fives? Suggest that she gives smaller helpings, cajoles, persuades and avoids too many rules.

Nanny as Disciplinarian

> If babies could speak they'd tell mother or nurse,
> That slapping was pointless and why;
> For if you're not crying it prompts you to cry,
> And if you are – then you cry worse.
>
> Roy Fuller,
> *Bringing up Baby*

It is a truism that people vote as their parents vote and bring up their children as they were brought up. In other words if *they* once experienced violence, shouting and swearing, they are not inhibited about treating their own child or children in their care in the same way. One of the main reasons for discussing the subject of discipline during the interview (see Chapter 4) is that attitudes are diverse and people hold strong views. It will now be obvious why a stable and happy family background is very important.

Norland nannies are taught that it should never be necessary to smack a child and they will refuse to do so regardless of the parents' wishes. Whatever you think is right, you must agree on a plan of action for dealing with a naughty child *with* the nanny. 'Please tidy your rooms quickly then there will be more time for a story/play/ Blue Peter.' Encourage the nanny not to stand for any rudeness to her and to make 'sorry' after a misdemeanour the absolute norm. Don't both bellow at the children in unison if you can avoid it.

Having decided between you on the course of action to take on discipline, there should be no public disagreement about an issue. Ask the nanny to stick firmly to an agreed policy. Don't let the children play one off against the other, but present a united front and talk about it later.

Nannies hate having their authority undermined, justifiably, as in the classic case of when the nanny says 'no' to another sweet and mummy comes in and consoles the doleful child with one. It is particularly irking when toddler manipulation wins out. Never succumb to the temptation to let the nanny know who is boss when it is not appropriate. Do not score points. You will repent in the leisureless weeks after she has left.

In an office, if a colleague is boring, irritating or behaving unreasonably, the bloke who sits in the next desk knows that he cannot attack him physically, however exasperating he may be. Yet in many families adults do hit their kids for those very reasons. Max Patterson, a past President of the PPA (Pre-school Playgroups Association) says that 'Much child abuse comes from parents' failure to perceive themselves as adults. They feel their child is being vindictive, so hit back in revenge, just as a child might react to another child.'

Even trained nannies with little practical experience may punish a child who is behaving in a way which is entirely appropriate for his age and stage, out of sheer ignorance. Correcting aggression with more aggression can only lead to confusion in the toddler. And he's more likely to be aggressive to his brothers and sisters so it can be counter-productive.

Many parents regard smacking as violence, and in a society where we agree that children should not be beaten at school the Norland approach seems reasonable. Those same parents admit to the occasional smack or wallop when at the end of their tether. It is for them a cathartic gesture, but a nanny should not need such an emotional outlet. For some parents, smacking is indeed a Sackable Offence (see Chapter 2).

If you give your nanny a lot of sole charge and anyone, be it neighbour, friend or distant acquaintance, mentions however obliquely and whistling the while, that she has seen your nanny behave in a way that she feels you might not have approved of, try not to dismiss her as an interfering old bag. It is not a subject people raise lightly. They don't have to be sensitive to know that you would far rather not hear bad news of your nanny, nor feel guilty about your own lack of judgement in having employed her. Investigate the criticism thoroughly and, if proved fair, be grateful and sack the nanny without delay.

Suggested disciplinary alternatives for your nanny to practise include: scolding, banishing from the room, sending up to the bedroom, standing the child in a corner, a quiet firm verbal reprimand eyeball-to-eyeball at the child's level, taking them aside and having a little chat, withdrawals of privileges and carrying through *any* threat.

Be aware that non-residential NNEB courses scarcely tackle the subject of children's discipline. The broad line is that nannies should take the lead from the children's parents. So give them one.

A long-established agent says that, 'The employer should assume that the children won't tell them how a nanny disciplines them. They are too frightened of what she might do to them next time the employer leaves the house.' A Scots employer warns: 'The awful truth is that nannies are more subtle and devious than we like to know. Discipline should be discussed, agreed on and stuck to.' She goes on to mention a nanny who was with her family for 18 months and when she left both the children were quite clear they didn't mind if they never saw her again. She never quite knew why, but always felt guilty that she had not been around enough to protect them from whatever the nanny had done to frighten them.

Parental child abuse is the one instance when the nanny is incontrovertibly within her rights to go against the rule of confidentiality between employer and employee, especially in a residential job. She would be likely to be sacked instantly but should be reassured that she is morally and legally in the right and that the law of 'unfair dismissal' was drafted to cover such an occurrence.

She may take her case to an industrial tribunal. PANN, the nanny's trade union, (see Chapter 17), would take up her cause.

It can arise that an employer feels uneasy about a nanny's relationship with a child. Do not suppress this reaction as being beyond the pale. There are cases when young teenagers are initiated into the joys of sex by a younger sibling's nanny. A live-in 'Mrs Robinson' is far from most people's idea of the perfect nanny. It's inevitably a Sackable Offence (see Chapter 2).

It is entirely natural that a toddler grabs or fondles his nanny's breasts, but even then she should gently reprove and remove his hand. A seven-year-old clearly should know not to do so. A nanny who permits or encourages such behaviour is guilty of abuse. A disturbed child may use the sexual contact of climbing into bed with a nanny often as a way of making himself feel safe and good. The carer should make physical boundaries for a child at a certain age – there are grounds for some minor confusion in the relationship, unlike that between parents and children who have the incest barrier to illuminate what is 'right' and what is 'wrong'. A tiny number of nannies who are not receiving physical or emotional gratification from an appropriate source may come to rely on children's affectionate gestures and insist on them.

One of the most common and heartfelt complaints from parents concerns the volume of the nanny's voice. They find this never more objectionable than when a nanny is chastising their offspring. Several mothers mention that they tell their nanny at the outset not to shout or insult the children; parents have no need to pay someone to do that for them. Verbal abuse is the first cousin of physical abuse, and can hurt some individuals a lot more. A nanny who continually yells at a child must go. It is not a pretty sight to witness a girl showing off her power over yours or another's child in front of other nannies and children. Object strongly and deal with it firmly – and quietly.

Nanny as Scaredy Cat

Irrational fears are part of everyone's upbringing but the last thing you need as an employer is a nanny who makes no attempt to hide hers in front of your children. A child is deeply affected by seeing an adult, and particularly one in whom he places his trust, obviously frightened or reduced to a jelly. It is not surprising that whatever has given the nanny hysterics is likely to give the child problems in the future. Spiders, flies, snakes, creepy crawlies, bats and mice are common bugbears. Water presents a threat to some.

Some people also dislike: black men, homosexuals, tattoos, seaweed, walking under ladders, flying, boats, cows, geese, horses, the dark, the heat, the cold, the wind, the rain, thunder, lightning, heights – and some of these people are nannies.

You asked her specifically in the interview if she had any particular fears or prejudices. Do not be too sympathetic if she now reveals herself to be an agoraphobe. She really should have told you before. You can't be expected to re-write the job description, as you would need to if you always go away at weekends and she is constantly car sick.

It is a good idea to talk about any fears or prejudices she has, but the important thing is for her to understand that she may not shriek in front of the children when she sees a spider.

Nanny as Potty Trainer

Usual thing: talk about it beforehand, have a party line and both stick rigidly to it. The subject and people's attitude to it is clearly related to discipline. Try to persuade your nanny to treat the training process as though dealing with the child's eating habits and not to get emotional, or bullying, and to avoid confrontation at all costs.

Try to instil into the girl the need for her to become the child's bladder or body alarm clock. In other words she must think about when and whether the child should/need/want to 'go'. Remember to standardize your vocabulary and check out the words the playgroup use. In the 1990s 'pee' and 'poo', 'willy' and 'bottom' seem to be fashionable and employed so universally that both employer and nanny can use them uninhibitedly.

Make sure that the nanny plays fair with your child and protects him from his own 'accidents' by always going out with a potty secreted about her person, as well as trainer pants and perhaps a disposable.

Don't let your nanny be relaxed about her own or anyone else's carpets – the stains are the worst. She must not blame the child nor use the popular but inept words 'dirty' and/or 'naughty'. Any trained nanny should understand why not, and if she skipped the relevant lectures at college, refer her to Penelope Leach, Dr Spock and, indeed, Freud.

Incidentally, if your nanny has not yet encountered the 'dirty protest' – when the child smears crap all over the cot and walls and eats what's left – if you are around, deal with it yourself. It is uniquely disgusting, particularly if you are not the child's mother. Don't stretch the vocational instinct to its limits.

Nanny as Educator

If your nanny or mother's help isn't naturally voluble, do try to get her to talk, talk, talk to a small child. It doesn't matter how trivial it is; like learning any language, practice makes perfect. If you think she is self-conscious and will feel silly having a dotty conversation about pink dragons-baggons and fiery blancmangey-mangey, talk to her about it and set a good example by making sure she hears you sounding silly too.

Get her to discourage stereotype roles. If she hears the four-year-old lad say to his two-year-old sister 'Girls can't be cowboys, only boys can', remind him that there are cow girls who are quite as capable of riding a bronco. Tell her not to ignore silly, impolite comments about other races even if they are meant innocently. She should make it clear that what has been said is unacceptable and should explain why unemotionally.

Books are the biggest boon to child entertainers. Most children adore being read to. It is a good thing to read to them after a period of activity. It can calm them down before a meal, or before going out, and, of course, before bed. No playroom can have enough books. Research affirms what common sense knows already: the more a child is read to, the better it is for his intellectual development, not to mention his reading skills, before, during and *after* he has learnt to read. Nannies of working mothers should be schooled particularly about the importance of lots of reading all the day through and if the parents can't be there at bedtime, the therapeutic effect of a quiet read of at least 10 minutes (the more the better, so long as the child is absorbed).

Encourage your nanny to tell stories as well as read them. Children can then add their embellishments. They love to hear about themselves; in written stories they identify with the heroes and heroines. It is easy to weave a story around them and their circumstances.

The nanny should encourage her charges who cannot read yet to 'read' books with her, to enjoy the pictures and tell the story with her and to her, to enjoy books on their own. Enjoying books helps a child concentrate, learn about people and situations and use the story and pictures as a spring-board for his own ideas and stories. All the time he is becoming familiar with letters, words and numbers. He is also developing his language and thought processes.

It may give your nanny satisfaction to see herself as much as a teacher as a carer. She will gain a sense of achievement, as will her charge, when she helps him learn the alphabet and how to count. Of course, she must be sensible and sensitive about it and not become hectoring, or insist that the child guesses letters when he doesn't want to.

Keep an eye on the children's tape cassette collection: does your nanny put on the same tapes (possibly her favourites rather than the child's)?; does she use them enough?; do you find a tell-tale cassette of her favourite rock group in the machine at the end of the day? Ask her about it. Encourage her to sit and read the book that goes with the tape with the child, rather than always leaving him to get on with it.

Nanny as Square Eyes

The use of TV and the video is a flashpoint for many parents and nannies. A few parents feel strongly that they want their children to sit in front of a TV for as short a time as possible, particularly when they have a nanny to amuse them.

Many parents are not happy about the amount of TV their children do watch, but find it a godsend. What a boon to plonk the little dears in front of a video of *The Wizard of Oz* on a wet Wednesday afternoon while you get on and prepare supper for eight, encourage them to watch Breakfast Time so the parents can have an extra hour in bed on a Saturday morning, or switch on Play School so that they can whizz round with the hoover. Some children come back pretty drained after a day at school and immediately 'veg out' in front of the telly for an hour and more – it's called being a 'couch potato' in America.

Other parents try hard to plough a middle course. They believe rationed telly is a Good Thing. They feel it widens a child's understanding of the world and how it works and familiarizes him with visual techniques like cartoons, hand and string puppets and animated models like Thomas the Tank Engine. They relish their children watching the wildlife programmes, anything related to what they are doing at school and generally approve of all the mass of colour, enthusiasm, imagination, skill and information that goes into a good children's programme.

Many parents find irksome the passivity of a child (always 'in a heap'), who watches the box for an hour or more. This is increased when the nanny is sitting beside the child filing her nails, talking to another nanny or reading a magazine. The parent may well break up the quiet scene if the sun is shining and the window is closed as well.

You may have touched on TV during the interview. Talk to the nanny again and remind her of your views, if she shows signs of wilfully ignoring what you asked her to do. Employers have every right to be tough about the telly if they want to be. It doesn't have to be used as a surrogate minder – not turning it off is a parallel to giving children daily doses of Phenergan so that they don't wake at night.

Agree that TV can be a life enhancer *if* she is responsible and selective about the programmes and channels she lets the child watch, if she watches *with* the child and if he is given the chance of talking about it with her afterwards. All this has to be spelled out most emphatically with a nanny who is in sole charge for long periods, particularly if the mother doesn't feel that the girl shares her opinion.

Nanny as Entertainer

Too many employers express discontent with their nanny's, mother's help's or even au pair's attitude to children's play. If a trained nanny doesn't show sufficient interest in, and enjoyment of, her charges' play, then she is a lot more culpable than an untrained mother's help.

Play helps a child develop practical skills, makes him think, calculate, ponder and use his imagination. It gives him greater understanding of the workings of the world and people. Play gives his limbs, lungs and muscles plenty of exercise; his senses – sight, sound, taste and touch – are continually stimulated through play. Last but not least, the trained nanny will have learnt how a child's play with other children and with adults contribute to the child's socialization, making him into an acceptable member of sociey who shares his toys willingly and with politeness, who doesn't kick, yell, snatch and scratch. Play enables him also to experiment with certain kinds of behaviour, reactions and emotions.

Good child carers *enjoy* playing with their charges, adapting to a child's ideas and wishes. She must be able to take a secondary role in a child's game while also being able to direct him to do something specific, like a puzzle or drawing a picture, at other times. Employers become annoyed when they are paying a trained girl £150 a week and she doesn't show initiative and imagination when with the children.

A nanny should think of herself as entertainments manageress and have something planned, either in her head or on paper, for most days. She also needs the flexibility to give up her fun-filled programme when the child is clearly too tired or just plain unwilling to do it her way. Play should never be forcibly directed.

If you are unlucky and have a nanny who isn't much good at entertaining the kids in a purposeful, energetic way, and it worries you, there is only so much you can do about it short of hiring someone else. Some girls will respond to suggestions and guidance, but if they haven't a great deal of imagination and minimal *interest* in their charges' high jinks, it will be an uphill struggle. If she has more than one child to look after, it will be a test of her skills anyway to make time for creative play. That is why it is always a bonus to hire a girl who has bags of energy. You want to avoid a nanny who feels like a wet rag having given the children breakfast, dressed and changed baby, cleared up breakfast, made beds and tidied toys and it is only 10 am.

However limited you may feel a particular nanny to be when it comes to amusing the children, it is worth writing down a detailed list of suggested activities. Don't leave it entirely to her to decide when to do painting/water play/playdough. It may happen once every four weeks, when it could happen once a week at least with a bit of guidance and nudging from you.

She may improve noticeably once she becomes used to thinking about ways of amusing her charges, and they will also draw the fun out of her and insist she does zany things with any luck. Parents can help a good deal by setting a precedent and doing things with the children which might not have struck her.

Remind her that play should be fun, varied and enjoyable. She needs to direct and stimulate the child while allowing him to express himself fully and do his own thing a lot of the time. If a child doesn't want to do potato prints today and he isn't just being contrary at the moment the nanny suggests it, leave it for another day. Tell her that play is for its own sake. Play is often about a child taking the initiative, or taking it with another child or an adult. It is also all about choice, and the player likes to be in control.

Like all employees, nannies and mother's helps prefer to use nice, new equipment. Imaginative entertainers can get by with remarkably little formal equipment to amuse a child. Some parents argue that too many primary coloured toys and games can inhibit a child's imagination.

However, it is best to be on the safe side when it comes to carers and, finances permitting, provide plenty of the following: shapes, sorters, nesting and hammering bits, bricks, puzzles, games, packs of cards, things to thread and make, things to construct and push together like Duplo, Brio Mec and Sticklebricks; toys to pretend with like toy soldiers, knights, forts, castles, zoos, a Noah's Ark, train sets and track, telephones, cash registers, cooking utensils, brushes and a dustpan, dolls prams, pushchairs, farm and wild animals, tractors and farm machinery, and on and on.

Make sure the nanny encourages plenty of constructive and creative play: cutting, sticking, printing, colouring, making scrapbooks, collages, mobiles; don't forget the ubiquitous egg box which has a thousand different uses, as have empty loo rolls, kitchen rolls and squeezy bottles. For imaginative play she could organize a dressing-up box, transform a clothes horse or playpen into a tent or purloin the kitchen scales and a collection of empty jars and boxes for the grocery shop.

Don't let the nanny deprive your child of his ration of messy play, be it digging in the sandpit, 'cooking' with flour and water in the kitchen, emptying buckets outside or from making mud pies in a discreet corner of the garden. Remind her that children also welcome quieter times with finger and toe games like 'Here's the Church' and 'This Little Pig', 'I Spy', opposites, and action and nursery rhymes. Whatever the activity, explain that children love attention and their play is enhanced if they have someone who is prepared to share it with them.

Nanny as Hostess

Tea, lunch, outings to the park, expeditions to museums or the zoo are more fun for both nannies and children if they are shared with their contemporaries. As an employer you encourage it within reason because it keeps everyone happy and busy. However socializing can be overdone, and is meant to be, after all, for the benefit of the children when it takes place with the nanny. Inappropriate ages and stages of children, some of whom may be unknown to you, are signs that the nanny is putting her social life before the children's.

However, bear in mind that many experienced nannies consider socializing on duty a perk. It is one of the few aspects that make nannying preferable to a nine-to-five job. They enjoy the necessary organization, catering and the alleviation of dreary routine and loneliness. Indeed, some socializing is to be recommended for nannies looking after babies and toddlers as they can become bored and out of touch with local life.

No mother likes to see a ring of gossiping nannies swilling coffee while the children go unheeded. Working mothers won't experience this exasperation, but it may well happen. One mother who works upstairs at home says she interferes boldly on this occasion but no other, and with a loud voice says, 'How about something that everyone can play? And less jumping on the furniture please.'

Too much emphasis on sociabilities is peculiar to large concentrations of nannies and children, i.e. in London. When children are old enough, about three years plus on average, they have reached the point when they can come and play on their own. Remind your nanny to invite the child alone.

If you have an inexperienced nanny, don't feel inhibited about vetting surreptitiously any friends she brings to your house and steer her away from the rough trade in the nanny world. You don't want her to pick up bad habits and a world-weary expression.

Chapter 7
Training

The ability to stick at a course for one or two years and come away with a qualification speaks of a certain dedication in a nanny. This stamina is less likely to be found in the kind of girl who may leave to serve in the local department store sale within six weeks of arrival. Some employers don't want trained nannies for many reasons, but all agree that attending a course bestows some maturity and more than a passing interest in the subject. One employer who has never had enough money to afford a trained nanny says, 'In my inexperienced days I pooh-poohed the need for a trained girl. Nowadays I think that someone trained is more likely to stay longer, be more professional and know more about ways to entertain young children. Another plus is that a trained nanny would not need the sort of intensive child care course that someone untrained has to go through for at least a month alongside me.'

Another mother who has always employed Princess Christian nannies says: 'I think training is vital. Not so much for the knowledge they gain but for their attitude to the whole job. If they bother to take a training course I think they have a genuine interest in children and in being professional.' Other employers have mixed reactions:

Standards seem low, but it's a mercy that there are any.

Training takes time and shows initiative.

All our trained nannies have been extremely efficient and organized.

How to do 65 different things with an egg box is not necessarily all you need, though of course splendid at times.

The nannies themselves are equally wide-ranging in their comments:

Lots of girls were doing the training because they couldn't think what else to do and they thought the jobs would be easy and well paid.

The courses were designed for the social services and didn't give me much idea about nannying.

I feel more confident as a nanny knowing I'm trained.

However, there is not much chance of nannies being treated as professionals unless a high proportion of them are trained. The untrained after a few years of experience acquire an honorary trained status, like Prince William's former nanny Barbara Barnes. The prevalent attitude that 'anyone can look after children' will not go away unless training and its standards are recognized, understood and seen to be excellent in practice as well as theory. The editor of *Nursery World* writes:

Training is often described as 'concentrated experience' and is a short cut to good practice which avoids many mistakes which may otherwise only be corrected by bitter experience. Formal training, when it is thorough, is a shorter route to excellence. It is not necessarily better than experience, however.

Trained nannies will at least have been exposed to many different theories about child care and should emerge with clear ideas about what is best for the child, rather than what suits his carer. They will have been taught about the emotional, physical, intellectual and social growth and well-being of an infant and, with any luck, may have picked up a number of professional tricks of the trade.The biggest objection to training is that a little knowledge can be a dangerous thing, especially if only partially understood and not put to the test with practical experience. Many employers and employment agencies complain that the trouble is that girls are given exaggerated ideas of their competence by training courses. Both groups agree that training course standards vary too much to make effective generalizations about the graduates.

Awards in Child Care

The CACHE Diploma in Nursery Nursing (NNEB) is studied by students at local authority colleges like further education and sixth form colleges, and at residential fee-paying colleges as well.

The first NNEB (National Nursery Examination Board) Certificate was awarded in 1946 and for the next 40 years it was the qualification for a trained nanny. Then in the 1990s there came a number of major changes. First, the award's name was changed to 'Diploma' though obviously the old 'Certificate' 'is still valid. Also, the course became open-ended, modular and continually assessed so as to be in the same format as National Vocational Qualifications (see below). Finally, the Board was metamorphosed to become CACHE (Council for Awards in Child Care and Education). This new body has a host of members like FRES (the employment agencies' trade association), the Pre-school Learning Alliance and the NCMA ((National Childminding Association). CACHE has a much wider brief than ever the NNEB had in that it administrates NVQs in Child care and Education and also in Playwork.

Because the NNEB initials are so well known, CACHE has kept them in the title of its two year Diploma course so that students emerge with a CACHE Diploma in Nursery Nursing (NNEB). A potential area for confusion is that CACHE also awards students who choose to do only one year's study with a lower ranking Certificate in Child Care and Education (CCE). Employers need to ask prospective nannies whether they have done the two-year Diploma or the one-year Certificate or indeed, if they are an older applicant, whether they have the old, two-year NNEB Certificate.

Employers need to know about NVQs (National Vocational Qualifications) awarded by the National Council of Vocational Qualifications . NVQs are a government initiative to give people with experience gained through doing a job, but with no formal qualification to prove it, the chance to acquire a recognised award: the NVQ. The idea of an NVQ is to show an employer that the applicant has had *practical* experience in the relevant field. It is not an academic qualification and assessment is centred around the individual's work. You don't even have to be in paid employment to be assessed for an NVQ, a voluntary helper in a play group could qualify. The crucial ingredient for acquiring an NVQ is that the person is in a 'workplace setting'. With NVQs it's not 'what you know but what you do'. Like the School Attainment Targets (SATS) where school children have to take tests in core subjects which are marked against a national standard, NVQs give a national standard in a great number of vocational skills.

As far as child care is concerned, a childminder, a playgroup worker or an experienced but untrained nanny of some years' standing are examples of people with bags of experience and who therefore can acquire an NVQ level 2 or even level 3 rapidly. They can register with an NVQ accredited centre (often an FE college) and start to gain 'modules' by being assessed at their place of work, and they put together a portfolio of 'evidence' in order to demonstrate their competence to NVQ assessors.

About 80 per cent of students – girls and some young men – taking the Diploma pass it, totalling around 10,000 a year, while about half that again obtain the Certificate. Around half of all graduates become nannies in private homes, while the other half work in private day nurseries, council day nurseries, nursery schools, hospitals and in state-run special needs schools and children's residential centres.

Happily for NNEB graduates, private day nurseries have grown dramatically all over the country in the last ten years, and so whereas before they would drop out of nannying after a year or two, now they can change direction and join a private nursery. Day nurseries offer an attractive package with the prospect of promotion, less hours, less responsibility and pretty commensurate gross pay when compared with a run-of-the-mill nanny job. Ultimately an NNEB could set up her own nursery.

CACHE course places are over-subscribed by three to one, which makes competition stiffer for entry into colleges with a good reputation situated in populous areas. The course is open to men and women full-time; it lasts for six terms and takes two years to complete. It can be taken over a maximum of five years, part-time. Students are mostly 16 years old at the start. Places are paid for by the local authority and a few get financial help with text books and travelling to college and 'placements'.

An applicant need have no qualifications of any sort because the course, in theory at least, is reckoned to be a 'vocational education'. But with demand high, many colleges cut down the applicant list by asking for a minimum of three GCSEs at grade C and above. Some favour pupils with English GCSE.

Diploma students take 18 short modules (C-U) and two extended modules (A and B) which run for the length of the two years, where all aspects of child care theory and practice for infants up to and including the age of seven are studied. The modules are rounded off by written assignments, which are assessed by college tutors and visiting external moderators. The extended module **A** covers the crucial practical side, representing 40 per cent of the course. Here students 'observe and assess' the young children they care for on their work 'placements', which take up two days a week. In extended module **B**, students learn how to plan activities to entertain children and enhance their development.

The short modules comprise:

C An introduction to the course, and lessons on the need for awareness of the 'social deprivation and discrimination' an NNEB may encounter at work.

D Caring: including hygiene, first aid, health and safety.

E Physical care and development.

F Emotional and social development.

G Health care (1) and studying for a First Aid certificate.

H Learning through play .

I Cognitive and language development

J Children's behaviour.

K Food and nutrition.

L Work with babies 0-1 years.

M Health care (2): childhood sickness and disease.

N Child protection: focusing on rights and procedures concerning child abuse.

P The nursery nurse in employment: what constitutes good practice, accountability, responsibility, employer/employee relations.

Q Child care and education in Britain with particular reference to the Children Act 1989.

R Everything to do with helping the child with special needs, as well support of his parents.

S Working with parents: the variety of parenting styles and attitudes in different social, cultural and religious contexts. All aspects of parent/child relationships and the role of the nursery nurse.

T The social and legal framework for children and families.

U Early years: how children are looked after as a group (for example in state and private day nurseries).

The child care theory taught for three days a week includes: health and nursing a sick child; safety; nutrition; a child's psychological, physical and social development; language progress, and learning through play. The details of the course can include useful items like cooking for children's parties, stocking a fishtank with tadpoles, setting up a child's bedroom and creating glove puppets.

There are more academic themes to do with current theories of infant problems, e.g. genetics and hereditary diseases, dyslexia, the only child, Down's Syndrome and other disabilities. Pre-menstrual tension, pregnancy, alcoholism, role play and imaginary situations, form filling and job hunting may also be tackled among other subjects.

Those students who take the one year Certificate don't do extended modules **A** and **B** to the same level or complexity, nor do they do as thoroughly modules **I** (cognitive and language development), **N** (child protection) and **P** (the nursery nurse in employment), **S** (working with parents) and **U** (early years).

Diploma and Certificate students can achieve a pass, merit or distinction on each module, which enables tutors to commend their star pupils as opposed to the lazybones who larked about in the back row. Employers looking out for a high flier in a new NNEB should count up the number of distinctions listed in her Diploma and note also in what topics an applicant did less well and ask her about them.

A girl with a CACHE NNEB Diploma is reckoned to have, to use the NVQ jargon, 'the necessary underpinning knowledge and understanding' equivalent of the NVQ in Child Care and Education at level 3. A one-year CACHE Certificate graduate is considered on a par with an NVQ level 2. Anyone achieving level 3 is deemed capable of working without supervison, like running a playgroup or being a 'sole charge' nanny for working parents, while level 2 suggests someone who needs supervision like a playgroup assistant or a freshly qualified CACHE Certificate nanny with little work experience.

It makes sense if employers find out from a recently qualified nanny applicant that she has done the **L** module – 'Work with Babies' – option and that during her two day a week work experience she was able to work with a mother and baby under a year old so that she knows something about work with a family.

It is recommended that a Diploma student works with babies of under a year for 25 days of the course and that she works with children who are one to three years 11 months for 55 days. It is reassuring for employers to know that most of them will spend the 25 days with a mother and her baby at home. Working with a family is the only option anyway in many cases, because there are not enough babies in day nurseries. CACHE says 'What we are emphasizing to course tutors is that they make every effort to get students to work with neo-natal babies in the home. These days so many girls take sole charge jobs and it's important that they have experience of a newborn. There is a difference between a baby who is a few days old and one that is several months old.'

Experienced but untrained nannies, day nursery workers and childminders can choose to do the NNEB Diploma. They can apply to the local FE college, and with the help of the tutors submit a portfolio of evidence detailing their previous experience which, once accredited, can reduce the number of Diploma modules that they need to take.

Likewise, an experienced but untrained nanny or day nursery worker (and only half of the staff at day nurseries have to have a qualification), or a childminder, can be assessed for an NVQ. They have to demonstrate their practical competence to assessors where they work (e.g. in their employer's home, at a day nursery or at their own home respectively), so they can build up their 'units of competence.' They need also to provide extra 'evidence' of their 'knowledge and understanding' of their work by collating a portfolio.

The NVQ in Child Care and Education

For this NVQ a girl will be assessed in 8 core subjects which have a lot in common with the CACHE Certificate and include 'Work with young children', 'Maintain a child oriented environment' and 'Maintain the Safety of Children.'

She will also be assessed in one of four 'endorsements' which will identify the type of experience she has. Thus she might choose: a) Work with Babies, or b) Work in Support of Others, or c) Work in a Pre-school group, or d) Work in a Community Run Pre-School Group. A nanny would be likely to choose a) or c). If she chooses a) she will end up with an NVQ in Child Care & Education (Work with Babies) level 2.

There are five NVQs at the higher level 3. There are 12 core units and the tougher ones include: 'Promote Children's Sensory and Intellectual development', 'Contribute to the Protection of Children from Child Abuse' and 'Promote the Development of Children's Language and Communication Skills'. There are five endorsements: a) Group Care & Education, b) Family Day Care, c): Pre-School Provision, d): Family Support, and e) Special Needs.

A playgroup worker would probably choose c) endorsement and a nanny would choose b). Once assessed the former would have an NVQ in Child Care and Education (Pre-School Provision) level 3, and the latter would gain an NVQ in Child care & Education (Family Day Care) level 3, both of which are equivalent to the CACHE Diploma in Nursery Nursing (NNEB).

CACHE and a Child Carer's Register

Following a couple of alarming court cases in the USA and the UK concerning nannies maltreating their charges (notably in the UK the case in which Carol Withers was convicted in 1991 for inflicting grievous bodily harm on the babies of two different employers), CACHE and the employment agents' association, FRES, have come under pressure to set up a proper register of working NNEBs and of child carers generally, which employers can check to see that their prospective nanny is *bona fide*, does not have a criminal record, and has the qualifications she claimed.

It is not known by many employers that CACHE is happy to check the validity of a Diploma or Certificate free of charge. Any employer or nanny can telephone with the award number and preferably the year and the college where taken. Carol Withers did the NNEB course at Chiltern College but failed the exams, and went on to do a decade of nannying. She told at least two lots of employers that she had (the old) NNEB Certificate. Unfortunately, the parents of one of the children she harmed took her at her word and didn't ask to see it, let alone check with the NNEB. If they had checked, the NNEB would have alerted them to her lie.

Rather than a voluntary register CACHE, ideally, would like a statutory register with proper power which all carers (including carers of the elderly, perhaps), would have to join by law. 'To work, a register would have to function like the General Medical Council which can call witnesses to a complaints tribunal when assessing doctors for alleged misdemeanours,' says Richard Dorrance, CACHE Chief Executive, who continues:

> With the best will in the world, any sort of voluntary register in our opinion just wouldn't be effective because we'd have to prove allegations made by the employer, This is a hard enough task for the police, and just not practical for CACHE.

For all the wishful thinking, however, a statutory register is a pipe dream, being on no political party's agenda at present.

Gripes about NNEB Training as Preparation for Nannying

(Gathered from employment agencies, employers, nannies, college principals and union officials)

- Too little properly-supervised practical experience.
- Inexperienced girls given exaggerated ideas of their competence.

- CACHE prides itself on the 'identical quality' of its 'standards of training' whether the course is taken in Newhaven or Newcastle, and claims it is much better on this than other awarding bodies, but there are still grumbles about the varying degrees of quality between courses.
- Not enough emphasis on work as a nanny in all its aspects.
- Health and nutrition not always adequately taught.
- Domestic skills not emphasized sufficiently, i.e. laundry, mending, etc.
- The employer/nanny relationship is still not tackled thoroughly enough.
- Apart from the agencies, there is no proper nanny-employer representation on the CACHE board.

Other Qualifications

NVQs have had an excellent effect on training institutions like City & Guilds, CACHE and NAMCW, because the courses they offered to students had to be re-thought, made modular, updated, improved and in some cases phased out so that the resultant courses met the criteria set by the NVQ Council. One of the important areas of which everyone connected with child care has become aware in recent years is the importance of early years' learning and how much a child benefits from learning through play. All in all an NVQ child carer is expected to know quite a bit about a child's social, emotional, physical and mental development. She will be made aware of, and know about, child abuse, special needs, non discrimination, child health and child-friendly surroundings.

The NVQ in Playwork

An NVQ in Playwork is designed for workers at play groups and after school clubs. There is level 2, which is appropriate for an assistant at a play group, and she is assessed as competent in 11 units, some of which overlap with the NVQs in Child Care and Education and emphasize the different aspects of a child's development.

Level 3 is designed for a more experienced person working as part of a team but also able to run a play group without supervision. This needs the candidate to demonstrate her competence in 15 units, with five of them overlapping with level 2.

GNVQ

A General National Vocational Qualification is administered by City & Guilds and is a vocational alternative to A levels studied by six-formers in schools at three levels. They acquire various units including ' Child Care', 'Business' 'Manufacturing' and 'Health and Social Care.'

Youth Training

The Training and Enterprise Council (known as the TEC) offers school leavers who have few or no GCSEs, or who cannot get a job, or who would like to acquire a skill, its Youth Training. This involves arranging up to two years' work experience in a plethora of businesses and trades ranging from accounting, carpentry, plumbing, sea fishing, hairdressing and catering to retailing, clerical work, building and warehousing.

Youth Training give youngsters 'credits' which they can give to an employer in exchange for training. They can get jobs at private or local authority day nurseries, at nursery schools, in hospitals, children's homes and the like. This way the youngsters acquire the necessary 'underpinning knowledge and understanding' to be assessed for NVQs at level 2 in Child Care & Education.

Students on Youth Training receive a training allowance financed by the TEC (everyone is careful not to call it pay), roughly equivalent to what they would receive on Social Security and employers may top this up if they wish.

From the employer of nannies and mother's helps' point of view, someone who has been on Youth Training may have acquired an NVQ in Child Care & Education. Even if she hasn't, she may have picked up some caring experience anyway. For example, in one or more assignments she may have learned to bath an elderly man, organized a game of cards for a group of pensioners in a day centre, or helped to dress and feed someone who is mentally handicapped. Thus she should have more idea of the demands and practicalities of caring for someone than the school leaver with no experience at all.

The Pre-School Playgroup Diploma

The National Association of Pre-School Playgroups offers a Diploma course which provides the 'necessary underpinning knowledge and understanding' to enable the graduate to be assessed for an NVQ in Playwork level 2 or 3. The Diploma takes three terms to complete, using one day a week, or in some areas two evenings a week.

NAMCW

The bulk of The National Association of Maternal and Child Welfare's students are school children aged 16 to 18 who study the NAMCW Certificate levels 1,2 and 3 in the fifth and sixth forms. From the nannying point of view, a teenager with a NAMCW Certificate to level 3 has learnt something about child care and is ready for practical experience working alongside her employer.

A few school leavers go on to gain the NAMCW Advanced Certificate, which is designed to suit mature students like childminders.

NAMCW also has a two-year Diploma course for students aged 16 and over who may not have been selected for an NNEB course, or who applied too late. It used to be regarded as a lower qualification than the NNEB Diploma but its course has been totally revised and updated so that it is now on a par with the Child Care and Education NVQ level 3.

A girl will probably be accepted for the course with as little as a couple of GCSEs. 'They should be highish GCSEs, because otherwise they can't cope with the theoretical parts of the course,' says a tutor, 'and they must demonstrate some interest in children, for example, they have done some babysitting.'

Those with the full Diploma are taught 'more than they need to become a nanny', one college tutor avers.

NAMCW regards itself as 'a stepping stone' to gaining NVQs. Because NVQs assumes work experience, the NAMCW Certificates and Diploma give young people a training that makes them able to register for an NVQ as soon as they get work.

City & Guilds

The City & Guilds of London Institute devises courses which are taught all over the country in various further education institutions. It has been providing education for youngsters of 16 upwards in practical skills like catering, plumbing, carpentry, decorating, hairdressing and upholstery for years, and its Certficates have been valued by both the public and private sectors.

Now it has 'gone NVQ' and its myriad courses are geared to providing the 'underpinning knowledge and understanding' to achieve NVQs at levels 2, 3 and even 4. It is the largest provider and assessor of NVQs in the country and it offers the NVQs in Child Care and Education (scheme 3034) levels 2 and 3 in competition with CACHE, though the content of the modules are pretty much the same .

The emphasis of its courses since the introduction of NVQs is more on experience gained in the workplace than in theory at colleges. A C&G course administrator says 'There is still teaching in college for students, but before there was more of the putting-a-nappy-on-a-plastic doll-style of teaching than today when it is essential that students go and learn in the work place – whether a private home, or a day nursery, or in a hospital.'

At NVQ level 2 C&G also offers nine different 'Care' NVQs (scheme 3033/3307-02), most of which are to do with care of the elderly, children in care, the handicapped and mentally ill. Each NVQ has a total of 11 units: six obligatory 'core' units and five specified 'endorsements' which include 'Domiciliary Support', 'Postnatal Care', 'Direct Care' and 'Residential/Hospital Support', all of which could be tailored to provide good experience with child care. The NVQ in Care at level 3 (scheme 3033/3037-03) involves eight core units and a choice of 21 different endorsements. The ones pertaining to children are Acute Care (children), Group and Foster Care, and Supporting Families.

Obviously, a girl who wanted to look after children would choose an NVQ in Child Care and Education, but employers may have an applicant who chose to do a Care NVQ and this would give her plenty of relevant skills which she could use if she decided on nannying rather than care for the elderly or handicapped.

There are a number of Care C&G courses which have been phased out with the introduction of NVQs which an applicant for a mother's help job might have. These include No. 3251 – Community Care; No. 3310 – Family & Community Care; No. 3241 – Caring for Children; and No. 356 – parts 1 & 2 – Practical Caring Skills.

The PCSC

The Preliminary Certificate in Social Care (PCSC), a two-year full-time course, is approved by the Central Council for Education and

Training in Social Work and is available to 16- to 19-year-olds and is geared towards care of the elderly. The CCETSW says, 'These courses allow young people the opportunity to learn about work in the social services, including work with children, and to see what career opportunities there are.' A would-be nanny with the PCSC should be taken seriously, though she won't have done very much child care.

BTEC

Although CACHE's NNEB award is still the only training of which most private employers have heard, it is no longer the highest ranking qualification for a trained nanny. The BTEC Diploma is of higher status.

Like the NNEB, The Business & Technician Education Council (BTEC) has been merged into the EDEXCEL Foundation to form a single awarding body. But the acronym BTEC has stayed to describe its full-time National Diploma in Childhood Studies (Nursery Nursing) and its part-time National Certificate in Childhood Studies (Nursery Nursing). The Certificate is designed for older, more experienced people in work where their job makes up for the more theoretical Diploma course. Both awards are equivalent to an NVQ level 3.

Other relevant courses include a National Diploma in Caring Services and one in Science Health Studies. Starting from scratch in the late 1980s, BTEC now has 8,000 completing its National Childhood Diploma and Certificate each year.

Unlike the NNEB, where students do not have to show any academic qualification in theory at least, four GCSEs are the minimum for acceptance on the Diploma, and English Language is preferred. The course appeals to the more academic 16 year old who wants to do practical training but is capable of 'A' levels. The Diploma is regarded as equivalent to two 'A' levels.

One tutor says, 'The great thing about BTEC is that it enables students to keep their options open. We find that about half go off to be nursery nurses or nannies and the rest go on to higher education for social work or nursing.'

Further Qualifications

While continuing to work as a nanny or a nursery nurse, a girl can take a course tailor-made for the NNEB and/or NVQ level 3: the

Advanced Diploma in Child Care & Education (ADCE) which can be done part-time or at evening class. Students choose six modules and have to write a dissertation. Those who have completed it say that they enjoyed greater job satisfaction having studied some areas of child care in detail (e.g. autistic children, problem parents and children), and they can go on into higher education if they wish.

Some nannies and nursery nurses want to do the professional qualification for social workers: the Certificate of Qualification in Social Work (CQSW). The minimum age for starting this four-year degree course is 20 and it is open to anyone. The Certificate in Social Service (CSS) is a two-to-three-year course of a lower calibre than the CQSW.

Residential and Fee-Paying Nursery Nurse Training Colleges

Fifty years ago there were more than 30 private nursery nurse residential colleges, but with the proliferation of free NNEB courses in technical colleges funded by local authorities, this number has dwindled, but the best known – the Norland Nursery Training College, the Princess Christian College, and the Chiltern College – remain the same.

All colleges offer the NNEB curriculum of six terms. Tuition and board at all three colleges costs between £8,000 and £10,000 a year. It is rare but not unheard of for students to win local authority grants. Princess Christian and Chiltern are both charities, while Norland prefers to keep its independence. Choosing to pay makes students and their parents take the course seriously. Also, because the graduates are so much in demand by employers, parents know that the investment will pay off. Apart from college pressure to do well, no parent is likely to allow their child to do it in a half-hearted way.

The three colleges all have educational requirements – they demand three GCSEs of grade C or above; or their equivalent. English Language must be one of these for Norland, whereas Princess Christian and Chiltern will accept the softer option of English Literature. All students who have their English Language or Literature GCSE are eligible to sit the Royal Society of Health Diploma in nursery nursing. All three colleges have been accredited as assessment centres for NVQs in child care. There is open access to this qualification to other people working in child care, for example childminders or employees in pre-school playgroups, and ex-students can also return to be assessed.

All students start at 17, although they can apply at 16, be accepted and go away and do something else for a year. The students live closely with each other 24 hours a day, away from their homes. They are supervised, live in a structured world and have to obey the college rules – not unlike an employer's house rules. Boyfriends are not allowed to stay overnight, smoking is banned in all of the colleges, and manners, appearance and general behaviour are corrected. The net result is the nearest thing to working in a private home.

Another major advantage that the residential colleges have over the public sector equivalent is that they all boast on-campus nurseries for under-fives so that their students can gain hands-on experience.

The emphasis on domestic science and home economics is evident in all three colleges. Every student will learn about additives, allergies and sugar-free recipes. There are also fancy aspects to the cooking courses including the use of woks and food processors. The same goes for needlework and crafts.

They wear uniforms and may receive badges. Reunions and newsletters flourish and the college in-house employment registries continue to place nannies for much of their careers. Any graduate guilty of conduct unbecoming that is investigated and condemned by the college, is struck off the register, with no hope of redemption.

The Chiltern College

Since our first visit ten years ago, this college has changed and expanded beyond all recognition, apart from the warmth of the welcome extended to visitors and its situation on a residential road in Caversham, Reading. There are up to 150 children in the college's daily care aged from three months to 11 years. Three buildings house an infant school, junior school and nurseries, and all are beautifully equipped. Chiltern has spent a fortune to bring itself up to date and has emerged as a wonderful springboard from which its students may launch themselves into any career in child care.

A managerial team of three, headed by Kate Beith, run Chiltern. She has three children and worked previously as senior lecturer at Chiltern before her promotion. The team also manages a workplace nursery for the BBC down the road. Some 40 per cent of the students live out. Past students return for weekends and other courses to update their knowledge. It is a hive of activity where everyone knows everyone's name and several have worked there for many years from the time they were students themselves.

There is a sophisticated multi-sensory room for Special Needs children, who may also come from outside nurseries to play there. Students no longer train in hospitals (mostly because mothers stay there for such a short period nowadays) but instead go to specially chosen professional homes for three days a week for six weeks.

Chiltern is the only private college to train males. One graduate is working as a nanny in a family with a Special Needs child.

An independent Chiltern nanny advisory job service has been run smoothly for some years by a full-time professional who finds employers and matches their needs to those of graduates. A contract, conditions of service and a professional salary are negotiated, and both nanny and employer are supported for the first year including occasional visits (see Agencies, Chapter 18).

The uniform is navy blue – skirts, tabards, trousers, aprons and plain black lace-up moccasins. In the evenings and at weekends students manage their own common room and its affairs and join numerous local clubs, classes and churches in Reading.

Norland Nursery Training College

Norland is synonymous with the trained nanny. Founded in 1892, it was the world's first nursery nurse training college. It is situated at Denford Park near Hungerford, in a gracious and imposing Georgian house set in its own 150-acre grounds. There are tennis courts, a chapel, an outdoor swimming pool and beautiful views of the Downs. It is the only residential college of which most people have ever heard. Norland has the largest number of graduates – 75 each year.

An unique feature is that the students receive 24-hour experience of residential child care. Members of the public who are going away on holiday can pay to leave their children up to the age of seven in a children's hotel at the college. The children who come to stay have their own small rooms. Each child is cared for constantly by one student nursery nurse; the aim is to give him a secure one-to-one relationship for the duration of his stay. She has a bed in his room. The visiting children also have a big playroom, a quiet sitting room and a dining room. They play in the gardens, sandpits and on climbing frames. It is designed to be as much like home life as possible and seems to succeed.

For those who may wish to consider this means of obtaining temporary child care, sending a child to Norland for a week *all in* costs about the same as a temporary nanny. Bonded mothers may throw a fit at the whole idea of abandoning their offspring thus, but those parents who do it are pleased with the service. Local authorities still make occasional use of the facility for respite care.

Additionally, there is a nursery school, after-school and holiday care, and several day-care units. Norland seems to head the field in its thinking and teaching on the subject of nannying in the private sector. Students are taught about child psychology and employer/ employee relationships in depth; in fact, all they need to know about the art of living in someone else's house. Their craft and needlework standards are high, too – students have to produce a smocked garment, a rag doll and clothes, a wall-hanging and be competent knitters.

Towards the end of the second year, students sit the Norland Final Exam and, in their first term, they take the NNEB Diploma and the Royal Society of Health Food Handler's Certificate.

Students who have passed all their exams, including the final Norland Assessment, become probationers. The Norland diploma and badge is not awarded until students have completed a year in a probationary post. A nanny can stay for longer than that with the family, nursery or nursery school, although employers must raise her pay when she is fully qualified. The college suggests a minimum starting salary, and holds a copy of the contract of employment. There is no pussy-footing with Norlanders on tax and National Insurance. They know just what the employer should be doing – so don't try it on and look foolish.

The probationer period is Norland's special invention and highlights its commitment to turning out nannies who are ready for and capable of the task – but only after they have had experience of working and living in a family for a year (or in a day nursery or nursery school). The probationary period is a clever way of avoiding employers' grumbles about newly qualified nannies. The basic tenet of the Norland philosophy is that a trainee does not become a nanny just by passing her NNEB exam, which is only one of several hurdles. This is an entirely different attitude from the local authority courses.

The vast majority of Norland probationers go into private homes. The principal, Louise Davis, says: 'The training was the first ever co-ordinated particularly for private homes, and there will always be an emphasis on this. The self-contained nature of

Norland College is such that each child-care section is finely structured and disciplined. We control our own standards of practice in every area.' It is a big plus that any Norlander having been put through the mill 'will not normally expect to meet such demanding tasks in such a variety of settings again'.

Students are distinguished by brown bonnets, black for winter. The rest of the uniform is brown and beige, except for some new Bermuda shorts and white polo shirts. There is a college magazine called *The Norlander*. The Norland registry is over-subscribed, so put yourself on the register months before you begin to need a Norland nanny and do not be at all surprised if you still fail to be offered one.

Louise Davis is a dynamic, efficient person, who leaves a lasting impression of dedication to the college and its fine traditions. She has a clear vision of excellence and is an ideal representative of the college when she lectures elsewhere and abroad. As a true professional herself, with both feet firmly on the ground, she sees her job as instilling the virtues of application and common sense into her trainees.

Princess Christian Training College for Nursery Nurses

The Princess Christian College was opened in Manchester in 1901 under the direct patronage of HRH the Princess Christian. Christened Helena, she was Queen Victoria's fifth child. She married Prince Christian of Schleswig-Holstein. Princess Christian was involved in many forms of charitable work. She was a founder member of the Red Cross in 1870 and set up Princess Christian's District Nurses in 1894. The Princess was keenly interested in the training college from the start through her involvement with The Gentlewomen's Employment Association.

Elsie Rigby took over as principal from the redoubtable Miss McRae in 1990. Her previous career has been in managing services for children, particularly in the care of the under-fives. She sees herself as building on the impressive reputation of the college and emphasizes excellence in the training of her students.

She says: 'I want this college to meet the needs of the 21st Century when so many things are happening in child care. Despite recession, many women are going back to work and there is a great demand for good quality nannies. I think the profession is beginning to be taken more seriously with the current shake-up in training, and the new emphasis on post qualifying studies offers interesting opportunities for NNEBs.'

Elsie Rigby is a confident judge of character and knows what she wants to see in her new students. 'Eye contact and body language I always watch because nannies must be able to communicate easily and, even by the age of 18, should display some sense of poise.'

There is a general feeling in the college that students are being treated as adults and adult behaviour is expected of them. Rules and restrictions are kept to a minimum and only imposed when strictly necessary. Elsie Rigby does not see herself as a pseudo-mother or guardian but as a trainer. She comments: 'My first responsibility is to make sure that each individual gets the most out of a very high-quality course. Then I hope I am also a caring adult who is happy to give sound advice either personally or professionally.'

She has distinct views about the NNEB course, which her girls study: 'I feel that nursery nurses provide an almost unreplaceable service in this country. The standard of the NNEB course is improving and I think it is both demanding and testing of my students. Academically it should be better recognized.'

The building in Wilbraham Road, Fallowfield (a suburb of Manchester), is a Victorian monstrosity, but this is mitigated by the fact that it backs on to a pretty park with a lake, lawns and a pets corner, ideal for the nursery children. The interior has recently been much improved and is far cosier and more personal than previously.

The college takes 28 students a year. Students have the day nurseries for various age groups organized into three nursery units – two baby units, two toddler units and a pre-school unit – all of which adds up to a 58-place nursery. Students wear uniform less than previously; it consists of brown dresses.

At least 95 per cent of the students become nannies. It is informative to listen to the principal musing on their role: 'The job of a nanny should not be underestimated. There is a wide variety of types of lives for nannies nowadays. My emphasis is on sharing the care of the child with the parent. There are enormous opportunities for travel and examining different cultures. While caring for a child, a nanny can get involved in a mass of community activities. They lead varied and useful lives and they have the great advantage of being able to improve their child care skills as they work.'

The college has its own employment register and students are encouraged to use it. Agencies are regretful. Graduates are issued with a beautiful brown testimonial book franked with the college imprimatur. There are blank pages so that future employers' references can be stuck in. 'They should be regarded as the passport to your career and should be kept safely. They cannot, under any circumstances, be replaced', the girls are warned. Employers are required to fill in an official testimonial form. It is then stamped by the college, which keeps a copy and the nanny is sent the original. Truly a reference worth its salt.

The three-year badge is awarded to nannies who have totalled five years' nannying, inclusive of their two years' training.

The Scottish College of Child Care

This little college was started in 1996 in a Victorian building in an Edinburgh suburb by Veronica Wilson, who was previously a teacher and then ran a nanny agency for six years. She has four children. She oversees two Emergency Mums agencies, the Nanny Service and a nursery for 35 children, from three months to five years old. She has 15 students each year at the moment and those who are not living at home or independently are housed locally.

Veronica Wilson says: 'I hope I have created a training facility which is a microcosm of Norland. It costs about £800 a term. I look for caring enthusiastic students who have a genuine love of children.'

The London Montessori Centre

The London Montessori Centre (LMC) is quite unlike any of the residential colleges, and quite unlike a local authority college NNEB course. It is a fee-paying daily NNEB college situated in the heart of London, just off Oxford Street. Its unique feature is that students not only achieve the NNEB Diploma but also take the Montessori Child Care and Teaching Diploma, for which they study simultaneously. Normally it would be a one-year course.

It is an expensive option, costing more than the residential colleges, possibly because it is not a charitable trust like the others, but a profit-making concern. 'You get a very good course,' says a Montessori teacher there. 'It is special to us.' Not only an excellent course, but two qualifications for the price of one.

Dr Maria Montessori (1870–1952) had both a medical and academic background and was the inventor of the Montessori teaching method. When Maria Montessori was a teacher, children sat in rows and learned by rote. She felt that they would respond better with more imaginative and indirect methods. She introduced a planned environment where a child could grow and learn by using her own patented devices: for example, counting beads in blocks of tens, hundreds and even a thousand. Through touching and counting the golden beads, the child is introduced to abstract arithmetic.

Unique Montessori teaching aids, include the famous Pink Tower with its fitting cubes, the Geometric Tray to help a child to identify shapes, the graded cylinders, beautifully turned in wood, and sandpaper letters that a child can handle. Music, dance and nature all have their place in her syllabus.

A Montessori teacher does not instruct in a straightforward sense, but rather directs children's natural activities so that they can learn spontaneously. With patience and the gentlest of guidance, she leads her children to explore and discover a carefully structured classroom, and lets them develop stage by stage at their own pace. The teacher should not, however, abandon the child to total free play. Today this kind of enlightened 'voyage of discovery' teaching is the norm; every nursery school, state and private, has plagiarized some aspects of the Montessori method.

The NNEB course at the Montessori Centre was started in 1984. One of the main reasons for the course's particular success was the excellence of its placements. This currently remains a major strength with an excellent nurturing atmosphere. By the late Nineties, the college had been taken over by Asquith Court schools, a consortium, which has injected money and resources into it, and it is still running happily under new management.

The College has a good scholarly atmosphere; it vibrates with activity and is full of Montessori teachers and students. There is a Montessori Nursery School on the premises, so NNEB students, alongside students from other Montessori teaching courses, can visit the school to do their 'observations' and some of their training.

Many students come from outside London and abroad and live in hostels or YWCAs. One or two may get grants. There is no room to provide any sort of social life within the college. 'But because it is a small group in a small college, all the students have lots of personal contact and involvement,' said a college tutor.

The Montessori method offers correspondence courses worldwide. In one year workshops were held in Penang, Bahrain, London, the USA, Africa, Trinidad and Malaysia.

Other fee-paying, one-year Montessori colleges can be found in Kensington, Wimbledon and Bournemouth.

Surrey College School of Child Care

This school started in 1994 in Guildford and offers a seven-month intensive Montessori diploma. It also runs nursery nurse courses of eight weeks', 12 weeks' and six months' duration. There is an introductory course of four weeks. The groups are small and intimate and 'you can't imagine how hard we make those students work in those six months'. Additional courses can be followed at Surrey College, so if a nanny plans to travel, she can add a language or a Teaching English as a Foreign Language (TEFL) qualification. The college is modern and well furbished and has good halls of residence. Alternatively, students can live with host families nearby. There is also a child care job shop which is run as a free service for students and employers.

It is too soon to comment further on the efficacy of these much shorter courses; in the next edition it will be possible to evaluate them better via feed-back from their alumni and the college itself.

Lucie Clayton Nursery Training College

Alice Lewes is no stranger to *The Good Nanny Guide*. We have followed her career from Norland nanny to nanny agent and now she runs short nanny training courses at Lucie Clayton, the finishing school in Kensington. There is a one-year course, a 12-week fast-track diploma, a one-week babysitting course, and a one-day baby and child life-saver course. Students may stay in the college's own cosy hostel on the premises. Alice is a particularly lively, conscientious and fun teacher, whose wide experience informs her instruction. She is aided by a senior paediatric Sister from a London teaching hospital. An inhouse Nanny Bureau finds the students jobs at the end of the course. If you believe in the value of a short course, this is a good one.

The Isle College, Wisbech

The Isle College, Wisbech, does not fall into any neat category. It is a residential course for some students; it does not offer the NNEB; it only lasts a year and there are those who say that its graduates are 'as good as Norlanders'. It has an intake of 20 students, of whom less than half are usually in residence. The college recruits nationally and though some students get local authority grants, most pay for themselves.

The nannies' course tutor is Sandra Ward, who has taught in nursery and primary schools and has employed nannies from the college in the past.

The course is designed to train students to be sole charge nannies in private homes. They study for the College's own Certificate. They also do in a single year a range of other courses: NAMCW's Practical Certificate in Infant and Child Care, the English Speaking Board for Nursery Nurses exam certificate, St John's Ambulance First Aid and the Royal Society of Health Food Hygiene certificate.

Sandra Ward comments: 'Apart from emphasizing the role of the nanny in the home, I have also introduced swimming, riding and languages to widen the course. We also encourage them to take driving lessons.'

The students have local placements and a number of employers go back to this little known college again and again for dedicated nannies.

Chapter 8
Au Pairs, Mother's Helps and All Sorts

Part 1: Au Pairs

This section deals primarily with au pairs, who work part-time, but as there are many foreign girls who work full-time, i.e. they are mother's helps, inevitably it covers both categories of child care. It is relevant to anyone wishing to employ a foreigner whose mother tongue isn't English.

'Au pair' is from the French meaning 'at par'. According to the Oxford Dictionary, it is 'applied to an arrangement between two parties by which mutual services are rendered without consideration of money payment'. In other words, the two services are equal or balanced. One of the earlier references in print to an au pair arrangement was in the 1920s where a German woman lived with a family and in return taught the children her language. Today an 'au pair' girl receives pocket money as well as board, as it is reckoned that so many hours' work a day cannot equal a straight swap of bed and board.

The chief characteristic of an au pair girl is that she is not British. She works part-time and she usually goes to 'English as a Foreign Language' (EFL) classes to learn English. Some employers talk about having an 'English au pair' but this is a confusing use of the term. What they mean is that they have an English *part-time* mother's help. The confusion comes about because many foreigners are mother's helps. They tend to stay longer than an au pair (for nine months to a year), and either don't go to classes, or go in the evenings if they are keen.

A great many au pairs are Roman Catholics, as they come from the Catholic countries of France, Italy, Spain and Portugal. Some Dutch, German, Swiss and Austrian girls are Catholic too. This may have no significance at all to the family that employs them. Many girls are lapsed Catholics or have chucked it entirely. Others still believe and are keen to go to Mass on Sunday. Some employers choose Catholic au pairs specifically because they hope that the chances of them being morally well-behaved will be higher. Sometimes they are right, and sometimes they are wrong. Certainly a *practising* Catholic is the best bet for these employers.

Au pairs have been a popular form of home help and child care since the war. One guestimate is that over 60,000 of them a year come and stay with British families. We are lucky to have access to this cheap form of labour in such quantity (unlike other European countries). The reason is because everyone wants to learn English – the international language.

Au pair plus

This is a term that has been made up by employers and employment agents to explain why the au pair is working more than the Home Office recommended maximum of five hours a day, six days a week. Some agencies offer to place a girl on an 'au pair plus' arrangement. In such cases some girls may work 36 to 40 hours a week.

Asked to comment on 'au pair plus', the Home Office says, 'It is against the spirit of the law for an au pair to work more than 30 hours a week and we don't approve.' However, many employers don't feel guilty about going for an 'au pair plus' if it is sanctioned by the agency, the girl is happy and if she is paid fairly for the extra hours. Since most of the girls who are 'au pair' are also members of the EU and can therefore work as many hours as they like, in most cases it is not an issue anyway.

Thousands of responsible employers, and irresponsible ones, choose this type of employment because it means they get help in the mornings – breakfast, lunch, and again for an hour or so in the evening around the children's bath and bed time.

For many employers who want to spend as little as possible on a home help who has nearly full-time duties, the au pair plus is the most cost-effective choice.

Demi au pair

This phrase, meaning 'half au pair', has been made up, like 'au pair plus', to describe the au pair who receives board and lodging and a very little pocket money for a few hours' work. In a sense this arrangement is closer to the spirit of the Home Office guidelines than the 'au pair plus', as the girl has plenty of time in theory to pursue her studies and her 'pocket money' is just that.

Some employers don't want five or even four hours of work a day from their au pair. They need someone to organize the children's breakfast and school rush, do an hour or so of housework a day and two nights' babysitting a week. Thus they like to pay a few pounds a week for about three hours' work a day.

So long as the au pair is fully aware of what type of job she is taking on, and has some money of her own to supplement the paltry sum, then the demi-au pair arrangement is not exploitative as such.

Unfortunately, all too often, the girl doesn't know that she will not be able to see the sights and keep herself in toothpaste on her tiny wage and she may think that this is a standard au pair deal. The other problem is that unscrupulous employers describe the job as 'demi au pair' in order to pay the minimum, when in fact it turns out to be a three-quarters au pair job.

Summer au pair

Agencies usually have more summer au pairs than jobs to go round. Lots of girls want to help in the summer holidays only. Many families find a bit of extra help useful during July and August. The au pair goes on holiday with them and has a much greater chance of being 'part of the family' than she does during term time. She also sees more of the British Isles, and/or even better, may experience a sunny spot in Spain, France, Greece or wherever for a couple of weeks. Mothers complain that just when the girl has got the hang of the family and her duties, she returns home. Others persuade her to stay on into the autumn with them. Agencies get cross, understandably, when a family doesn't pay them anything extra for a summer au pair who ends up staying six months or a year.

Which foreigner may work here?

NON-EU AND NON-COMMONWEALTH NATIONALS

Foreign girls who are neither part of the Commonwealth, nor part of the EU, or the European Economic Area, who come to the UK to do any kind of work for remuneration must apply for a work permit. Thus for example, Brazilian, American, Mexican, Japanese, Filipino or Chilean nationals, who do not have a work permit and are full- or part-time mother's helps, are 'illegals'; they are breaking the law under the 1971 Immigration Act. This does not stop them finding work with British families without difficulty.

Many non-EU and non-Commonwealth nationals have little or no chance of obtaining a work permit, but thousands of them, particularly in the big cities, work in hotels, restaurants, shops and pubs as domestic servants and as full- and part-time mother's helps. Many of them enrol in 'English as a Foreign Language' classes or other educational pursuits which enable them to have their stay extended without much trouble by the Home Office.

Most employers of those who cannot get work permits report that they don't have difficulty with the authorities. If their mother's help has signed on at a local college and can show the Home Office that she is registered for so many hours a week to study, there isn't a big problem in getting her passport stamped for a further period. Some foreigners take a trip abroad when their 'leave to remain', as the Home Office calls it, is about to expire. They re-enter a few weeks later and often are allowed to enter for another six months.

The police require that au pairs from outside the EU and Commonwealth citizens must register (fee payable) with them within seven days of arrival. They need to take their passport and two passport-sized photos to their local police station or, if in London, to the Alien Registration Office.

According to the Immigration Act, the au pair scheme is an arrangement under which an unmarried girl or boy (boys were included in 1993) aged 17 to 27 inclusive, and without dependants, who is a national of Andorra, Cyprus, Bosnia-Herzegovina, Croatia, Cyprus, Czech Republic, Faroe Islands, Greenland, Hungary, Liechtenstein, Macedonia, Malta, Monaco, San Marino, Slovak Republic, Slovenia, Switzerland and Turkey may come to the UK to learn the English language, and to live for a time as a member of an English speaking family. At time of going to press, Poland was not part of the scheme.

Nationals of the European Economic Area (i.e. European Union members and Finland, Iceland and Norway), can enter the UK to study or work where they like and are not bound by au pair scheme rules.

A girl or boy admitted under an au pair arrangement has no claim to stay in the United Kingdom in some other capacity. When the immigration officer is satisfied that an au pair arrangement has been made, he may admit the visitor for a period of up to 12 months with the strict instruction not to take any other employment. If the visitor has already spent time in the UK as an au pair, he or she may be admitted for a further period as an au pair, but the total aggregate period should not exceed two years.

The Home Office guidelines supplementary to the Act on the au pair arrangement (which it will send you) say firmly that an au pair is not a domestic servant but may help in the house for *up to* five hours a day for pocket money. Suitable tasks would be light housework and taking care of the children. She or he should have two days each week completely free and should be free to attend language classes and religious services. The guidelines point out that the light household duties which the au pair does as part of the 'arrangement' are not regarded as employment.

COMMONWEALTH COUNTRY NATIONALS

Nationals of a Commonwealth country receive special treatment. They can work outside the work permit system under the 'Working Holidaymaker' scheme. A Commonwealth national, for example, an Australian, a New Zealander or a Canadian can enter this country on the Holidaymaker scheme. It allows them to stay in the UK up to an aggregate period of two years on the condition they have sufficient funds to return home, do not intend to have recourse to public funds (i.e. will not claim social security) and wish to do some paid work. The scheme says that their employment is meant to be incidental to an extended holiday in this country. In other words, it sanctions Australians and New Zealand girls taking work as mother's helps for short periods as part of their Grand World Tour.

Exploitation

Many employers do not want to know about the Home Office guidelines on au pairs. Once a few employment agencies were vague or inaccurate about the number of hours recommended, but by the late 1990s most agencies were protecting their girls from over-demanding parents. But even so it remains the case than an au pair can be, and often is, gravely exploited.

Just asking her to do, for example, an extra hour a day, five days a week, pushes her weekly hours up to 35 and she has thus become an au pair plus without any of the 'plus' money. Thousands of au pairs are grossly underpaid for the number of hours they work.

Many agents tell us again and again how they will not place an au pair with a family where both parents work full-time. Too many parents, anxious to keep child care costs to a minimum so that the second salary isn't eaten away too much, ask their au pair to do far too many hours looking after one or more children on their own. This can prove to be a dangerous sort of economy.

The case of Louise Woodward, an 18-year-old English girl who took a job as an au pair in Boston, USA, in 1996, where one of her charges, Matthew, was shaken to death, made his working parents and countless others round the world think again about how much they depended upon and expected from very young child carers. Au pairs are inexperienced in life and in child care and shouldn't expect to be burdened with too much responsibility for too many hours at a time. What such a family needs at the very least is an experienced mother's help, either British or from the EU, and she needs to be paid properly for full-time work. The least a mother's help can expect is around £120 a week net in London, a bit less in the provinces.

The trouble is that hundreds of au pairs arrive, usually in London, with no contacts or friends, and take the first job they are offered simply to get a roof over their heads. They go and stay in hostels like the YMCA or a convent but because they have little money, they do not 'shop around' much. Even the cost of going to interviews in Greater London adds up. If a mother offers one a job, she usually takes it, even if they know there are too many hours involved. She may have liked the sound of another job, but it is a risky business hanging on in hopes that the family will choose them rather than someone else.

Another problem is that too many employers make the job sound a lot more agreeable than it is. They say airily, 'Oh and then there is some housework, mostly hoovering really. I'll tell you about that if you come to us.'

Prospective employers use euphemisms and weasel words which merely sketch in the girl's duties without spelling them out. An employer would be less likely to indulge in this bad habit if she was interviewing an English girl, but because the foreigner misses subtle use of the language, she is unlikely to challenge the exact meaning of, for example, 'some housework, mostly hoovering really'. Having said this, many mothers do mean just that – hoovering and not much more. For many, however, this seemingly inno-cent phrase is another way of saying, 'Well, we have a 12-room house and whilst the children are at school I expect you to dust, hoover, wipe, tidy, straighten, spit, polish, plump up, fetch, wash, dry, iron, sweep, sew, not to mention chop, boil, steam, fry, grill, wash-up, dry-up – you name it, Cinderella.'

Parents forget to mention that they will expect her to walk the Labrador twice a day on the Common. They don't say that the two step-children come and stay for a large part of the holidays and she'll be looking after them too. They play down the things they want her to do. They describe the job in such a way that it sounds quite leisured, when in fact she is on the go non-stop. They don't say, understandably, that they are thinking of splitting up. So the poor girl is perplexed by the icy atmosphere and cryptic conversation whenever He is around.

Some talk about 'lots of free time' but this can just not happen or not often enough. Many au pairs take literally the phrase 'and of course you'll be one of the family', and they are hurt and feel left out when it becomes clear that she is 'one of the family' on duty, and a lodger in the top room when she is not.

One phrase that employers take literally and most au pairs don't know about is the notorious 'mucking in'. It is a useful catch-all which employers use constantly. What many employers mean when they use it is that they expect the au pair to roll up her sleeves and do everything she is asked to do with a good grace.

Employers like to think they are pleasant, caring people, and particularly so when they are looking for live-in help. A great many are. A big proportion, once they have hooked the girl, forget, often, about all their good intentions to give her a reasonable time. These self-occupied types are in a hurry, have their own worries, and don't really want to know whether she enjoys their hearth and home.

If au pairs are asked to do long hours caring for many children for too little money, some of them leave. Others decide to stick out their six months with the devil they know. They put up with a lot more than other untrained carers, and console themselves by being able to visit a few tourist sights and enjoy themselves in their free time meeting friends and going to discos.

Employers of nannies and British mother's helps have to be a lot more careful and considerate, otherwise these girls will leave. An employer often gets away with cutting corners with a foreign girl.

Au pairs are the most exploited group of in-home child carers. They come from abroad, their grasp of the language is often minimal and it takes them a while to compare the arrangements that other au pairs have. They do not stay long anyway so it isn't worth their while to find a better job and hand in their notice to the old battle-axe. Human nature being as selfish as it is, the result is that many, many employers expect their au pairs to work more hours and have much greater responsibility for children, housework and animals, than they should.

In an effort to reduce the numbers of exploitative employers, many agencies emphasize the necessity of the au pair to do light housework only, and the need for her to be treated as a daughter of the house, and, as the Home Office guidelines say, not as a servant.

Agencies also remind prospective employers that the au pair may also need help in finding English classes. Making these points enables the agencies to remonstrate more effectively with erring employers who ask their 'slaves' to do too much.

Au pairs' grumbles

- Wanting a simple written work schedule
- Not being paid on a set day
- Not knowing exactly when is her 'time off'
- Having pay docked when ill
- Not being given plenty of notice when asked to babysit
- Being given too much responsibility when both parents work
- Having too much involvement with the children instead of doing the job *with* the mother
- Not being allowed to take enough part in family life
- Missing family and/or boyfriend
- Feeling isolated because the family lives somewhere remote with bad public transport

---

Au pair considerations

SOCIAL STATUS

Many employers are chastised by agencies and au pairs, quite rightly, for their off-hand approach to the girl in question. Because au pairs are young and usually new to this country and the family is, in effect, *in loco parentis*, they must be treated as social equals. Nannies do not have quite the same status, though many families attempt to give it to them, and a good many succeed. Thus an employer can say without guilt to a nanny or English or Australian mother's help, 'Could you give yourself supper in the evenings or eat with the children at 6 pm? And please, can you vacate the communal areas like the sitting room at night as my husband and I need a bit of peace and quiet together? – thanks.'

With a professional nanny, an employer should not have to say any of this; the nanny will just melt at dusk. There are countless instances of less professional nannies who should know better who manage to hang around in the evening. Time and again polite employers grind their teeth but still find it difficult to be direct and say bluntly 'Please go elsewhere.'

In contrast, with an au pair the much-used phrase 'one of the family' does have to mean that to a greater extent than when used somewhat euphemistically with a nanny. Remember that the point of coming to the UK for the au pair is that she wishes to improve

---

Employers' grumbles

- Their difficulties speaking, reading and understanding the language
- Conversation with them can be tiring
- The fact that many of them are not domesticated ('Does her mother do *everything*?' wails an employer)
- The way they break machines
- The inability of many of them to drive a car
- Their lack of initiative
- Their difficulty in adapting
- Their different cultural habits and mannerisms

---

her English and wants to practise on you. Care of your home and the children are a means to an end as far as she is concerned. She must have an opportunity to talk to you, and the conventional place for this is around the supper table. Because she is on a par with a teenage daughter she expects to eat with the family and no self-respecting employer can deny her this.

Many employers try to avoid this duty by encouraging the au pair to be independent in the evenings. They let her catch up on her English conversation during the day when sorting the dirty washing with mum. Some girls are not particularly keen to have to make stilted conversation while masticating their hostess's idea of *boeuf bourguignon*. Others are tactful and know that hubby and wifey yearn to have a moan about the office, the size of the gas bill this quarter and what their darling Rosie got up to today at school, *alone*. These sensitive souls let them get on with it and take a tray upstairs.

Some employers, often new to the world of au pairs, are admirably conscientious about fulfilling their role as hostess with the mostest in a foreign land to the extent that the au pair is always in tow, even when they have friends to supper.

One couple was amused, but slightly put off, when their friends' Belgian au pair joined what they thought was going to be an intimate evening. 'First she had supper with us, so we all had to take turns in being polite and try to extract a sentence from her. Then she joined us in the sitting room afterwards and sat there like a lemon. By this time we had all given up trying and just ignored her. It wasn't good.' Presumably after one or two more of such evenings the employer reviewed her generous 'one of us' policy.

Many employers are good about eating with the au pair if they are on their own, but say firmly if they are having friends that the au pair must eat in her room or early so that she is not queuing up for the fridge when her hostess is trying to stop the mayonnaise curdling. A good litmus test on this sort of issue is to ask yourself what would you tell your teenager to do? Many parents would ask them not to join the boring oldies for supper and say that they were to steer clear of the kitchen after 7 pm because Mum will be flapping.

THE LANGUAGE PROBLEM

The big problem *all the time* with employing foreign girls is one of communication, which is why a few specify 'good English' in their advertisements. Some au pairs can understand barely a word of English, let alone speak it coherently.

The first-time employer of an au pair with poor English has to remember to speak slowly and to *show* her how to do things rather than just tell her about the ironing, the washing etc. The quickest way she can pick up her household duties is to watch how you do them. Always remember not to give too many instructions at one time. The chances are she will concentrate for the first bit and not have a clue about the second half, and of course she is likely to say yes, she has understood all you said.

One couple went to the theatre and rang home in the interval to find out if the Danish au pair was coping OK. 'The children all right?,' they asked, 'Ya,' she said. 'No problems?' 'Ya.' 'Is the house on fire?' 'Ya, ya' came the enthusiastic reply.

Explain to her the potential seriousness of her saying 'Ya', she has understood, when she hasn't. The instructions may involve something important about the child she is looking after, like the correct cleaning and mixing of bottles, or the temperature of his bath, or how to clean a dirty bottom properly. She may say she understands your run-down of what you suggest she does if the house does go up in flames. Make sure that she does. This doesn't mean she will perform as you instructed her in an emergency, but it may increase the odds. At least you can say to yourself after some ghastly happening that you had run through the drill with her properly, and feel better about it.

Some mothers are relaxed about the communication problem of au pairs. They hope that through signs and demonstration the language barrier will be surmounted, and it often is. By the end of the girl's stay, she should be able to understand most domestic vocabulary.

Others find all this too time-consuming and exhausting, especially if they have more than one child. One mother called a halt to an interview almost immediately. A speechless Spanish girl had brought a friend to act as an interpreter. The mother told them both briskly that the interpreter wasn't going to live with them as well, so that the arrangement would never work.

The responsible employer who does not speak English as a first language should make this clear to the employment agency and any au pair she interviews. As quoted above, the Home Office requires that au pairs stay in an English-speaking family, but in practice an au pair can find herself listening all the time to Chinese, Japanese, Gujarati, Hebrew and Arabic among other languages.

One au pair told us that her first job in the UK was with a charming but completely incomprehensible Chinese family living in Windsor. A foreign girl working for a non-English speaking family in London, for example, may encounter extraordinary difficulties with language, and diet and custom as well. Unusual dietary habits are rare but it can be something of a shock for an au pair used to smörgasbord to eat nothing but Kosher or Chinese food. She may also resent being asked to comply with eating and cleansing rituals if she has not been told about them before joining the family.

CLASSES

The au pair expects her employer to do a little homework on her behalf about her 'English as a Foreign Language' (EFL) classes. Go straight to the local Yellow Pages and look under Colleges.

The local Further Education college is a good bet for EFL courses, though the further away from a metropolis, the less likely it is that the college will run such a course. In London and towns like Brighton and Bournemouth, popular with foreign students, there are plenty of privately run language schools which charge commercial fees. Some have special cheap au pair courses. State colleges, particularly in London, are hugely popular because the fees are inexpensive. In order to get a place it is often necessary to register the term before.

If your au pair or mother's help is able to get a place at a state college usually she can study for two hours a day either in the morning or the afternoon. If she is from the EU she will pay very little per term. If she is non-EU the fee will be much higher.

MONEY

The Home Office now talks about a 'reasonable' amount of pocket money for the 30 hours she works. There used to be huge variations in au pair pay, but just as with nannies, hiring au pairs is becoming more professional. She is also expected to cope on her own more and more, rather than the traditional working alongside the parent. The London rate is £35 as a minimum up to £45 for 30 hours.

Payment varies depending on the demands of the job. An au pair with one small child to look after could expect to receive less than an au pair with three children under six. An au pair who joins a family that has a cleaner may well find that she receives a bit less pocket money, because she doesn't have to do much housework. Pay drops a bit the further from London or a city the au pair's family lives. Likewise, in the country, employers expect to pay an au pair less than the top rate, though often living there is much less of an enticing proposition for her, unless she loves fields and views.

An au pair is not paid enough for her to have to pay National Insurance Contributions and tax, though she is free to make voluntary contributions, and this makes sense if her EU country has a reciprocal agreement about social security payments with the UK. If she wishes to pay National Insurance, get in touch with the local Social Security office about how she goes about this. Not surprisingly, 99.99 per cent of au pairs do not want to do such a thing.

TIME OFF

By now readers must be clear that au pairs are meant to work a maximum of five hours a day. They must have two *full* days off a week. Many employers are naughty about giving the au pair a complete two days off, and many shift about which two full days off depending on their needs. This is all right within reason, but it isn't fair if an employer tells her on a Saturday that she can have next Wednesday off as the parents have organized a squash session for Sunday morning and she'll be needed to see to the children.

As with a nanny, an au pair can expect to be asked to babysit two nights a week on average and it is courteous to give each other ample warning when either of you intend to go out (see Chapter 5). An employer who wants her au pair on duty on quite a few Sundays must make this clear at the interview, saying that she can have a day off in the week instead. The employer must also reassure the girl if she practises a religion that she may take time off on the Sunday to worship. This way the au pair can make up her mind beforehand whether she is prepared not to be free when her friends are, and she is less likely to flounce out when messed-up weekends affect her social life.

HOLIDAYS

One of the advantages of au pairs is that if they stay only six months, then they can't expect to receive any paid holiday, and they don't. The rationale behind no paid holidays is that the au pair experience is not a job as such and it is part- time anyway. For all that, a case could be made for some paid holiday after a six months' stint, and some generous employers do that with a successful au pair in the form of a cash bonus when she leaves.

There is moral pressure on employers who hire an au pair for nine months and more to give some paid holiday as well as about two weeks of unpaid holiday. Conscientious employers of foreign mother's helps who stay nine months to a year give them two to three weeks' paid holiday. Many employers do give au pairs unpaid leave during their stay, often at Christmas.

PERKS

One of the few perks of being an au pair is that, if she is with a responsible family, it will show her the sights or at least tell her how to get to them and be pleased to hear all about it afterwards. 'Being nice to the au pair' can be a chore, but it shouldn't be shirked, if you feel that she would appreciate it. Some are highly organized and independent and, mercifully, their one idea is to escape from the family in their time off. Kind employers take her out and about with them on their outings. They take her to other people's parties, lunches, drinks and even weddings. They take her to the Tower of London and Alton Towers and Madame Tussaud's. Less kind employers rather hope the girl will get on with it off her own bat.

In London all this is less of a problem as it is there on her doorstep, after all. Some employers make up for five months of touristic neglect by treating the au pair to Chatsworth or Blenheim in the rain or something else they want to do that they feel sure that she will enjoy too.

In the country even the less kind employers feel they should help out a bit as travelling to tourist spots and even the local town can be expensive and complicated. No employer wants a moping au pair and, as with the nanny, enlightened self-interest pays. Au pairs can feel lost and homesick, especially if they have just arrived in the country. Make full use of her agency friendship circle, if there is one. Check out a copy of the *Foreign Student and Au Pair Magazine*, which she might enjoy. Introduce her to other au pairs and nannies so that she can make friends with whom she can go for a walk or to a pub, or whatever, which can make a huge difference to her contentment.

THE CHILDREN

Somewhat curiously, au pairs are associated in people's minds with housework rather than children. Perhaps it is because this is where she differs greatly from the nanny. The latter only brushes up against housework when it is linked to her charges. The au pair cannot escape. Also, many parents choose the vastly cheaper au pair option when their brood have reached school age and they feel that their full-time nanny or mother's help is not needed any more. It may be also because women who hire au pairs when they have young children are around much more than they might be if they had a nanny. These mothers concern themselves with the children while the au pair does the chores.

SOLE CHARGE

Apart from the part-time nature of an au pair's work, she is also very much less capable of 'sole charge' than the experienced or trained nanny. Au pairs can only be an option for working parents if all the children are of school age. Then her time can be split into a breakfast/get them to school shift and a collect them from school/tea/bath/bed shift. This gives her the day to go to classes.

More and more au pairs find that the mother has some part-time work which she does somewhere else in the house while the au pair is in semi-sole charge. The mother is around and can appear if she hears yells and screams, or if she wants to see how the au pair is managing. Generally, the modern mother – working or not – tends to spend a lot less time working with the au pair looking after the children and doing the chores than she did in the past. Modern gadgets, machines and carpets have reduced the grind.

Many agencies warn mothers that an au pair should not be expected to be in sole charge much, and certainly not for long periods. In practice many of them are, and often for most of the time they are on duty. Mothers should be aware that the quality of child care can be a problem with untrained girls whose prime aim is to live in a foreign country for a while; many of them are not interested in enhancing a baby's or a child's play. An au pair, like a nanny or a mother's help, can leave a baby lying in his cot for longer than you would and listen to her music for an hour or two alone in the play room with a toddler left to entertain himself. It is also important to feel pretty confident she has the *nous* and competence to cope alone (see Chapter 6 for Emergency Drill and Sole Charge). However wonderful you think she is, remember she is foreign and if the child was streaming blood or the house was burgled, she would be under more strain than a British mother's help or nanny.

Parents often underestimate the skill it takes to keep small children tearless for long periods. They have developed their technique over several years. They know their children very well, their little ways and how to deal with them. The au pair is unlikely to have looked after two children on her own for any length of time before. She is probably unskilled in her timing of when to feed, play, encourage a child to go to the lavatory, and when to put him down to rest. Remember that her knowledge about what to do with a whingeing baby or child may be minimal.

Another aspect which isn't important until the children are over a year, is the need for the au pair to get on with, and talk to, her charges. It is far from ideal for a child aged between ten months and five years not to be able to practise his own language learning with an au pair who has pidgin English.

Many mothers don't expect an au pair whose English is not good to be able to read books to the children, or have those delightful discussions with three-year-olds upwards about the mysteries of the universe – what is thunder and why is it so hot at the top of the house on a summer's day? Many parents of two- to five-year-olds give up having au pairs and foreign mother's helps for this reason. They don't want to risk their children's language development.

Loads of experienced employers with small children solve the problem pretty much by taking only the Norwegians, Swedes, Danes, the Dutch and the Germans. These girls usually speak good English so that they can converse with a child and read to him comfortably too. Some girls of these nationalities are bilingual and, ironically, speak better grammatical English than many British.

TRAVELLING

Some agencies say that their clients will pay a girl's fare to and from Britain, but no employer should be expected to provide this perk. The odd generous family does so. One mother went so far as to pay an unseen Brazilian girl to fly from Rio to be her mother's help. Unfortunately the girl was a complete disaster and only stayed with the family six weeks.

It is sensible to give an au pair from abroad plenty of help and instruction about how best to get to her destination. Families should try to meet her at the airport or station. Apart from the courtesy, she is sure to be burdened with luggage. In London she can be asked to jump in a taxi and the employer can pay on her arrival. It is mean in the extreme to let a 17-year-old au pair arrive at Heathrow to be met by a message telling her to get to Elstree, an outer London suburb. There was no crisis at the girl's employer's home to warrant this behaviour, just a lack of warmth and help-fulness for which British hostesses of au pairs have a reputation.

What type of au pair?

There are two types of au pair and foreign mother's help. There is the sort you are most likely to want and the agencies certainly prefer to place. She is usually 18 or 19, and is fresh in every sense – new to the country, new to the language, new to adulthood, new to men and she may be someone who is still under the influence of a no-nonsense mother who 'knows what is best' for her daughter. This type of girl tends to want genuinely to improve her English and enrol in classes. She may be taking a year off before going on to some sort of further education, or to train for something like nursing. She is likely to get on with her parents and siblings and come from a stable background.

This is the old-fashioned, traditional sort of au pair. This type was the norm throughout the 1950s and 1960s. Then Britain joined the EEC in 1971 and this opened the door to the second type, the EU national who is free to work in this country indefi-nitely in any capacity she chooses. This group chooses to live abroad for years rather than months. It is almost exclusively a London phenomenon. These girls may do all sorts of different jobs, one of them being an au pair or a mother's help for a spell. They are usually older – 20 to 25; they may be as old as 28 or 30.

There is also the non-EU national who can come within this second category. She is often from South America but could be from Japan or elsewhere in the Far East and is probably seeking work as a mother's help or an au pair illegally. She probably won't have a work permit but has registered at language classes in order to receive permission to stay in this country from the Home Office.

This type *can* make an excellent au pair and mother's help. Part of her attraction is that she knows about the British way of life, can speak the language quite well, has already experienced an English household and may know quite a bit about children. Because she is older than the fresh flower sort, she is more mature and may have graduated to a *steady* boyfriend which is a bonus. Many of this kind of 'mature' foreign girl take daily nannying jobs and return to their flat and their boyfriend in the evening.

There is a big 'but' with this category of au pair, however. Unlike her younger counterpart of the Alpine pastures or the farm in Holland, she is likely to be streetwise, and know all the pubs, clubs and discos of London from High Barnet to Morden. She is likely to have had several boyfriends while she has been working over here. Often she no longer goes to classes because her English is good. So her motives for wanting to live with a family to help with the children and the housework are very different from the traditional au pair's.

This sort of au pair is looking, primarily, for cheap board and lodging. If she is a good sort, this approach won't necessarily interfere with the way she does her job, but the odds are higher that her latest steamy relationship may get in the way, as it can do with living-in British nannies and mother's helps.

If she is a bad sort, she will be hell to live with and is to be avoided at all costs. She will regard your home as a place to while away the daylight hours before the gaudy night begins.

One employer remembers landing just one such au pair member of the café society: 'She was an Italian who lived way beyond her slender means, caught taxis everywhere, and spent hours in the bath lolling in Floris. We felt we had a would-be fledgling Bianca Jagger in our midst, but without the looks. She spent her pocket money on charity ball tickets which seemed to clash too often with our plans to go out and eat a humble pizza. She had to go'.

What nationality?

Many employers are prejudiced either for or against particular nationalities. It may be the result of a bad experience with a girl of a particular nationality but often it is not. Age-old xenophobic comments about different nationalities come up time and again.

The Germans and Austrians are highly popular and highly prized for their grasp of English. They are also described by a string of adjectives, not all complimentary, including: organized, intelligent, matter-of-fact, no-nonsense.

The Swiss are sought after because their English is good, provided they come from the right bit of Switzerland. Not surprisingly, people praise their precision and reliability, like clocks, as well as their industry.

The Dutch are popular, along with the Scandinavians and the Germans. Their English is very good. Employers tend to be a bit wary of French au pairs, but they do respect them for their ability to work hard and get on with whatever needs doing. Some mothers say they have come across several who are too detached, and too keen to look after Number One to make ideal au pairs. Often mothers grumble about how they do the job to the letter rather than the spirit. Superior, glum and grumpy are some derogatory adjectives used about them.

Belgians tend to get tarred with the French brush, but nicer things are said about them.

Highly praised for their excellent English accents and grasp of idiom, Scandinavians are about the most popular group. Mothers seem to be prejudiced pro the Swedes, Norwegians, Danes and Finns. Somehow Scandinavians are associated in employers' minds with attractive things like blonde hair, snow, enlightened attitudes to ecology and child care, and a healthy vigorousness.

Spanish, Portuguese, Brazilians, Argentinians and Chileans are generally reckoned good sorts, warm and tremendously hard working. Many mothers say these girls are warm and good with the children partly because many of them have at least three siblings. Some employers find the differences in culture and manners of some of the girls hard to take. A few say they can be moody, gloomy, stormy and sulky. They all grumble about the girls' poor English and accent.

Italians are popular and considered gentle, charming and good with children. Often they have much better English than you might expect.

The pros and cons of hiring a foreigner or going native

Whether to hire a foreign or an English mother's help – part- or full-time – is a conundrum. Many employers experiment a bit to begin with before settling on one or the other. Many parents are quite sure that they prefer their own nationality without ever trying a foreign mother's help, largely on the grounds that they can speak English. To a lesser extent, they feel that there has to be more in common and that it is easier, generally, to get on with someone from one's own country. Others find foreigners socially and culturally more relaxing to live with.

Some members of the middle classes say that there is a higher chance that an au pair from Europe will come from a similar background. A foreign girl is less likely to turn up her nose at her employers' foreign food like chilli con carne, pork spiked with garlic, and lasagne. In fact, au pairs tend not to be fussy eaters and many seem to exist on yoghurt and fruit. Many young English girls are keen to try new foods and take an interest in menus which are not all chips, peas and fried chicken, but the odds are that a foreign girl will be happier to eat yesterday's murky stew re-heated.

There is more likelihood that a European may be cultured and keen to visit museums, art galleries and historic monuments. She may well go to see the same films, plays and concerts as her employers and enjoy discussing their merits afterwards. It is not important if the mother's help or au pair doesn't share any of her family's interests and enthusiasms, and loads of them are not into culture, but if it matters to you it is a definite bonus to have a kindred spirit around.

Sometimes employers can experience culture shock with girls from poor, unsophisticated families in parts of France, Italy, Spain and Portugal. One Kensington mum recalls, 'I sacked one and all my friends laughed. Her table manners were too awful to live with. She would put her knife in the honey pot, lick it, and put it back again. Ugh.'

Foreign girls are less aware of differences in income and class than British girls. Many parents reckon that this makes living with them more comfortable. It is less necessary to be aware of what you say about politics, class and money when living with someone who probably doesn't understand a good deal of what you mean and whose frame of reference can be very different.

One mother who had employed foreign girls in the past remembers her first, and probably last, 18-year-old English mother's help:

It dawned on me that, however nice Sheilagh was, she might have arrived from Outer Mongolia. She came from a Scunthorpe working class family with a lot less money than us.

It was her *attitude* to living with us that was different from a foreign girl's. She was perfectly polite, and good with the children, but I felt she thought our way of life was not hers and she didn't aspire to it either. After Sheilagh left we went back to the Ingas and Petras. Quite frankly they are less lumpen and didn't watch the box so much. Sadly, we have more in common with a girl from across the Channel than with one from north of the Humber.

Where to find an au pair or foreign mother's help

Au pairs can be found by word of mouth, by going to agencies, contacting various convents and organizations who run hostels as well as the churches of different countries, (see useful addresses), by putting ads in local shops and schools and by taking an ad in *The Lady* (see Chapter 3). The advantage of an ad in *The Lady* is that, provided you live in and around London, you can interview applicants, rather than having to rely on a telephone conversation.

It is not necessary to be paranoid about the 'experienced' au pair who has already found her feet in the capital and avoid *The Lady* entirely. In fact, there are loads of 'nice' girls who do come straight from home to London. Often two friends make the trip across the Channel together, book in at a hostel or convent, or stay with friends or even a relation, and go and buy a copy of the magazine. Often a girl's home town convent may have contacts with one of the London convents, some of whom put girls up and will help them to find a job.

OUTSIDE LONDON

Parents who don't live in London, its environs and the Home Counties have much less choice. Many resort to provincial agencies, and failing those, London agencies. Some place an ad in *The Lady* and suggest that the girl makes a long trip, probably from London, for an interview and agree to pay her return fare. Some try to save money by taking a chance and suggest that the applicant who sounds the most appealing on the phone comes 'blind', without a face-to-face interview, and both the family and the girl try each other out for a week. Others take a sophisticated route and get a friend to advertise in a foreign newspaper and field applicants long distance.

It is worth enquiring from a town or village's twinning association if there are any girls wanting to stay with an English family. Getting in touch with the local school or college language department can reap rewards too. If the family lives in a town or close to it, there's a chance that there will be enough entertainment for the au pair to be happy and to stay. But for a family living in deep country, away from easy transport and other young people, the odds are long on finding an au pair who will stay six weeks, let alone six months. Even the use of a car, an essential for the country au pair, may not make enough difference.

Country folk keen to land a long stay au pair could well benefit from the effort of putting an ad in *The Lady*, and interviewing girls personally at a friend's home or at an accessible spot such as the Commonwealth Institute in Kensington High Street, or the Indian Tea Centre in Oxford Street. Then the employer, clutching photos of her husband, animals, children, house and grounds, can explain to her face to face what a country job entails.

Others have the luck to secure a girl who genuinely likes views and quiet.

Proper transport is essential. One Devon mother's Finnish au pair found the twice-weekly 20-mile trip by lift and bus to the city for her classes, and not being able to stay on and have fun in the evenings, frustrating. Very soon she flew from her unidyllic nest to the convenient pavements of Plymouth.

Part 2: Mother's Helps, Australians, New Zealanders and Others

Mother's helps

A mother's help can be British or foreign. Most are British, a significant proportion are Australians or New Zealanders and a good many are from the European Union or beyond. There are lots of 'illegals'. The main advantage of a mother's help is that you do not pay for training. She is a lot cheaper than anyone trained and that includes CACHE, NAMCW and City & Guilds (see Chapter 7).

Many employers like the fact that a mother's help may be young and malleable and they feel more comfortable living with someone who in no sense challenges the way they live. One mother says, 'Oh no, I couldn't cope with a smart, trained NNEB, quite apart from the cost, I'd have to redecorate the bathroom and get a cleaner.'

One of the characteristics of a trained nanny is that if she is any good she is, by definition, going to hold views about how your child should behave and should develop. A few employers dislike anyone else having views about child rearing; they really want someone who does it as they do.

Employers also like housework to come within the child care package. Mother's helps hope to be asked to do 'light housework' only – they breathe a sigh of relief when there is a cleaner already for the heavy stuff. This means they won't have to mop the kitchen floor, scrub the loos, wash down the paintwork, spring clean, wash the front door step, hoover the stairs or polish silver and brass. If the family hasn't got a cleaner she can expect to do all these things.

However, housework today isn't *that* heavy in most modern, centrally heated, carpeted homes. The traditional idea of a mother's help is that the mother is, broadly speaking, around to be helped. Although many mothers leave their children to be looked after by the mother's help, whilst they go out to work full- or part-time, reputable employment agencies frown on this practice, unless the girl has had considerable experience.

After several years (three at the very least), experience may make the girl feel that she is on a par with her trained counterpart and with some justification. There are plenty of mother's helps with one or two years' experience who reckon they are as much a nanny as someone trained, and they don't hesitate to describe themselves as such. Most mother's helps are better supervised than left free range. A mother's help will do anything alongside a mother like cleaning the car, spring cleaning the sitting room together, washing the windows together – that sort of thing. With you helping she will even clean the swimming pool or manoeuvre the puppy pooper scooper round the lawn.

A job shared is a job halved, as far as the mother's help is concerned – from the employer's point of view it is a job done properly. If the employer acts like Lady Muck and reclines on the chaise longue reading magazines day after day, the housework will not be done well, if at all. A few mother's helps have a natural aptitude and enjoy housework; they are never happier than when sorting out the airing cupboard and reorganizing the marmites and marmalades. Some mothers have trained their daughters as excellent housemaids. The vast majority are just plain bad at it and bored by it and do it far too quickly and superficially for good results. They are either naturals or they aren't, so try not to get indignant about their myopia and lack of vim.

It helps to cheer up the whole housework experience if you give a mother's help all the modern cleaning gadgets you can afford, like a cylinder cleaner for the stairs and a sleeve board for the ironing. Make sure that old cloths get thrown away and don't be mean about the Ajax supplies and newish bog brushes.

Another bonus about a mother's help is that an employer can ask her to help with the cooking for the family and the washing up. Thousands of them can't boil an egg, but it is quite legitimate to encourage her to do it as best she may and, if she is foreign, try her national alternatives. Katharine Whitehorn, in *How to Survive Children*, says, 'Much easier are mother's helps who mop floors as well as tears. If you've hired them for qualities of cow-like tranquillity you absolutely don't have yourself, it's unfair to be furious if they take an hour and a half, reflectively stirring the water with one hoof, to do the washing up.'

There is a species of daily mother's help who is rather like a childminder on your turf. She is untrained, probably local and experienced with kids, having brought up a few of her own. Some families, often one-parent who work full-time, don't want a nanny but a housekeeper: someone to collect children from school, cover for the holidays, do the housework, washing, ironing and shopping. Such families often have live-in British mother's helps who fulfil this role. Unlike most mother's helps, she will probably work for you for several years – more like the job span of a cleaning lady than that of a nanny.

Whatever her age, the untrained mother's help should have the same qualities, ideally, that you look for in a trained nanny (see Chapter 3). The essential stuff about liking children and being capable of spending most waking moments in their company all apply. Be sure that she is equable and sensible, responsible and that you *like* her. Do not compromise yourself or your children just because you aren't paying the earth.

One of the most important things to remember about an untrained, inexperienced girl is that she may have no idea about the importance of safety indoors and out. Buy her the Red Cross book and lecture her at length, regardless of her age or her experience with someone else's family (see Chapter 5).

Another common problem with a younger mother's help, as with the new nanny, is homesickness (for remedies see Chapter 5). You are employing someone young enough to be your daughter and she may have not have had any sort of training or relevant experience since leaving school. British mother's helps tend to be young – 17 or 18. For many girls it is their first job. Employers should try to recall how crassly they handled their own. One experienced employer says, 'I always keep closely in touch with her parents if she is under twenty. If I have problems with her, I will need their support.'

The big problem with the 17-year-old English girl is that as often as not it is a toss-up between serving in the local chip shop, making beds in a hotel, or nannying. Many an employer doesn't realize that her mother's help has not yet made any clear plans about the future. It is quite likely after several weeks in the job, when her employer is just beginning to relax, that the girl will smile sweetly and announce without a blush, 'My mum says there is a good job going at the local DIY shop. I think I'll give it a try.'

A few mothers have had the enlightened idea of encouraging their mother's helps to pursue some child-related training by correspondence and in night classes, with the intention of broadening their experience and expertise. Some examples include a Pre-school Playleaders' course, a Montessori correspondence course and night courses at the local council college in storytelling, cookery, kids' clothes making, smocking, toy making and puppet workshops.

Australians and New Zealanders

Agencies and employers are unanimous in their enthusiastic support of this group. One agency says: 'If I could afford to ditch every British nanny and only deal with the Aussies and Kiwis I definitely would. They are trouble-free, happy, sensible and reliable – no wonder we all love them!'

Australians and New Zealanders present only two major drawbacks. They may not want to stay for longer than six months, though it is more usual by the late 90s to persuade them to commit for a year than it was a decade ago. But they may not know how long that may feel in reality and leave sooner, whatever they originally agreed to do. The wish to travel is urgent and the Antipodean is definitely working to finance this desire worldwide for a year or two. However good they are with children, employers must psych themselves to accept the fact that they are transient treats.

Aussies and Kiwis are good fun to employ and they are mostly gregarious. This is ideal for energetic large English families living in the country. Most people who choose Australians and New Zealanders like to stick with an agency with whom they build up a good relationship.

Australians and New Zealanders are particularly prized for their initiative and ability to 'muck in'. No one seems capable of an analysis of this essential commodity without mentioning housework. They are reckoned among the Seven Wonders because they will wield a scrubbing brush without throwing a fit. To enumerate the qualities of Australian and New Zealander mother's helps is to list the shortcomings of the British nanny.

Another striking feature is that the Australians and New Zealanders are older – mostly in their early or mid-twenties – and often trained, not as nannies, but as nurses and teachers and in a whole host of other professions. Thus the employer more easily accords them respect. They have lived away from home and have crossed the world, so they have a better chance of being more amusing and sophisticated company than the average British mother's help or nanny. All of which means that communication is more direct. Antipodeans are legendary for their plain-speaking and their Pom employers are quite keen on it within reason because it can reduce friction. Polite/disorganized/timid/ employers find it a relief to hear a sensible Kiwi announce that she will be doing X, Y and Z this morning.

Typical attitudes not commonly manifested in English girls include an amazement that employers don't do the jobs they want to hire people to do themselves. Although Australians and New Zealanders are happy to be employed as mother's helps, house-keepers and 'couples', they don't think that those jobs are worth having, apart from the money. 'It's not like that at home' is a phrase commonly on their lips. 'Why can't she do the work herself?' As one agent says:

> They ask me questions as often as not and I say because they have enough money to get you to do it. I have to explain that English employers are not much interested in discussing the ethics of who should be doing the job; they just want someone, preferably not them, to get on with it.

There are darn few Australian nannies in Australia, so most Australian mother's helps/nannies will never have done the job before. They may have no idea whether they will like nannying. They will probably do it anyway, and make the most of it for six months, whatever they think of it. As one mother says, 'It is an experiment for them. They have to live in to have a roof over their heads. They are over here to experience anything new and it certainly *is* different.'

Many Aussies and Kiwis think that British children are spoilt. They find the lack of discipline strange and the fact that children are not punished for misdemeanours is not in the least to their liking. If you are the mother of a fragile flower, have a chat with the Antipodean mother's help about how you do and do not expect him to be treated. Most employers who deliberately choose Australian and New Zealand help tend to share their stoic, no-nonsense attitudes; that's why they get on so well.

Australians and New Zealanders are more expensive than an English mother's help – it would be cloud cuckooland to rate maturity highly and then not expect to pay for it. They earn around £135 a week to live in. The onus is on the employer to arrange tax and National Insurance, but most don't let this responsibility weigh too heavily – they'll be gone soon and that's that. They mostly do not expect to do elbow-grease housework and tend to go to families that keep cleaning help. They prefer not to have their readiness to 'muck in' tested daily.

The whole class thing does not raise its ugly head. They sound different; they're foreigners; they do things differently, for the same reason. That's how employers see it. Many a public school employer misspent a year or more Down Under on sheep stations – even Prince Charles went to Geelong. They dreamed dreams, lost their virginity and got legless under the stars in the outback, so the vibrant tones of an Australian mother's help bring back happy memories.

There are quite a few short training courses in child care available in Australia and New Zealand, some better than others. Several British agencies have links with them and others just deal with employment agencies there. Says one, 'The only name we can rely on is the Tricillian hospital in Sydney. The nurses are brilliantly trained from there.'

There are several well-worn paths to agency doors. Look up the specialist agencies who deal mostly or entirely with Australian and New Zealand help and skim through the list for other agencies who are keen to attract Antipodeans. If you want to avoid agency fees, advertise in the free weeklies designed for Aussies and Kiwis living in London – *TNT* (see Useful Addresses), *New Zealand News* and *New Australasian Express*.

The agencies are more than capable of sending a fax to check references in Australia and you should foot the bill for them to do so. It is obviously silly to risk taking a girl off the street without a reference just because she lives so far away. There are bad apples, but there are very few stories about Aussies and Kiwis behaving badly to their employers, which is creditable given how footloose and fancy-free they are actually while working here.

Employers and agencies say:

They are bright and cheery and not evasive and depressing like so many English girls – even interviewing them is a positive pleasure.

They turn up and start work within hours of ringing the agency; that's what I like best.

I'm crazy about them. They just watch what you are doing and then do it better.

The moronic British mother's help is such a nightmare by comparison. We always have Australian graduates and they are such a help and so nice to have around.

Babysitters

> Ma's out, Pa's out,
> Let's have fun,
> Pee, po', belly, bum, drawers.

Anyone who has a real-life nasty story about a helper certainly has one about babysitters. The most popular and infamous tale concerns the parents arriving home early because they forgot their keys/got the wrong night/had a migraine, to find their babysitter with her boyfriend in the kitchen – both giggly and passing joints. The oven is on and the door is ajar. Then they see the tin foil stretched over the baking tin stir. Ripping it off, to their horror their six month baby is revealed in all his chubby nakedness, smeared with lard and with an apple in his mouth . . .

The story has a lesson for many parents who do not make much effort to check out their babysitters thoroughly. Funnily enough, someone who is paying £175 plus a week for a swish daily nanny may often hire an agency babysitter they have never seen before in their lives. She is handed the children, the house, all the goods and chattels, and the employer assumes blithely that her burglar boyfriend will not arrive ten minutes after they go out for the whole evening.

There is no law to prevent anyone of any age babysitting in England and Wales, nor is there any law that says parents may not leave children alone in the house when they go out. In Scotland the legal minimum babysitting age is statutory at 16, which doesn't stop thousands of families flouting the law. Many responsible parents south of the border believe (wrongly) that the law sanctions a child who has reached 14 to babysit other children, and happily give their children permission to earn some extra money in this way. What English law tries to be clear about is parents' 'duty of care' to a child, so it is only when their child is considered to have been neglected by becoming harmed in some way (which may involve a babysitter) that the police start asking questions. It is only when a babysitter is 16 years old or more that he or she can be held responsible, before that a child's parents are to blame for any mishap, whether they were present when it occurred or not.

An NSPCC representative comments, 'The law says that unless a person is over 16, he or she cannot be held responsible for the care of a child. The law on neglect is adequate, but babysitting should be specifically mentioned.'

The ad in the local shop looks fine. 'Responsible, experienced 14-year-old for babysitting'. Look at it again. How well would the average 14-year-old cope with a fire when there are only two minutes to extract the children from their beds? How would she cope with a frightening phone call, an odd caller or a burglary? And how would you feel afterwards about yourself, her and her parents should a tragedy occur? Is it worth risking this kind of anguish or guilt?

Choose a 16-plus local girl, whom you and the children know well, trust and like. Alternatively, find out about the local babysitting circle or start your own. The latter is a group of mothers, often as many as 20, who babysit for each other free of charge. Some groups dish out tokens which may be cashed in when it suits. Whoever it is, hand him or her an emergency drill written out clearly – the hospital name, surgery number and doctor's name, instructions for an ambulance driver, where you are for the evening and leave your phone number *always*, even if you are going to a cinema, theatre or restaurant. Leave also the phone numbers of close friends or relations who live nearby. Parents should not take advantage of a babysitter by leaving them to cope with a child who is already sick and who is unlikely to settle down to sleep.

Do make sure that your children know babysitters well enough so that if they wake up and are sad or thirsty, or have wet their bed or whatever, they can ask the babysitter without feeling too miserable that their parents are not around. Tell your sitter what pet names your children may have for their needs.

Decide beforehand what you feel about the babysitter's boyfriends or girlfriends coming to join her in your absence and state your view. The general rule is no to men, yes to girls. As for drink, if you like, fill a wine glass and make it clear that that's all that's on offer.

Agencies are expensive, not ideal nor in some magical way more reliable than a local arrangement. There are a few which earn their

fee and a very few who guarantee a babysitter after an annual sub-
scription to their service. Then their babysitters, who are trained
nannies, will make their own charge as well, so the total is not an
option for many people. 'A' level students, nursery school teachers,
the greengrocer's daughter, the health clinic assistant, student
nurses from the hospital, the teenage daughter of a neighbour or
friend – all can be contacted via postcards in shops, clinics, hospitals and schools, and if they live near you will charge half that price.

Other people's nannies are the first choice for people who are
without them. Employers of nannies get very annoyed with
approaches from comparative strangers and acquaintances on the
school steps and in the park. As an employer, it is quite OK to say
'no' flatly. Most are kind and say yes, then they curse their stupid-
ity, when the nanny is kept out till 3.30 am by neighbours and is
not fit for work the next day.

Supper – ham and salad, no sweat – should be provided. A
working TV is vital. If you know you will be later than midnight
offer her somewhere to snooze, preferably close to the children, or
suggest she brings her overnight bag and you will pay her until
midnight. Otherwise, when you return, either you drive her home
or pay for a taxi. Always err on the generous side; round up her pay
to the nearest hour. If you treat her well consistently, it will pay off
in the long run.

The granny substitute or proxy mother

Some employers don't have mothers who make perfect grannies
and they do not want to leave a nanny, mother's help or au pair in
sole charge of their children whilst they go away with their husband for a holiday or on a business trip. So they sometimes want
to employ a granny substitute to oversee the household.

There are agencies who deal in these super grans (see Agencies
for details). They are mostly about 50 to 60 years old, can drive,
have had children of their own or are retired nannies and are
entirely capable of running the nanny, the house and your children
smoothly in your absence. Make sure that you check her references thoroughly and invite her to meet you and the family before
your departure.

Chapter 9
Friction

Stress and Conflict

Control yourself,
Contain yourself,
And if you can't,
Restrain yourself
Then try to act
Agreeably on the whole.

Life is much too short
To spend it in a huff
Try to imitate
the guy who laughs
When things get tough.

Cleo Laine at Carnegie Hall

If you are bad at communal living, having a resident nanny or mother's help may be a helluva strain. One full-time working mother (who therefore sees comparatively little of her nanny) speaks for many when she says:

> The nanny/mother relationship appears to be full of conflict. You want long-term commitment, but few of us like the children feeling more secure with the nanny than with the mum. You want them to be mature, but you reserve the right to treat them as teenagers. You don't want your own position challenged, but you expect them to behave as you would if you were there.

Very few people can be said truly to *need* a nanny. Employers hire one of their own free will and the mistake most of them make is to think that money will somehow buy them immunity from problems.

If you hire a super-experienced and highly trained girl to live in and look after your children, you will cut out many of the obvious stresses. But there will always be some friction, disagreement, problems of adjustment and personality differences. And that is just for starters.

Friction can cause fire, but the fuel which provides ignition is what any good employer, keen to keep a nanny or mother's help long-term, needs to analyse thoroughly. Nannies and employment agencies report that if employers behaved more fairly they would have a much better chance of nannies staying longer. Employers say that if nannies were better prepared by their training colleges and/or agencies for the realities of living-in posts, they would cope with the strains better. It is pragmatic to learn to become a better employer. Examining the problems is far from having a self-indulgent wallow, or an excuse for a grumble.

Carelessness, thoughtlessness and selfishness on either side are the root causes of stress. As Juliet Solomon puts it in her book *Holding the Reins*, 'Employers are permanent volunteers, nannies are temporary mercenaries.' Too often employers forget this and demand too much of the people who care for their children. Employers can also become dismissive and disdainful of the work the nanny is doing. Employers must respect the nanny's job. They have to take an interest in her and, while expecting her to be as professional as possible, they should not lose sight of the fact that she is human and fallible.

One parent says glumly, 'Normally most start off mediocre and stay that way or get worse. You straighten out the worst niggly aspects of their behaviour; the rest you ignore or get used to.' Another takes a more robust line, 'I don't like kids in dirty clothes, so I tell nannies their standards aren't high enough and I put the clothes in the basket myself. Most of them tend to slacken off when they get to know the routine – I'm afraid familiarity does breed contempt very often. I have only had one nanny who maintained very high standards for two years.'

One can pinpoint periods during a nanny's employment when she is likely to be less than satisfied with the status quo and may well leave unless you take precipitate action. Mrs Davis of Norland says, 'It is human to slacken off after six to nine months and it is harder for the employer to reprove by then.' A London employment agency says that employers should watch out for the New Year which is a natural time for reassessment and itchy feet. One mother says, 'two years seems to be the limit for everyone and they start to tail off well before then.'

Mrs Baxter who ran an employment agency for twenty-five years says, 'What nannies are told at interview often turns out to be untrue.' The biggest cause of stress in nannies is when employers transgress their initial arrangements, particularly when it comes to the Big Four (see Chapter 2). It amounts to a denial of a nanny's rights when an employer chooses to welsh on a contract, written or otherwise. It is also the ultimate sign of your lack of respect for her professional status.

The Nanny Connection agency in London says its 'biggest beef is with parents who take advantage of time off. It is the nanny's day off and the mum says, "Can I just run down to the shops while the baby is asleep?" The nanny doesn't want to refuse. Three minutes later the baby wakes, three hours later mum returns.' It is quite interesting how disingenuously employers may phrase such unfair demands – they are well aware that they are putting the nanny in an impossible position. They have set up the request in such a way that she cannot say no without feeling mean.

It takes quite a lot of gumption for a young girl to say in response to the question 'You haven't got anything special on tonight have you?' 'Well, not special, but I put it in the diary a week ago that I was going out . . .' The naughty employers still persist: 'Oh right ... well do you mind awfully/just this once/my husband never usually gets back this early/we just want to go for a quick drink on the river....' At this point a nanny may agree to cancel *her* visit to the pub by the river, and it seems positively defiant for her to reply 'I'm sorry, but I need to take a break and get out of the house.'

This is just as bullying as bellowing at someone. Anyone would resent such trespass on their free time which makes them renege on arrangements and let friends down apart from being a dampener on the morale.

Even when the Big Four (see Chapter 2) are conscientiously adhered to, nannies may still not be happy with the reality of the arrangement that you agreed mutually. For example, the Nannies of Kensington agency says that in living-in jobs nannies always want more evenings off. It doesn't matter that they know they are obliged to do three or four evenings a week babysitting. That doesn't stop them wanting to go out more than they can. One Norlander explains that many nannies, including herself, never relax when they are in the family's house. For her, unless she had shut the front door behind her and was tripping down the path, she always felt she was on duty.

A natural victim of a family that always needs help is a nanny who has the misfortune to land an employer who is desperate without many hands to tend her children elsewhere. Her waking nightmare is to find herself alone with a child. Open any door in her house and there will be another starched uniform performing some duty. The mother is a mass of white silk and Worth by night, a vision in a mink bed jacket and a tangle of telephones till noon. She is always frantically busy having her toes/portrait/jacuzzi painted. She just hasn't a moment for her children, though the shih-tzus are spoilt rotten and as neurotic as she is. No wonder many nannies insist on working for parents who are out of the house all day.

Nannies' comments are particularly tolerant of their employers' neuroses, hang-ups and egocentricity, though a few naturally enough have pithy criticism of their behaviour. Many of them think that they and their friends are exploited, often not a lot, but nevertheless put upon.

> I get annoyed by their guilt feelings [sole charge] and their need to spoil the children and the lack of discipline.

> One family treated me like a piece of furniture and never considered my feelings at all.

> My employer is very untidy, she leaves her clothes all over the house, it drives me mad having to pick up her blouse in the playroom.

> My employers lack basic common sense, the father eats noisily and hates children, and the mother reads *The Hobbit* to her daughter aged four.

Symptoms of Friction

Employers' paranoia and the Lucan Solution

Employers do get neurotic. They fear that their nannies don't like them and are rude about them behind their backs. Sniggers stop as they enter, tearful phone calls to the parents abound, the air is filled with melancholy sighs and speaking silences, the Sit Vac page of every magazine is propped up on the coffee pot, and rather posh voices on the phone ask for Miss X. Employers' paranoia sets in.

Either this is all your fault, or she's making it feel that way for her own purposes. Your husband doesn't see as much of her as you do, so get his point of view on the evidence and ask him to tell you if you are going off your head. The Lucan Solution (remember he sought to solve domestic strife with murder and killed his nanny in error) threatens and the nanny is unaware that you have taken in all these details, and have been reduced to a gibbering wreck. She's sending out distress signals; you are ignoring them outwardly by virtue of your stiff upper lip and attempted maturity but you're crying inside too.

Your husband agrees that you are mad, 'but not to worry about it and do let's get some sleep. If I hear about that blessed girl again … oh for the day we won't need them any more.' Sure, but what about *now*? In fact, husbands can be tremendously helpful if they want. They can deal with potential potholes like pay, overtime or holidays. They can ask the nanny to be considerate/understanding/more sensitive. It is often easier for her to take this sort of thing from the husband rather than from the old hag.

Ring the agency which supplied her for advice, and don't hesitate to call the college that trained her. The three residential colleges encourage employers to ring them with their problems. Local authority college tutors are not meant officially to arbitrate and you can but try.

Snooping

At this point, several mothers confess that they have become obsessed by the need to have their suspicions confirmed. After a sleepless night, as soon as the nanny has taken the children out, the mother sneaks furtively to the nanny's room. Looking out for the full nappy bucket on the top of the door, which is luckily ajar, she enters the nanny's room and carefully, so as to escape detection, reads private letters and a diary and searches for any other incriminating signs. The waste paper basket is a magnet.

Snooping may take different forms – from eavesdropping to rooting through her personal belongings. Why is it done? Again there are many reasons. You may indeed need certifying; you may actually have nurtured a viper in your bosom (and very uncomfortable too); she may be a bit underhand (but not seriously so) or she may be on the move and is trying to let you know, albeit ineptly.

One mother felt that the nanny was acting oddly, but 'I couldn't put my finger on it. The only interesting item I found was a lesbian mag in the drawers under her bed. I had to keep checking for my own peace of mind and I used to go up once a week.' Diaries provide good ammo for the mother who suspects her nanny is conducting an affair under her roof. One employer was horrified to discover that her nanny had been having regular sex with her boyfriend in the house while on duty. According to the diary (which also sported gold stars as a score system recording each time she and her boyfriend made love), the tireless couple had climaxed sensationally on the landing outside the bathroom door while the children were in the bath.

One of the problems is what to do with these ill-gotten gains of insight? The person who can't face talking to a nanny normally about mutual problems is not likely to be any more capable of confronting her with the evidence of her wild sex life and explaining how she came by the information. Most find excuses, however lame, to sack forthwith.

Nannies snoop too, but more from nosiness than paranoia. They probably just want to get to know the nature of the beast.

Snooping is outrageous, unprofessional and the temptation to do so should be resisted. It is symptomatic of a badly conducted relationship which is close to divorce. Once again it speaks of a total lack of moral courage. Employers will not like themselves any better for resorting to such low conduct and ought to deal with each warning flare as it goes up. If a nanny sobs or sighs – ask her what is wrong. If she is silent and uncomfortable – ask her if she is happy and what you can do to help her. Don't let mountains grow out of molehills, discuss any problems. It may take an effort and a bit of grit, but employers must bite the bullet, deal with problems as they arise and not let them fester.

Sources of Friction

Unrealistic expectations and prejudices

Even after months, intractable employers and nannies may still cling to the stereotypes they first dreamt up for each other. This is particularly common when either employer or nanny is new to the game. A newly qualified nanny may have been told by other nannies, her tutor or her mother that employers are exploitative. Regardless of how the employer behaves, she may remain wary and untrusting. An experienced nanny may have encountered genuine exploitation and be once bitten, twice shy.

If she still selects the children's crockery and cutlery from the draining board, and leaves your cup and saucer, she is making a point. Enter your well-practised 'Let's have a chat' mode: compose your words, smile, and catch her eye. More like confrontation this time, as long as your conscience is clear that you are a good and fair employer. Say, 'What is the point you are making?' If the reply comes back like a Dalek: 'I-am-an-NNEB-I-do-not-wash up-for-my-employers,' you either accept this mean-spirited reaction and think the worse of her, or realize that this is what people mean when they talk about 'mucking in' in their advertisements, and resolve to include this elusive quality in *your* next ad. This by-the-book attitude does not make for happy give-and-take. After a time of you giving and her taking, you'll feel like an exploited employer and will have had enough.

Having said all this, many nannies do feel that this sort of nit-picking behaviour has to be resorted to as a desperate measure to stop employers taking advantage of them. Some employers never get beyond treating the nanny, or mother's help, as a resident slave, and even with employers who think they are fair, the nanny will find herself doing more and more, unless she takes a stand. One Australian notes acerbically, 'The English are up themselves. They will get you to iron their silk knickers if they can get away with it.'

Some nannies may set up in competition with the mother in several different ways. One mother says, 'If I have ever felt jealous of the nanny's relationship with my children, it is because I was intended to feel jealous.' Another says: 'Some nannies try to score off mummies.' A third comments 'I've not felt jealous much, well, perhaps a teeny weeny twinge once or twice.'

It is pretty much the employer's responsibility to discourage any nanny from usurping her role as a mother, housekeeper and social secretary. It is difficult if you are working to show a nanny proper appreciation if you are also feeling resentful that she has run your home, from dealing with the gas man to taking messages from your girlfriends. She may know more about your life at home than you do, and this makes some employers not just jumpy, but positively paranoid. This can stem from general feelings of guilt and wistfulness from which some working mothers suffer because they are not watching their child grow up in every tiny way.

The most unkind way that this guilt manifests itself is when a mother wants to deny the reality of leaving the house and the children in the care of someone else every day. She doesn't want to visualize or think about what goes on in her absence and therefore she ignores the nanny in an attempt to block out the importance of her contribution. Not surprisingly, the nanny becomes desperate for attention and tries to encourage the mother to read about her children's day in the log that she keeps for that purpose, and generally take an interest in their daily lives. The mother feels that the nanny is deliberately rubbing in the details of all she has missed, and is curt and dismissive. It must be soul destroying for a committed nanny to have to deal with such unbalanced behaviour.

Regardless of how incompetent/uninvolved/unloving/chaotic the nanny may think, or even know, her employer to be with the children, her training should have prepared her to care for them as their mother directs. One college principal instructs the girls to 'remember that parents' wishes should always be adhered to, even if you are horrified by the way a child is being brought up. Bide your time; gain their confidence; it is not possible to make an impact on a child's upbringing immediately.'

Both nannies and their employers agree that the nanny's contract or work agreement (see Chapter 17) cannot be prescient about the small details and coruscations which can make both sides unhappy. Either party may be irrational and nit-picking and the other will either have to live with it and kowtow to their foibles or tell them they can't stand whatever it is and they must change it. It is not the individual niggle that matters *per se*, but rather the cumulative effect, which, when allowed to snowball can metamorphose into a Sackable Offence. One Norlander tells us that, 'It is not the big issues that curdle a relationship; they are contracted for and discussed. It's just the petty things.'

There are stories of employers who wash eggs before cracking them, always keep leftovers (from bacon rind to half a cupcake) and recycle everything, refreeze the fish pie, pelt marauding cats with oranges from the top storey and insist that the nanny do so too. They ask her to say they're out when they're in, take a Fort Knox approach to locking every door, boil bathmats and flannels, and, as a child's tenth cold of the term starts, huddle the family under a huge towel to inhale Wright's Vaporizer and press the nanny to join them.

The nanny's problems: physical

Nannies' and mother's helps' health, diet and general ability to look after themselves effectively can cause considerable trouble to her employers. At the interview (see Chapter 4) you may have screened the nannies for anorexia, bulimia, epilepsy and any psychiatric problem. Amenorrhoea and dismenorrhoea mean respectively not getting periods and getting them painfully. Menorroghia is when a girl gets them very heavily. If your nanny suffers from any of these afflictions, take them seriously and insist that she sees a doctor. The sad thing is that, although she may be helped with treatment, it is quite possible that she has a long-term problem which may disqualify her from nannying.

You obviously will not be overjoyed to find that your nanny is out of action for two or three days a month or, almost as bad, when she complains loudly and moans about her period. It is most difficult if she is accustomed to retiring with pots of tea and hot water bottles. PMT (pre-menstrual tension) is a buzz word and can pro-

vide a good excuse for bone idleness. Alternatively it may be for
real and you should be sympathetic. Not easy, this one.

If, having talked to her, you feel she is making a fuss about the
whole subject, tell her you think so and that you would be glad if
she would take a couple of Panadol and get on with her life without involving everyone else. Mention that it helps communal
living if some things are private.

Another important aspect of health is diet. What, how, when
and where a nanny eats will tell you a lot about her. It will affect
you if she eats too much, too little, too often or finishes packets,
jars, the last tomato, crust, bit of paté/dolcelatte/chocolate ear-
marked for you or your husband. If she is prone to this sort of
thoughtlessness, suggest that she asks before swiping anything of
which there's not much left.

Nannies' and mother's helps' grumbles

- Not being paid on time
- Being given too short notice for babysitting
- Last minute change of plans
- Employers interfering with the nanny's handling of a child
- Employers cluttering up the kitchen/playroom,
  particularly while gassing with friends
- Employers not making up their minds
- Employers forgetting repeatedly to do something they said
  they would
- Employers getting drunk
- Employers shouting at and rowing with each other
- Employers saving up several grumbles and bringing them
  up unexpectedly
- Always running out of lavatory paper, cleaning aids
- Old, inefficient machines, e.g. vacuums
- Employers being mean with the heating in winter
- Having to leave everything tidy always

If you try to lend a willing ear to the nanny's latest attempts to
slim, it may pall when you watch her nightly flit to the chip shop
with her mates. Try not to be irritated; remember that she is young
and her good intentions will often fail, but you don't *have* to listen
to them. Say once, 'I have heard it all before and I'll only want to
hear again when you have lost three stone.' One mother bet her

nanny '£20 a stone and she lost three in no time'. Recommend .
Weight Watchers and let them monitor the progress if you are
plagued by a diet bore.

If you hired a fat nanny and she lacks energy and has a lazy outlook then that's too bad. If she gains weight noticeably while
working for you, then it should concern you and it needs to be discussed. Say you are worried about her health and wonder whether
her weight gain has been caused by too much children's tea or,
heaven forbid, bingeing at midnight from loneliness /unhappi-
ness/homesickness?

It is sensible to steer clear where possible of subjects like diet and
menstruation, because it can cause a confusion of roles; a professional nanny should not need a substitute mum or a new best friend,
so however fond you are of each other, deliberately distance your-

---

Employers' grumbles

- Not emptying the disposable nappy bin
- Pretending the nappy pail is infinitely expandable
- Not washing up immediately, entirely and thoroughly
  (employers are bad about this as well)
- Allowing thick dust and deep litter to gather in the
  children's rooms
- Allowing toys to get smashed or lost because they haven't
  been properly organized
- Not saying if the buggy/pram/high chair needs repairs
- Not dressing the children properly – grubby and/or
  unmended clothes, unpolished shoes, buttons hanging by a
  thread, inadequate clothing
- Children's unbrushed hair, dirty and uncut finger nails,
  tidemarks round the neck and behind the ears
- Unswilled, unrinsed, undisinfected and unscrubbed potties

---

self. Period pains are the kind of thing she can talk to friends and
family about. The insidious aspect of confidences is that they need
to be exchanged and the employer, who may be naturally reticent
about her personal affairs, can find herself making all kinds of revelations and, later, be cross with herself for having been too intimate.

Do not treat her as a teenage daughter, she may become one and
you will both resent it in the long run. One agent is well aware of
the converse problem: 'Some mothers depend on the company of

the nanny. They don't realize how much they rely on it until their kids go away to school. Then it's just as sad for them not to have a nanny around any longer as it is to have the children away. They can get quite depressed.'

Several mothers have been alarmed to hear their nannies refer to them as 'mummy'. It starts off with the nanny making it clear to the children who she is talking about, but can wind up with an employer wishing the ground would open and swallow her when the nanny calls her mummy in front of the milkman or granny. A few think the appellation is cosy.

A nanny who smells or has bad breath is a major horror for employers. The latter are deeply embarrassed and often don't know what to do about it. If they do not find the courage to talk to the girl about her problem, they stop spending much time with her, don't include her in family gatherings, and will shun her in many little ways. All this behaviour may be misinterpreted and cause extra stress all round.

Start the fresh air campaign with heavy hints. Open windows, stand well back, prime the children to mention it if they have already complained and you can rely on them not to cite you, give her soap, have a go at bringing the pomander back into fashion, and grab a clothes peg as she enters the room. Seriously though, you may already be searching for excuses to get rid of her on other grounds, because the stench has become unbearable and that for you has become a Sackable Offence.

Dread it as anyone does, compose your words and your smile, catch her eye, take a deep breath and say, 'I think I have noticed recently that you possibly aren't using enough deodorant? . . .' (Pause to check the effect of this thunderbolt. Has she twigged instantly that you are talking about her B.O. which she is acutely aware of? If not, and that blank expression is set, take another deep breath and blunder on.)

'It really matters to me that my nanny should smell nice and fresh. I do hope you don't mind me mentioning it, but we *really* need to sort this out together . . .' (Has it suddenly penetrated? Is she scarlet and sobbing? If so stop, mop her up saying that it's all going to be all right *now*.)

The reaction may be swift and unpleasant: don't be surprised if your careful phrasing has insulted her deeply and/or she can no longer look you in the face, and she tells you she's off. Many employers don't attempt to solve this problem, because of the high odds that she will resign. It is an upsetting subject and no fun for anyone to have to deal with.

The nanny's problems: professional

OVERLOAD AND UNDERLOAD

A nanny doesn't have to be physically ill to let the job get on top
of her, and the prudent long-term employer will be well aware of
periodic job dissatisfaction caused by overload and underload.
When you hear your nanny's voice becoming more shrill and less
patient with the children and she looks worn out, give the poor
girl a break. When she returns from her longer than usual weekend, sit her down and talk to her about how to deal with the problems. If she says she feels too busy to do anything properly, either
she needs a lecture on time and motion or she is overloaded, in
which case you must decide jointly where to prune her schedule.

The other side of the coin is underload. This can happen to nannies who are looking after just one baby or whose charges are
away at school for most of the day. She is lonely and bored (her
best friend may have just left for Canada), and she may do her relatively few tasks either inefficiently and lackadaisically or efficiently and thoroughly as usual. Either way, you must take action.
First, do a bit less yourself and think about ways to keep her occupied. Maybe her mornings could be spent with another family?
Would she like to start a playgroup or song and dance group with
a nanny friend to amuse your baby's local contemporaries? Or
maybe you haven't realized yet that you don't need a nanny any
more.

Both overload and underload can produce hypochondria.
Headaches, making heavy weather of heavy colds, flu and endless
upset tummies are all symptoms of the nanny needing a break or
planning a complete change of scene where your lovely home and
family do not feature.

Fitting in with the family

FATHERS

One lurking drawback to the family – and far too many nannies
discount his impact until too late – is the proud sire of her
charges. Although countless fathers are supportive, appreciative,
kind and helpful, many of them are the opposite and can be
boring, obstructive, humiliating and arrogant, and also can
undermine the sterling work their wives have put in to keep the
nanny with the family for that extra year. Some are genuinely dis-
tressing to a nanny.

Nannies are buoyant and sensibly dismissive of some types of dad. One's party piece for her friends is to take off her Hooray Henry employer preening himself in his Puffa jacket. He caught her at it once and 'his sense of humour could *just* take it'. One employer humiliated his nanny at a large lunch party by insisting that she sing 'that marvellous teddy song'. She refused but has never forgotten it.

One fat dad always came down to breakfast in his underpants. The nanny reports, 'I didn't know where to look in the mornings. I find it hard to talk to the man of any house, but it's worst when you see too much of them.' A mother's help remembers one horror who 'ate noisily and hated kids'.

During the nanny's first week fathers need to be reminded to be better about sharing the house. A score of nannies mention being burst in on by a dad wandering round the nanny's part of the house or flat. Some stopped being amused when he walked in on their ablutions too regularly with a stupid grin, and others were crosser still – with as much dignity as they could muster from the lavatory seat. If the poor wretched nanny can pluck up courage to mention his odd behaviour, a wife should not take umbrage but put locks on the door and insist that her spouse is more thoughtful in future.

One nanny had just got the children out of the bath and dressed, when she had to answer the phone. She returned to hang up the towels and let out the bath water to find a plump pink father waiting expectantly for her return. 'Will you scrub my back for me?' It's not so jokey if you are 18, it's your first job and you will need a good reference when you leave. On top of this his wife may well greet tales of mass bathtime with cold scepticism.

FAMILY ADDITIONS

Even something apparently simple, like a new baby that everyone is expecting, can cause a lot of change. The employer may be post-natally depressed, unexpectedly possessive and a bit dotty. Her husband may be moody or uncommunicative. The existing children will certainly react to the new arrival, who may present his own problems. The nanny is expected to show more initiative and do more. She may also have to cope with a maternity nurse, and possibly, if the mother is usually out of the house, the nanny has the added strain of getting to know her better and differently, for the first time.

Even though her extra duties were outlined in advance of the baby's arrival, the nanny may find the added workload exhausting and more than she expected. Many agencies mention the fact that

some NNEBs are loath to look after babies – they know it takes a
lot of time and effort and they do not like the restrictions of late
feeds and the general mess. One tutor on the Birmingham NNEB
course says that she 'would like to see more training on the course
in the 24-hour care of young babies'. Norlanders have an advantage in having had experience of this, but then even they are under
supervision.

Unless your NNEB has done this work before, don't rely on her
training and leave her in sole charge of a new baby. Employers are
frequently outraged to discover that their trained nanny doesn't
know what she should be doing with a new-born.

TEENAGERS

The major problem nannies may have is their inability to cope well
with the varying age groups of modern-day extended families. In
much-married clans the children may range from nine months to
19 years. An insecure nanny will not cope well with teenagers' lack
of respect and deliberate disruption of prescribed routines. Co-
existence is precarious, when a nanny is taunted by teenagers
whose prep they cannot understand. They have little in common
and can do each other quite a lot of ego damage. Much of the time
employers ask nannies to do things for teenagers that they should
be doing for themselves and nannies find the humiliation unbearable.

Employers should be aware of the probability of a clash between
nanny and teenagers and tell both that the nanny is not there to
service their requirements unless she chooses to do so. She should
not boss them about or control them at all, that is their parents' job.
When nannies are babysitting everybody at once, parents should
issue strictures directly to teenagers with dire threats of docking
pocket money if they muck her around. She will leave if you don't
back her up. When the inevitable conflagration threatens, remind
your semi-grown up children that they threaten *your* freedom by
their lack of cooperation with your domestic arrangements for 'the
little ones'. This makes you angry and they should understand that
stress levels will rise to the family's detriment.

GRANDPARENTS

The relationship between the employer and the grandparents will
set the tone of theirs with the nanny. Relaxed and loving grandparents enjoy their grandchildren and welcome the diversions and

fun they provide, and may often be a great source of support to mother and nanny in time of crisis. But a prolonged stay with the in-laws, particularly if enforced by unfortunate circs, may cause too much tension. Employers mention the following problems with grandparents during any length of stay:

> My mum is surprised that they have as much as two days off a week. In her day it was more like one a month and she often says so.

> My mother-in-law cannot understand why I need help. She had four children without any.

> They'll never get used to Christian names and no uniform. I keep nannies and grandparents as far apart as possible.

> I always hire an Australian temp to go with my children to their grandmother. Otherwise my nanny would leave me – no one could stand such barbed comments. I explain the difficulties, pay the earth and stay well away myself.

Most grandparents want to be involved with their grandchildren, but this does not give them the right to make life more difficult by interfering with your *modus vivendi* with the nanny. When she is staying with them along with the children, it is sensible to warn her of any old-fashioned views and foibles. It is probably also a good idea to prime your mother to curb her tongue and let the nanny do it her way unless she is floundering. In fact, if they are both told to live and let live, and that the other 'can be exasperating', then the chances are they will get on splendidly and even strike up a sort of friendship.

The best grannies have been trained to say: 'Young families today work harder and need all the help they can get' and they will not wish to rock the boat, but be supportive.

Change

Any psychiatrist will comment that change is stressful. Nannies and employers don't find it as good as a rest because it involves changes of job description.

MOVING HOUSE

One employer complains bitterly that her nanny resigned rather than move house with the family. This seems unreasonable. If anyone's job relocates it is not taken for granted that the employees move without a murmur. Indeed, they can be offered redundancy.

Moving house is a terrific strain on everyone. Builders can cause unforeseen horrors. You may have to find an interim place to live. It might be a cramped flat, a damp cottage in the country, or with the grandparents. New thinking, instructions and discussions – in short, complication.

YOUR VISITORS AND FRIENDS

Grandparents, step- and half-brothers and sisters, visiting cousins and friends and ex-wives or husbands may all come to stay – some for a long time and, on occasion, for ever. Inevitably, this will mean more work for the nanny. Do recognize the impact this has on her job description, and talk about it before she approaches you. Encourage friends who leave hordes of children at your home to tip her generously. If a step-child who is an irregular feature of your life comes to stay for the holidays increase the carer's salary for the duration, unless you genuinely intend to take on the extra work yourself.

If you take the nanny on holiday, or to stay with friends, you'll be lucky if she can handle the change professionally and allow you to enjoy it too. Staying in other people's houses means that temporarily the nanny is living by someone else's House Rules as well as carrying yours around in her luggage, and gains another boss to boot. This can lead to trouble. One nanny says, 'We went away to stay with friends of my employers. The lady sent me out to the kitchen and treated me like a little nobody worth nothing. She told me I could probably find "something in the fridge" if I was hungry. She went on treating me bad all that weekend.' Whether the hostess was being off-hand or was just flustered by the numbers she had to feed, this is a good example of unhappy weekending.

By the by, weekend and holiday exposure to your friends and the ways that they treat their nannies are familiar trouble spots. Do not have post-mortem chats with your nanny unless they are entirely complimentary. To pre-empt the possibility of your good nanny picking up bad habits from a friend's sloppy one, drop a little hint that you *did* notice Mandy forcing lettuce down a child's throat with a fork, so you mentioned it to her employer, your friend. End of conversation.

DIVORCE AND REMARRIAGE

Divorce, separation and remarriage affect nannies greatly and that's an understatement. If they don't like it, they won't lump it

and off they'll go. Some will stay because they take to the new partner or lack of one, and others stay just long enough to tide you
over the initial upheavals. This is extremely obliging, particularly if
they aren't mad about the new regime and probable extra responsibility. The least you can do is to pay them more.

It is reasonable to expect a nanny to adapt readily to temporary
changes. But how long is temporary? If you want to keep her,
make her feel part of your plans, give her extra time off and don't
be arrogant enough to assume that she will go along with all you
do uncomplainingly. It's fundamental to any job that you check
out employers before working for them. If the nanny's boss leaves
her partner or swaps one for another, the nanny may wish to
reassess her position. If her parents get divorced or remarry, similarly expect her to be affected and try to make it possible for her to
spend more time at home for a while.

DEATH

Death is difficult to deal with for everyone concerned. Obviously
an employee must be given time off to attend any relative's funeral,
and she would be required to drop her plans and help you in similar circumstances. If an employer has a wasting disease, or develops a disability, the nanny will be in the extraordinarily awkward
position of deciding whether to abandon the family, or stay on and
risk martyrdom. Try and make it easy for her. Tell her your hopes
and fears without any pressure on her to do what would suit you
best. Spell it out that she is not to feel she must stay and also, that
life will be very different from now on.

The death of a child – or even a terminal illness or grave injury –
may be more than your nanny can cope with. In these circumstances, many nannies do leave and they can't be blamed in any
way for wanting to get away. Like falling off a horse, a nanny might
come to terms with her sadness and shock (and misplaced guilt on
many occasions), if she lived through the grief with the sad family,
but that's her decision. A cot death is uniquely traumatic.

It is embarrassing at one level for a nanny to find herself unable
to work happily with a recently bereaved employer, who may be
unapproachable and withdrawn in his or her grief. More compli-
catedly still, if the wife dies, the nanny has suddenly to deal with,
in effect, a new employer in the widower. He'll be a novice at the
job and may not have much idea about anything domestic.

If you discover that your real need now is for a responsible
housekeeper or more mature carer for your children, explain

gently to the nanny that because the situation has changed so completely she should find another job. She will probably be relieved you brought it up first.

A NEW SIDE

Both employers and employees may reveal a 'new side' of themselves after several months or years of employment. This 'new side' may result from historic problems which emerge or re-emerge in a new form, or are thrust upon either party by fate or an act of God. A 'new side' is almost always a darker side.

Employers' problems which may impose on the nanny include: alcoholism and attempting to stay on the wagon (imagine her having to listen to a drunk dad beating up his wife and wondering what to do if he starts on the children next); unemployment (so she may be stuck with a depressed hulk under her feet who is keen to help with the children now and again); nervous breakdowns and recuperating from illnesses can also keep employers at home unexpectedly and require attention and effort; very pregnant mothers who have given up work to have their baby and who interfere with the status quo.

None of these events are likely either to have been predicted, or their possibility to have been revealed at interview. In other words, circumstances do change. And for nannies too.

You may discover too late that the nanny's reportedly happy family life is tragically the opposite. One mother mentions her nanny's revelation on the doorstep, having been sacked for losing her temper repeatedly with the children, that she had been abused by her father as a teenager and this had made her cruel, she thought.

The 'social smoker' of six months ago may turn into a smoke stack. The glass of wine in the evenings may become an empty vodka bottle in her waste paper basket and, you note with growing alarm, that there weren't any friends to share it with last night. The quiet, controlled admonition to the children has turned into a harridan's shriek and the neighbours are complaining. The shrinking violet of yesteryear is only reflected in her electric purple boob tube (and how *they've* grown, as your husband remarks nonchalantly . . . daily), and you recognize with a sinking heart that men and the discos beckon.

A frightening 'new side' to the carer may be in drug use. One agency reports that when they rang to check that the nanny was getting on well with the family, the grandmother was irate. 'Getting

on well? I should think not indeed! I sacked her myself within
days of her arrival. I came in from shopping and found the new
nanny rolling about on my daughter's bed with an Irish labourer
who was meant to be wallpapering and there were hypodermics all
over the place. I look after the children now so no one has to see
those kind of disgusting things again.'

But there is a lighter side, and employers were interesting in
their general consensus that nannies' and mother's helps' confidence grew in the job. But, as one mother reported, 'Of course, any
20-year-old changes a lot in a year in new circumstances, so expect
it and hope for the best.'

Remember the House Rules?

You have either forgotten about these by now (in which case turn
back to Chapter 2) and that is why you have friction problems, or
the nanny has adhered to the whole bunch of House Rules up until
now and things are beginning to slip. This may start to happen at
three or six months or any time thereafter. She is probably not
doing it to test your memory, the restrictions are just getting to her.

Decide with your mate whether you mind maintaining your
carefully constructed edifice of strictures as continued self-
defence. You may want to rethink certain aspects of them. For
example, you may now feel secure that you have netted a real
goodie – a responsible nanny with a ton of energy who is well
capable of getting up at 7 am after arriving home at 1 am or later.
So, don't let this rule slide, giving her good reason to think that all
the rules were a hollow show of strength at the start. Tell her that
you noticed that she came in later than you both agreed last night,
but that you have thought about it and have decided to trust her
judgement about her bedtime for the time being. Does she think
this is a good idea and she won't abuse it, will she? This is good
gamesmanship and it is fun to be seen to be generous and it didn't
cost you a thing. Nice one, Cyrilla.

It is worth saying that the best nanny/employer relationships
seem to be based on a good deal of give and take. Nannies are great
ones for not sticking to what their agencies, colleges or bolshie
friends insist are their rights – if they like you and you are clearly
not out to exploit their kindness, they will want to do many little
extras for you. In return, after praise and thanks, next time you can
show her that you really appreciate her flexibility, and it will be
your turn to be more easy-going as well, and if she has any sense
she won't take advantage of you either.

If all the House Rules are being bent and broken all over the shop and you haven't had the energy to enforce them for a month, don't put off the day of reckoning any longer. Either she lives the way you want under your roof or she goes. Unless you have changed too and anything she wants has become the rule. This is popularly described as 'trusting her totally'.

Quite how an employer can misjudge a character totally after months of living with someone is illustrated by the mother who liked and trusted her nanny implicitly. She allowed her to have friends to stay; she could go anywhere in the house; she was left in sole charge of the children while the parents went on holiday. So imagine the mother's horror when her bank manager queried some strange-looking cheques. It emerged that this much prized nanny had been adding noughts to her salary cheque and had forged her boss's own cheques. In all she had embezzled £3,000. Her employer was flabbergasted. Although history doesn't relate, it might be argued that this nanny was not a natural law breaker. She was just tempted by the ease of access to her employer's cheque book and could resist anything except temptation.

The epitome of a disaster nanny is summarized briskly: 'Over several months she broke in to the wine cellar, hid the empties in the various loo tanks, flooded the house, and fled with the best jewels, leaving the children unattended.' Employers may be forgiven on occasion for thinking that they cannot win. It is just a matter of how badly they lose.

Finding Solutions

Louise Davis of Norland advises her students to: 'Be sponge-like, absorbent. Recognize the kicking the cat syndrome. You've got to be fairly tough-skinned and ignore someone being curt at the end of a long day. It is not aimed at you.' For the average nanny this is pretty grown-up stuff. Many employers assume too much *savoir faire* on the part of their nannies. They forget that the young are often gauche, crass, shy, easily embarrassed and sensitive to humiliation.

Employers love to think that they 'shoot straight from the hip' and 'tell it like it is' with 'no holds barred' to 'clear the air' or 'have it out' – in other words, nothing short of a stand-up fight with their nanny or mother's help. This is bullying, self-indulgent and rude, though entirely human. The cathartic effect will be short-lived and if she answers back, you have real problems.

Although your attack may have been caused by over-reaction to a misdemeanour which affected the children, you have no right to shout at someone. You may deeply upset a young nanny by such behaviour. Remember that this would be most unlikely to happen in an ordinary job. Also, once you have rushed in and blown your top, there is no room for manoeuvre or face-saving if mitigating circumstances later emerge. After all, your whimsical husband *may* have given the go-ahead to some daft scheme. A salutary reminder is provided by one nanny who says, 'Any employer who's rude to an employee risks losing them. Most employers treat you badly at some time; I've learned never to let them do it twice.'

Even if nannies mean to be polite, they sometimes get it wrong as far as the employer is concerned. Many an employer is genuinely hurt when having taken trouble and given the girl a beautiful birthday present, or announced a handsome pay rise, she hears (just) a mumbled 'thanks' in response. And that's all she does hear about it.

Another obvious example of unintentional rudeness is when a nanny brings her friends to your house and you meet them in the hall. They advance crab-like, talking to each other over their shoulders and ignoring you. Finally the employer plucks up courage to say a tentative 'hello'. They barely respond. In time she will see how you make a point of introducing your friends to her and with any luck get the message. If she doesn't and it bugs you, tell her.

Don't think of it as confrontation. Try not to churn half the night or victimize your husband. Deal with the problems the moment they emerge. Do not ruminate or bore the mothers on the school steps or your colleagues at lunch; just say what is bothering you to the person to whom it matters, and try and teach her to do the same.

Don't forget to *listen* to what your nanny or mother's help has to say. It can be effective to say as little as possible to start with, hear her out. This way you learn a lot quickly. It also gives you time to prepare your response. Try to see the problem from her point of view. Why is she so fed up/cross/irritated? Be alert to what she is *not* saying. Often the unsaid may provide the clue to solving the problem.

When in doubt about a moan or a request, buy time. Before thinking about the query at all say automatically, 'Ah, I'll have to think about that/ask my husband/check in the diary.' The carer should use the same ploy too when she is being asked a favour or being asked to change her plans. If you have said yes to some plan and you later regret it, don't hesitate to say, apologetically, that on further reflection you have changed your mind.

Social graces are at a premium between employer and employee, especially with a living-in nanny. Many employers fail to have them at times when annoyed by their nannies. In spite of your natural desire to remonstrate in indignant tones, it is actually more productive not to sound cross and overbearing. If you can do it with a smile so much the better. Like Scott and Oates in the Antarctic, the need for self-sacrificing tolerance and courtesy is great. When the going gets tough, the habit of good manners will rescue you from ranting and raving regrettably.

Employers often moan about their nannies and mother's helps not showing enough initiative. Try not to be put out if she has done something off her own bat for once, but it is not quite how you would have tackled the problem. Try to praise her as enthusiastically as you can. Once bitten she'll be shy of doing anything similar again.

The art of saying what's wrong

Whatever happens, try to issue instructions and admonitions pleasantly. It isn't always easy to smile when you are in a hurry, frothing with fury or just plain tired, but it makes so much difference. It's a vicious circle; the nanny does something important wrong again, the employer has said it with a smile several times before and she doesn't want to give her a ticking off but feels she must, so she becomes tense, her brow furrows and in a strangled voice she deals with the whole thing badly. Rather than risk an eruption which you will regret and anyway could have been better phrased, (and that can be just as tiresome after the event), go somewhere else, think quietly about it, let time pass and compose your features into some semblance of sanity before tackling the subject once more.

Mrs Davis tells her students to start their complaints or gripes with the words 'I feel' or 'I prefer' or 'It upsets me when' and this is a sophisticated defusing device. An employer can take a leaf out of her book. When a nanny says 'I thought you said' or 'I didn't think you'd mind if', take a deep breath and then put her straight, politely. Some mothers report their paralysis when it comes to asking their nannies not to do something in a particular way, as well as general instructions. Such phrases as 'I wonder if you would mind?', 'Do you think you could?', 'It would be so marvellous/terrific/helpful/kind/useful if', 'Would you be an angel/duck/dear/pal and . . .', 'I'd be so grateful for . . .' , do help to oil the wheels. This gush helps a nanny feel that she's not being got at and/or merely the recipient of a string of orders.

Don't get too subtle by cloaking your every need/wish/command in this way. She may interpret such flannel as you not meaning what you say. If she thinks you said 'It would be nice if you did X, but I'm not bothered if you don't get round to it today', then you overdid it. One parent admits to 'gabbling nervously and burying the instruction in the middle of a stream of chat'. In this case, the girl may well miss the instruction.

Eye contact means just that. Don't save up all your criticisms for long journeys where you can look straight ahead for hours, and don't issue instructions with your head in a broom cupboard. Two mothers reveal that these are their favourite venues for a ticking off. Closet employers will find that this cowardice is impractical and self-defeating. Apart from shopping lists and written reminders, don't resort to memos. Blasts should be delivered personally. Just as you ought not to yell, so you mustn't write hate mail to the top floor. This verges on the loony, but lots of people do it. If you find it therapeutic and it orders your mind, write it down, have it around for a few hours, but throw it away eventually.

Employers who wish to remain calm and reasonably happy with their nanny *have* to be tolerant and remember that they can't change a personality and turn it into a robot that mind reads and doesn't answer back. They indulge in too much ascribing of blame. Employers, like nannies and everyone else, find it difficult to admit they are in the wrong.

Postscript

It may be helpful to remind employers that the five stages of any project are popularly held to be:

1   Enthusiasm
2   Disillusionment
3   Panic
4   Search for the guilty
5   Punishment of the innocent

Try to be the kind of employer who recognizes that we are all human. Second chances given your nanny's youth and probable immaturity should be considered, unless she has done something that is *totally unacceptable*. Find out exactly why and how things went wrong, talk about it, sleep on it, and see if it won't suit both of you best if you forgive her. Remember priorities. The children may love her and she may be conscientious and kind to them; you are made of sterner stuff than they are.

Chapter 10
Maternity Nurses

Maternity or 'monthly' nurses are often an employer's first experience of having a nanny in the house. There is serious confusion among some parents about what a maternity nurse is: many think that she has a special qualification in the care of newborns. This is rarely the case; nearly all maternity nurses are just experienced nannies. However, a maternity nurse has specific functions and is specifically treated.

Are They Worth It?

What's the point of having one? Opinion is sharply divided about maternity nurses; people either think that they are an indispensable part of the first few weeks of a baby's life or they can't imagine anything more idiotic and intrusive than employing one because they want to do everything for the baby themselves. One SRN mother says: 'I'm far too bossy to want anyone else and I always breast feed for months, so why bother?' And another: 'I didn't realize I'd feel so possessive; I couldn't bear anyone but Chris [her husband] and me to touch her. Next time I'll just hire an extra pair of hands to do the chores.'

Mrs Baxter, who used to run the eponymous agency in Peterborough, felt just that way with her five babies and says that there is far too much pressure on young mums from their friends to have maternity nurses. She reckons that they interfere unacceptably and that people should ignore such a silly fashion and have faith in their maternal instincts. She preferred to provide 'confinement helps' as an alternative – they walked dogs and other children, cooked, and helped do any odd jobs which you dread, leaving the mother free to look after the baby herself.

Nevertheless, many employers are sold on the whole idea. New mothers, especially those who want to be fit and well and back at their desks swiftly, say they appreciate a crash course in babycraft (or indeed a refresher course if there is a sizeable gap between the new arrival and its sibling). They also like the peace and rest that is made possible by the extra help.

One devotee claims maternity nurses are 'a treat that everyone should try and afford. She makes an enormous difference to the happy running of the house, and yours and the baby's peace of mind.' Another confesses, 'I feel at a low emotional ebb having had a baby and need the comfort of someone else in full control. Not everyone can give birth in the paddy fields or behind a bush and get up and go straight on as though nothing had happened. Some of us have caesars and they need a lot of recovering from.' A third says, 'I wanted each baby to have that special care and attention that I would not have the strength to give them having just returned from hospital.'

A few mothers say that they always return to their mums after their babies, or their mums come to them to help out. One maternity nurse appreciates this need and says 'to be any real use, we must be a lot like their mothers'. Some families' old nannies come out of retirement to deal with any new baby born to the family, its cousins and occasionally old friends.

You can claim on BUPA or PPP for the fees if your maternity nurse is an SRN or a registered midwife and if you have had a caesarean or other complications at birth.

What sort do you want?

Different types of maternity nurses fall roughly into two categories: old and experienced, or young and inexperienced. With a first baby most mothers are reassured by someone extremely experienced, organized and disciplined to teach them all about the baby. Many maternity nurses admit to far preferring the simplicity of the first time around. 'The best thing in the world is working with a first baby. Both parents are starry-eyed, all the equipment is new. There's such magic with number one.'

With later babies, it is more important that the maternity nurse is friendly and relaxed with the other children, and, though she is unlikely to give you much help with them, she should be prepared to include them in walks and bath-times and teach any nanny already in residence the ropes, so that the takeover will be smooth.

Good heavens, whatever next? A maternity nurse when you've already got a nanny? You must be mad/rich/spoilt, your in-laws may say. Ignore them, they haven't got to deal with the nanny becoming too exhausted from night duty with the baby to be pleasant to the other children during the day. But you certainly need someone who will deal tactfully with your nanny and not put her nose out of joint. This is a common problem exacerbated by the maternity nurses' characteristic grouse that young nannies don't work hard enough nowadays and they may say so too often and too loudly. This sort of professional competitiveness is tiresome; don't let the maternity nurse stir up trouble.

Some old nannies say that present-day NNEBs are snobby about their lack of training and one comments: 'I make sure I never cross swords with them. I know how to conduct myself. I just think, I'll keep off the grass with you my dear, and I am pleasant but never intimate with them.'

Many people are wary of traditional 'old-style' maternity nurses. The employment agencies often concur. One warns: 'I'm not doing maternity any more because too many of the old ones are a bit mental and I could never persuade them to retire before they became a liability. It was so awkward and cruel to be saying constantly that I didn't have any jobs for them, but it was the only safe thing to do.' Another reports: 'They are very nanny-knows-best and try to pressurize mothers to bottle feed so that they have complete control.' The last states: 'The old dears are complete pains in the neck. All the mothers think they are ghastly and even if someone dies in the house, their attitude is as long as the baby's OK that's not their business.'

Christine Hill, an obstetric physio who runs excellent ante- and post-natal classes from her house on the river in Chiswick (see Useful Addresses), says that her mums 'are frightened of them and the babies probably are too. The young ones may create an uncomfortable feeling of the blind leading the blind, but anything is preferable to living with a battle-axe.'

There are too many horrifying stories of old maternity nurses who are over the hill and don't know it for employers' and agencies' reactions to be hot air. The point is that if you choose a mature and experienced maternity nurse you will be well-advised to make sure that she is fit in wind and limb and capable of doing her job professionally, and looking after *you*,which is part of it.

Both employers and agencies agree that the good maternity nurses are like gold dust and a bad one is such a nightmare that you are better off doing the job yourself.

How long before the birth should you find one?

Everyone is agreed that about nine months' warning of the baby's arrival will already be too little notice to net the best maternity nurses. They are snapped up the moment the little poached egg shows up on the pregnancy DIY kit and the wise mother will interrupt her 'gynae's' speech of congratulations to ask if she may use the phone to book her special treasure.

One mother whose baby arrived a month prematurely and thus neatly evaded the dates for which the maternity nurse had been booked, hired a replacement from her hospital bed. 'It was incredibly lucky. She was much better than the one I'd planned to have, whom I'd had before.' Most people are not so fortunate.

Where do you get them?

The grapevine hums with news of gems: 'My dear, she refused to take a minute off for three weeks and even the dog got breakfast in bed.' One maternity nurse has been employed exclusively by word of mouth recommendation for 12 years and says: 'Employers can check up on me with their friends. But I can also check up on them. It works both ways.'

Don't automatically assume that because X and Y like someone that you necessarily will too. You may discover entirely different attitudes in dealing with the baby, your husband, your fridge, other children, granny and a host of other details which make her entirely unsuitable for your family. Someone else's old nanny, however much revered by 'her' family, may not prove in the least good news as far as you are concerned. Having employed her, which everyone insists is a huge favour to you whatever the price, you may fall out with old friends if you decide that she is a self-opinionated old bag who needs a constant audience.

The grapevine occasionally contains a bad apple who continues working for 'everyone' by a sort of Emperor's New Clothes con trick combined with years of Chinese whispers. Someone once said she was fantastic, so no one along the line explodes the myth. If you do, you'll find several people back along the chain of recommenders who gave her glowing refs but readily concur with your criticisms of her shortcomings. They didn't want to be the first to mar the dossier and probably thought something was wrong with *them* for not liking her.

Several of the employment agencies (see Chapter 18) have maternity nurses on their books, and one, Pembroke Maternity Service, is run only for maternity nurses by an extremely experienced and well-qualified ex-maternity nurse. The agency is small with a nucleus of highly trained old-style nannies, but can also provide young trained nurses too. You can also advertise in *The Lady*.

What do they cost?

The range in the early 1990s seems to be from £220 to £450 a week. There are also daily maternity nurses who charge about £45 a day. They all pay their own insurance and National Insurance contributions because they are self-employed.

Maternity nurses to twins must be some of the most heroic women on earth. They command the highest salaries and may safeguard your sanity in the first weeks of unrelenting bawling and feeding, burping and changing. Employers of these martyrs are pathetically grateful for their calm and confident support. 'We would never have lived through it without her' and 'She made us see that there would eventually be light at the end of the tunnel' and 'always a gentle smile for each little face at 3 am – what a saint!' Don't haggle if it means losing one of these. It is uniquely hard work, and if you have just performed the miracle of multiple birth no one needs a good maternity nurse more than you do.

Payment is obviously negotiable, but if she does not start on the day on which she was booked, because the baby is late arriving, or you are stuck in hospital with complications of whatever kind, you must be prepared to pay her at least half pay for the first week of waiting and, after that, full pay even if she has not started.

Many maternity nurses complain that employers are extremely mean about this. The 'waiting' period is a grey area as far as payment is concerned and employers must resist the temptation to take advantage of this and not pay the nurse properly while she waits for you and the baby to do what you said you would do, and she is unable to earn her living elsewhere in the meantime.

Many Australian and New Zealand nurses do maternity work and are attracted to the high wages which enable them to travel soon after they have saved enough cash. No one would argue that it is money for jam, given that the restrictions of keeping a baby's hours preclude any social life during a job.

How much time off?

When your maternity nurse has worked for you for a week she is entitled to 24 hours off each week. She is on duty 24 hours a day.

How long will you need one?

> Four weeks is the ideal time . . . don't hand over so completely that
> you are scared to death of her leaving and haven't a clue what to do
> with the baby because she hasn't let you touch it since birth.

> Six weeks. Both times.

> She stayed on for two years because she fell in love with the baby and
> then the gardener, whom she eventually married.

> We sacked her after three days; she was a tiresome old woman who
> drove me up the wall and it was mutual.

Some maternity nurses understandably don't want to do such concentrated work stints for longer than a month, though others
prefer the continuity of an extended stay. There is no ideal length
of stay; it depends on each individual and how much you are the
victim of hormonal upheavals and emotional exhaustion,
demanding husband or jealous children. Some mothers feel they
need protracted support at this time.

What exactly does she do?

The Pembroke Maternity Service issues some guidelines to an
employer entitled 'The Duties of a Maternity Nurse'.

> The maternity nurse is a professional whose responsibility is the wel-
> fare of the mother and baby. This is a 24-hour-a-day job. She is not a
> domestic servant for family cooking, cleaning, washing and ironing,
> nor is she responsible for the care of other children in the family.
> She is responsible for guidance and help in all aspects of feeding
> together with teaching a convenient routine to you and the baby. She
> is responsible for the tidiness and cleanliness of her room, the baby's
> room, the nursery bathroom and the nursery kitchen. All the baby's
> washing and ironing and care of clothes is also her responsibility. She
> will undertake simple nursing care of the mother if necessary and will
> advise on a suitable diet for breast feeding mothers. She will ensure
> that you get as much rest as possible throughout her stay so that you
> are 'back on your feet' by the time she leaves. Meals are normally
> taken with the family and, when possible, she will offer to help.

Agents and mothers agree that you should never employ a maternity nurse without a proper interview at home before the birth.
You should do this well in advance. If you are a first-time mother,
ask her to give you a shopping list for the baby. She is bound to like
particular brands and have preferences for special items of kit, so

you may as well humour her. If you have done all the shopping for a previous baby, show her what you have done already and make sure she uses it and doesn't utter a word of disapproval. Some maternity nurses despise disposables. Old-fashioned nannies also don't like baby-gros. They love beautiful shawls and long nighties and hand-knitted cardigans which they handwash far into the night as obsessively as Lady Macbeth.

Show her where she is going to sleep and how much other space you can allot to her in the house. Many maternity nurses do sleep with the baby, but if they do, then it's specially important to give them somewhere else to sit in the evenings.

Ask the maternity nurse about her qualifications, where she trained and *always* check references. Does she smoke? Talk about whether you want to demand feed or 'get the baby into a good routine'. Does this mean that she recommends you leave the baby to yell all night/at all? A very few take the toughest possible line and just shut the door and let the baby cry at night without going near it: one mother says she had to sack one devotee of this Draconian discipline for a week-old baby – both she and her husband cracked on the first night and asked the nanny to leave immediately.

Will she support you if you hope to breast feed? Sometimes a maternity nurse will come and wake you with a sweet-smelling baby and you return it to her to be burped and settled, while you snuggle down next to your burrowing husband, or she wakes you and you go and join her. Will you have the baby between you in bed or on the floor beside you in a basket or elsewhere? All these details will inform her what sort of mother you will be to work for. Any information you can give her about what you do and don't like will help prevent stress after the baby's birth, when you may be feeling exhausted and intolerant.

How much do you think you will want to be looked after? Breakfast in bed? One agent says, 'No one wants to be running around with trays for every meal, but to provide coffee and tea to mothers is common courtesy.' Some nannies can be bossy. Decide if you can stand it. Some people positively welcome it, find it relaxing and consistent with their recent institutionalization in hospital and thrive under the nurse's strict regimes.

All the rules are for your own good; it's just a question of whether you will agree to being dictated to or have an uneasy feeling that you are old enough to make up your own mind and the nanny may be overly enjoying her ability to do that job for you. They may enforce rest in the afternoons, refuse visitors, deny your relations a peep at the baby which could unsettle its routine and even prevent you from driving for the first three weeks or so.

This last injunction concerns post-natal amnesia and general dottiness, which is quite as common as depression but much less talked about and is, of course, impossible to quantify in advance of the birth. Hormonal changes can cause debilitating worry to any woman at this stage; to be cherished by a good maternity nurse can provide a wonderful bridge with reality. One mother describes the process as a 'need to grow back a hard shell or a new skin if you will. I do feel entirely vulnerable for several weeks after having had a baby.'

Talk to the maternity nurse about what sort of care she intends to provide for you and set clear demarcation lines of duty between her and the existing nanny if there is one and likewise the cleaning lady. Who will wash and iron your nighties? You may be glad of clean ones daily when you arrive home.

A maternity nurse will usually expect to be treated as a member of the family. One says: 'If employers don't feel they can eat with me then they shouldn't have me.' A peculiarly intimate relationship may develop so that you may feel the need 'to pour your soul out' as another put it. But maybe you will be quite yourself after the birth and that self will be as resilient and organized as ever and the last thing you will feel like doing is having to talk to a maternity nurse.

If there are separate catering arrangements for your existing nanny, it can be difficult to make an exception to the House Rules for the maternity nurse. Use your judgement having met and sized-up both individuals, but don't on any account be bullied into something you won't be comfortable with. Remember the remote possibility of skinlessness and be resolute now.

Young maternity nurses may not be fully conversant with the proper means of sterilizing bottles, because they have always had made-up bottles to give babies in hospital during their training. One agent says this causes so many complaints that she recommends that the mother show the maternity nurse precisely how she wants it done.

Any professional maternity nurse will recognize the need for the new mother and father to be alone, both with the baby and without. One old hand says, 'Some fathers get embarrassed if I watch them kissing and cuddling the baby, specially if it's a boy, so I always melt away.'

The Pembroke Maternity Service insists that their maternity nurses wear some kind of uniform, even if just a tabard, partly so they are treated like professionals and partly to guard against the risk of infection.

Agree the terms, the time off, the pay, and the exact day you want to start hiring her. Most mothers say that they like the nurse to arrive at home before her return from hospital to set everything out and bully the husband into turning up the heating or generally making the house babyworthy. Some ask her to come to the hospital to collect the mother and thereby attempt to avoid a sibling's instant jealousy by letting the maternity nurse be the one who fusses over the new baby at the start and introduces it into the household, leaving the mother free to be warm and loving with the other child/children.

One maternity nurse was funny about the problems of jealousy in the first few weeks.

> Lots of dads hardly come near me or the newborn. They find the baby's arrival very messy and traumatic and strange and don't know how to react at all. The odd thing is that dad is invariably ill during the first month, just a little toothache or feeling a bit off-colour, but it's always because he doesn't feel he really has a role to play and wants a bit of extra attention.
>
> I don't encourage them to stay at home for these imagined ills. I pack 'em off back to the office and am a bit brisk to protect the mums. No more trouble from *you*, I say quietly and they look at me in surprise like naughty boys.

Some maternity nurses are queasy about circumcision and particularly request not to work in families where it is the norm. This is coupled with complaints from maternity nurses that many mothers are exploitative. This means, by their definition, being asked to walk dogs, do the household cleaning, washing and ironing, being expected to clean out grates, look after the toddler, and make family meals. Then, they say, this type of employer has the nerve to quibble about the agreed salary and time off. Don't earn a maternity nurse's disapproval unless you want them to leave you holding the baby, which they certainly will do, and with the full backing of their agency. Unless *they* offer to do anything other than the baby, you should not demand it as of right.

This is far from saying that many maternity nurses are not immensely obliging and helpful in a million uncalled-for ways, as many mothers report:

> She reorganized my store cupboards and did everyone's mending which had piled up over five years.

She arranged flowers terrifically well and was sweet to my invalid aunt who lived next door.

She was a gem and a strong gem to boot. She pulled a box spring double bed through a first storey window and moved loads of furniture with my husband.

One maternity nurse who has worked with babies for 30 years says:

I like parents who love and enjoy their children. I am happiest when it is easiest to leave knowing that the baby will be happy and secure and its needs considered unselfishly . . . I like an interesting, relaxed atmosphere, reasonable space and light and a grandmother's house in a pretty part of the country.

Maternity nurses are understandably driven mad by 'flighty mums who insist on breast feeding but refuse to express and then go out shopping or for a lunch date. They arrive back so late that the baby is screaming and impossible to settle and I feel much the same way.' 'Some new mothers are so silly; in the end they force me to make rules, so it is better to start with a few,' says another.

One mother wonders why maternity nurses ever do the job: 'It is an odd life. One minute she is so much needed and wanted and so close to the family and the next off she goes somewhere else and is virtually forgotten within weeks.' One maternity nurse of many years' experience replies: 'At long last I have discovered the depth of my feelings for these little scraps and why. I love them desperately and they never push you away nor make you feel unwanted and neither hurt nor reject you by look or by touch. I'm very secure in my baby world with each baby individually looked after by me and I really feel loved in return.' Many others simply reply, 'I just love/adore/am crazy about babies.'

Finally, the seeds of the relationship between mother and maternity nurse may grow into a lifetime of reminiscences for the whole family. Several maternity nurses report that they have been invited to be godmothers and/or are always invited to the christening, usually back on duty for the day. There is a special toast to her at the celebration afterwards and the treasured photos live in serried ranks round the maternity nurse's sitting room at home. Most employers say that their children always receive first birthday cards from the maternity nurse, and they particularly look forward to her visits so that they can hear the old stories again about how they behaved at three weeks at 3 am in the morning.

Chapter 11
Special Needs

Agencies which specialize in finding nannies and other help for children who are physically and mentally handicapped come and go with alarming speed. They mean well and most *do* very well for a short time and then collapse, but not for lack of business. Over ten years we have watched them flourish and expand and just as suddenly disappear because their proprietors could not take the emotional, financial or physical strain of dealing with parents of children with a mass of special needs problems who encounter so many difficulties in all areas of their lives with which they need support, advice and help.

In the agency section of the book it is saddening that we only have one recommendation – excellent and professional as it is – Network Special Needs Agency, which is run by tremendously experienced and sympathetic Lucy O'Donnell.

Only a few ordinary agencies will even attempt to help, though most assure you that they do. They are particularly hopeless at providing temporary help. One mother told Lucy O'Donnell that although she had rung 50 agencies before Christmas to try and get a fortnight's respite care for her cerebrally palsied daughter – she did not receive a single call back. Mothers say that they also get nannies for children with special needs by contacting the heads of the residential training colleges (see Chapter 7) and their local NNEB colleges. In both cases they ask if there are any students on that year's course who particularly want to work with children with special needs and whether the course tutor recommends them personally. Some handicaps can only be dealt with by qualified nurses who may be contacted through the relevant agencies, by advertising in the *Nursing Times* and via hospital notice boards. Some mothers use *The Lady* and *Nursery World* and the local press. They are unanimous in their recommendation that anyone with a handicapped child is upfront about it in the ad. They also put up cards in One O'clock Clubs and leisure centres.

The range of different kinds of children with special needs is vast. Nannies are needed to help with slow learners and backward children, cerebral palsy, Down's syndrome, children with short life expectancies for a variety of different reasons, having a tracheostomy or colostomy, mentally and physically handicapped, blindness, deafness, tuberous sclerosis, low IQ, hyperactivity, car accident victims, multiple sclerosis, congenital heart and respiratory problems, cystic fibrosis, fits and epilepsy, behaviourally difficult, microcephalic, sickle cell disease, haemophilia, AIDS, paralysis, children on ventilators and on kidney machines, with pacemakers, tracheal oesophageal fistules, paraplegic, tetraplegic, quadraplegic – there are as many therapies and treatments.

Mothers and nannies should try to keep themselves aware of facilities which are specially aimed to help the handicapped, like special needs days at adventure playgrounds. Play Matters/The National Toy Libraries Association runs a string of toy libraries, often mobile, for the disabled and the disadvantaged. It was the brain child of Jilly Norris, a Froebel teacher with two handicapped sons. Special toys for the handicapped are impossible to find and borrowing them from a toy library makes sense.

There are several magazines and newsletters dealing with subjects relating to the handicapped. The best known newsletter is *In Touch*, which links families with other families nationally and internationally who have types of handicap in common. A magazine was started called *Special Children* which deals with children with special educational needs. Contact-A-Family in London co-ordinates local groups nationwide so that they can get together for various activities and it also puts parents in touch with other parents to pool news and views on rare handicaps.

An adult usually has to accompany a handicapped child on specially organized holidays for the handicapped, and this is where a nanny could step in and give the child's parents a breather.

What Sort of Nanny?

Some of the best nannies are 18-year-olds who have been doing voluntary work since well before they left school. Others may be 25-plus nannies who have usually done a course and have worked in residential and respite homes. These girls may especially appreciate the responsibility of caring for two or three children, having grown used to dealing with so many with insufficient staffing.

Employers also say that they look for:

> Someone who understands my need for a break from my daughter and who is not as emotionally involved, though capable of being kind and reliable. Katie is autistic, quite tall and often violent. She terrifies me, but I love her. Can you imagine what it is like to love a child who may attack you with scissors from behind a door as you walk into a room? People don't understand.

> Handicapped children need someone with a lot of patience who is prepared to repeat a task endlessly and to encourage self-help.

> You definitely don't want someone who can't form normal relationships and thinks she is doing you a favour. It is not good to have a nanny who immerses herself entirely in your child without outside interests. No weirdos.

> I'm always grateful to my young nannies for providing a hurly-burly sort of atmosphere. It is good when they are not too protective. A mother can never stop being so.

One nursery nurse speaks for many when she says:

> I enjoy looking after the handicapped. It is a varied and rewarding job – the children are delightfully brave and loving. The frustrating thing about it is not being able to help the child communicate when they have no language ability. It is so sad not knowing what is wrong when one of them starts to cry.

One employer spoke movingly of her need for a special nanny to look after her special needs child:

> She's got to believe in God or something beyond this physical world and she must be jolly. She must also know that I need a bit of mothering, and if I feel despairing and am in tears at the kitchen table, she should not be fazed by it and just understand that sometimes the depression is total.

A special needs nanny agent says:

> The girl must not be judgmental about how the parents are dealing with their children. She must not be critical. When parents reach rock bottom, I put in the best girl I can find. At the start they may be saying that they never want to cope with their special needs child, but they find themselves with a bit of freedom away and gradually come back to the responsibility.

Her duties

Duties of nannies and mother's helps are described respectively:

Nannies   Will be trained and/or very experienced with children, capable of sole charge of children and of every aspect of their care and upbringing. The duties and salary will vary, as will time off, from post to post, but a nanny may expect to take care of children's meals, entertainment, bathing, supervise homework, attend therapy sessions, stimulate intellectually and physically, take care of children's laundry, clean their rooms, her own nursery/playroom, some babysitting.

Mother's helps   Will not be expected to cope on their own for more than a few hours, will participate in all aspects of the running of the home and of the children's care, plus some housework, ironing, cooking etc. and some babysitting, and to participate in the child's therapy sessions.

One example

Edwin is three and has congenital heart and respiratory problems, and a tracheostomy. He needs 24-hour care; his mother works part-time. She has to hire two trained SRNs and they need to have had specific experience; for example, some SRNs do not have tracheostomy care knowledge. So far he has had 21 operations. Below is reproduced the daily routine that she gives the nannies on arrival:

08.00   Edwin wakes. Has atrovent nebulizer (1 ml atrovent, 2 mls saline) and physiotherapy. Bath.

08.45   5 mls Septrin (take off syringe, squirt it into mouth), two drops of fluoride (orally).

Breakfast: four dessertspoons of Readibrek, one tin of fruit, daily dose of Wysoy. Warm for one minute in microwave. Fill beaker with Wysoy and encourage him to drink.

09.30   Second nebulizer – .5 mls of Bricanyl. Additional physio as necessary. On school days the above schedule needs to be earlier so to be ready for 9.15 – omit second nebulizer. [Nanny takes Edwin to the local Montessori nursery school and stays with him there.]

12.00   Atrovent nebulizer and physio. Change of tracheostomy or before tea i.e. whenever stomach is empty.

12.30   Lunch – a combination of mashed potato, baked beans, ravioli, mince, mashed carrots. (Saturdays my mother will have cooked him vegetables already, so no need to take food to her, only Wysoy.)

14.00   Bricanyl. Nebulizers to be given a minimum of one hour apart. Rest: put him in bed with tape recorder, and dummy and he'll have a good sleep.

16.00   Tea – baby rice, semolina, rusk, custard etc. (Dependent on bowels fruit can be omitted or added.) With tea – after it has been heated – add 5 mls of Ketovite liquid and 3 crushed Ketovite tablets.

17.00   Atrovent nebulizer and physio.

17.30   Bath or good wash, get Edwin ready for bed.

18.30   Supper – as for lunch – savoury or vegetables, followed by pudding if hungry. Again try and get him to drink.

19.15   Bricanyl nebulizer.

19.30   Bed – put Edwin to bed with a dummy, tape recorder and room humidifier. He should be connected up to Aquapack for at least five hours each night. Nappies at night.

Overnight – suction and physio as necessary.

Edwin's mother says that her nannies have many duties.

> Apart from physio, suction, administering drugs via a compressor, a nebulizer and orally, they take care of all the equipment, cleaning, sterilizing, connecting it up, making sure it works, ordering replacements, spares and servicing: they also teach him to maximize his potential and do as much for himself as he can; use sign language and communicate, take care of clothes and all the usual nanny duties, emotional as well as physical.

Her pay

The Disability Living Allowance from the state comprises an Attendance Allowance which is paid from birth and graded in three levels according to the severity of the disability, and a Mobility Allowance, which starts at the age of five. They total about £70 per week. There are also discretionary grants which are awarded according to how persuasive and pushy parents can be in fighting their own corner and how sympathetic an individual authority wishes to be.

If a mother is close to breakdown, the social services may allocate funds for someone else to help with a special needs child, and that carer could be permanent. Some local authorities, looking at the fact that institutional care can cost them £50,000 a year, are beginning to grasp the benefits of underwriting a nanny's salary to provide care in the home. They also pay for respite weekends and longer periods in residential homes.

Whoever you employ, it is desirable to pay generously especially if you expect your helper to do more than average duties, which you probably will. Even with no sole charge, there is the extra responsibility which should be reflected in her salary. Try to give her as much free time as possible if the care is intense. The pressures are great and a nanny's burnout can be high in these jobs. Enlightened self-interest pays off. Think how hard everyone finds it to anchor a nanny normally; a mother of a handicapped child can do without the extra strain of frequent recruiting.

Her special needs

Remember that the carer of a handicapped child has a greater need to have a social life and to be able to 'get away from it all' than the average nanny or mother's help. A girl who looks after a child with special needs by day and who watches nothing but TV by night, needs your attention. In London more and more nanny groups have sprung up, and increasingly in the provinces too. Parents are increasingly open to the idea of socializing with other parents of handicapped children and many nannies do the same and pick up tips about 'how Suzie is persuading young Dominic to feed himself' alongside much-needed practical and emotional support.

Nannies may have to deal with unpredictable and complex reactions to their charge from the parents and other members of the family. As parents have become more open in their reactions to their handicapped children, most siblings are more helpful in these families, but there can be exceptions. Some siblings may treat the handicapped child like the runt of the litter. They may be embarrassed in public and cruel in private. Some are disgusted by their sibling's deformities and anti-social behaviour. They may resort to disturbed attention-seeking antics. It can be serious. Siblings may react by failing to progress properly, manifest psychosomatic disorders like asthma and migraine, truancy and anorexia. Nannies may be more able to cope with this than the child's parents, who are likely to be overprotective and overwrought by their other offspring's unkindness to their vulnerable 'baby'.

The vulnerable baby syndrome presents problems itself. Some nannies listen to mothers talking glibly about the need to bring the child on and further his development, but watch with dismay as the mother insists that her 15-year-old handicapped son wears dungarees and a Mickey Mouse T-shirt more suitable to a toddler. One mum still baths her not very backward daughter who is now in her twenties. Very few mothers can bring themselves to be honest about the fact that they prefer dealing with their handicapped children as babies and young children. Some mothers are happier for their child to mix socially with those younger than themselves as their handicap is less obvious. Often parents feel threatened by their handicapped child as he or she becomes older. The question of what plans to make for the young adult's middle age looms too close not to want to disguise the reality.

In so doing, mothers deny the nanny or mother's help her proper role. The nanny may recognize sooner than the mother that Simon is ready to use a knife and fork and can just about cope without a bib. This is not easy; the girl must brace herself in the interests of the child to have a gentle talk with his mother.

A family may resent their child's handicap so much that they deny diagnosis for a long time. Nannies find it extremely difficult to deal with this head-in-the-sand behaviour, which may do the child no good. Those working with handicapped children may expect less leeway from their employers if they muck about with the House Rules. The parents are jumpy by definition. They are steeling themselves not to feel guilty about delegating the care of their much loved and often totally dependent burden, anyway. So any signs of an irresponsible attitude trip off all the alarms and nannies may expect their employer to blow a gasket.

Nannies should realize how great is the long-term anguish of the parent of a severely handicapped child, and how different the parent/child relationship can be from the ordinary. A special bond which can exist between the parent and her handicapped child is illustrated poignantly by one mother who says:

> When the time comes and my end is near, I would like my child to leave this earth with me. I hope I shall find the strength to ensure that. I know many parents of handicapped children who have this feeling. I brought the child into the world, and I will see that I don't leave him behind, alone.

Mothers and fathers should be sensitive to the nanny's probable devotion to her charge. She will be as distressed as they after the child has had an operation or painful therapy. She may have given the child everything she's got, but it is in the nature of his handicap that he deteriorates and dies. The family does not have a monopoly on the emotions summoned by the sadness and helplessness of the child's plight. A family must try to share with the nanny the misery of knowing that while there is still life, there *is* no hope in some cases.

Finally, one agent for special needs nannies says, 'The best nannies who care for a severely handicapped child are those who work because he is here today and that is as far as she thinks. She does her best to develop a fine degree of sensitivity and endless patience and to be intuitively connected with developing the invisible. She must be in touch with a different mental realm about which she has faith but no knowledge.'

Chapter 12
Nannies Abroad

Any nanny who has an urge to live and learn from the rest of the world, the nerve to leave home for a time, and the desire to earn more money than others in her field of expertise will want to try working abroad for some part of her career. Some girls are employed by English people working abroad, some go with foreigners for whom they have worked in the UK, and others take the biggest plunge and seek employment with the natives who live where they fancy living. As one thriving agency reports, 'all our top nannies go abroad'.

Some nannies go abroad to work for Europeans in their respective capitals, but jobs there are more frequently for mother's helps or au pairs, groups who want to improve their language, are not specially qualified to look after children, and who are not there for high wages and glamorous perks. Mrs Baxter, recently retired after twenty-five years as an employment agent, says: 'I only send British girls to be au pairs in Europe, not to the USA or Canada, it wouldn't be any good for them. In Europe they gain a language and a different insight. The British who live on the Continent often choose to employ a British nanny or mother's help. But it is difficult to find a girl who will live abroad successfully.' 'Rushing home to mother for the weekend is an expensive and major expedition, friends have to be made from scratch, the basics of a foreign language mastered and understood, and a whole culture grasped and accepted. This is no joke for an English girl,' writes one correspondent from Brussels who has employed trained and untrained British nannies there for over five years.

The extent of culture shock depends on the country in question – some countries, like the USA, Australia and Canada, while they may present surprises and challenges, are less of a shock than working in Riyadh, Moscow or Bombay. Almost everyone wants to go to America, and most will settle for Paris, Rome, Bermuda and places warm. However, if you live in Belgium, Holland, Denmark and Germany, you have to work rather harder to find someone. (Incidentally, some nannies are irritated that whether a girl works a five-hour day with some babysitting or is a trained or experienced nanny – if she is foreign and looks after children in Europe, she will be known to one and all as an au pair. *Rien a faire*.)

What Sort of Girl is Good at Working Abroad?

The kind of girl whom employers value when living abroad is a little different from her British-based counterpart. It is just as important to find someone with whom you will get on as someone who is good with the children. The employer, like it or not, is *in loco parentis* for her, ultimately responsible for her behaviour to the community (in which the family are themselves foreigners) and you will be handing out advice and giving help more often than if the job were in the UK.

While the new recruit makes friends and finds things to do, the wise expatriate employer should provide a warm and friendly atmosphere so that the girl does not become homesick and lonely. 'A happy nanny means happy children, which means happy parents – something too easily forgotten by many,' says the experienced Brussels employer.

The nannies to avoid are those who want to go 'abroad' just because it is. They are the ones who put Marbella at the top of their list. 'They have a vision of themselves spending every night in a different disco. If they do they will fall asleep the next day while the baby chokes to death on the telephone wire,' informs a jaundiced mum from the Costa del Sol.

The nanny should be able to list positive reasons for working where the employer lives – wants to learn the language, visited the place on holiday, liked it and wants to see more of it (and has some real idea of how it might be out of season), has friends and relatives there (a big plus since she is unlikely to be lonely), is going to settle down in England and wants to do something else in a year's time and to broaden her horizons before doing so. Going abroad just because there is nothing better to do at home is not ideal, but it doesn't necessarily mean that the girl is bad news. Running away from anything is more a recipe for disaster, but you will need to be a canny interviewer to intuit this.

The girl has to be mature, another thing that is hard to tell at once, and preferably with some experience of living away from home. No employer needs the additional worry about a nanny's safety in a strange city when she has still not returned by 5 am. Is she packed and on her way East via Marseilles or smooching with a local lad two blocks away? Willy nilly, the nanny becomes an ambassadress and a flagship for the family in which she works, and she is a reflection on her employers. Foreigners are *always* high profile and in the public eye because the natives are acutely aware of them, at least initially, and specially in tight-knit communities.

There is one major drawback for some British nannies working abroad for the locals. They go because they want to improve their grasp of the language of the country, but their employers hire them because they want little Hiro or Jean-Claude or Angelo to speak good English. Actually, not just English but 'pukka English' as one employer requests on the application form. All over the world agencies report that there are families who are rich enough to employ a nanny and choose to do so regardless of the availability of local 'help' – amahs, ayahs etc – and the reason they do? They want their child to be disciplined, well-mannered and speak the Queen's English. The Mary Poppins image is ingrained worldwide.

When and how to find her

The best time of year to look is, as in the UK, either in the New Year or in June/July/August. This last period coincides with the close of the academic year and is a time when pre-university or post-university girls (who can make bright mother's helps) are looking for work. Newly qualified NNEBs are on the market, and nannies whose charges start school in September and are no longer needed, are looking around for a new post. The chances grow dramatically less good as the year progresses with only a brief upsurge of availability at the year's end.

There are many ways of finding a nanny to work abroad. The well-worn routes are to put an ad in *The Lady*, use a British agency (but you have to reckon with higher fees than for domestic place-ments), advertise locally or by word of mouth. It is hard for those living abroad to get to England and usually a nanny is found by advertisement, short-listed by letter and interviewed by telephone. The lack of personal interview can make for a high degree of dis-appointment and discontent on both sides. There is really nothing to recommend it and it is *not* the only way to do it, just the easiest in the short run. An alternative is to ask a friend or relation in your own country to interview for you, although this is never a perfect answer because so much depends on personalities.

Good Business Arrangements and Other Anchors

Once you have ensnared your paragon, consider drawing up a work agreement(see Chapter 17). Talk it over slowly and carefully. This is particularly necessary if the family or the nanny is not English, since they may have differing interpretations of the same job description.

It is sensible to check local salary rates with friends and other employers and also with one or two English agencies. Salaries must always be fair and will depend on all the usual considerations plus the cost of living adjustment for whichever country you live in. When estimating this, consider the cost of local cinemas, transport, discos, cafés or whatever entertainment is appropriate. If the nanny is not paid the going rate, she will soon discover this when she meets local nannies, and the combination of finding her feet and thinking that you are being mean may provide the impetus for a swift leavetaking.

Work out with her how she wants to be paid. Half in sterling into an English bank account for saving, and half in local currency in cash for spending, is a popular method.

If the choice is in sterling, agree an exchange rate which you will review according to its fluctuation. Do not forget to take out medical insurance to cover medical and hospitalization costs, find out about the EEC National Health reciprocity agreements, but don't assume they'll be adequate and not bother to find out when an insurance top-up is necessary.

It is doubly important to make an effort with a new nanny if you live abroad and especially so if you are a native of the country. Even buying a bus or train ticket for the first time in a foreign language can be daunting. 'I hardly said a word to my Spanish employers for the first month,' says one nanny who worked in Madrid,' then the toilet paper ran out and I had to tell them. I couldn't get away with miming it, could I?'

European Posts

Brussels

Choosing someone to work in Belgium is hard work. Unless the nanny rejoices in 'O' level geography or, possibly, economics, a predictable number of British girls have hardly heard of it or think of it in terms of the Common Market, or a well-lit autoroute to other more interesting places. Nannies who have worked there like it.

Brussels is a small, friendly city and easy to get around. There is an au pair club which is busy and welcomes every nationality. There is the opportunity to learn or improve French (Dutch and German too since these are the other two national languages), but this is by no means necessary since many Belgians speak English.

There is plenty of night-life which is not prohibitively expensive, and an English language magazine, *The Bulletin*, which reports on life in Belgium for both the expatriate and local community. If she wants to travel, it is only an hour to most of Belgium's borders.

Rome

Advertising on the English church notice board or in the one English language bookshop – 'The Lion' – are favourite places for nannies lost and found. There is a bi-weekly English language 'paper' called *Wanted in Rome* which is free and financed by people placing ads in it. Most nannies prefer to be in the centre of Rome, though if enough carrots are dangled – higher pay and use of a car – they will take jobs a bit further afield.

The social life there is boosted by American Marine functions which are frequent and popular, and there is a club called 'Meeting Point', ostensibly for any English speaking person, but usually frequented by nannies, au pairs etc. The English church is quite a good cosy base for new nannies – although nothing is officially organized, cups of coffee after services can lead to friendships or at least a place in the choir!

Most nannies, mother's helps and au pairs go to the Dante Alighieri, the Italian language school, at the start to get a smattering of Italian (important for emergencies, particularly medical). Most British employers keep their girls for the contracted year, but conditions may be attached to a London/Rome/London ticket for a minimum stay of six months. There is a local au pair/nanny agency in Rome, but the British do not use it because it is prohibitively expensive.

There are nannies who stay for years with the English family who recruited them; but on the whole young families seem to prefer either a full-time Filipina, who also babysits, or a part-time daily plus a mother's help or an au pair.

Paris

The unique portrait of a British nanny in France is provided in *The Blessing* by Nancy Mitford and almost nothing was right with the place as far as she was concerned: 'Well, dear, we've had nothing to eat since you saw us, nothing whatever. Course upon course of nasty greasy stuff smelling of garlic – a month's ration of meat, yes, but quite raw you know – shame, really – I wasn't going to touch it let alone give it to Sigi, poor little mite.'

Present-day nannies love working in Paris. Mostly they take sole charge jobs for high-powered French mums. They meet initially at the English church and the vicar's tea parties. There are jobs with the international set here and many nannies jump on a bandwagon which may take them all over the world. Paris, like London, is one of those cities where, if you have six houses worldwide, you probably have one in each of those capitals. The lyrics of Peter Sarstedt's Sixties hit 'Where do you go to my lovely?' are played out for real by a few.

Oslo, Copenhagen, Stockholm and Amsterdam

The reason that most English nannies and mother's helps like working in these capitals is that there are lots of friendly young people, almost all of whom can speak English. They are also not far away from England.

One Dutch employer says, 'Why do they come? By the time they are about 20 they have been working for four years already as a mother's help in England, so they are glad of a change. They work a 12-hour-day and they are good workers, the English. We have had six of them – one every year for the last six years. No complaints.'

Madrid

A few Spanish aristocrats and British expatriates have nannies in Madrid, but most other employers employ *chicas*, Filipina or Spanish women who provide child care along with housework and cooking. Some English and girls of other nationalities come as au pairs and are usually unhappy because they are treated as maids. Some working mothers in Madrid send their children to private day nurseries – *Jardins de l'infancia* – and their care is supplemented by relations and friends volunteering to fill the gaps.

Marbella

It is remarkable that so many agencies mention Marbella as a particular nanny favourite. English nannies may be employed there by beach bums and bank robbers. They meet on beaches or at Sina-

tra's Bar in Puerto Banus. The English language newspaper called
The Sur has details of local nanny jobs.

Athens

There are shipping types who employ British nannies but they do
not tend to treat their nannies at all as they wish to be treated.
Nannies report that they won't stay to be pushed around like
skivvies. They are unimpressed by the huge houses and staffs,
beautiful islands and big salaries, and before long they go.

West Germany

Many British nannies have boyfriends in the British Forces in Germany and want to go and work out there to be near them. This
causes a lot of problems for employers because the girls want every
weekend off snuggled up with their beloveds, and if either of them
gets fed up, they are stuck with each other and often make employers wretched as well.

One colonel's wife in the British Army of the Rhine comments:
'Do not hire a Sloane Ranger type. The number of eligible bache-
lors will make her the centre of attention and you the employer
will trail around with your children in her wake while she is ogled
and feted by every man in the regiment *and* you'll be told how
lucky you are to have her.'

Another colonel's wife agrees and adds, 'At least in England
there's every chance you will not know the nanny's boyfriend.
Here we always do. It is exasperating that instead of scarpering
through the window into the night, they insist on facing my husband honourably, having been pulled out of the nanny's bedroom.
We used to dread going home. All the subalterns were round this
one like bees round a honey pot.'

Switzerland

Plenty of nannies go and work for expatriate English and American families, located principally in Geneva and Zurich or some
way towards the mountains outside Geneva in picturesque vil-
lages like Crans Montana. They have a wonderful time out there,
skiing and enjoying the scenery, and the opportunity to learn at
least one or two languages.

It should be noted that it is illegal for British girls to work in
Switzerland, though many do.

Far Away

Tokyo

American and British families employ British nannies successfully here. Some hire local girls who are used to being maids but who also help out with the children. Chinese amahs and Filipinas are popular in Japan. The Tokyo locals are not keen on looking after other people's children, and it appears that ex-pats sometimes resort to island girls.

There are a few bad stories about Japanese employers who are sometimes over-strict with the House Rules – 'more like house arrest actually' reports one nanny. 'Even the agency suggested I take refuge in the British embasssy with my luggage so that they couldn't get me back. They really behaved horribly to me and I was scared I would never get away. I would recommend anyone doing this kind of trip to make absolutely sure they hang on to their passport for dear life.

South Africa

'Even Harry Oppenheimer has black nannies, but then he would, wouldn't he?' says one Jo'burg father. 'There is a different tradition in Zimbabwe. In South Africa, almost everyone reckons that if you can hire a local houseboy, nanny and maid all for the price of one English nanny, the choice is simple.'

South America

Nannies have a good time working for the locals in many countries in South America and for expatriates too. In Sao Paulo, Brazil, there is a small community of British nannies – the older type, 30-plus, working for rich Brazilians and reportedly 'having a ball'.

One British ex-pat in Rio reports, 'There are still maids available all over South America, I never needed a nanny while we lived in Brazil, Chile and Argentina. We just needed babysitters if the maid wasn't there, or too busy for any reason. We occasionally hired a European if my husband and I had to go away together and leave the children, just to oversee the household of local staff. The great thing about the beach life in Rio was that everyone took their children to the beach and we all looked after them together.'

Hong Kong

Many expatriates have had amahs because they refuse to pay more than £400 a month for British nannies. One employer who was herself raised by an amah says, 'I was in her charge from the moment I came back from the hospital as a baby. She slept in my bedroom until I went to boarding school. I now have an amah in Sussex.' It seems that amahs for ex-pat families are on the decline and Filipina maids are in the ascendant. North Americans cannily advertise for Filipinas in Hong Kong newspapers.

The fact that Hong Kong is glamorous and remote appeals to the British nanny or mother's help. Most employers who have 'stayed on' insist a nanny joins the family for a minimum of two years. They usually advertise in *The Lady*, interview in the UK and return with their catch. One long-time Hong Kong resident says: 'There are two nanny agencies that have good reputations here – Rent-a-Mum and British Nannies – and they recruit locally. Both operate on a minimum four-hour rate, which is a bit more than £4 an hour.' One wistful London agent notes, 'There are about 60 British nannies working there at the moment, I could place hundreds, but there aren't enough British mothers there.'

Nannies meet each other up and down the Peak and also at the English church. 'The amahs spoil the children with too many sweets and fizzy drinks; I want an experienced and well-trained nanny. It is less easy otherwise for children to rejoin their contemporaries in England after a few years here,' says another resident.

Hong Kong is a hard-living, hard-working place and some girls complain that their employers are so busy at work and out so much in the evenings that they don't give their nannies much time to enjoy the night life. 'It's only the nice ones who bother to introduce you to other nannies; sometimes it quite suits them to keep you apart for as long as they can. I left one just like that,' says one experienced nanny there. But how long will they all remain?

Australia

Only a few Antipodean employers want to afford to pay the flight fares for nannies to come and work for them. It is much the best, if a nanny can afford it, for her to pay her own way there and then find an agency. There is quite a lot of work available for nannies, especially in temporary jobs. Sydney and Melbourne seem to be where the greatest number of Australian employers live and occasionally the Brits who are working out there for a year or two take a nanny with them.

Australians increasingly want other Australians to work for them and the nanny training courses are supplying them. There are a few rich farmers who live in the outback who hire British governesses rather than send their kids to state schools. 'They are usually nice girls, who probably ride and cook as well as teach,' says one Australian employer.

The Middle East

Regency Nannies agency says: 'Middle East clients collect Norlanders as status symbols. It is nothing for them to collect three or four on their yacht in the south of France. Some of them are offered wonderful presents like £1,000 for a new dress if they are all going out that night.'

Louise Davis of the Norland College says, 'I tell them there is little time off, and it is often very lonely and they may spend a lot of time stuck inside without any opportunity to see the country.'

For some girls it is a culture shock. Sometimes they are virtual prisoners, in fact they are much safer than they would be with a family in England. They are shepherded from place to place in limousines and there is no question of them being mugged or raped. But they are not free to do what they like and they have to be careful what they wear. Their passports are taken away and they have no exit visas from whatever country they are in. These are suitable posts for much older girls and many Arab families want women in their 40s and 50s. They can earn a pile of tax-free cash which is fine as long as they fully understand the drawbacks.

One employment agency says: 'It is not worth our while. Without contracts you just don't get paid. Often the nannies don't either. The Arabs flatly refuse to sign contracts and women have no rights under local law. Our biggest debt is from the brother of a bloke who came to London the other day to see the Queen and the Mall was shut for his procession. It just makes it more difficult to collect.'

A Norlander who has worked for a Middle Eastern head of state reports: 'They went abroad a lot and it was extremely lonely and hard work. Lots of money, loads of other staff to cook and clean and transport us. Let no one think that work in this part of the world is a soft option. I have enjoyed my years with the family very much, but I reckon I earned every penny.'

The agencies generally say that their nannies like working in Istanbul and in Cyprus.

Russia

Following the disintegration of Communist USSR, there are many new opportunities for curious and adventurous nannies to experience Russia and the new Republics, where for the first time since 1917 Western bankers, businessmen, consultants and diplomats are going to live.

Very few trained or experienced nannies in the past have wanted to join Western expatriates in Moscow, understandably, because of the alien and restricted lifestyle. Before the collapse of Communism, families took out mother's helps with no child care experience, but who were interested in the Soviet world because they had a degree or degrees in Russian. But as Russia and the new Republics close to the West, like the Ukraine, and those on the western seaboard, like Lithuania, become more accessible, it is probable that more 'ordinary' British nannies will want to go. However, now that there are millions of locals who are able and anxious to be nannies and housekeepers to foreigners, most Western nannies may be priced out of the market, as they are in the Far East.

One mother of five, wife of a diplomat in Kiev, has hired a middle-aged, thoroughly capable Ukrainian as nanny, and has another stalwart compatriot as housekeeper and cook.

North America

Canada

Many British nannies go to work in Canada. Employers advertise for them locally, use an agency or try putting their need out on the grapevine. 'You can trust the word of your friend or acquaintance more than that of the agency lady,' says one experienced Toronto mother. 'There are more bad agencies than there are good ones and, when I say bad, I mean from the nanny's point of view as well. They don't ask the right questions of either side so they are not satisfactory and a complete waste of time.'

Many people deal with an agency which has contacts abroad who will bring the girls from various countries. They choose a nanny from a file, present an offer by letter and the agency makes all the arrangements (immigration, medicals, visas etc.).

But as one mother says, 'What I have never been able to overcome is that I'm choosing a very important person in my life based on a picture and an application form. There is no opportunity for subjective opinion before the girl is on your doorstep. Also if you need someone in a hurry, it does take 90 days. There are always lots of girls looking who are already here. So probably as many employers pick a girl who is available immediately as get them straight from overseas.'

When girls go to Canada with a job offer from a Canadian family, the air fare is usually paid for by the family, though not always. The local agencies in Canada charge one month's salary (gross), as their fee. It is more expensive for a Canadian employer to hire a nanny through a British agency, but some do it.

The term 'nanny' is used much more loosely than in the UK. In Canada it means more in terms of pay scale than actual duties. Trained British nannies can – and do – do housework in Canada. Unless a girl makes it clear from the start that she is not prepared to do it at all, some housework will be expected of her. The mother's helps, as in the UK, do laundry (including the family's), light housekeeping, cooking, driving and ironing.

The salary seems to be more dependent on age and experience than in the UK. The range for a live-in nanny who drives and does light housework is (gross) from $1250 to $1600 (exclusive of health insurance) graded on experience and references. The figures are in Canadian dollars. She cooks, shops, car pools, does the laundry etc. for two or more school-age children.

There is a Nannies' Friendship and Information Centre in Toronto which is enterprising and well organized. It puts nannies in touch with other nannies and deliberately tackles the usual problem by 'giving each girl a word of advice and reassurance to let them know that they are not alone and to give them a chance to see Toronto and possibly other cities in Canada without the great trauma of homesickness, which is the main reason why girls go home before their contracts are fulfilled,' as its newsletter explains.

The hours of work, time off and living conditions are more specific there than in England. A working week is 50 hours maximum (this is occasionally abused) with a required two days off per week, 36 hours of which should run over Saturday and Sunday (this rule gets elasticized as well).

The Canadian nanny requires private accommodation (own bathroom too) by law. All statutory holidays, two weeks' paid vacation a year and Worker's Compensation paid by the employer and usually health insurance are all the responsibility of the employer.

USA

For the British nanny, the lure of the USA is as much a wish to experience the excitement of a New World as the desire for exceedingly gainful employment. Unlike Arabia, which does bring out the pure materialist in the British nanny, America appeals because there is no language barrier and life there seems larger than life here.

Despite high salaries, American women have stayed away from becoming nannies in droves; the indigenous nanny profession has only just been born and is slowly gaining respect and recognition. Until it does, the cream of nanny-employing Americans import their nannies from England.

The problem is that it is *illegal* to bring a foreign nanny into the USA. The US authorities have always required any alien, including a nanny, coming into the country to work to have a work permit. Employers of illegals working in the USA are responsible by law. The onus is on them to 'verify' the employment status of anyone hired for a job. This law applies to everyone.

All the papers must be in order within three days of the employee starting work. This precludes an earlier loophole when American employers did the basic minimum necessary to procure a green card and just putting the wheels in motion made the girl legal – a bit like getting a new tax disc for a car here.

Violation can carry a fine for employers of up to $2,000 for each employee who has not got the correct papers to prove the person's identity and employment status. Second offenders can expect higher fines and you hit the jackpot of $10,000 on your third offence. In theory, violators can be sent to jail.

British employment agencies report that their trade has not diminished one whit. Business as usual, meaning that they conspire with American employers to get their nannies past the Immigration Officers (INS) at America's airports.

Many British agencies do a bit of illegitimate work of this kind, if the price is right, though none will go on record as saying so. One agent shows what risks Americans, regardless of their position in public life, will take to hire the English nanny of their choice: 'I have a regular client who works in the White House and this is the second time I have sent him a nanny. If he is not bothered by the threats, who the hell is? Believe it or not I have just placed two nannies in the families of Congressmen in the space of eight weeks.'

An amalgam of many British employment agencies' views on the issue runs thus: 'No one, touch wood, has been fined yet; no agency has been put out of business, no employer has had to pay the big max fine; no nanny has yet died under interrogation by an immigration official. Let us get the problem in proportion and not be too hypocritical.

'People go on about how dangerous it is for nannies to go to the States to work illegally, do they have any idea that there are *thousands of them* at it? Many Americans could not care less what they pay, they just want an English nanny. All the old sobersides in London say they bet they have a miserable time there . . . that's hard to do in New York on £500 a week for pocket money.'

British employers or Americans who have been living in the UK for a while (and have employed a nanny for not less than a year) may take nannies with them to the USA legally. The nanny's passport will be stamped specially since she is then designated a member of their staff and a dependant of theirs. She will be bound to work for that family or become an illegal if she leaves them and does not immediately return home. Agencies sometimes backdate contracts so that an employer moving from the UK to the USA can take a nanny with them.

There is a severe nanny shortage in New York, Boston and Washington. 'People are crying out for them and could not care less how they get them,' one Bostonian comments. The risks that people take to procure British nannies are greater now that the immigration authorities have taken this new line of making the employer responsible for, and equally guilty with, the illegal.

All You Need is a Green Card

Are you sitting comfortably? Now the system works like this. A green card is what every nanny wants and is most unlikely to get. It entitles the holder to live and work legally in the USA. Barbara Binswanger and Betsy Ryan explain the process succinctly in their book *Live-in Childcare*: 'There are six preference classes of immigration visas. Domestic workers come in under the lowest, or sixth preference class: the one for skilled and unskilled labour in short supply. Only 10 per cent of all immigration visas can be issued to people in this sixth class, or about 27,000 domestic and other workers per year. If you are trying to bring in a nanny from overseas, she will get no special treatment and be lumped in with the group.'

Doing it legally and getting a green card is a Herculean task, seemingly designed to be frustrating, difficult and complicated. You have to prove that a local unemployed US national is not available to do the job adequately instead and then the red tape and your problems have hardly begun. That process of 'job certification' comes with the need to prove that your nanny has had at least a year's experience of work. Then you have to advertise in your area for three consecutive days and file your job with the local employment office. Then you have to find convincing and legalistic reasons for rejecting the applicants. After that, you must wait while the decision is reached on a regional level as to whether your job certification application has been successful.

Still with us . . . ? You won that round and now you have to run the gauntlet of the Immigration and Naturalization Service (INS). They instigate various further checks and procedures and then you wait some more. According to Binswanger and Ryan again: *'It takes about two to three years to get a green card'* (our italics).

Only expatriate Brits need to agonize further over more of the labyrinthine details of this subject – buy Binswanger and Ryan (see Bibliography) if you do. Suffice it to say that it is a bind. *The Lady* and *Nursery World* have refused for ages to allow any mention of America in their ads. It is clear that the INS legislation and punishing fines are *really* meant to deter Mexican, Puerto Rican and other foreign workers – but the long knives have been pointed directly at nannies and their employers too.

Two women appointees of President Clinton's Administration were unable to take up their posts because it was discovered that both had employed illegal immigrants as nannies and had not paid their tax and national insurance. Many American women are in serious jeopardy of being exposed for the same misdemeanour and, as a result of the outcry, men will henceforth be screened similarly. Nannygate has been a nasty shock; British employers take note.

What British Agencies Do About It

Understandably, no agency worth investigation by the authorities admits to sending nannies to America. Almost every one with international contacts and foreign business does place nannies there. A few deal exclusively with the above-board channels – nannies for diplomatic families, bona fide long-term employers moving from England to the US and the legal au pair programmes.

The Au Pair Option

British and English-speaking Europeans between the ages of 18 and 24 can go for a limited time to work in America. The two programmes working at present are The Au Pair in America Program sponsored by the American Institute for Foreign Study Foundation and The Au Pair Homestay USA under the aegis of the Experiment in International Living.

Au pairs get in to America on 'cultural exchange' visas which are valid for a year. There are quite strict rules governing both programmes. The candidates must have had secondary education, some relevant experience or training in child care, hold a driver's licence and be verifiably healthy. The programmes' 'Code of Conduct' prohibits drug use and drunkenness and insists on good notice being given to the host family of any travel plans. Emphasis is placed on politeness and correct behaviour on both sides. Host families apply three months in advance of the date they wish the au pair to start and all applicants are screened in Europe.

The au pairs' responsibilities are more onerous than those expected of the au pair arrangement in England (see Chapter 3). They do a 45-hour week and their job description is similar to what a British employer would expect of a mother's help (see Chapter 3). The cost to the host family is about $150 a week.

How Was It For You?

Cecil Woodham-Smith in *The Great Hunger* wrote that the Irish who went to America discovered three things. First, that the streets were not paved with gold; second, that they were not paved at all, and third, that *they* were expected to pave them. It is exactly the opposite case with nannies. That is why they risk the huge potential unpleasantness and embarrassment of being found out and deported: the simple fact is that they love it.

Most American employers are generous, considerate, appreciative and determined to keep their nannies and show them a good time. The standard of living is much higher than in Britain and employers are keen to share the luxuries of their lives unstintingly with the angel who cares for their children. The stories of magnanimity are legion:

I didn't just get every weekend off; they used to fly me to wherever I wanted to go in their private plane.

I saw everything there was to see all over America with my employers. They were set on me seeing the sights.

The weather was so great wherever we were. If it got bad we moved to a house somewhere else where it was better!

It is not easy to find the homesick, lonely and exploited comments in that bunch or most others that we heard, though they were not uncritical or without a slight wistfulness for the old country.

But for all her nostalgia, one nanny knows exactly which side her bread is buttered: 'With the favourable exchange rate I'm better off working here and sending money home when I can, than living and working in England. I can imagine a time when constant life in the fast lane of the rat race will wear thin, but it hasn't happened yet.'

Apart from the East Coast market, the nanny scene thrives in the West as well. In Los Angeles, especially Hollywood, the rich and famous have British nannies. The somewhat less rich hire Swedish, French and Swiss au pairs. Anyone else who can afford help has Mexicans, Guatemalans and other Hispanics, who are paid peanuts and do everything. One LA lawyer comments, 'We are both lawyers. We risk a helluva lot each time we hire an English nanny from here on in. It is virtually impossible for us to get them here legally. By the time we succeeded the children would have grown up.'

The Malibu beach set give their nannies a lovely life. They are paid about $300 a week, have nice cars and/or a chauffeur at their disposal, and they socialize in the Tudor Tea Rooms and the King's Head in Santa Monica.

The American nanny

The nanny profession in America in the mid-1980s seemed to be becoming organized at last. Nanny conferences, nanny agencies and training schools sprang up and a dozen or more nanny books were published. Many of these still exist, but the new International Nanny Association foundered by the early 1990s, and there is no obvious focus or forum for the nanny profession.

The market for nannies in the USA is enormous – estimates range from 10 to 250 job orders for every nanny or mother's help available. The big question is: Will the women of America become nannies in sufficient numbers to supply the domestic market? Recruiting them into child care has been difficult. The main reason that the INS has pushed so aggressively for tighter legislation to support its efforts to exclude aliens may to some extent reflect the current American belief that any idiot can babysit. It must be admitted that the legislation has been a shot in the arm to the US nanny industry.

As Deborah Davis, editor of the excellent and now defunct *National Nanny Newsletter*, wrote: 'Until we perceive that the work of the child care provider is a legitimate profession, our society will continue to reinforce the low status and low pay of the professional nanny. We need to make clear the distinction between babysitter and professional nanny before the career of the in-home child care provider can be viewed as a viable job option for American women.'

Chapter 13
Why She Left

... Children I am very cross. Mary Poppins has left us ... It's outrageous. One minute here and gone the next. Not even an apology. Simply said 'I'm going' and off she went. Anything more preposterous, more thoughtless, more discourteous ...

P. L. Travers,

Mary Poppins

At the interview you discussed how long you wanted your nanny or mother's help to stay. Indeed, if there was a work agreement you will have written it down nicely i.e. 'We hope that you will stay at least one year.' Most employers make the big mistake of thinking that nannies will stay for ever. Trained nannies may stay as long as two years, a few stalwarts may manage a couple more, but the average is a year to eighteen months.

One agent is extremely jaundiced about the swift turnover. She says, 'They are a fickle lot; they get itchy feet. Like gypsies, they amuse themselves better by keeping on the move.' Employers should not be offended when after a happy co-existence the nanny murmurs one day, 'It's time to be off.' The nature of the job and its restrictions mean that it is only bearable for many nannies if they keep moving, particularly for those who have ambition. They feel they are going places, and they well may with another family that goes abroad on holiday and generally offers a more pleasant and exciting package. Often the grass *is* greener when the next employer is richer.

Some employers do not want their nannies to stay with the family for longer than a year, however good they are, because they fear that their children will become too attached to them and be very sad when they leave. The incidental advantage of this policy is that employers get a good feeling of being more in control of events as the chances are better that a nanny completes a year. The disadvantage is that the mother suffers the recruitment process every ten months. It is partly for this reason that when February comes round again and the nanny is still with them, employers rejoice.

Employers don't chat easily with their nanny about the possibility of there being another world outside and the likelihood of the nanny wishing to rejoin it. Not talking about it is superstitious and ostrich-like. One mother, having clocked up a record two and a half years with her nanny, brings up the subject regularly, partly because she knows that all good things must come to an end and she wants to be the first to know when. It's also good psychologically, and much less stressful. If you can give the children a long lead-in to the whole idea, there is less upheaval.

Any employer gets cross when a nanny does not fulfil the agreed length of stay. Some employers are themselves the cause of the move and if they have transgressed the Big Four (see Chapter 2), repeatedly or generally abused a nanny's willingness to 'muck in', she will leave before they planned and is quite right to do so. If a nanny leaves under these circumstances, some people get their own back unfairly by either not writing her a reference at all, or writing a bad or equivocal one, which is transparent in its lukewarm list of duties done. This is rough treatment to a young girl who has served the family well for over a year. The seriousness of this petty reaction to an inconvenience cannot be overstated. Her next employers will take a dim view of a gap in her CV, and she is defenceless against such evidence.

The employer can reasonably feel that she has been let down if the nanny resigns before her agreed time is up, because she feels merely tired of the job, or has been offered a more interesting one by someone else. It is too bad for the employer if the girl's mother is suddenly seriously ill and she wants to leave to nurse her. Other Acts of God which are exceptions are: employers moving house, bereavement, divorce – any major change in her job content or its atmosphere (see Chapter 9).

Louise Davis, Principal of Norland College, advises her students:

> If you have decided you want to leave, don't be persuaded to take a fiver a week more. If you want a salary rise ask for one, if you want to leave, go. Employers shouldn't offer a little extra once a nanny has said she is off, it's too late by then. If she'd really rather have left then her nannying is not likely to be as good as it ought to be.

Employers are bound to have a shock when their carer gives no sign of wanting to leave and then out of the blue gives a month's notice. If lines of communication have been properly maintained both employers and employees will give each other much more notice of long term plans than a month. However, the accepted minimum *is* four weeks' notice.

In theory, both sides agree that lots of notice is a great idea all round but as another nanny put it: 'In my first job I was over-worked and underpaid. I gave two months' notice as we'd agreed. I now think that that was a mistake because my awful employer made those months feel like an eternity.' If relations have disintegrated so that you try not to meet in the passage, even four weeks will be miserable, and most of all for the children. Let her go, pay her off and, if you can afford it, call the agencies for a nice calm capable temp, while you start interviewing for a replacement.

Employers will be relieved to note that a nanny cannot take them to an industrial tribunal for 'unfair dismissal' until she has been with them for two years.

When employers want a nanny to leave without working out her notice, they vary enormously about how much they pay her in lieu. The honourable, who have spelt out these terms in a contract, pay the nanny her entire notice period, i.e. in many cases, four weeks' pay. Others don't behave so well, depending on how aggrieved they feel and pay just a week or two, or not at all.

Employers' stories about nannies leaving without notice make fantastic reading. Apparently trained nannies leave their charges unattended at midnight and scrawl inadequate notes left on the hall rug to say they have gone. Some don't even bother to do that. One nanny says she has never forgiven herself for doing just this in her first job. Even a babysitter, who hadn't any excuse for not liking her employers, so brief was their acquaintance, abandoned two children aged three and one in a big house in Richmond. The three-year-old girl went out into the snow to tell a neighbour that her little brother was playing with the logs in the fire . . .

One employer of a North Country NNEB had gone out with her husband to the office dance. She and her husband returned at 3 am and kissed the children good-night. In the morning they found a note from the nanny in her bedroom saying that she'd left because she was homesick. Later they learned that a neighbour had heard a car drive up and away again, minutes after their own departure for the evening. Three little boys under five had been left alone for most of the night. Too late to sack her even if they could have; she was a candidate for the Lucan Solution.

Time to Go

The vast majority of nannies and mother's helps never dream of behaving irresponsibly and leave after giving notice for a wide variety of normal reasons, like these, say employers:

To get married.

To be a nurse.

Went back to Australia.

To become a daily nanny for more money.

Because we moved house.

The girls give additional reasons for leaving:

After a long stay with the grandparents, my employers started to take me for granted. They began to come home really late in the evening and generally put a lot more on me.

I left the job because I found it too hectic and it was hard to get holiday pay.

I left because there were four kids including twins and no routine. The final straw was that I was expected to clean up the dog mess all the time.

Many nannies remark that it is very sad to leave, especially the children. It's often more of a wrench than they think, though with experience they learn to distance themselves effectively.

Nannies and mother's helps who leave under normal circumstances should be reminded that any show of being upset, however touching, will not help the children get over her departure. The best precaution is to warn the nanny that you will preoccupy the children while she makes a quiet exit. Floods of tears, ululations and breast beating are not the ideal final memory of a nanny for a child after two happy years. That's not how grownups behave.

The last few weeks or days before a carer leaves are always a touch fraught even when she has behaved impeccably hitherto. Don't put up with a slide into anarchy; it won't help the new incumbent to have to reinstate the routine and, again, it just isn't professional. It is odd how often employers and nannies, the light at the end of the tunnel approaching fast, fall out for the first time over the silliest things.

Try to keep the parting sweet. It's not as simple as it sounds. Most employers find it trying to listen to too much whoopee about the nanny's new job and lovely plans, especially in front of the children. Charts with the days crossed off are tactless. If she hums 'Show me the way to go home', try to join in the refrain.

It is hard for a child to understand fully why the nanny is leaving him and it is extremely important that he doesn't interpret it as rejection. It can be a painful parting and parents must not try to minimize the pain that a child may feel for their own purposes.

Jeanne Magagna, child psychotherapist at the Tavistock, says:

> A good nanny prepares the child for separation from herself when it is time for her to leave. It is traumatic for a child when a nanny leaves – a crisis to many children when the nanny has been there for 18 months or more. . . . Children feel psychologically dropped at the carer's departure, which is very bad for their self-esteem and confidence. Parents should acknowledge children's acute anxiety and share their sadness.

Don't wait till the morning of the departure to discover that her room is a horrible mess. Suggest she occupies herself constructively in giving it a thorough spring clean. Get her to take down her pictures, posters, scarves and mementoes – it may give her a slight twinge that the place needs redecorating. If she is a brick, give her a paintbrush. Ask her to change the sheets and towels for the next nanny. Diana Forney, a Norlander who is an independent consultant to the nanny profession in America, recommends to nannies: 'If you are responsible for cleaning your own room and bath, do a thorough job. Small details speak well later for your recommendations.'

Remember that both of you want to part friends, draw a line under the whole experience and sign off neatly. Employer and nanny will then congratulate themselves on having won through, without a stumble when the winning post was in sight.

References

Don't be lazy about giving your nanny or mother's help a reference. Even if the nanny forgets/hasn't the sense/or simply doesn't know about its importance, be correct, write one without being prompted and give it to her before she leaves. Don't waste any lick on the envelope, she'll be dying to read it. It is sloppy to say that you will send it on because you haven't found time to write it. You may never get down to it and then what does she do?

Carve half an hour out of your life to compose an effective reference. Now you have to judge her character and how well she has done her job. Your composition will affect her future job prospects. Her livelihood may hang on your words. The business should be taken seriously and be given a bit of thought.

Agencies complain that nannies manufacture their own references all too often. For this reason a few employers take an extreme view and mistrust them completely. To avoid any possibility of identification or an edited copy being made, use headed paper if you have it, state your telephone number and post code and include any title or professional initials. The traditional way to address the unknown reader of the reference is 'To Whom It May Concern', with the nanny's name in full, underlined underneath.

Remember she will read the reference. If you have grave reservations about her and she hasn't been wonderful for any reason, you have three choices. One is to write a straightforward vitriolic blast which will almost certainly end up in your dustbin before she leaves. Another is to go to her and tell her frankly that any reference you could bring yourself to write would do her no good and that you have no intention of perjuring yourself on her account. Third, admitting that you should have parted company months ago, you can chicken out and fudge something to keep her happy – and employed.

It is as hard to know how to write about the mediocre nanny or mother's help. It is easier to write a string of superlatives, or a grudging line or two, than to compose a carefully worded, non-committal couple of paragraphs. After all, writing references is the art of omission. You pick out what they do right and leave out what they do wrong.

You may choose to damn with faint praise, or to write with such obscurity that the recipient has to read between the lines. This is bad news for any future employer. The nuances are likely to be misinterpreted and also be an impenetrable code to someone with a different educational background or to a foreigner.

It might be preferable to keep it short and get out of the problem by merely summarizing her job description and saying that she fulfilled it and that she was honest and hard working. The drawback with this is that she is likely to sense, and be disappointed by, your brevity and you will feel rotten. That's why people do the clever-

A glowing reference

(An actual reference for an experienced mother's help from a couple of working doctors in Hertfordshire)

Mary was employed as a nanny for two years and is leaving to further her career. During this period of time she has undertaken a number of other duties and has thus fulfilled a wider role in support of our children and family. In all respects I have been completely satisfied with Mary's work while she herself can only be commented upon in terms of the highest praise.

Mary's great asset is her outgoing, but not overbearing personality. She gets on well with the young and old alike and is sensitive and mature beyond her years. In particular, our family is impressed with her adaptability, yet she is able to interest and entertain children extremely constructively whilst maintaining firm discipline. Her training in catering has stood her in good stead and she is an excellent cook both at the family level and also for entertaining.

I am also bound to speak of her selflessness and her capacity to accept responsibility. My expectation of Mary has been more than fulfilled and all our family are saddened and sorry that Mary has to leave us.

clever thing and write to confuse. They have helped perpetuate the not-so-very-vicious circle of average nannies with average standards. But doing it doesn't boost the image of the profession or give it much respect.

If you write a prevarication of a reference, at least issue an open invitation that anyone who would like more details about the nanny should ring you forthwith. Make this a Belisha Beacon on the page.

Keeping in Touch

Once your nanny has left, all the inhibitions have gone and if you always felt that she was a kindred soul you may continue to be closely in touch with her for ever. One nanny was overcome when she learned of a small bequest in her favour in an old employer's will, who labelled it 'to my most faithful friend, our loving nanny'.

It's more surprising that au pairs remain family friends and across great distances too. Most employers say that they maintain contact with the vast majority of their successful nannies for some time.

Where Are They Now?

> Other people's babies
> That's my life! Mother to dozens
> And nobody's wife.

Happily, nowadays most nannies want to get married, have children and do. More and more don't want them too soon, so that they can experience different things – travel, work in a nursery school, run their own nursery, set up an employment agency, become a daily nanny or a childminder.

One thing the majority of them say they *don't* want is to have a nanny to look after *their* children. The main reason for this is that they expect to enjoy bringing up their children themselves. One nanny is enchanting: 'I wouldn't have a nanny free of charge. Children are so small, I couldn't miss out on the happy funny times bringing them up.'

Finally, one nanny seems to have marked, learned and inwardly digested much:

> I hope that I will be married or, if not, travelling somewhere in five years' time. I think nannying has made me realize that having children too soon in married life is wrong. Enjoy marriage with your husband alone first. If that works well, then go ahead with children.

Chapter 14
Childminders

One of the best things to have come out of a wider choice of child care in the last ten years is a greater awareness of what constitutes *good* child care. Choice promotes more competition and thus standards are raised all round. For example, some private day nurseries now offer hair cuts, French, dancing or swimming and so have one up on their rivals who do not. A childminder knows that she is competing against day nurseries so she is less likely to yield to temptation and relegate the child's entertainment largely to the TV or video while she gets on with her own life relatively unhampered.

Increasingly, standards-conscious parents are abandoning old-style minders in favour of energetic young women who read the parenting magazines, know about child development and put theory into practice with their own children. Happily, much child-minding today is practised in a healthier world of fresh air and fresh foods with more cerebral stimulation in the form of reading, games and making things.

The 1989 Children Act states that anyone who, in their own home, looks after a child under eight for pay or reward for more than two hours a day *must* be registered to do this with the local social services department. Close relatives (usually aunts, uncles and grandparents) are exempt from this rule. The Children Act specifies the number of children a childminder may look after simultaneously: no more than *three* children under five years, and only one of those under a year old. Alternatively, she may care for a total of *six* children of five to seven years, or look after a maximum of six children under eight, in which case no more than *three* can be under five years of age. All these numbers must *include* the carer's own child or children. Local authorities have the right to set a limit to the number of minded children over the age of eight.

There are 110,000 registered childminders, and parents choose childminding more than any other form of day care. Ten years ago

there were less than half as many. Gone are the bad old days when
there were thousands of unregistered women who 'took in' children like washing and got away with it.

Although there are plenty of women who 'mind' on and off for
short periods, who don't want to run the gauntlet of form-filling
required by the social services in order to register, fewer and fewer
parents are prepared to employ an unregistered carer for their
child for any length of time. The decline of the unregistered carer
has partly come about because councils have tried hard in recent
years to promote registration and present it in a positive light: i.e.,
it makes sense for both parties that the carer is *bona fide*. Credit
too should go to the campaigning work of the National Childminding Association (NCMA), which was the pioneer in making
childminding a profession worthy of respect.

Once again, it is *illegal* for a childminder to fail to contact her
local authority and apply for registration, and she can be prosecuted for not being registered. Strangely, the parents of the children she minds can't be prosecuted for using her, an anomaly
which the NCMA has queried. There are many positive reasons for
a minder to make the effort to register with the local council. Once
registered, the council should put her in touch with other minders
who may be organizing activities in the area. She should have
recourse to the social services' officials – such as Under Eights
Officers, Childminders' Advisers and Day Care Officers – who are
responsible for all aspects of child welfare.

The local authority may well be able to offer help and support to
registered childminders in the form of 'drop-in centres', toy
libraries, pre-and post-registering training courses, and the loan of
equipment, such as fireguards and double buggies. Councils vary
enormously as to how much effort and what resources they allocate to childminding. Some do the absolute minimum, but the vast
majority now have a good support service.

Councils work closely with the NCMA and encourage childminders to join the Association. Thankfully, the image of the illiterate, scruffy, fag-puffing minder with hordes of children loosely
scattered around her on kerb corners is now almost extinct.

The Registered Childminder

It cannot be stressed enough that new mothers and fathers intending to leave their offspring with someone else must go for the best
they can afford in whichever field of child care they choose. Child-

minders are interviewed by the social services, who check that their home is safe, secure (doors and gates shut and lock properly), warm, hygienic, and has suitable equipment, such as staircase gates and fireguards. Childminders, and anyone over the age of 16 living with them, have to answer various questions pertaining in particular to their health and whether anyone in the household has ever been involved in violence or child or drug abuse.

Someone in the house with a police record (or married to someone with a police record), will not automatically be turned down, depending on the nature of the record, and time lapses are allowed for some offences. The police run a criminal record check on everyone over 16 living in the house.

The Under Eights Officer assesses the relevance of a particular offence (for example, shop-lifting ten years ago would not affect registration), and its effect on the prospective childminder's suitability. Registration does *not* mean that the minder has received any sort of seal of approval from the council about her ability to provide a high standard of child care. Registration may simply mean that the childminder has been asked to buy a fireguard for the sitting-room fire which the children use as a playroom, and a guard for her cooker hob. But it is no guarantee that these will be used every day.

Once accepted, the new childminder receives a certificate of registration and pays a small fee. The social services must visit her once a year to check that all is as it should be. The premises are re-registered each year, for which there is a small charge. Some councils do turn down applicants or strike minders off their registered list; and some are a lot more choosy about whom they register, and keep on the register, than others.

Although a council does not have to give reasons for rejecting a candidate, the candidate may appeal. So the reasons for rejection have to be ones that will stand up in court, should the case go that far. It is tough to deny someone access to legal earnings. Thus officials are under some pressure not to turn down a person who meets the basic negative criteria to do the job, like not being married to a criminal, not having some illness or physical disability and having adequate, hygienic surroundings for the children to live and play in. She may well not have many shining positive characteristics that give the registrar a gut feeling that she would make a first-class carer of children. But under the present legislation the registrar cannot allow her or himself to make the sort of value judgement which might lead to the childminder being denied her registration.

The Children Act itself does not spell out exactly what it means by a 'fit' person to care for someone else's children. The Department of Health guidelines on childminding criteria are the most explicit to date. They state that local authorities should take into consideration whether the prospective childminder has had any experience of looking after young children or the elderly; whether she has any qualifications or training; whether she can give warm and consistent care; whether she has knowledge of multi-cultural issues; whether she is able to treat children as individuals; if she has health and mental stability; whether she has integrity, flexibility and carries no record of abuse of children.

Why Do Childminders Do the Job?

Many mothers do not want to go out to work or cannot find work, or if they can, it does not pay enough to have something over after paying the child care costs. So many turn to childminding. They enjoy looking after children and are pleased that their own have some company. They like to feel wanted and they want to be more than just a housewife. Many feel that if they are looking after one or two of their own already, the more the merrier. Last, but most important, the job does bring in cash each week.

A childminder who is caring for two children, not to mention however many she may collect from nursery and primary school, can earn £150–200 a week. From this she has to deduct expenses – heat, food, disposables, etc. Childminders pay their own self-employed tax and National Insurance and might be able to claim up to two-thirds of their income as expenses against tax.

Who Uses Childminders?

The idea that childminding was forged for the poor by the poorer, is out of date. Today relatively few parents who use childminders are semi-skilled manual workers; more are in professional or managerial jobs. They are paid enough to be able to afford a childminder and often this type of care is the only option for them if they have no relations living locally. The upwardly mobile 'nuclear family' have often moved away from their parents' neighbourhood so they have no local grandmother around the corner to help out.

The women who use childminders tend to be younger than the childminders – in their late 20s and likely to be in an early stage of parenthood with only one child – according to Peter Moss in his *Review of Childminding Research*. He goes on, 'Mothers are likely to have had more education and to have more qualifications than the minders they use ... there is little evidence about the 'match' of minders in terms of colour or ethnicity ... childminders are more likely to have been born in the British Isles than are the the mothers of the minded children.'

A growing proportion of the professional middle class use child-minders. A small but significant number of childminders are popular among this group in inner cities, and particularly in London where more mothers with young children continue to work. Many houses and flats in London do not have a spare room for a live-in nanny or mother's help. Where the artisan cottages of Fulham, Balham and Kensal Green have been gentrified, the next-door neighbour may double as the cleaning lady or the childminder or even both.

The NCMA comments: 'Childminders are popular with doctors, teachers, health visitors and social workers – curiously, all community-based professions. There are no statistics yet, but they may come across childminders in their professional life, see how they operate, like it and decide it could work for their children.'

The Pros and Cons of Using a Childminder

Although childminding is no longer a cheap option, especially in Greater London where fees level peg with day nurseries and often exceed them, it has many other advantages. The minder is almost always a mother herself, so will be experienced in child care. You can tell quite a lot about the quality of care by watching the minder's own children, her home and the toys and activities she provides. The child is likely to be one of several, to enjoy the company and learn to be sociable and share the toys. It is good for children to have the experience of another environment in which they feel at home.

The consistency of care is a great advantage – the minder has probably lived in the area for some time and is unlikely to move, so the child is likely to benefit from several years of uninterrupted care from one person. This is in marked contrast to the day nursery option and to the live-in or daily nanny. One mother quoted in the *Parents at Work Handbook* says that she is 'now in a position to compare the relative merits of childminders and nannies and I have to say that, for me, the childminder wins hands down. What I have come to appreciate is the sheer lack of organization involved when employing a childminder.'

A childminder is a bit more flexible than a nursery or a crèche, although, quite rightly, childminders resent parents being late to pick up their children. How can a childminder broach the ticklish matter of overtime pay?

One of the major, insurmountable drawbacks of childminding is the fact that a mother is more of a client than an employer of a childminder. She must largely go along with the minder's views on, and standards of, child care. Moreover, the minded child (or, for that matter, the child at a nursery), cannot ask a friend home for lunch, or visit a friend's home for tea easily. This form of socializing can be a most enjoyable pastime for many children aged three upwards. It is a good idea to talk to mothers who have used childminders for some time to get an idea of what to expect, be aware of, and what to look out for.

One mother tells us: 'When I went to meet the childminder, everything was sweetness and light and there were lots of toys and games around. Over the next few weeks I kept thinking that maybe they had been put away before I went to collect Jason, because I didn't see them again. So I asked Maggie to show me where she kept them. There was some blustering and rudeness, but it became clear that they had not been hers; she must have borrowed them for our meeting. I took him away; how could I trust her after that ?

Many childminders see their role as caring for children. They don't see themselves as educators; they don't reckon to be the home version of the Montessori teacher, or even the NNEB who knows about child development in all its manifestations. There is more chance that the minder will take a somewhat *laissez faire* approach to the child's play and enthusiasms. If she has three children under five to look after, feed and take to the lavatory, it is not surprising that she may have little time to sit on the floor and play with them. It is even less likely if she is fitting in her washing, ironing and cooking the evening meal for her family. You can't expect her to be Superwoman.

As one ex-childminder put it: 'There is the good, the bad and occasionally, the ugly, in childminding'. There is also the mediocre. A mediocre childminder is not good enough for your child and it may not be at all easy to detect one at the outset. The onus is on mothers to be vigilant, and expect the best rather than accept the indifferent. The NCMA advises: 'There are lots of excellent childminders with modern ideals and ideas. But we do recommend that mothers shop around a bit and do not take the first childminder on offer.'

What it Costs

Childminding appeals to many parents because it is cheaper (although the difference is closing) than daily nannies and often less than a nursery. Whether or not it can also be considered good value depends on the quality of the minder. Childminding is better paid now than in the past, as parents and minders have grown to expect more from each other. Childminders offer a better service and parents are glad to pay properly for it.

The cost per hour for different childminders varies enormously depending on the part of the country (a big city, a market town or deep country) the minder lives. Costs will also vary with the quality of care. If a childminder thinks she provides a first-class service which rivals the day nursery down the road, she will charge a similar fee to the nursery.

Childminders charge what the market will bear. Thus, in an affluent part of town charges will be higher, but that is not to say that a childminder won't tailor her fees for, for example, a hard-up single mother. A 50-hour week will be anything from £85–£140. The NCMA has a useful table of lowest and highest amounts per hour, ranging from £1.70 to £3.00.

From that the childminder will deduct such expenses as toys, safety equipment for the house, the food the minded child eats (many take their own lunch) and disposables if she provides them (most don't), special baby needs (zinc and castor oil cream, bibs etc), fares or, rarely, petrol for special outings like the zoo or museums.

Where to Find a Childminder

Research shows that most mothers seeking childminders do not shop around and they tend not to interview more than one candidate. She is often recommended on the grapevine or is someone they or a friend know. 'Hauling around lots of addresses with a small child is daunting, especially for women who in any case often feel anxious or guilty about leaving their child,' says Peter Moss. Some mothers who have made the decision to return to work after having a baby feel vulnerable, and, in a curious way, actually resist finding out all about various sorts of child care. It is as if, by opening more than one door, they may find themselves overwhelmed by a whole range of options and choices which they haven't got the energy, time or resilience to think through and deal with. Some are plain lazy; others too sensitive; some are aggressive and some are just foolish. Whatever the reason, many cannot cope initially with the effort required to seek out a really good minder.

Even with the best will in the world, in some areas there are very few childminders available and a mother may be stuck with someone less than ideal. The first thing to do when beginning the search for a childminder is to ring the local social services and ask for an Under Eights Officer. He or she will have a complete list of the district's registered childminders. He should also be able to tell you who is a member of the NCMA and try to match you with not just any minder but the type to suit you.

If you have an unhelpful response, write direct to the NCMA (enclosing an sae) for a list of local groups. Your health visitor should have some ideas. Also, if you live near a borough boundary, contact the neighbouring council for its list of childminders. Childminders make themselves known by: advertisements in the local paper (it is a good sign if they quote their registration number), newsagents, laundromats, one o'clock clubs, schools, clinics and local shops. They also leave their names with staff at the local clinic and tell the health visitor that they are looking for children to mind.

Any local NCMA group probably operates a vacancy list. Also it is a good idea to place your own advertisements in all these places locally. As with all ads in public places, it is advisable not to give your name, just the telephone number and as many details of your needs as can be fitted on to a postcard.

How to Choose a Childminder

Parents should leave no stone unturned when interviewing a registered childminder. Scepticism, albeit heavily camouflaged, should be uppermost. After all, when did the council officers last check that all is just as it should be in the childminder's home ? This, incidentally, is something a prospective client can ask the childminder herself. If she has nothing to hide, and wishes that an inspector would call so she can show off her new plastic slide in the garden, she won't be put out by *any* prying questions.

The childminder needs to be able to communicate with both parents and children. She must be able to tell a parent about any problems with their child or deal with a parent who takes her for granted without souring the atmosphere for weeks. She must also support the whole ethos of a working mother. She should co-operate with other childminders and the authorities as well.

Membership of the NCMA

One of the unfortunate aspects of childminding is the word 'mind', which sounds like the definition of a part-time activity where the woman minder gets on with more important domestic tasks simultaneously. Child 'carer' has a much nicer ring to it. In the 1980s the NCMA made such advances that the word 'minder' began to shed its former bad associations. It helped to remove the low status of childminding by making it more professional and respected as a worthwhile option for care of working parents' children.

All childminders who take pride in their profession should be members of the NCMA, if only to flag to parents that they take their job seriously and that they, like GPs and the British Medical Association, have the back up of a professional body. Membership gives peace of mind to the minder and to parents. When difficulties arise, the childminder has recourse to the NCMA's 24-hour legal advice phone line, a help line three afternoons a week and a telephone insurance query line four days a week.

Many join simply because it offers a good insurance package. All registered childminders have to have public liability insurance and several companies offer competitive rates (contact the social services for information). Many join the NCMA because of its comprehensive insurance package. Its public liability insurance cover includes :

- accidental bodily injury or death to children in her care.
- legal defence costs.
- loss or accidental damage to minded children's property up to £250 (e.g., a lost coat or damaged buggy).
- alleged abuse of children where 'actual' injury has occurred.

The NCMA also offers standard legal expenses insurance in the event of a criminal prosecution for alleged child abuse where there is no 'actual' injury or damage. There is also extended legal expenses insurance which covers the childminder in a dispute with the parents over her contract. Childminders do have problems sometimes over payment and don't pursue the issue in a small claims court because of the hassle and expense. Childminders can also buy house contents and building insurance specially tailored for them.

As one childminder says: 'Doing everything thoroughly and on the level is important. I was so relieved that I had when I looked after a child who died a cot death. It wasn't at my home but it was terrible and a lot of questions were asked. Quite rightly. Thank goodness I was properly insured and everything was correct.'

Membership also means receiving the NCMA magazine four times a year. Called *Who Minds?*, it aids efficient childminding with discount offers of cash books and attendance registers, childminding contracts and an accident record book. Incidentally, parents looking for a childminder can access the NCMA's national database of registered childminders and there is also a helpful book, *Choosing a Childminder: A Guide for Parents*, and a video.

The NCMA comments: 'Childminding can involve providing: love, play, security, food, time, warmth, attention, outings, routine, stimulation, sympathy and protection.'

The interview

It is often best *not* to take the child along to the first interview with a prospective carer, especially if you intend to see two or three, which is thoroughly recommended. It makes it easier for you not to further the relationship without affecting your child, and, if you do want to do so, arranging the second interview also serves as time for reflection. Once you have found a gem, then take your child to meet her on your second visit and check out whether the childminder continues to gain points by handling him well. The interview will obviously vary according to the personality you encounter. The childminder should ask you a lot of questions, too. You will both be hoping that your priorities and wishes coincide well enough for a successful partnership. You will not necessarily see much of each other during this relationship, but that makes it all the more vital that everyone concerned is entirely happy with it.

Comments from mothers include:

One problem with childminders I have each time I've needed extra child care and gone interviewing is that you have to take your child out of a spacious, pleasantly decorated house with lots of toys and interesting things to stimulate him and put him into a much smaller sitting room and kitchen with fewer toys and a smaller garden.

You have to accept that the prospective childminder, however nice, is definitely going to do things her way and you can take it or leave it. So far, I've left it.

I had live-in Australians for my first three children and only discovered the usefulness of childminding for part of the day for my fourth. Leaving a child with a childminder you like for a relatively short time is just fine.

We sent Marie to a good nursery, but since then I have met one wonderful childminder who manages to bring up three children of her own quite beautifully in a fairly cramped space. But I would have chosen her for Marie if I had met her earlier.

What I want is a carer who shares my views about child care and with whom I have something in common. The trouble is that most childminders are not middle class and I feel the whole lifestyle is too different from ours to be comfortable with.

Assuming that the childminder is able to provide the basics for your child's physical wellbeing – enough warmth, space, light and fresh air – you need to assess quickly what *type* of childminder she is. If she is older, say 40 plus, there's a higher chance that she may be cuddly, but with the old-style 'I let them get on with it' approach. She may give herself away by saying, 'Oh yes, there are plenty of puzzles in the cupboard', and you may pick up from that dismissive sentence that she is not likely to do many puzzles (or anything else) with the child.

A childminder needs to be as close as possible to an ideal: a warm, intelligent, switched-on entertainments manageress who really puts her job of caring for your child well before her own shopping and housework. You want a childminder who is prepared to make your child's 10-hour a day stay with her worthwhile. One of the key things you need to decide is whether the childminder is 'hands on'. Do you believe that she actually *plays* with the children, does a jigsaw, plays lotto or snap, paints a picture, draws with him, reads lots to him, makes models with plasticene and playdough, sings nursery rhymes, etc?

Check with the Under Eights Officer as to whether the council provides a short training course for childminders – more and more do, and ask if the childminder you are interviewing has been on one.

With any luck the Council's Under Eights Officer will have briefed you on several minders and there'll be enough choice for you to have already rejected the no doubt nice but uninspiring ones. Assuming that you wouldn't be meeting the childminder unless you knew that she was registered, the next thing to discover is whether she is a member of the National Childminding Association (about half of registered childminders are members). If not, why not? Often the response is that she doesn't feel any need to be, which loses her a few Brownie points. One childminder said reassuringly that the few other childminders within walking distance of her home got together often as friends to compare notes.

By definition, a childminder is a busy person who is likely to be keen to keep commitments down to a manageable minimum – and all clubs take up time.

One of the first things to ask her is whether she takes in more children apart from her own for after-school care? If she does, think seriously before pursuing it. The NCMA comments: 'Often a child who was minded by one of our members before going to school comes back after school each day, until his mother returns from work. This can work well for everyone. The school-age child enjoys the company of his minder and can help out with the younger ones. We wouldn't recommend that a mother reject a minder who takes in one or two schoolchildren for a couple of hours in the afternoon. But it is something that she should know all about and it would be a good idea to discuss the matter with the council's Under Eights Officer. Ask the council officer concerned whether he or she knows if the childminders he has available do take in older children after school and if he doesn't know, get him to find out.

Questions to ask her

1 Is she a member of the NCMA? If so, get her to tell you all about her involvement.
2 Does she take children to playgroups and/or local activities?
3 What previous work experience has she?
4 Does she have any qualifications, child-related NVQs or other?
5 How long has she been childminding?
6 Does she mean to do it indefinitely or does she want to go out to work soon?
7 Does she practise any religion? (always interesting this one)
8 What are her views on discipline; would she smack, shake, or shout at him?
9 What are her views on sweets (would she reward a child with a sweet or crisps?)
10 What about manners – 'please' and 'thank you' and others?
11 What about TV and videos? What does she let them watch? When and for how long? What does she do then?
12 What about vegetarian or ethnic food?
13 When does she do her shopping? What about her housework, washing and ironing? (The ideal answer to this one is when every other person who works and doesn't have a cleaner does it – at the weekend or before or after work).

14 What hours do her grown up children and/or husband keep?
    Will any of them be around during childminding hours? How
    old are they and what do they do? (Try to meet all the house
    inmates and have a chat to see what they are like).
15 Is there a dog (not ideal with small children around) or a cat?
16 What arrangement does she make when she, or one of the chil-
    dren, is ill? Can you still bring your child if he is ill?
17 What does she do when she wants to take a holiday? What
    about Bank Holidays?
18 Will you be paying her throughout the year? Is there a retainer
    fee during half-term and school holidays when your child stays
    at home?
19 May you pop in when you can?
20 What is her procedure if a child has an accident?
21 Has she got any other jobs? Many do and their childminding
    can be affected.
22 What is her worst swear word in front of the children?
23 How and when will she expect to be paid?

Anyone who has interviewed a childminder knows that it is neither possible nor sensible to bombard her with 1001 questions.
Having said which, try to chat her through them, because you
certainly need clear answers however you procure them. One
Under Eights Officer says: 'We tell childminders that they must
expect to be asked what may seem to be intrusive questions and
that it's right that parents ask lots of them.'

Sometimes it may feel as though she is doing you a favour by
taking on your child rather than someone else's. Often there are so
few available childminders a mother has to think positively about
an interviewee and literally hope for the best, even if in an ideal
world she would not be her first choice. Many of her answers will
probably solve your other questions. If your gut feeling is that she's
for you, then you can ask her more questions at a second interview.
If you feel after the preliminary questions that she's not the one,
wind up the conversation as fast as you can.

It is important that you understand every aspect of her requirements. If you feel that she's the one, before you get committed ask
to study her contract and acquaint yourself with any extra fees and
idiosyncratic stipulations she may have. One mum comments:

> She was charging top whack anyway and once we agreed to take each
> other on she started telling me about Bank Holidays, retainer fees and
> nil flexibility on pick-up times. Phew, I rather wished I'd kept looking!

A childminder ought to volunteer views which coincide with your own and if she does not, then she should treat your child as you wish him to be treated. The core subjects of optimal childrearing should not be ducked – discipline, potty training, nutrition, safety, etc. You also need to ascertain that the childminder is not going to give your child the benefit of any prejudices which you do not tolerate – racism, xenophobia, or sexism, for example. It will be far from ideal if the child has to witness anti-social habits like smoking, swearing and blaspheming. If you care about the *quality* of the care, you have to try to find someone as like you as possible, whose views coincide with your own. Easily said.

Questions to ask yourself

- Does her home look clean and safe ?
- Are you happy about the space, in view of the number of children minded?
- Was the TV on when you arrived?
- What was her line on TV? Do you feel confident that when she says that she doesn't have the TV on much, that that is the actual case? Does she show videos?
- Are there lots of toys, and preferably some educational ones, about?
- Does the garden look pleasant and have any play equipment?
- How often, when and where does she propose to take your child out?
- How old are the other children that she minds ? Will they fit in well with yours?
- Where will your child be changed/rest/go to the lavatory? Some councils insist that the child rests on the same floor as the minder i.e., the minder cannot be in the sitting room with some children while one rests upstairs.
- Is she sympathetic and receptive to any illnesses, abnormalities, special diet or allergies, fears or particular favourites that your child may have?

Here is the NCMA/Open University list of things which children do that some childminders say they find hard to tolerate :

- make a mess with toys
- get dirty
- refuse to stop and look before crossing the road
- exclude another child from play because of skin colour or sex

- tease other children
- are rude after being told off
- refuse to tidy toys away
- hurt another child
- break someone else's special toy/object/book
- won't walk on the pavement when out shopping
- call a black child names
- run around indoors
- take food without asking
- bang on windows
- tease or hurt an animal
- tell lies
- constantly try to get attention
- fight with other children.

Think about the implications of this list. Is your child guilty of much of this irritating behaviour? Warn the childminder about his peccadilloes if you know trouble finds him fast. Encourage your childminder to list her likes and dislikes as well as making your preferences and expectations clear.

Discipline

Most parents don't want a childminder or a nanny to lay as much as a finger on their child, however fed-up and cross the carer has become. The NCMA has a 'no-smacking' policy. It says, rightly, that smacking another person's child is neither acceptable or necessary and it wants its members to be on the same footing as foster carers and playgroup and nursery workers who are not allowed to smack.

Here is an edited version of the well-argued reasons why, according to the NCMA, childminders don't need to smack, and it is just as relevant for parents, nannies, grandparents and all child carers, too:

Set limits from the start – there should be clear house rules about behaviour. Simple, consistent rules are very reassuring to children who will accept them if they understand the reasons for them.

Build children's self-esteem – shaming, humiliating and hurting children teaches nothing positive. If children are used to getting attention with good behaviour, they won't need to seek it with bad behaviour.

Set a good example – children learn values and behaviour from adults. Be considerate, polite and honest in dealing with children rather than smacking and shouting which sends clear messages to the child that physical force is a good way of getting people to do what you want.

Bad behaviour, not bad children – it's the bad behaviour that's rejected. It's important not to bear grudges against children and to treat them with concern and respect and to resume a normal affectionate relationship with them when an incident is over.

Getting to the end of your tether? No matter how patient we are, there comes a time when we just can't reason any more. Put the child in a safe place, clap your hands, punch a cushion, have a cup of coffee to put yourself into a 'let's start again' frame of mind.

Be consistent – say no and mean no. It helps if children know that we mean what we say.

Manage behaviour without smacking – if the situation is dangerous, the Children Act permits the use of 'reasonable force' to protect the child. Grab the child, say 'no' loudly. If a tantrum is in the offing, remove the child from the immediate area until he calms down. You can restrain him gently until the tantrum subsides, then cuddle him to soothe and reassure. Losing control is frightening enough for young children without adult reaction compounding it.

Help children to be good – children want to please adults who are important to them. Help with positive discipline and encourage rather than scold, shout or smack.

A few final points

Every childminder has by law to keep a record of each child's name, date of birth, parents' names, emergency telephone numbers, whether the child has any health problems and whether he takes any medicines. A good childminder will keep a record of every bump and scrape and tell the parents about how they happened immediately. Ensure that she also has the child's doctor's phone number, a record of the infectious diseases he has had and his immunizations to date. Work out together a fail-safe contingency plan for emergencies.

If a childminder isn't asking you questions, get her to do so by saying: 'Is there anything you'd like to ask about us?' She should want to know as much as possible about your child – his personality, what he likes doing, his habits and stage of development.

With any luck she will encourage you to send the odd toy and comfort object along with him. She should assure you that she will make it easy for you to talk to her about problems and express any worries you may have. Don't forget that it is not unknown for a childminder to turn *you* down, probably because she doesn't think that you and she see eye-to-eye sufficiently. If she does, don't persuade her otherwise: respect her judgement!

Many minders and mothers favour contracts nowadays; the NCMA has one. It does not have to be a complicated document, but should mention the hours and the pay. As with in-home child care, a contract can cut out a lot of resentment at a later stage.

Peter Moss of the Thomas Coram Institute reports that 'The pleasures of minding centre around the children and the dissatisfactions around the parents ... major sources of friction are money, hours, feelings of being used and differences of opinion about child care ... in general, parents appear less critical of minders than minders are of parents.'

To summarize, babies and toddlers may spend happy days with an involved, well-balanced, conscientious childminder and it can be a most successful form of care. Contact and communication between mother and minder must be energetically maintained by both. Parents and childminder must be sensitive and sympathetic to a child's need to settle in gently to the new routine.

The first week or two can be difficult if the child is over a year and may cling to his mother on the doorstep. It is best to put him in the minder's arms and go promptly. He will cheer up after a while and soon get used to being left.

It is a good idea, as soon as the child is old enough, to arrange for him to go to a playgroup or nursery school. This enables both minder and minded to get away from each other for two or three hours during a long day. It will break the routine for the child and may mean that some parents need to be less concerned about the amount of varied entertainment and stimulation their adored offspring receives week after week.

Chapter 15
Day Nurseries

State Day Nurseries

In this country the majority of state day nurseries, especially in cities, are used by local authorities to provide care for children who are on the 'At Risk' Register. These children are so described because their family background and circumstances are such that they may be physically and/or emotionally 'at risk'. This means that social workers decide that it is best for the child to spend most of his day in a nursery and away from his parents and home. There are long waiting lists for the remaining places, which are usually filled by the next children 'in most need', or who are considered to be 'high priority cases'. These euphemisms carry a certain stigma for the parents who use state day nurseries.

In rougher areas of some inner cities it is possible to find local authority day nurseries where there are no 'normal' children. Nor would most caring parents wish them to be there if there were other options. Some parents cannot afford the alternatives and state day nursery charges for day care are minimal. A West London mother, a Yugoslav who emigrated to the UK fifteen years ago, says 'I could have put my daughter in a local authority day nursery because I am alone and in a small flat, but I would never put my child in such a place. I am lucky, I pay only £70 a week for her to go to a community nursery where the places are subsidized to an extent by the council, and the children are all from ordinary homes.'

Another working mother from Camberwell says, 'I managed to get my daughter into a local authority day nursery. It was all right when she wasn't walking, but then the competition with the other children was too much. She kept coming home scratched and was knocked about a bit. She was always getting infections and they wouldn't take her when she was ill. I took her away and sent her to a childminder.'

A third got a place for her little boy in a Marylebone council day nursery because ' he hadn't slept at night for two years. Me and my husband were going spare. The social worker was very sympathetic. Both of us work and getting her a place at the nursery was such a break.' State day nurseries are usually open between 8 am and 6 pm including school holidays. Some take children from six weeks to school age.

In the past there have been some fairly grim inner city nurseries which took children from disadvantaged homes, for example, where the mother was the sole parent and went out to work in poorly paid part-time jobs.

Astonishingly, a significant percentage of full-time and part-time working mothers leave children unattended at home or in the 'care' of older siblings. The social services have helped to keep this situation to a minimum by giving the children places in state-run nurseries. One nursery officer comments: 'Many of them are at risk of not developing properly – they don't talk or behave like kids of their age. They often have very poor concentration spans. They all need a rest in the afternoons; most drop asleep in front of a TV as the wee small hours approach.'

It is difficult to argue that there is much benefit to ordinary children in being solely in the company of these unfortunates.

There are still such nurseries today, but there are also many more reasonable local authority day nurseries which are catering well for a mix of working and middle class children, and where there are only a handful of 'at risk' children, who benefit greatly from being with children from more normal homes.

As the number of households rise where both parents work full- or part-time, parents have been forced to take the initiative and set up new day nurseries – often in tandem with charities, businesses and state-run institutions, like hospitals and colleges. In many instances this has been done with the blessing of the local authorities so that a 'partnership' is formed whereby the council subsidizes each place by contributing a quarter, or even half, of a nursery's running costs.

Community Day Nurseries

These have often been set up by a community – like those living in a group of tower blocks – and their aim is often to provide an alternative to exisiting care in a specific way. Many community nursery organizers feel strongly about racist and/or sexist bias and some challenge traditional organizational methods by working together as a collective.

All the staff are paid the same and there is no hierarchy. Children attending a community nursery live close by. One of its attractions to parents is that it doesn't carry the stigma of the state nursery where some parents feel criticized by staff. They also resent the minimal link between parents and staff in many state nurseries. The community variety are trying to change all that.

Parents are treated as partners with the staff in the care of their children. They are on the management committee and can influence decisions about the way the nursery is organized. The committee decides on wages and these can vary enormously, but are competitive with childminders' fees. They can be based on a percentage of the parents' income, so that the better off pay more. Alternative forms of care, like community nurseries, mean a great deal of hard work for staff and parents. Time has to be spent organizing, campaigning and approaching charities, businesses, parents and local authorities for funds to keep the nursery solvent.

Workplace Nurseries

In the 1980s it was thought that by the end of the century there would be thousands of workplace nurseries, but their growth has been very slow and the numbers are still small. The idea of a workplace nursery is appealing with many parents welcoming the chance of seeing their children during the working day. Its disadvantage, as with all out-of-home care, is not only the sweat of the early morning rush, but the trip into work accompanied by a child or two, instead of parking them with a childminder round the corner from their home. And then parent and child have to run the gauntlet of the evening rush hour.

The workplace creche pioneers in this country during the 1970s included the Kingsway Children's Nursery and the Chandos Place Nursery, both in central London. Today they are in effect private nurseries, though some of their places are subsidized by up to two-thirds by the parents' employers. Bigger companies tend to be, and can afford to be, more philanthropic, like Midland Bank which sponsors over 1,000 places around the country. The Body Shop provides its workers with a state of the art nursery at its headquarters in Sussex. Other progressive companies like Walker Books, a successful publisher of children's books, have their own nursery on site.

The City Child Nursery broke new ground when it opened in 1988. It remains a rare collaboration between the Corporation of London's social services department, Islington council and property developers. The developers were granted planning permission for a Barbican site, so long as they included a 30-place nursery and agreed to underwrite it for ten years. The tenants of the property are American bankers, Merrill Lynch, who agreed to pay two-thirds of the cost of a nursery place for any of their staff who wanted to place their children in it.

'One Euro-bond dealer married to another asked me if the crèche could be open 24 hours? I replied that we aim to provide high quality *day* care facilities. Just think of that poor child's routine. They obviously need a live-in nanny. We are only providing one option – obviously it won't suit everyone. But it is one way of sharing domestic and work responsibilities peacefully and we welcome as much parental involvement as parents want', comments Susan Hay, a founder of City Child.

Although the City Child would like to help employers open other nurseries, (Spitalfields and Docklands have been mooted), the fantastic expense of real estate in these places and the high costs of running a nursery, not to mention a firm's subsidy of children's places, militate against companies wanting to become involved.

Institutions with plenty of space like schools, sports centres, universities and hospitals have set up crèches. If the institution is big enough, like the BBC, staff places are subsidized. St George's Hospital in Tooting, south London, has a nursery for all its staff which caters for shift work. In school crèches, teachers pay the going rate, but it is of great advantage to have their children so close.

A much simpler and cheaper solution has been developed by the National Childminding Association and the insurance group Allied Dunbar in Swindon. Childminding in Business liaises with 40 local childminders who reserve places for the children of Allied Dunbar staff. The NCMA hopes that there will be many other such arrangements in the future.

It is always worth checking out a workplace nursery. The standards are often high and the staff well motivated. If it has a vacancy or two, a local child may be eligible. Workplace nurseries received a boost when the tax which employees had to pay on their employer's contribution to the cost of the nursery place was abolished. At a stroke this reduced the cost of child care for employees and cut the administrative red tape for employers too.

Sadly, it is just because there are so few workplace nurseries, and a belief that it will be a long time before there are many more, that the government felt able to waive this tax. Another problem with the whole scheme is that it is not always easy to work with a perk which ties the user to the job so closely. Occasionally it is possible to arrange to keep the nursery place for your child should you decide to change jobs. The National Child Care Campaign, the Workplace Nurseries Campaign, City Child and Parents at Work all campaign and lobby to increase workplace nurseries (see Useful Addresses).

Private Day Nurseries

In the 1990s private day nurseries came of age. From being a fairly rare sight outside London in the 1980s, they have sprouted everywhere in cities and towns and sometimes in farmhouses in the country. There are now a few 24-hour nurseries which have, in effect, a children's hotel on the premises. The pioneer in round-the-clock care is London's Pippa Poppins. Day nurseries are a lifeline to the 'career' mother of one child and sometimes two children, who hasn't room in the house for a live-in nanny and who rejects a daily nanny, who takes more organization and supervision than a nursery. She returns to work after anything from six weeks to six months and is able to leave her precious bundle with, in most cases, a well-run nursery. A part-time working mother can choose to leave her child a whole or half day, once, twice or every day of the week.

Now there is more choice, expectations of, and the quality of, nurseries has risen. They are expensive to run, needing high staff-to-child ratios, so they are mostly more expensive than childminding, but are often competitive compared with daily nannies. The cost of a nursery varies, but the normal range is £80-£120 for a 50-hour week and plenty of examples of £150-£170 plus in the capital. Be sure to enquire about extras. Many nurseries charge extra for swimming, dancing, etc – others roll them up in the total (higher) bill.

A drawback, which is not confined to state day nurseries, is the prevalence of infection. One mother who is a doctor says ' There are higher instances of respiratory and gastro-intestinal problems wherever there are large groups of small children, unless hygiene is scrupulous.'

One mother says 'My son goes to an excellent local private nursery in Fulham – we are incredibly lucky, there are two of them that are equally good in the Fulham Palace Road and Moore Park Road. Hilary runs my son's in a converted flat and she really brings the children on. There are about ten children. They charge £25 a day, so I send him whenever it suits me – about once or twice a week, and he is as happy as a sandboy'.

Private day nurseries for two to five year olds can be an excellent option for working parents who can afford them. With a child in a good day nursery, there need be none of the worries associated with a nanny or a childminder. There is no risk of young Freddie having to endure his nanny's or his carer's rock music tapes.

Although it is harder to make a mistake in choosing a nursery, there are degrees of good nurseries. Some nurseries have all their staff qualified to NNEB and above. Although local authorities can have good practice guidelines and encourage nurseries to have all their staff qualified, the statutory minimum is that only 50 per cent need to be qualified, so many nurseries keep to this to keep costs down. There can be negative changes in staff, atmosphere and morale, so parents take their children away earlier than they intended. Nurseries lose a lot of children when they reach three years plus, when they leave to join state nursery and primary nursery schools. However, many nurseries still care for their charges after school and cater for the older child in the school holidays.

Checking Out The Private Nursery

As with all types of child care, do not vet just one nursery. Compare several, which will give you a feel for what is on offer and how well it is delivered. You will be happier with your final choice if you have done your homework and know that although the nursery you settle on isn't perfect, it is the best of the lot near you. In many cases there may be only one that is close enough to home. Try not to plump for the nearest one, if there is something better a bit further away: many parents drive quite far so as to use a preferred nursery.

The only way to judge a nursery's quality is to see it in action. Keep your eyes wide open and chat to all the staff. Be sure to visit when all the children are *in situ* so you can chat to them about their training. Always ask about staff/child ratios. The statutory minimum for 0 to two years: one staff member to three children;

for two to three years: one staffer to four children and for three to five years: one staffer to eight children. Good local authorities encourage better ratios, ie, one to three children under 18 months, one staffer to five children aged two to five years.

As with interviewing childminders, there is a limit to the number of questions you can ask in an hour. Two visits at different times of the day are a good idea to check consistency of care and organization. There just isn't time to get through a long list of questions in one visit and others may suggest themselves after the first. On the second visit you can be definite about which wins your best of the bunch award. The lists below should help to focus your own thoughts on what you want and expect from a nursery:

- Consider the size, shape, light, airiness of the room(s).
- Does this place have a happy, purposeful atmosphere? Are the children full of life? How much noise is there?
- How much time do babies spend in their cots and playpens?
- Do the children receive well-balanced meals when they should?
- Are they getting enough rest? Is there a rest area that is quiet and conducive to a zizz?
- Are babies cuddled and fed carefully, with their carer concentrating on them exclusively?
- Are the children reasonably clean?
- Are there too many of them with coughs and colds?
- How does the nursery clean toys, changing mats, mugs etc?
- Are there enough toys/games/books/tricycles and other equipment?
- Do they paint, draw or model in plasticine and playdough?
- What does the nursery offer in the way of exercise?
- Can the children go swimming and/ or singing and/or ballet?
- Do firemen, police, St John's Ambulance visit?
- How large and well-equipped is the garden?
- Are the walls crammed with artwork?
- Is what the children are busy doing better than I could provide? Is the room humming with an activity which I could not possibly match?
- Is there a common policy on discipline, potty training, manners?
- How do they discipline children?
- Are children encouraged to enjoy letters and numbers? How much pre-school learning is there? Pre-reading games, writing and arithmetic?

- Does the nursery have a 'philosophy' on this? Is there indeed a curriculum where children learn in a systematic way how to write and read?
- How much one-to-one attention will a child receive?
- Is there a small room where a child can do something alone or quietly with a nursery nurse?
- How structured will the child's day be? Are there specific times when the children are read to, go outside, listen to music, enjoy free play?
- What does the nursery do when one or more of its staff are ill?
- Do parents and staff meet and discuss the child now and again?
- Who really runs the place and directs what will happen next? Are they good at it?

Nobble other parents on the subject of how they are treated by the nursery. Are they kept at arm's length and their input ignored? One mother says: ' It is vital to chat to every member of staff and get a clear picture of lines of command.'

Sally Provence, a professor of paediatrics at Yale, writes from her own experience of managing a day care centre for babies and young children, about the requisites for their good care. Her list, quoted in *Mother Care Other Care*, includes:

> opportunities for the child to act on his environment: materials and opportunities to hammer, paste, colour, cut, sweep, dress, wash, build, mash, throw, kick, mix, stir, beat, pedal, run, dance, strum, jump, skip, button, zip and spit. Young children need these to feel effective and competent. Also an enriching atmosphere: good relationships with caregivers who are consistently available, affectionate, patient, good listeners, good talkers and enthusiastic about the child's achievements. Every child deserves somebody to be excited about the first time he walks and the first time he rides a tricycle. And [there should be] limits, prohibitions and expectations for conformity: just as children need opportunities to express themselves, they also need to learn limits on their behaviour which will make them acceptable members of their society. Children do not come into the world knowing the social rules; adults must teach them. Firmly enforced guidelines for behaviour, especially those aspects which affect safety and others' rights, are essential in any child care situation.

If these requirements coincide with your own and the place seems to be running pretty much along these lines, this may be the nursery for you.

One full-time working mother took her little son from six months to three years to a private day nursery and says 'He had a wonderful time every day. He loved his carers and they became fond of him. He did so much creative play and enjoyed his peers' company tremendously. As my only child at the time, I was certain that he had a much better time there than he would have done with me or with a super-duper nanny or childminder.' That's how it will feel if you get it right.

One area it is important to discover all about at an early stage is the nursery's approach to pre-school teaching. Be sure that it matches yours. It is now accepted that children benefit greatly from 'early years teaching' and it is reckoned important that there are periods during the day when they should have structured play, so that nursery nurses and other staff can ensure that they learn the list of 'core' skills, which include number and letter recognition, pen control etc. Different nurseries emphasize different areas of development and some feel that children should discover the world on their own with a minimum of guidance.

There is an understandable feeling among many parents that if they are paying a considerable sum each week for their two and three year old's care, there ought to be efforts to encourage his development, and that it is a good thing that reading, writing and arithmetic are introduced to him sensitively, sensibly and soon. More and more nurseries provide for early learning, particularly in London where there is a higher proportion of the professions using nurseries. They sometimes choose Montessori-based theories.

One head of a tremendously popular nursery in Battersea comments : 'I can't see the point of not encouraging three and four year olds to be aware of the three Rs. Some of them are so keen to master simple sentences, they lap it up. It has to be an advantage to have grasped the principles of reading by the time they go to school.' Other nurseries feel very strongly that this should be an age when children are not pressured nor their lives much structured. But, like it or not, the trend is to educate young children, and there is likely to be greater emphasis on learning for the older children.

The LEGO National Child Care Directory, which is a very useful database of UK private nurseries and nursery schools (obtainable from the library, see Bibilography) has helpful suggestions for good practice in day nurseries and guidelines for assessing their quality. We list an edited selection. Although few parents would be able to ascertain all the information, it is worth being aware of the issues they raise .

Suggested Good Practice for Under-fives Day Nursery Care

The nursery shall conform to at least Department of Health guidelines – even if a local authority permits some relaxation in its own standards.

All staff shall be paid no less than two-thirds of recognized local authority rates for their equivalent positions.

All permanent staff, except those engaged mainly in catering and cleaning, shall be trained to at least a fully qualified two-year NNEB level.

No more than one student, or trainee, shall be present at any time in the day-care facility.

Insurance cover for child death or injury shall be maintained – giving a minimum of £500,000 for serious disablement and £1 million for staff liability.

All children shall be registered when they enter and leave the facility, and fire drill is to be called once a month.

A development record shall be kept for each child, showing their progress on several key cognitive, affective and sensory motor skills.

Each child shall be read to by staff at least once a day.

Children shall be given drink, rest and access to toilets on demand.

An outside play area shall be provided giving at least as much free space as that required inside and containing at least three pieces of well-maintained fixed equipment, safety surfaces and a grassed area.

All children shall be encouraged to clean their teeth after meals and snacks.

The nursery shall be cleaned thoroughly at least once a day and toilet/kitchen areas cleaned and disinfected at least twice a day.

All meals shall be carefully balanced to give a healthy nutritional diet and, in the case of full day care children, receiving lunch and one other meal or snack, the food will provide at least 50 per cent of the World Health Organization recommended daily intake of vitamins, essential minerals and protein. A doctor or qualified nurse shall be 'on call' throughout the day and no child shall be allowed to be in contact with other children once an infectious illness is evident.

Guidelines for Judging the Quality of Day Nurseries

To quote the LEGO/National Child Care Directory:

Department of Health and local authority guidelines establish minimum space, staffing and facility standards – largely in quantative terms, but to judge whether a nursery is well run and effective, it is necessary to go beyond them and to consider a wide range of factors.

Here are more LEGO/NCD questions to bear in mind:

Location

Is the nursery:

- In an exposed position, on a northward facing slope (not much sun)or in a depression (poor outlook, less light)?
- Located in a residential or commercial area?
- On, or very close to, a major road with heavy traffic and noise fumes?
- Easily accessible by car and foot?
- Does it have adequate parking facilities well protected from children?

Children's development and welfare

- Are the children formally registered as they arrive?
- Are children monitored for their personal and emotional development? Is this information formally recorded and made available to parents?
- Does the organization operating the facility adopt a particular child development philosophy (eg Montessori)?
- Is a sickness record made and parents in general alerted to any contagious illnesses contracted by other children?
- Does a doctor regularly attend the nursery to carry out preventative medicine or is there one on call?

Range and nature of experience provided

- Is there a wide range of play activities – inside and outside?
- How long are children allowed to watch TV/video each day?
- Are the children taken out on trips during the year? If so, how frequently?
- Do staff take part fully in play and games activities or do they just oversee them?

- Are new toys and games frequently purchased and old/worn toys removed (unless a child is particularly attached to them)?

Culture and atmosphere

- Would you say the atmosphere is happy? Warm? Quiet? Efficient?
- Do the children move around freely during activities?
- How closely are they supervised?
- How noisy is it? Do staff raise their voices to gain attention?
- What happens if a child does something wrong? What is meant by 'wrong'?
- What happens on rainy or cold days?
- Are the children confined to one or two rooms for long periods?
- Does the nursery contain a social mix?

Management

- Does the head of the nursery look like someone in charge and generally trustworthy?
- How frequently is the nursery inspected by the local authority?
- What are the opening hours? Is the nursery open all year? What about Bank Holidays?
- What happens if a parent is unavoidably delayed and is late picking up the child?
- What is the maximum time a child can be at the nursery – per day, per week?
- Is there a management committee? Does this consist of 'worthies' or is it largely run by staff, parents and any sponsoring organizations?
- Who decides to appoint staff? Who has the final say? (It should be the Head). How bureaucratic is the process?

Staff calibre

- Are all staff qualified to at least NNEB Diploma/NVQ level 3?
- Has at least one member of staff been trained as a nursery teacher/SRN?
- What is the qualification/background/experience of the head of the facility and directors? Does this contain a significant business management element? How much previous experience have they had in child care (outside family commitments)?
- Does the Head also operate/run other nurseries? If so, how many? Where are they located – are they geographically dispersed across local authorities?

- What are their other business interests? How much time does this take up?

Equipment

- Is there plenty of equipment for: outside/inside play; staff record keeping (files/a computer); kitchen functions; laundry functions?
- Is it carpeted? Are visitors asked to remove shoes in the baby unit?
- Are children expected to sit and crawl on hard floors?
- Does the nursery keep a change of clothes for each child? Does it have its own store of underwear for emergencies?
- Are children given drink on demand? How frequently and how well are they fed?
- Are stairs and access points to the outside and kitchen areas protected by safety gates?
- Do outside play areas have protective safety surfaces?

Decoration

- Does the *external* decoration of the building look satisfactory (i.e. no rotting window sills, chipped doors, poorly operating door mechanisms)?
- Are the nursery's grounds dirty or litter strewn? How often are they cleaned up? Is there a member of staff responsible for maintenance/gardening?
- Is the internal decoration satisfactory (i.e. heavily chipped paintwork, peeling wallpaper)?

Value for money

- What are parents/employers/sponsors charged per child?
- Are charges to parents means-tested?
- How do charges compare to the local rates for childminders and nannies?
- Does the overall cost include food, drink and consumable items?

Illness

- What happens to children when they are ill?
- Is there a sick room?
- How ill do they have to be to be sent to it or home?
- How soon are parents expected to respond to a child's sickness?

Parental involvement

- Is a brochure available to parents setting out the philosophy of those running the nursery and essential facts about its operation i.e. hours of opening, costs, meals provided etc.
- Are there staff/parent meetings?
- Are parents involved in a management committee? If so, how democratic is their election?

One of the best things about a day nursery is that working parents are less worried about what their child is actually doing during the day and whether the child is receiving enough stimulation, a constant concern when they hire a nanny or childminder. It is a lot easier for a nursery nurse to do her job properly when there are plenty of other staff. Parents know about the structure of the day, when children have free play, when they do a project or craft, have a story, have one-to-one, eat, go outside etc.

What strikes the visiting parent going round most nurseries is the air of industry. Each child is doing something constructive most of the time. Even with free play there should be plenty of toys to play with.

To What Extent Do Nurseries Differ?

Nurseries do differ, though it's often hard to pinpoint exactly how and why. A crucial area is the quality of the staff. Because of local authority stipulations the parent knows that there is a definite ratio between the number of children and carers, and that half the carers have to have at least minimum qualifications. The higher the percentage of staff that are NNEBs *at a minimum*, the better – and more expensive – the nursery. Some nurseries employ very experienced school teachers and again their high salaries are reflected in the fees. Parents know that the nursery building itself has been passed by the authorities as a fit place for children to be.

Parents have to assess whether the carers are doing their best to make a long day for the children varied and fun. Because nurseries are mostly run by NNEBs or BTEC graduates, they all know about entertaining children and aiding their emotional, mental and physical development. So it is not surprising that a nursery will provide most of the opportunities and items that enhance play and learning through play (listed by Sally Provence above). All nurseries have lots of sessions for making things, cooking, painting and drawing, reading and being read to, singing and singing games like the hokey cokey. Every nursery has a range of popular play things like shapes and sorters, the Brio wooden train set, stickle bricks, octons, plasticine, duplo and lego, miniature cars, diggers and dump trucks, dollies, dolly buggies, a dolls house, a home corner, dressing up clothes, tricycles and other wheeled toys.

Given that the basics which should make every nursery good enough are there, the parents base their choice on the gilt on the gingerbread: the extras like good food cooked on site, emphasis on activities like ballet classes, cooking, swimming or gymnastics, not to mention a visiting hairdresser. Just like schools, another decider is the attractiveness of the building itself, the size of its garden, how staff look (fresh and bright), and their manner (attentive and polite), how they react to questions (patient and helpful rather than unsure and defensive) and above all, how they treat the children (lots of cuddles and giggles).

One parent says 'I was shown around the nursery by a pleasant looking NNEB who seemed cheerful and confident about who she was and what the nursery was doing. She had done some nannying and had been at the nursery for about four years and obviously enjoyed the work.'

Venues vary enormously. Some nurseries are low ceilinged and feel cramped. Others have a huge advantage if the building lets in plenty of light and has a pleasant aspect and there is easy access to its garden. Most nurseries are not purpose built, so that the layout is constrained by the limitations of the building which could be a church hall or several portakabins run together in a school's grounds.

For example, in Kingston, Surrey, there are two nurseries owned by the same business which cost the same (£17 a day for two-years and over). One is housed in what looks like a small aircraft hangar with no windows, so there is no natural light and the place has a slightly claustrophobic feel. In its favour it backs on to a sports ground and there are several acres to walk in and explore. It also has the use of a huge gym owned by the scouts. Its sister nursery, about two miles away, is in a church hall which is a lot more pleasant. But its separate baby room is truly cramped so it would not score highly for the mother of a child under a year. All in all, choosing between the two is a bit of a toss up. The factor that forces the choice is that the church hall nursery can only take a child all day on Wednesdays and Thursdays at present, so the aircraft hangar is the winner.

Some nursery managers are houseproud with a visual sense and some don't possess either virtue, so there is no doubt that some nurseries look scruffier than others. This is partly to do with the dec-

orative state of the building and also its layout. Many nurseries want
to keep prices down, so decoration comes far down the list of priorities. Nevertheless, parents are looking for reassurance all the time
that they are doing the right thing for their child and a nursery that
looks neat and clean and well loved makes an impression.

Some of the most impressive nurseries visually are those in a large
old house which has been converted to a high standard, and where
the mantlepieces and period details have been kept to give a homely
feel right away. Well-lit, carpeted nurseries done up in bright cheerful colours with good quality fittings for the basins, loos and the
children's tables and chairs help, as does enough central heating
and open windows on a sunny day.

It is easier to have a super clean nursery if it has been virtually
purpose built for the job. Nursery nurses find it easier to do a better
job faster if there is plenty of good, easy-to-use equipment and
modern conveniences to help them. So the nursery which has
higher fees doesn't have to penny pinch and this creates a virtuous
circle whereby wealthier parents like its upmarket feel and so they
send their smartly dressed children there, and in no time it's known
as the glossiest nursery in the district and has a two-year waiting list.

Kitty Mason's Holland Park Day Nursery in West London is one
such nursery and she charges a staggering £168 a week for two year
olds and older. She set up the nursery because there was nothing
available for her children. She says her fees are high because she has
high calibre staff whom she pays well and the children have an
action-packed time with lots of activities, outings and pre-school
learning. The nursery is very flexible on hours and there's a babysitting service so parents can pick up children, for example after the
theatre or a meeting as late as 11.30 pm.

'Finding high quality staff is the key and it's difficult,' she says, 'I
interview 100 applicants and give ten of them a trial week. If a child
can't remember the carer's name after a day then she's not making
enough impact. I am not put off by age, I look for charisma and role
models. Parents want paragons not just good carers. I choose the
best of the NNEBs, though many applicants are not of high enough
quality, also Montessori, and at the moment I have two who have
done teacher training.'

Baby Care

Working mothers who need to find a nursery for their baby of as little
as six months old in order to return to work must be very organized

ahead of the birth. There will not be much choice in nurseries that take very young babies and most nurseries have waiting lists, partly because nurseries' baby units tend to be small with around nine to 12 babies. One nursery nurse comments: 'We had nine babies at one time, but that was too many and we're happier having just six.'

Whereas a two and a half to three year old can cope with being left all day away from his home, it all becomes more problematical with babies and toddlers, not least because of infection. Although a baby won't be 'homesick', there is less consensus about whether very young babies in creches are a good thing.

The norm for most nurseries is to accept babies who have reached six months (when many mums' maternity leave comes to an end) though quite a few take babies of four months. There has been media coverage of the rights and wrongs of leaving babies and children under two years for eight to ten hours at a time looked after by a group of people rather than the one-to-one relationship the baby experiences with a mother or childminder, and the possible psychological damage this cutting of the umbilical cord might inflict. To mitigate this many nurseries adopt the 'key worker' system whereby each child or baby is assigned to a particular carer so there is continuity for the child and there is at least one person whom he knows and who understands a lot about his personality.

One carer put her finger on it with 'the trouble with babies is that when one cries they all start to cry and unless a nursery has plenty of space, which it usually doesn't, it is hard to avoid a room full of crying infants at times.'

So parents have to be doubly cautious as well as confident that wherever they're leaving their baby is excellent. Warmth, light, fresh air and space are very important. Also it's a plus if there are plenty of different sleep rooms so babies can have their naps without being disturbed by others. Some nurseries keep their babies completely separate, but the Chandos Nursery in London makes a point of mixing ages and its staff believe the older ones give important stimulus to the tinies.

Babies being subjected to staff chopping and changing, it is agreed, is not desirable and managers try hard to keep staff changes to a minimum. It is worrying when a very experienced NNEB trainer and owner of two nurseries commented to us: 'I think babies under two in nurseries is a very bad idea. I'd always have a nanny for my children at that age. Why do I accept babies at six months? Because it is what so many parents prefer and I haven't got to the point when I impose my personal views on their choice. But it is not ideal, not really suitable.'

Chapter 16
What Really Matters

Politics and Crusades

The Americans describe jobs in terms of their 'comparable worth'. The Californian *National Nanny Newsletter* presented the argument thus: 'garbage collectors get good pay and benefits (better than teachers in some communities); they also have uniforms and titles such as 'sanitation engineer'; zoo keepers and janitors receive more pay than nursery school teachers. Judging from the US Department of Labor Statistics, child care is still at the bottom of the list, coming after home nursing aides and maids in the "value to society" scale.'

Scarr and Dunn in *Mother Care Other Care*, who have contributed much to the thinking of this book, say:

> Many have pondered the low status of work with children and blamed it on the distance of child care from the realms of power and money. We want to propose another explanation . . . that children, especially babies and young children, are devalued by their close connection with women. In our view it is the low status of women that has tainted work with children, whether done by men or women.

We agree. It is the case that while many battles have been fought and won in the name of women's liberation, crucial battles over what women *and* men should do to make family life run smoothly have scarcely entered the lists. Most of the subjects we raise in this chapter concern these areas. Working parents and quality time with their kids/ domestic juggling; paternity leave and more time off for dads routinely to be supportive of partners and offspring; tax breaks for employers who pay nannies out of post-tax income and are thus twice penalised; good state day nurseries for everyone from birth if required (especially and genuinely necessary for one-parent families) – these are just a few of the unresolved issues which should affect both men and women and legislators.

Since this book was first printed there *has* been progress in child care and many of the things we campaigned for are now concerns of the media and politicians.

The most current in the late Nineties was the government's voucher scheme for all four-year-olds to be partially funded to attend playgroups, day nurseries and nursery schools. This is a shaky response to the need to provide nursery education for three to five year olds because it *is* apt and important that three-year-olds are included in the scheme, which itself is uneven in what it offers – who can compare a village playgroup with a fully fledged Montessori nursery school?

There has been a huge increase in the number of private day nurseries. Now parents in small provincial towns have the option of a day nursery. In 1993 the plight of 'latch-key' children was recognized with generous government funding of £60 million for out-of-school schemes which have grown nationwide from 300 to 3400 in six years thanks to the Kids' Clubs Network. Even this is just the start of addressing the problem – there were 800,000 latch-key kids still uncatered for and unsupervised. A kids' club for every primary school should be the aim, not to mention secondary schools when older children have different but no less urgent needs – wouldn't most 13 year olds prefer to be with friends on the streets rather than home alone and meant to be doing homework?

On training, the National Council for Vocational Qualifications (NVQs) have subsumed and shaken up the traditional training courses. They can be studied over several years, all at once or in bits and there is a new emphasis on education of children rather than just their care. Nannies and childminders have easy access to these whether they take the CACHE Diploma in nursery nursing or the NVQ equivalent at level 3. In a nutshell, women and men who have gained hands-on experience in child care can finally feel good and impress their employers with paper qualifications which dignify that experience.

Most women are not secure enough in their jobs to say to their colleagues, 'I must go home to my family *now*'. (Fifty per cent of mothers already go out to work in the UK – the highest percentage in Europe. Twenty-one per cent of families have two working parents). When they do say this they know that it reinforces men's view that women who have children can't be relied on. Many men disapprove of the idea that their employee is working when she has children at home. All this continues to be unfair. Women are not 'reliable' because their careers become inevitably disrupted by the conflicting commitment to their children. They mostly therefore work and earn less and their pension is smaller.

Tax fiddles

The Revenue is now targeting nanny employers who dodge tax. They have been scrutinising nanny ads in *The Lady* and *Nursery World* and tax returns from households in which both partners work and where child allowances are collected and investigated. It is also liaising with nanny agencies to ascertain who is hiring nannies.

If the government were to make the employment of domestic help a tax deductible item which the employer could offset against his or her income, there would be every incentive to pay a nanny's tax and NICs fully.

Day nurseries

1997 was the year that the UK began to attempt to match other European countries' organization of a decent nursery education system. While other countries provide nursery places for almost all their three and four year olds, we are still only planning to make room for only two-thirds of ours through the much trumpeted nursery voucher scheme. Many of these places are often in overcrowded primary school reception classes, playgroups or day nurseries which may not offer much in the way of education. There are not enough quality places available to meet the number of vouchers issued. A huge injection of public funds is needed and neither political party wants to find *that*, however much energetic lip service they pay to the theory of universal nursery care.

The lack of state child care for a stressed, often single, parent for children from birth to age four is a disgrace, which forces this parent to live on benefit. If this need is not addressed we will deserve a future in which Two Nations no longer communicate – rich and poor, black and white, educated and uneducated. The nation has focused on child abuse and on horrible instances of cruelty to children in recent years. Social workers have been castigated for not doing their difficult jobs better. But families who have no money *have* no choice.

The mother has to go out to work. She strives to be superwoman with no support – she shops, cleans, washes, feeds and cherishes and may spend six to ten hours a day out of the house working either full- or part-time. That is the norm for a surprising number of women in Britain today. It might be worse – her husband may walk out on them next week. The children may have to be left in their cots. Sometimes the woman across the hall looks in to see that they are all right. Along comes the social worker and suggests, rightly, that the children should be in care if their mother cannot organize things better.

How can a working mother be blamed for leaving a child alone in a house and at risk of injury, even of death, when she cannot find, or cannot afford, anyone suitable to help out with her children under the age of four? We have said that nannies make mothers better mothers by giving them some free time and/or the chance to work without worry. Universal day care should provide a similar service for everyone.

Many mothers emerge from the relentless chores of child rearing, feeling, understandably, that they don't want to be involved in any aspect of it ever again. It's someone else's turn to gripe and then *they* are too busy. Still nothing gets done. Parents, local authorities and Westminster have failed to make any radical changes in children's care for the under-fours and not enough yet for latch-key children.

Childminders

Local authorities should ensure that registration can be regarded as a mark of ability to provide a *good* standard of child care. Not enough people are deemed unsuitable for the job – arsonists and smokers are screened, but the authorities don't make value judgements about the childminders' ability to enhance play and thus development. Many are 'hands off, stand well back, get on with their own lives and the money is good.'

The Department of Health guidelines (attached to the Children Act) on what councils should bear in mind when deciding what could constitute a good childminder are a step in the right direction. Also local authorities' Early Years departments are increasingly informative and helpful, and most insist on pre-registration training for childminders. Health visitors and baby clinics are more clued up and supportive.

Babysitters

In Scotland a law prohibits anyone using a babysitter who is less than 16 years of age. In the rest of the UK parents can leave anyone of any age to babysit. The police only become involved if there is any suggestion of 'neglect' and a child is injured or dies. Parents are legally responsible even if absent, unless their babysitter is aged 16 or over. The NSPCC, which receives many calls from worried parents about necessary age limits, recommends that babysitters attend the Red Cross seminars which exist to point out the possible crises and how to deal with them.

Police records

It is now possible to check that your nanny has not got a criminal record, just as councils get the police to check childminders. New Scotland Yard says, 'Quite a lot of employers get their prospective nannies to go to their local police station and request a copy of their criminal record from the National Criminal Record Office.' It costs £10 and takes two weeks. If the computer cannot find one, the report will be blank. It is a cumbersome way to deal with the matter, which reflects increasing concern among employers. It should be a normal matter of local police routine. Christine Little of FRES comments bleakly, 'It is better than nothing, but nannies may have done things for which they have never been charged'.

Following the infamous Carol Withers case (see Chapter 7) , the initiative of the Nanny Umbrella – Parents at Work, CACHE and FRES among others – to campaign for some sort of national child care register. These bodies cannot agree on its form or its powers. All carers, both of children and of old people, should ideally be registered. A voluntary scheme would not have any teeth, a statutory alternative would work better, but no government will make it a priority because of the expense and policing required to make it work. It's pie in the sky, but it remains an issue.

The Americans have produced a star wars idea which effectively spies on nannies with hidden video cameras installed in the home. If nannies are relaxed and conscientious about their doings, this works well and gives parents peace of mind and disposes of the constant worry that they have that their nannies are neglecting or mistreating Junior in their absence.

Agency black lists

Given that the possibility of a national register of carers is remote, nanny agencies should co-operate more with each other nationally and agree some form of early warning system when they spot a nanny who should not look after children. FRES does do this, but too few agencies think it is worth their while to belong to FRES to make its list adequate.

Nanny Networks

It would make nannying much more enjoyable and satisfying if an organization took responsibility for a nanny's need to share problems and be supported professionally. Nanny networks are commonplace in America. Some agencies are conscientious and altruistic and put nannies and au pairs in touch in their locality, regardless of whether they placed them or not.

The nanny organizations, PANN or NANN (see Chapter 17) should mastermind a proper nanny club and encourage nannies to go on refresher courses. Discontented nanny gripe sessions are rarely attended by fulfilled, busy nannies who might otherwise raise low morale and fire their contemporaries with their enthusiasm for the job. Fortunately, now that NVQs can be studied part-time and at home, there is more to challenge the lively nanny. But these happy nannies say that they would welcome going to well-organized evening seminars from time to time. An editorial in *Nursery World* comments, 'Nannies are isolated from their professional colleagues and they are constantly in danger of forgetting what good child care practice is.' This is too true to be good.

Over the last ten years since we first wrote the *Guide*, much has changed and largely for the better. Nannies and employers *have* become more professional – the former are paid a lot more in a recovering economy where more new mothers than before have gone back to work. They think hard before exploiting their nannies, they pay their taxes properly nowadays in the main (especially at the top end of the market where big sums make fudging harder) they respect their needs and working conditions and weekend work is largely a memory. Maybe in the next decade we will virtually see the end of nannies living in? From both sides a growing need for privacy plus a curious trend among the super-rich to run their own errands so as not to feel so out of touch with reality, means that it is probable that the daily nanny will reign supreme in the future.

But the exploitation of au pairs is still rife – they are the Cinderellas of the profession and there is a growing demand for them. It is common to hear that they are working a full day for £45 a week and babysitting many nights. In the country it is worse because the girls are isolated and powerless to do other than leave.

Chapter 17
Nanny Nitty Gritty

The Work Agreement

By the 1990s employers were beginning to realize that the more professional they were in their dealings with their nannies, and indeed, their mother's helps, the less stress, trouble, misunderstanding, guilt and resentment everybody had to suffer. Until recently it would have seemed too like litigious America to be so pompous as to commit a nanny's duties to paper. Surely everyone knew what they ought to be doing, didn't they?

The Americans have recently started to create training for nannies, but already employers' attitudes are way ahead of their British counterparts. Work agreements are the norm in the USA. Barbara Binswanger and Betsy Ryan in their useful book *Live-in Child Care* say: 'Many parents, even those who negotiate office contracts with ease, find ironing out similar agreements with their live-in helper time-consuming, embarrassing, or even trifling. But don't allow yourself to fall into that trap. A clear financial arrangement made at the outset . . . will pave the way for a smooth relationship . . . you and your prospective live-in helper can negotiate an equitable salary arrangement with a minimum of hidden upsets later on.'

The UK pioneer in nannies' conditions of employment statements was the Norland College. It protected its probationers from exploitation in their first jobs by drawing up its own neat and formal agreement. Also, the Federation of Recruitment and Employment Services (FRES) has adapted its domestics' statements of employment' for a nanny. (Send an s.a.e. to FRES to receive a copy, see Useful Addresses).

Some conscientious employment agencies have created their own, although some agents still don't like contracts. An agent says, 'It's a two-edged sword; both sides can get too specific and rigid, and flexibility and common sense is jeopardized.'

Most British employers have not yet adopted the written statement of employment. The new converts now swear by them. The point about it seems to be that with any luck no one ever refers to it again, but the niggly points which may eventually cause friction have at least been considered and discussed before any contretemps has blown up. Apart from anything else, it forces employers to think through the whole business of having an employee in the house and helps to make them behave professionally towards the nanny. Likewise it will also bring home to the carer that she is doing a proper job with responsibilities and duties to which she has agreed. Both parties have had to focus on their expectations of the job. A contract provides a psychological rein on thoughtless behaviour on both sides.

It should be mentioned that several nannies say that they think nannies choose this profession because of their love of children and dislike of red tape and routine. Some employers reckon that they want their relationship with their nanny to be warm and informal and they are disturbed by the formality of a contract.

The contract that one employer draws up with a nanny or a mother's help may be extremely long or very brief. It would be absurd to detail every little preference and minutiae of the routine, but just as silly to omit salient detail. There is a golden mean dictated by common sense and how much the job is shared with the employer.

Working mothers are well served by having a contract and drafting it carefully and fully. Their nannies say that it helps them a lot to have a written routine and clear guidelines about the mother's expectations of their child's day. You might as well extend a written routine to a contract.

Under the Employment Rights Act 1978, after 13 weeks in any job, employers must give their staff a 'statement of employment'. It is binding in law but is more a statement of intent by both parties. In other words, there is no reason for either side to be scared of it. The idea of the statement is to give the employee some protection against his employer so it has to contain certain basic terms and conditions of the job.

However, it is toothless as far as the law and the outside world is concerned in the sense that you can still sack the nanny without *any* notice within the first year. After a year the maximum she can claim in law is a week's pay in lieu of notice. Unfair Dismissal legislation is not relevant to nannies unless they are part of a staff of over ten. The statement of employment is not chiselled in granite and unchangeable: an employer in consultation with the nanny can discuss changes.

Nannies and mother's helps should not be asked to commit themselves to more than one year with the family. Miserable nannies, anxious to leave but bound by their contract, should be released from it and let go for the children's sake.

Try not to reject the whole scheme as a time-consuming bore. Think of a work agreement as a useful tool for both employer and employee. They should not be considered the sole preserve of the pukka nanny, as they are at present in this country. The good reasons for having one apply to any kind of child carer who comes to your home. This is a proven way of reducing friction and gives you a better chance of a long-stay nanny. It does not have to be typed. It need not extend beyond one page – a list or long note will do fine. All the details should be discussed with the nanny by the employer before being written out neatly, and then both parties sign it.

What the shortest statement of terms of employment might include

(If you choose to have a statement then all those asterisked must be included by law)

- Names of employer and employee*
- The employee's job title*
- The date the employee starts work* and her expected length of stay
- Hours of work* (you don't have to be specific about this one; 'variable' would do)
- Period of probation
- The salary: amount, how and when it is to be paid*
- National insurance and tax
- Sick pay arrangements
- Time off: the number of days and weekends off in a month
- Paid and/or unpaid holiday and bank holidays*
- Pension* (this must appear in the statement by law even if there is no pension and there is unlikely to be; with 99 per cent of nanny jobs the employer writes 'no pension')
- Notice on both sides*
- House rules
- Sackable Offences, discipline and grievance procedure*
- The date

- The employee's signature confirming that she has received her statement of employment*

Some employers include additional items like:
- Overtime or additional payments, if any
- Salary review (when and the amount)
- Oral and written warnings before dismissal
- Dress (if uniformed, the employer pays for the upkeep and replacement)
- Description of the girl's accommodation
- Which appliances she may use in the house
- Car arrangements (who pays for what)
- Telephone (who pays for what)
- Entertainment of guests (boyfriends, girlfriends)
- A list of duties (especially outlining anything other than childcare, like feeding animals, housework, shopping, doing accounts etc)
- Availability for travelling (for long periods away from the family's home)
- No holiday to be taken until she has worked for three months
- Joint referral of disputes to the agency who placed the carer and agreement to abide by its arbitration
- Babysitting (not more than two friends to accompany or whatever)

The statement can be amended by both employer and nanny at any time.

Since our research shows that a high proportion of employers do not pay full tax and national insurance on behalf of their nanny and thereby break the law, spelling out these details on paper is not sensible. If a nanny agrees that only part of her salary is declared to the Revenue, presumably these details will also be fudged in the contract.

A Specimen Work Agreement

Joanne Marden's work agreement as living-in nanny employed by Hugh and Emma Blackwell of 27 Ashley Gardens, London SW1.

Joanne starts work on 30 April 1998. She agrees to stay for a year, which is renewable because Emma would prefer a two-year contract. There is to be a four-week probationary period. Joanne will

£160 NET
200.78 GROSS
INC 25.69 TAX
15.09 EMPLOYEE'S NIC
14.02 EMPLOYER'S NIC
214.80 TOTAL

a/c Shipley
a/c PD132
329.

a/c DOM
629.74

0091815517
3500

09978291300
NS6775 82C
*

EMPLOYER'S

HELPLINE

0345 143143

£175 net is cash

= £223.37 gross

= £245.69 total

inc. 30.98 TAX
17.39 EMPLOYEE'S NIC *

22.32
EMPLOYER
NIC

do the usual nanny duties looking after Tom (five) and Martin (15 months) and she will keep the children's hours.

The salary is £. . . gross a week. Joanne's NIC is £. . . a week and her tax is £. . . a week. Emma pays this £. . . a week on Joanne's behalf. After tax and NIC, Joanne gets £. . . a week. (Emma also has to pay £. . . towards Joanne's NIC.) Emma will pay Joanne £. . . a week in cash. The remainder will be paid once a month by standing order into Joanne's account at the Nat West. Emma will give Joanne four weeks' sick pay a year from when she arrives. Joanne will have weekends off. Joanne will get three weeks' paid holiday a year including Christmas and New Year, but excluding Bank Holidays. Both sides agree to give each other one month's notice.

Our House Rules are: no boyfriends in the house; girlfriends to stay by permission only; telephone used after 6 pm except in emergency; home at midnight if working the next day; no gossiping about our business; no high heels on duty; no smoking at all.

Instant Sackable Offences: stealing or lying, neglect or cruelty to the children, boyfriends in the house. We would sack for these things without notice.

Joanne will help Tom look after his hamster. We need her to come with us to the US annually for six weeks in the summer. We will go on holiday for two weeks a year alone and for a few weekends – Joanne and the children will mostly go to Granny in Bath.

Insurance

Motor

If the nanny or mother's help is under 25 and has no 'no claims discount', and/or has a conviction for a driving offence, an employer is likely to have to pay more to insure her to drive his car. The odds increase sharply if she is to drive in a city. Do not assume that if you have 'any driver' insurance she can jump in the car and drive it. Always check with your insurer whether she is covered. An au pair with no UK driving experience will elicit an extra premium.

A nanny's own car must be insured 'for business purposes' rather than 'for pleasure' if she is ferrying your children around. This could be very significant if she had an accident involving them.

Public liability – the employer

Suppose your nanny or mother's help was in a room in your house and the ceiling collapsed, or shelves avalanched down on top of

her, or she was electrocuted by one of your appliances. Who
would pay her compensation for her accidental bodily injury
(including death, disease or illness)?

You will be pleased to know that anyone who has home contents and building insurance is *usually* covered for 'accidental
injury through negligence' for an *unlimited* amount for anyone
who is not of his immediate family, like a nanny (or a visiting
nanny). This is called 'public liability' insurance and it is to do with
an accident occurring because of the *employer's* negligence.

For example, if the ceiling collapsed because the employer had
put his foot through it while in the loft, or the shelves weren't fixed
properly, or if the carpet was loose, then the nanny's claim might
be successful. If, on the other hand, she overloaded the bookcase
so that it was sagging with her exercise weights, then the accident
wouldn't be put down to negligence on the employer's part and the
nanny could claim only if she had 'personal accident' cover. As
this sort of insurance is expensive, few nannies have it.

If the employer has house contents cover which includes 'accidental damage' insurance, then if the nanny damages an orna-
ment, spills bleach on the carpet, or burns a hole in the sofa with
her cigarette, he can claim for replacement or repair of the item.
Incidentally if a nanny's, mother's help's or au pair's cigarette
burned the house down, it would be treated the same as if your cigarette was the culprit.

An employer can arrange extra cover – either 'standard contents' or 'accidental damage' cover – for the nanny's possessions in
his home.

Public liability – the nanny or childminder

Childminders have to take out 'public liability' insurance and
more and more nannies take it out too, so that they are covered for
up to £1 million if the children in their care suffer accidental bodily
injury or death. Contact childminder and nanny insurance brokers : Morton Michel (0181 765 1067). Nannies who join the nursery nurse union, PANN, get public liability insurance, and if they
join the NCMA they have access to its own cheap public liability
insurance scheme.

Professional negligence

Public liability and personal accident insurance should not be
confused with 'professional negligence' cover. This is a subtler

kind of liability linked with the nanny's competence as a professional. Rather as with a doctor or a surveyor, professional negligence revolves around the professional giving 'advice' that proves wrong. So far as the nanny is concerned, roughly speaking, if she gives advice which is acted upon which has a bad outcome, then she could be sued for professional negligence. For example, a child is sick and the nanny takes the initiative and advises the mother that Calpol is what is needed. But it turns out that the child has meningitis and is rushed to hospital . The parents could sue the nanny for her wrong advice which constituted, in their opinion, 'professional negligence'.

Buying professional negligence insurance is very expensive so agencies don't encourage it and few nannies take it out.

Suing

The subject of suing is not one on which anyone wishes to dwell – employer and employee alike. Most employers in the UK don't give it much thought except as something to which they might resort in extreme circumstances when they felt that sacking a nanny was insufficient punishment and/or recompense for professional negligence on her part.

Most couples are adamant that they would never consider suing. They say the reason for this is that they feel that they should take the ultimate responsibility for anything a nanny does, and so suing would be inappropriate. Others squeak with indignation, 'Would you sue a member of your family?' Some say, 'It's a risk you take'; others chime, 'Accidents will happen and I think it's bad luck when the children have them with the nanny.'

According to one insurance broker 'parents wouldn't dream of suing before anything goes wrong, but as soon as there is a problem and their child has had an accident with the childminder or nanny, the first thing they do is go straight to a solicitor.'

In a rare instance a lawyer, Anita Longcroft of Chelsea, London, sued her son's nanny Sheila Beeson (a state-enrolled nurse) for alleged child neglect. Mrs Longcroft claimed that Miss Beeson had thrown eight-week-old James through the air at her during a row. Mrs Longcroft caught him unharmed, but lost the case.

Many people have heard of the ancient aphorism 'a master may not sue his servant'. But nannies know that, in this increasingly litigious age, they can be sued by their employer, for the law is quite clear that an employer can sue an employee for being negligent (in legal terms 'master and servant' are synonymous with 'employer and employee'). Thus in principle it does make sense for a nanny to take out professional negligence insurance.

A nanny, like any employee, is contracted to perform her duties with proper care and reasonable skill. If an employer can show that she has failed to do this, then he has a chance of winning a court case. Thus she could be sued under a contractual claim. In *any* job, the employee has to carry out his or her duties with reasonable efficiency and care. This is implicit in all arrangements where one person works for another for payment and it prevails whether it is written into a formal contract or not.

Having said which, ironically, an employer would be likely to sue a nanny *only* if she had public liability and/or professional negligence insurance (and therefore the money to pay the compensation if her employer won the case).

Employers suing employment agencies

Good employment agencies have substantial professional negligence insurance. If an employer takes on a girl from an agency and she steals the T'ang horse and is found to have a criminal record, her employers might try to sue the agency that placed her with them for not screening her thoroughly.

Temporary nannies are often covered by their agency. To date there have not been many claims made against an employment agency as a result of the behaviour of one of their nanny placements, but disgruntled employers can complain to the Employment Agency Standards Office. Phone 01923 210706.

Income Tax and National Insurance

Ask most parents about tax and National Insurance contributions (NICs) for the nanny or mother's help and they groan. If anyone is doing it, it is usually the wife, though some husbands do help. The most painless solution is to hand over the whole thing to the accountant or to one of the payroll companies like, Nannytax, that specialize in the tax and NICs of nannies and mothers' helps (see Addresses).

In virtually all cases, people who employ nannies are by definition employers and have a duty in law to organize the employee's tax and NICs if they are paying them a minimum sum or more each week. The minimum usually changes each year, so one of the first things you need to do is to find out from your local tax office what the current threshold is.

You have to enquire from the local social security office the current pay threshold for National Insurance. This changes most years and it is set lower than the one for tax. But in both cases, the rate is well below what people pay their nannies.

An employee has to pay the State's National Insurance contributions (NICs) to ensure she is eligible to receive maternity and unemployment pay. It is the employer who has by law to deduct the girl's contributions from her gross pay each week. Also, the employer has to contribute from his own pocket towards his employee's total National Insurance payment. He pays just a bit less than whatever NIC the nanny has to pay.

The importance of the distinction between 'gross' and 'net' pay

It is crucial to get absolutely clear with the nanny whether you are paying her 'gross' or 'net'. 'Gross' means *before* tax and NICs have been deducted; 'net' means *after* they have been deducted. Many employers make the mistake of talking about their nanny's pay in net terms. For example they say, 'She's earning £100 a week.' Often they mean this is what she 'takes home', i.e., net.

Talking 'net' pay is not good, but is universally prevalent. It is dismissive of the importance and worth of tax and NICs, and the nanny should not be encouraged to think in these terms. It underplays the fact that the employer has taken time and trouble on the nanny's behalf to ensure that her tax and NICs are paid. Focusing on net pay allows the nanny to think only in terms of take-home pay. In an ordinary PAYE job she would know her gross wage or salary and how much had been deducted and why.

Talking 'net' is very common among nannies and indeed their trainers. Even heads of residential training colleges still talk about so many pounds a week 'clear' rather than encouraging their girls to think in terms of a gross salary.

In order to give the nanny or mother's help some idea about how her wages compare with 'the real world', it is worth considering talking about an 'annual' salary at the interview, and again when you offer an applicant the job. For example, you could say: 'I intend to pay you £6,500 a year which works out at £125 a week (for 52 weeks) before tax and NICs'; tell her what these amount to and how much her net or 'take home' pay will be. And remind her so that she can appreciate that you are being as professional as possible that she is entitled to so much sick leave (two to three weeks) and so much paid holiday (three to four weeks), plus all Bank Holidays. Don't forget to tell her that you are paying your contribution to her National Insurance each week as well.

The mechanics of paying the nanny's tax and National Insurance

Employers have to deduct tax from their employee's pay. The Inland Revenue accepts payment from a nanny's employer each quarter. At the same time, the employer must pay over her contribution to the nanny's total NICs and also the nanny's contribution. If the nanny has paid a minimum amount of NICs each year, she is entitled to statutory sick pay, unemployment benefit and state maternity pay, as well as getting a year closer to qualifying for her state pension.

There is a Simplified Deduction Scheme especially arranged for employers of one or two people, but if the nanny is earning gross pay of over £240 a week, then PAYE should be used, rather than the Simplified Deduction Scheme.

Those who want to use the Simplified Scheme need to ask to be sent a starter pack and it is *vital* that you ask for the name of the tax officer and the telephone number and address of the tax office responsible for your district. It will help him if the employer can give him the girl's P45, the form that her last employer should have given her on leaving, stating her paid tax to date, her tax code and other bits of information.

A nanny who had a nanny job immediately before joining the family won't have a P45. Nannies and mother's helps are often on 'emergency tax'. This means their taxable pay is constant throughout the year, to make it easier for the employer to work out her tax and NICs. Thus the tax office doesn't have to know previous tax details immediately, though if a nanny wants to claim allowances, she needs to complete a tax return.

It is a good idea to have photocopies of everything you send to the Inland Revenue to do with your nanny's tax and NICs, then if there are any queries, maybe years hence, you will have evidence that you did it all correctly. The tax office should send you a new employer's 'starter pack' containing:

- A4 card headed 'Simplified Deduction Scheme' with instructions and current tax tables (ref: P16).
- Form 16A, which every employer should complete when taking on a new carer, and send it to the tax office.

- The Simplified Deduction Card (ref: P12)
- A green National Insurance table booklet (ref: CA37) with the employer's Helpline: 0345 143143

In a letter you receive with the starter pack you should be given a name and extension number to contact if you need help.

Payslips, to fill and return to the Inland Revenue with your quarterly tax and NIC cheque, will be sent separately and will show a specific Accounts Office reference number.

The tax officer will also give you two reference numbers: the tax district number (this appears at the top of the Deductions Card), and an accounts office reference which you use when filling in the quarterly pay slip.

At the top of the Deduction Card the tax officer will have filled in the nanny's tax code and the amount of tax-free pay she receives, as well as the Tax District number and a reference number, both of which you need to quote in all correspondence.

The card looks more daunting than it is. If you find you are sitting too long at the kitchen table trying to fathom out the information, ring the Helpline: 0345 143143 or make an appointment to see a tax officer and talk over any problems together.

Once you know the nanny's gross pay each week and how much 'free pay' (as the card calls the nanny's tax-free pay) she has each week, working out and logging her net pay is not difficult. Nor is selecting her NI contributions from booklet CA37.

Once you have done this, completing the Simplified Deductions Card should take 10 minutes once a quarter. Work out the figures before she arrives, and then set up a standing order to be paid into the nanny's bank account each month.

Many nannies ask sensibly for a payslip stating the details of their earnings each month and it is a considerate thing to do. Mrs Davis insists that the employers of her Norlanders do so. 'It is illegal not to,' she says, 'and it is the only tangible proof they have that they have paid their NICs and tax.'

At the end of the tax year

The tax year ends on 5 April each year. The employer fills in a P37 form (which the tax office should have sent him) which is a declaration of the employee's total tax NICs and sick pay paid in the last tax year. Then at the end of the week in which 5 April occurs, he sends the P37 and the Simplified Deductions Card to the tax office, and at the same time sends the tax and

NIC cheque to the accounts office. The tax office will send him a new Card.

Each time a new tax code for the nanny is issued (usually at the end of each tax year), the tax office will send a new Simplified Deductions Card. Whenever an employer receives a new Card, he must start using this and send the old one to the tax office.

When she leaves

As soon as the nanny or mother's help serves her notice, inform the tax office that she is leaving. When you have paid her last wages, send the tax office her Simplified Deductions Card when she leaves, and a cheque for any outstanding tax and NICs.

Some employers have been confused when their nanny has asked if they could fib and confirm, when the social security officer rings, that she was fired for, say, incompetence, even if she left quite amicably having served her notice. If she doesn't join another family straight away, it is only if she has been sacked that she can receive social security instantly. If she left a job of her own accord she then has to wait several weeks for unemployment pay.

Incidentally, make quite sure that an unscrupulous mother's help whether British or from the EU or an au pair who is an EU national, is not claiming social security while working for you. One employer was most taken aback when her German au pair asked innocently, 'Do you mind if I go on collecting social security?'

'Girls from overseas don't have to pay tax and National Insurance.' True or false?

Many parents think, quite mistakenly, that to employ a girl from overseas, say from Europe, and for some odd reason more particularly a girl from Australia or New Zealand, exempts them from having to pay tax.

It is remarkable how often the happy employer of a New Zealander will say with a smile, 'And of course, because she is from Auckland, we don't have to worry about tax.' Total poppycock. Just for the record, no overseas visitor, including an Australasian or a Canadian, has a special tax arrangement with the UK which exempts them, miraculously, from PAYE and NI.

Certainly, there are reciprocal tax arrangements between Britain and many countries whereby a person resident in this country *and* paying tax will not be asked to pay tax in his homeland. But that is something quite different.

The myth has grown up partly because foreign mother's helps are often not employed for a full year, and sometimes with Australians and New Zealanders it is as little as four months. So in practice many foreign visitors just don't pay tax and their employers are happy to go along with the act that the Revenue is unlikely ever to catch up with them.

Although in an ideal world the Revenue would love to make sure tax dodgers paid up, in practice, as far as mother's helps are concerned, a tax inspector has got more pressing problems than to chase back tax from an itinerant Australian. The chances of detection are even smaller than when an employer skips paying an English girl's tax and NICs. Before you can say The Taxman Cometh, these mother's helps are off on their travels again or have returned home, or come back to the UK after a spin round Europe three months later.

The single person's tax allowance

The single person's tax allowance is another reason why few employers pay a foreign girl's tax. The allowance means that the mother's help, like everyone who has to be on PAYE, earns a proportion of her salary *free of tax*. If she doesn't work part of the year by leaving the country after a few months, she should get that taxfree part of her wages back at the end of the tax year. Getting this tax rebate may be difficult if the girl has gone back to Australia.

Many employers feel that if the girl is no longer with them, there is no chance of the Revenue knocking on their door chasing back tax. But be warned, the tax man has statutory powers to collect tax and NICs from the employer, even if the girl in question has left the family.

Even though the Inland Revenue would prefer the authors to drop any reference to employers' illegal behaviour in failing to pay tax and NICs for nannies from overseas, the purpose of the book is to explain the facts, though we in no way condone what is practised.

Not paying NICs for an overseas girl is not the immoral act that it is for a British girl. If she is a Commonwealth national she is allowed into the country under The Holidaymaker Scheme, provided she is self-supporting and doesn't apply for state benefits like social security and unemployment benefit.

Different types of employer: how they deal with tax

There are three types of employer when it comes to the nanny's and mother's helps' tax.

1 Those who pay tax and National Insurance in full. This is the minority. They know their local tax officer well, or their accountant does, and they pay the lot. We need spend no more time on them except to award them a rosette.
2 Those that do the total fiddle. This is the type who have such a phobia of red tape and resent handing the taxman money that has already been taxed.
3 Those who semi-fiddle. There are thousands of nanny hirers who do a bit of both. They feel unhappy about the total fiddle, and so arrange a part declared/part undeclared tax system for their nanny. Often the employer pitches the declared level a bit above the minimum earnings level for tax. The rest is paid in cash or sometimes in kind (free petrol). A likely split would be declaring £100 a week for tax purposes and giving the rest, say £40, in cash or kind. Bonuses for hard or extra work are often paid in kind by the canny employer. Thus handsome presents – a watch, a designer jersey, a facial – are acceptable to both parties.

Some employers don't feel bad about not paying full tax and argue that it is absurd for anyone earning as little as £100–£120 a week to have to pay any, but they do see the point of paying NICs. Unfortunately you can't dodge one and not the other. So they say, with enlightened self-interest, that they will declare a chunk of her salary and pay tax and NICs on that, so in effect secure full benefits at a reduced rate. It is all Black Economy and unprofessional, but the mutual benefits that accrue make it popular.

Most employers shy away from crude words like 'evade'. It is not something they talk about much in mixed company anyway (who knows if the man at the next table is a tax inspector?). They don't talk about 'fiddling' the nanny's tax either, but this is what thousands of employers do. No nanny should be fobbed off by lazy employers' mutterings about 'self-employment', which means that she is responsible for paying her own tax and NICs. Nor should employers accept a nanny's statement that she regards herself as self-employed. It is very rare that a tax inspector accepts a residential nanny as self-employed.

Fortunately employers are becoming more responsible, ironically, partly because there are such large sums involved that it's simpler to pay a nanny by direct debit than stuff an envelope with wads of £20 notes in an Arthur Daly fashion. Now that experienced nannies earn a reasonable salary on a par with their peers, they are more aware of their fiscal rights. Highly paid nannies assume, rightly, that there is no question of anyone ducking the rough one-third of their gross salary that goes to pay tax and NICs.

If at the interview a nanny or mother's help finds that a prospective employer evades the subject of tax and NICs, warning bells should ring. She should make it clear what she expects in terms of pay and conditions and if the employer still can't tackle the topic in a sensible manner, however much the interviewee likes the family in other respects, she shouldn't take the job.

A nanny who finds that what was agreed at the interview does not happen in practice should insist on a proper discussion immediately. The advantages of drawing up a contract before a nanny begins work are obvious.

Why it is important to organize tax and NICs

Although the temptation to forget about tax and NICs by both employer and nanny is understandable, neither are treating the job professionally and it shouldn't be shirked. One of the secrets of the successful employer/nanny relationship is that they treat each other with respect and the business of caring for the children is looked upon by both as a serious, professional job, with proper pay and conditions, including tackling the boring old PAYE.

Christine Little, head of FRES, comments: 'We feel strongly that employers should pay their nanny's tax and NICs. The nanny loses out in the long run. Just because it is cheaper not to pay tax and NICs, doesn't mean it is right.'

Sick Pay

Statutory sick pay (SSP) is only a small contribution to making up a nanny's salary when she's ill as it is less than half the average nanny wage. It is a flat rate which changes each tax year.

The nanny only becomes eligible for SSP after four consecutive days of absence from work. There are no DSS rules about producing a sick note, but there are three waiting days before SSP can begin to be paid. Thus if a nanny fell sick on a Monday then she would not be eligible for sick pay until the Thursday so for the Thursday and Friday of that week she would be paid two-fifths of a week's SSP.

The importance of an employer making a sick pay arrangement

Many employers fudge the issue of sick pay. They don't like to
think about the possibility of the nanny becoming ill, and when
she does they often resent it a great deal because it inconveniences
them, and they loathe the girl for lying in bed while they have to
drop everything to take over the child care.

As usual it is best to make quite clear what you are prepared to
offer in the way of sick pay at the interview. If an employer doesn't
mention it, the nanny should do so, once she has been offered the
job and the nitty gritty about pay and conditions is discussed. Sick
pay details can be spelt out in the statement of employment, so
there is no doubt on either side.

An employer should think about the unfortunate eventuality of
the nanny falling sick, and should work out the necessary contingency plans, including how long the sick pay is to last, and how
much it will be each week.

It is reasonable for a living-in nanny or mother's help to expect
four weeks' full pay while she is sick (though many employers
don't offer this), if she is intending to stay with the family a year.
The longer she has been with them, the longer caring employers
are likely to carry her until she is well and back with the children.

When is she eligible to claim sick pay

A nanny on a contract of less than three months is excluded from
SSP. A temporary nanny is likely to have arranged with her tax
officer to be self-employed, so the temporary employer has no
obligations in law to her when she falls sick.

As far as the employee is concerned SSP is treated as pay by the
Inland Revenue, so the employer has to deduct tax and NICs from
it as he would from the nanny's salary, and the employee receives
it net in the same way.

The red tape when sorting out her sick pay is not as straightforward as it is when paying a nanny's tax and NICs. Any cries for help
should be directed at the Social Security Advice Line.

Those wishing to claim SSP will need to ask the local DSS office
to send the employer's manual on SSP (Ref. CA30) and a SSP tables
booklet (CA36). It is a good idea to get from the local DSS office
booklet N1244: 'Statutory Sick Pay: Check Your Rights' for the
nanny.

There is a column in the Simplified Deduction Card where the
gross amount of SSP has to be logged if it has been paid during the

completed quarter. If an employer pays out SSP during the quarter, most of it can be reclaimed from the NICs of the same quarter. In other words, at the end of the quarter the employer adds up the *gross* amount of any SSP the nanny has received in that quarter and deducts it from the usual total tax and insurance cheque that she pays to the Revenue each quarter.

The State will pay back 80 per cent of the sick pay paid out by the employer for the first six weeks of illness, after that small employers (i.e. nanny employers) can claim 100 per cent relief.

An employer must *by law* keep records of SSP in a form comprehensible to a DSS officer for at least three years after the end of the relevant tax year.

British and foreign mother's helps and au pairs

If trained professional nannies have difficulties when it comes to sick pay, the grey area develops into a thick fog with the untrained mother's help with not much experience, foreign mother's helps and au pairs. With disingenuous but understandable logic, an employer feels under less pressure to do the decent thing when she is employing someone untrained and less well paid.

Anyone working full-time for a family should have some sort of sick pay deal, and, if staying for a year, should receive four weeks on full pay as the pukka nanny expects. The case of the au pair is again slightly different because she is there for a short time and works part-time, and the issue of sick pay doesn't pose a problem. If she is seriously unwell she packs up and goes home.

In a family where an au pair is staying for six months and is off sick for a week she will probably have no pay docked. An employer might insist that a mediocre au pair, who is limping through her six months with no laurels, make up the time lost. The same employer might ignore a few days' sickness in an excellent au pair who did more in a day than some do in two. Ideally, it is always best to err on the generous side, it makes everyone feel better.

Trade and Professional Associations and Unions

The Federation of Recruitment and Employment Services (FRES)

FRES is the trade association for private recruitment agencies of every kind in the UK, including those who specialize in providing nannies, mother's help and au pairs. It was founded in 1930 and aims to 'represent its members to government and opinion-forming bodies and helps to raise standards by which agencies operate'.

FRES has a seat on CACHE representing the interests of private sector employers. It is a good sign if an agency has taken the trouble (and expense) to become a member of FRES. The FRES booklet states clearly the minimum requirements expected of its members. They are all laudable ones that should indeed be met by any self-respecting, reputable agency.

But there's the rub. FRES lists 54 nanny member agencies nationwide, many of which are very small. Of the two to three hundred in existence, many are long-established good agencies who choose not to be members of FRES, believing that it has nothing to offer them. However, FRES, run by Leonard Allen, Christine Little and her staff, does provide a useful service informing agencies about contracts of employment, tax and National Insurance, setting up an agency and a mass of legal technicalities and valuable legal advice when necessary.

The best thing about patronizing an agency which is a FRES member is that it will have been alerted to bad nannies (and bad employers). A member can complain in writing about either and FRES will include the information in its next monthly mailing. This is known loosely as 'the FRES blacklist'.

The National Association of Nursery Nurses (NANN)

NANN is the nursery nurses' professional association. It has about a thousand members who pay a small annual membership fee. It holds a conference once a year and an annual seminar. There are branches throughout the country which are formed wherever nursery nurses have the energy and find the time to run them. They organize social and educational meetings.

The idea is 'to encourage nursery nurses to keep in touch with modern methods of childcare and to stimulate interest by postgraduate lectures and conferences.' The sort of topics discussed include children with special needs, parents as professional partners, and new government legislation on childcare.

The Association is geared almost entirely to the nursery nurse in the public sector. It has very few nanny members and does not really cater for them, but wishes it did. There is, however, a leaflet issued giving guidelines on a nanny's pay, duties, holidays, hours of work etc. It is run by committed nursery nurses with full-time jobs who have little time even to keep it ticking over. It falls far short of being a proper support group, but any working nanny can contact NANN (see Useful Addresses) and discover if there is a local branch.

The National Childminding Association (NCMA)

It was partly to counteract childminding's appalling public image that back in 1977 the NCMA was started by a group of childminders, parents and interested organizations.

The NCMA objectives are: 'To promote the provision of day care, recreation and education of young children; to promote good standards of childminding; to advance the education and training of childminders and to conduct research into all aspects of care, recreation and education of children under eight.'

The NCMA is now a serious force in the growing debate about how the nation should be caring for its children, with its membership totalling 55,000, exactly half the number of registered childminders. It is partly funded by the DSS but its contribution is declining, and the NCMA relies more and more on the support of its members who pay a fee for membership.

Parents can nominate their childminder for the NCMA/Peaudouce National Childminder of the Year award.

Trade unions

Employers may be unaware that nannies can belong to unions. There are very few nanny members as yet, but it is important that employers know about nanny unions. The unions' idea of promoting professional standards and good pay and conditions should not put off a good employer. Union membership does not automatically turn your nanny into a red under the bed. She may just be taking the job seriously and every employer can be glad of that.

As the Professional Association of Nursery Nurses (see below) states: 'Employees have responsibilities to do the job for which they have been employed. If they fail to do the job or breach their employer's trust in any way then their employer may take disciplinary action against them.'

PANN

More and more nannies are joining the Professional Association for Nursery Nurses (PANN). It is a section of the Professional

Association of Teachers which is not a member of the TUC. It is the first union to attract the residential qualified nanny, though most of its membership consists mostly of nursery nurses in the public sector. Graduates of CACHE, NAMCW and BTEC can all become members. PANN is proud to say that 'we don't believe in strikes and we are the only union that is run by nursery nurses for nursery nurses.'

Like NANN the National Association of Nursery Nurses, it issues guidelines on pay and conditions. It is keen to promote the necessity for a contract for the nanny. It has its own lawyer to give free advice to members. There is a sliding scale of inexpensive union fees, depending on when a nanny joins during the year. PANN believes in solving problems by discussion and provides a 24-hour telephone service to give advice on problems (see Useful Addresses). Members receive union support in the event of a dispute with employers.

PANN says: 'The care of young children is a very demanding job. Nursery nurses will only improve their pay and conditions when they can demonstrate that they are fully qualified professionals.'

UNISON

The administrative, professional, technical and clerical staff union, UNISON, is the nursery nurses' union affiliated to the TUC and is on non-speaks with PANN. It has more pay negotiating clout than PANN and attracts most of the NNEBs working in the public sector.

Chapter 18
Agencies

Choosing and Using an Agency

An agency should save the employer time, frustration and hassle. Their experience of screening hundreds of applicants a year and talking to hundreds of employers can make them the ideal people to make a good match between the two. It is an inspired new development that several of them meet not only all their nannies, but all their clients as well. They should provide qualified applicants, check references carefully and act as honest brokers, if problems arise after the nanny or mother's help has been placed.

Agencies use recruitment methods which are much too expensive for individual families to contemplate. They maintain contact with training colleges all over the country, many visit them and have good relationships with tutors.

George Bernard Shaw said that theatre-goers should not leave their critical faculties outside with their coats; so it is when an employer speaks to an agency. Just because you are paying them to do their job, and probably you will never meet, doesn't mean that it doesn't matter whether you like them or not. Trust your instincts and decide if you react well to the voice on the telephone. If you find it too authoritarian, too stupid, too snobby, too easy-going, ask to speak to the manager, and if you don't like her either, don't use the agency. If you can't get on with them instinctively before any money has changed hands, you will not respect their services as negotiators and mediators later.

A good agency will ask a lot of questions. Don't be defensive about the number of bathrooms. Don't exaggerate. Sally-Anne Lloyd of The Nanny Connection says that she likes 'employers who sound as though they have thought through all the details before they lift the phone. They describe the nanny's room precisely, and they don't make it sound as though they are doing the nanny a huge favour.' Agencies use the phone all day for screening purposes. They are quick to suss out any sham.

Some agents provide excellent aftercare and their intervention, when requested to deal with a problem, can save much misery and difficulty. An agent with 25 years' experience was rung up not long ago by an employer who couldn't stand her nanny loping round the house with bare feet and putting them up on her polished furniture. The nanny said that she thought she could do as she pleased as far as *that* little detail was concerned. The agent was asked to mediate. She spoke to the girl 'Whose house are you working in? Do you think you are at the seaside?' It was an explosive issue, and if handled badly would have been a surefire case of 'for the want of a shoe . . .', but the nanny respected her agent's view and is still in residence.

Questions to ask an agency

An agency isn't used to being asked many questions by employers, so these will be a good test of keenness to help.

- Where do the applicants come from and how do you find them?
- What does the agency *mean* by the terms 'trained' and/or 'experienced'? Do they have a minimum age?
- How much do its nannies cost to employ per week? (Don't let an agency tell you that you can't afford one, that's your business.)
- What is the agency fee, their refund and/or replacement policy and guarantee period?
- How would they describe their interview methods? (You want the Spanish Inquisition and some indication that they do turn down some applicants.)
- Do they check all references properly? By letter or phone or both? How many references do they require and from whom will they accept them? How old can the references be? Do they require a complete record of the girl's working life?
- What after-care does the agency provide? What are their general attitudes to employers and nannies? (Few agents maintain their balance sitting on that fence.)

Beware:

- One-woman bands working from kitchens or front rooms mushroom and vanish monthly. Aftercare and repayment of registration fees are unlikely
- Registration fees may be a rip-off unless you receive a list of available nannies by return post
- Bad agencies attempt to charge the would-be employee. This is illegal
- Bad agencies are too lazy to check references. The employer should always double-check
- Bad agencies don't offer aftercare for girls they have placed. This is unprofessional. (Good ones will also provide a list of other local nannies, and abroad too.)
- Bad agencies may attempt to lure your nanny to another job once she has been with you for some time
- Bad agencies do not give an adequate guarantee period. Less than six weeks is silly
- Bad agencies risk your privacy and security by sending out detailed lists of employers' phone numbers and circumstances
- Bad agencies send girls abroad without proper instructions, briefing or back-up
- Bad agencies put pressure on a nanny or employer to accept a match for the sake of their fee
- Bad agencies crack up jobs to be something they ain't. (Working in a theatrical family *may* be glamorous or *may* involve extra long hours and tension while actors are 'resting'.)
- Bad agencies never see the girls on their books. Personal interviews make happy placements much more likely.

What Employers Say About Agencies

The only employers who have words of praise for the agencies are those with good nannies who feel that the agency fee was well worth it and that the agency saved the employer trouble by doing a good job. Employers are often as resentful about agency fees as they are about their nannies' salaries. Do what you can afford and shop around. If the cost is not the point compared with your aim to find a competent loving professional to care for your children, then you are quids in, in every sense but literally.

There are many agencies who provide an excellent service, but it will be your bad luck, and theirs, if they have not got anyone suitable at that time whom you like. A lot of it is skill. A lot of it is luck, for the agents and the employer.

> I can't stand high-handed staff. It never matters how much you can afford, they always say that's not enough.

> I don't think they screen the girls or check references properly.

> I just call six or seven and hope for the best.

> At last I have found a brilliant one. I send so much business their way that they sent me a bunch of roses last month.

> I always use agencies so that there is some comeback if the nanny is unsuitable. I don't think I'm a great interviewer and I value their experience.

> I like agencies run by ex-employers of nannies best, and occasionally those run by really professional ex-nannies. They have the best grasp of the problems.

> One agent told me that if she had a ventriloquist's dummy which said it could drive, she would place her twenty times over right away. It's hard to forget that view of agencies.

Agencies Specializing in Nannies

The agencies listed below have been generous with their time, not just with this chapter, but with advice for many angles and ideas in the book as a whole. The comments are personal, as is the choice. None of the largest has been excluded, but the list is far from exhaustive. We have deliberately not included a few agencies in this edition because employers could find nothing good to say about them. Should readers find that their favourite has been neglected in this edition, we would welcome comments and suggestions.

Fees are classified as 'below average' if less than £350 for a permanent residential nanny, 'average' if between £350 and £550, and 'above average' if more than £550–£1500 and more. The same phrases have also been used much more loosely in connection with proxy mothers, babysitters or maternity nurses.

Addap Personnel, 42 Newmarket Street, Falkirk FK1 1JQ Tel: 01324 636101
Fees: well below average.
Mrs Adele Pickles runs this delightful agency, which is the only one that anyone recommends in Scotland. She has been dealing

with nannies since 1986 and the majority of her clients get NNEB trained nannies from her and occasionally maternity nurses, temps and mother's helps.

'We get lots of calls from London. I send more mature girls there mostly to avoid homesickness problems. We liaise closely with the local NNEB college and everyone is carefully interviewed.'

Anglo Nannies London, 20 Beverley Avenue, London SW20 0RL
Tel: 0181 944 6677
Fees: average.
In 1989 Mrs Omur Yeginsu started placing nannies in England and abroad. She provides a full menu of daily and live-in nannies, trained and mother's helps, Antipodeans, au pairs, maternity nurses, babysitters and temps, and also sends English teachers to Turkey as governesses. She also sends nannies abroad to Turkey, where she has an office and a strong nanny circle, and to Germany, France, Switzerland, Far East and Middle East and to America, but only with a permit. She is highly recommended for maternity nurses.

'We handle business in a professional way in a proper office. We keep careful records and run the show honestly. We know this is a service job and we work very hard to get good results.'

Annie's Nannies, (main office) l43 Chatham Road, London SW11 6SH Tel: 0171 924 6464 and (subsidiary) 69 Caversham Road, London NW5 2DR Tel: 0171 267 6432
Fees: average.
This interesting and innovative business is run by friendly Annie Prior, who was a professional musician and then in PR, before starting the agency seven years ago. They are the only agency who offer daily nannies *only*. They have every variety of daily nanny , mother's helps and nanny shares, full-, part-time, permanent and temps. This agency produces some uniquely helpful paperwork for both nannies and employers – interview questions from both angles, details of a babysitting club, a comments form for remarks about their service, an excellent specimen contract and details of an insurance service.

'Our nannies range from 18 to 50 and have to be more flexible than ever before'

Bees Knees/ Impec Agency, 53 Church Avenue, East Sheen, London SW14 8NL Tel: 0181 876 7039
Fees: average.

Mrs Crane started this agency in 1980. Her clients are mainly local, but her nannies and au pairs come from all over the world. She has built up a regular clientele and provides both daily and live-in nannies, au pairs and babysitters, housekeepers and domestic dailies. References are always checked before placement.

'As the mother of two small children, I understand the problems and am a good listener. My success lies in personal service. I never raise false hopes.'

Bellamy Nannies, Office 27, London House, 271 King Street, London W6 9LZ Tel: 0181 748 3838
Fees: average and good value for more than a decade's experience in Central London.
Proprietor since 1984, Mark Rolo is a favourite with *Guide* readers. He is happy to be surfing again on the surge of successful nanny business which characterizes the end of the Nineties. He offers nannies, maternity nurses, Australians and New Zealanders. About 50 per cent of his business is now abroad and mostly in Europe, where his girls are very well paid 'articulate and look the part; they also teach the children to speak English'. They have fixed rates instead of taking a cut of the nannies' salaries, which ensures that they do not press employers to raise them for the agency's benefit. Mark is chatty and thorough and fair.

Bligh Appointments, 131/7 Earls Court Road, London SW5 9RH Tel: 0171 244 7277
Fees: average and above average.
A two-tier structure comprises a two-month guarantee and replacement scheme for £650 plus VAT or you can choose to pay a straight £400 plus VAT as a flat fee. Louise Bentley, who trained as a teacher and did nannying for six months when she arrived here, runs this cheery place. They deal with Australian, New Zealand and South African nannies and mother's helps. Their office in Sydney helps them to check out references. They interview everyone shrewdly and carefully. Temps and part-time available too.

'Our nannies are much in demand because they are flexible and willing to turn their hands to anything. They are keen to learn and kind of worldly by the time they've crossed it to get here.'

Bunbury Domestic Employment Agency (Everybody Needs Somebody), Foxdale, Bunbury, Tarporley, Cheshire CW6 9PE Tel: 01829 260148
Fees: below average/average.

Proprietor since 1972, Leila Potter is a redoubtable personality whose clients are loyal and admiring. Bunbury is deliberately run as a rather offbeat and extremely personal service. She produces all sorts of staff and every assignment is treated as a challenge. Her successful 'Rosey Rota' system for Alzheimers' sufferers is typical of her positive approach. She lectures at NNEB colleges, her service is quick, efficient and always accomplished with style and fun. This all makes using this nanny agency an amusing experience.

'I think our proxy mother service is pretty good. We have a nationwide appeal nowadays. Most mothers are working which makes the nanny scene friendlier. We don't like to be too business-like.'

Canonbury Nannies and Nannies Plus, 12a Haven East, l46 Dalston Lane, Hackney E8 1NG Tel 0171 923 9978
Fees: average.
Denise Bailey, mother of three, has taken over from Amanda Drury and runs three branches in Islington, Mill Hill and Hackney. She runs daily, live-in and shared nannies, a few maternity nurses, temps, part-time, proxy mothers and au pairs.

'Many of our nannies have lots of experience so you can call on them for any job. They aren't cheap but they are tremendous.'

Care At Home ('Cura Domi'), 54 Chertsey Street, Guildford, Surrey GU1 4HD. Tel: 01483 302275
Fees: above average.
Robert Flatt, Helen's son, has taken over the agency. They have a large team of professional carers whom she does not call nannies. All the managers are trained nurses and the emphasis in this company is on professionalism and total dedication to the children with special needs in their care. It is impressive.

'We recruit from all over the country. We provide 24-hour backup. We try to make it possible for these very dependent children to live to their greatest potential. We are as responsible for that child as if he were our own.'

Childminders, 9 Paddington Street, London W1M 3LA Tel: 0171 935 3000 and 0171 935 2049
Fees: average.
Going since 1967, this agency is under the same ownership as the Nanny Service. The manager is Julia Eason, a Norlander. It provides babysitters *only* from a pool of 1,500 people who operate all over London and the suburbs. This is the largest agency of its kind in England and, they think possibly, in the world. They have 300-

500 bookings a week. There is an annual membership fee of £35 plus VAT and they charge less than £3 per hour on weekdays, more on Saturdays and as a daily rate. Parents must reckon on hiring for a four-hour minimum and paying for their fares. They have many long-standing members who are happy with this service.

'We have masses of student nurses from all the major teaching hospitals, nannies and teachers on our books, and lots of otherwise experienced people and we are very busy every day. We vet everybody thoroughly and they are all over 19.'

The Chiltern College Register, Peppard Road, Caversham, Reading, Berks RG4 8JZ Tel: 01734 471847
Fees: above average.
Chiltern graduates join a supported nanny scheme, run by friendly sensible Carryl Sabine, who has been there for 22 years. She visits prospective employers to discuss their precise requirements and then, from her two-year knowledge of students' needs and personalities, Carryl makes a short list. Employers are guided with salary, tax, NI and house rules if required and for a year – 'but actually indefinitely' – support is given 'to iron out the creases'. It seems to be working very well, though unsurprisingly there are not enough nannies to meet demand.

'We have thirty jobs for every graduate. I try to make sure they get the one that will suit them best individually.'

ComputaNanny, 206 Hammersmith Grove, London W6 7HG
Tel: 0181 746 1108
Fees: well below average.
Started in 1991, this new and effective idea for an agency has been successful and is admired by employers. It is run by Nicky Baly, mother of three with a refreshingly upfront, friendly approach. The computerized service costs £225 and aims at a high turnover and low fees. References are checked, but girls are not necessarily interviewed. Nannies and mother's helps, Australians and New Zealanders are a speciality.

Cotswold Nannies, Lilac Cottage, Bisley, Glos GL6 7AF Tel: 01452 770076
Fees: below average.
Camilla Despard has been working here for five years now and keeps the place both successful and cosier than many London agencies. She provides nannies, mother's helps and maternity nurses. Good interview and back up.

'We have an office in Australia and we make the girls come to England for a minimum of a year and the English go and work out there too on the same basis.'

Delaney International, Middleton Lodge, Munstead Heath Road, Godalming, Surrey GU8 1AR Tel: 01483 424343
Fees: above average.
Proprietor since 1991, Marcia Delaney, an ex-lawyer, one-time au pair in France and has hired her own, has stopped doing au pairs and moved into nannies. She does things thoroughly and well, but charges for it. She specializes in Australian and New Zealand mother's helps, many of whom have done a short nanny training there and she has agents down under who work exclusively for her.

The Dulwich Nanny Agency, 40 Chancellor Grove, West Dulwich, London SE21 8EG Tel: 0181 761 2973/333 7486
Fees: average.
Started more than three years ago, Samantha Franey and Gabriella Vianello run this popular agency which covers the whole of London. They were both nannies for seven years and their experience certainly helps them help employers and nannies to deal with each other equally. They are soon opening another branch in Hampstead. They deal in nannies of all kinds, maternity nurses and temps, both here and abroad, and about 40 per cent of their nannies are Antipodean.

Elder Recruitment, Emberton House, 26 Shakespeare Road, Bedford MK40 2ED Tel: 01234 352688
Fees: average.
Elizabeth Elder has run this agency for 16 years and her experience is much appreciated by locals in Bedfordshire and elsewhere. She is an agent for Au Pair in America and deals in nannies, whom she recruits from the good local colleges, and in au pairs.
'I look for someone who will fit in with the families round here. I can see at a glance if they will share their values and standards.'

Family Match Ltd, 12 Southgate Street, Winchester, Hants SO23 9EF Tel: 01962 855799
Fees: average.
Jenny Warner has run this agency since 1993 which provides nannies, mother's helps, au pairs and maternity nurses. It is growing, and locals regard it highly.

Fry Staff Consultants, 48 Gravel Road, Farnborough, Hants GU14 6JJ Tel: 01252 540761
Fees: below average.
Proprietor since 1971, Mrs Eileen Fry knows she prefers professional trained nannies whom she places more in the UK than in Europe these days. She also provides mother's helps and maternity nurses.
'I like serious girls. I'm always available to help them should they need me. I give them long pep talks, but I pick the nicer ones and they know how to behave. I have always had very high standards'.

Global Au Pairs and Nannies, St Brides House, 32 High Street, Beckenham, Kent BR3 1BD Tel: 0181 650 4860
Fees: average.
Anne-Marie Skupien has moved into the business of nannies because so many of her clients needed to be told that they should not leave au pairs in sole charge of pre-school children and she felt she must offer an alternative. Her au pairs are especially well tended – she runs coach trips to touristic sights often for any au pairs locally who want to go.
'There are more bad clients than there are bad au pairs. But there are problems with nannies too. It is very hard to get live-in ones at present and they are extremely demanding.'

Harborne Nannies, 106 Greenfield Road, Harborne, Birmingham, B17 0EF Tel: 0121 428 4944
Fees: average.
Caroline Cofman has run this agency since April 1996, but she first qualified as a nursery nurse in 1982 and has worked as a nanny, in a post-natal hospital ward and in a nursery. She has two children as well. She mostly has qualified nannies on her books, and they are mainly daily and local.
'Only Norland tells students to learn to drive. I can't place the ones who can't. Around us, people don't just want drivers, they want people to be car-owners as well.'

Help At Hand, Enterprise House, 113 George Lane, South Woodford, London E18 1AN Tel: 0181 530 8464/989 5164
Fees: average.
Barbara George, who used to work with June Warriner the former owner, took over the business in 1995. She supplies nannies, mother's helps and au pairs, and is an agent for Au Pair America.

Hutchinson's, 33 Princes Gate Mews, London SW7 2PR Tel: 0171 581 0010
Fees: just above average.
Frances Hutchinson has long experience as an agent and an excellent reputation. She has excellent maternity nurses and experienced nannies available for London and abroad. This is a professional and efficient service.

'I'm not into computers. We see all the applicants and the girls and I am determined that in the people business it is vital to get a good match of personalities. We have very few failures, an even 95 per cent success rate.'

Hyde Park Nannies, 2nd floor, 85 High Street, Winchester, Hants S023 9EH Tel: 01962 841234
Fees: average/above average.
Jennifer Harrison has run this large, busy agency since 1990, although it has been operating much longer. She provides any private household staff including qualified or experienced nannies in the UK and abroad. She gives a unique five-year guarantee on the fee and this is a popular agency with London employers. Pam Holmes runs their temp and maternity business from a London base at 31 Huggins Place, London SW2 3UQ Tel: 0181 671 1399.

Imperial Nannies, 25 Thurloe Street, South Kensington, London SW7 2LH Tel: 0171 581 1331 and freephone 0800 614465
Fees: above average.
Sarajane Turnbull owns this thriving agency which started in September 1996. They check references and are equally solicitous about both clients and nannies and, uniquely, were determined to turn down bad employers as well as bad nannies. They only offer 21 plus girls, who have had a minimum of a year in private service. There is also a sister agency called **Maternally Yours** (on 0171 581 4994) which specialises in maternity nurses.

Janet White, 67 Jackson Avenue, Leeds LS8 1NS Tel: 0113 2666507
Fees: below average/average.
Janet White is a Canadian who has lived here for more than 20 years and started her agency in 1978. It provides mother's helps, nannies, maternity nurses and au pairs both in the UK, Europe, Canada and many other places in the world. She is also a regional organizer for Au Pair in America.

'I screen them carefully and always think "would I like you to look after my children?"'

Kensington Nannies (also Nannies Kensington), 49/53 Kensington High Street, London W8 6ED Tel: 0171 937 2333/3299
Fees: average.
Mrs Teeling-Smith and Gilly MacWilliam own this agency and the latter has worked there since 1976. Long established and well respected, this establishment agency provides nannies, mother's helps and maternity nurses both in the UK and overseas. Many Australians and New Zealanders are available through them. This is a perennial favourite with employers and nannies alike.

'Nothing's changed except that we've got fussier. We see at least 15-20 girls each day. We interview carefully and welcome nannies with the right attitude.'

Knightsbridge Nannies, P.O. Box 7772, London SW6 2YN Tel: 0171 610 9232
Fees: above average.
Julie Bremner has taken over this agency. She has temps, maternity nurses, mother's helps and nannies working both in the UK and in top jobs abroad.

'There are a lot more jobs than nannies now. I have a good pool of Princess Christian and Norlanders'.

Koala, 22 Craven Terrace, London W2 3QH Tel: 0171 402 4224
Fees: average.
Australians and New Zealanders are handpicked by Catherine Mansel Lewis and Dale Headington at this busy agency. They have nannies, mother's helps, a few cooks and housekeepers.

'We are fairly stringent. We don't feel any pressure to take anyone who's not right. We have built up a good reputation that way.'

Lifesavers and Ideal Nannies, London House, 271/273 King Street, London W6 9LZ Tel: 0181 748 4868
Fees: average.
Karen Murphy has more dailies than live-in nannies and parttime, temps and shares, mother's helps and maternity nurses.

'I am honest and realistic and insist that employers and nannies are too. We interview everyone.'

Lloyd's Agency, 32 Kensington Place, Newport, South Wales NP9 8GP Tel: 01633 216710
Fees: below average (twice gross weekly wage).
Gaynor Lloyd set up this mainly domestic staff and nanny agency

in 1989, largely because when she had her son she couldn't find a good Welsh child care agency. It is now the largest and longest established agency in Wales, and places nannies and mother's helps everywhere, and sends British girls abroad too.

Mill Race Nannies, 5 Victoria Road, Sevenoaks, Kent TN13 1YD
Tel: 01732 742987
Fees: below average.
Karen Smart and Hilary Burdis run this very good small agency, which started in 1985. They offer nannies and mother's helps, and their speciality is Australians and New Zealanders. They acquire the latter from Rangi Ruru Nanny School, Auckland, which is the first (3-month) course in nanny training in New Zealand. Employers and girls swap detailed requirements and descriptions and the nannies pledge to stay for a year. It seems to work well.

Monroe Nannies, 34 Brook Street, London W1Y 1YA Tel: 0171 499 8867
Fees: above average.
Jane Street has run this agency since 1984. It specializes in trained and experienced nannies, mother's helps and maternity nurses available for work in London, Europe and the Middle and Far East. Over 50 per cent of its work is now international. They recruit only half their applicants. Interestingly, Jane says that nannies working for families in the home counties are, for the first time, now earning the same as their counterparts in London. This is an up-market and professional business.

'Our clients want vocational nannies who want to make a commitment. The salaries reflect these mothers' desire to have and pay for proper professional child care.'

The Nanny Agency, 38 Ridgeway, Epsom KT19 8LB Tel: 01372 722519 and other branches in Kensington (0171 938 2299) and Muswell Hill (0181 883 3102).
Fees: average.
Four years ago Nina Kaye began this conscientious, likeable agency. She not only meets all the nannies who apply for jobs, but also all her clients as well. This is not loose talk but good practice adhered to also by her franchisees. They offer a reliable support system for both employers and nannies. Their clients are very appreciative.

'Lots more regulation for agencies and checking out nannies like childminders would decrease the horror stories'.

Nannies Incorporated, Room 317, The Linen Hall, 162–168 Regent Street, London W1R 5TB Tel: 0171 437 1312
Fees: above average.
Annie Martin owns this company and is mostly to be found in their branches in Paris or Brussels, but Sarah Simpson runs the nanny section in the London office. This is a swish and extremely impressive set-up started in 1989. The emphasis is on maternity nurses, which are excellent, but they have nannies as well. This is a very employer-friendly agency and highly recommended by many.

The Nanny Connection, Stern House, 85 Gloucester Road, London SW7 4SS Tel: 0171 835 2277
Fees: average/above average.
Sally-Anne Lloyd worked as a nanny and then at The Nanny Service for five years before setting up this agency in 1987. She has attracted a lot of Australians and New Zealanders on to her books, along with NNEB nannies and a few mother's helps and temps. The agency reflects the owner's bubbly, bright, practical nature, continuing to maintain high standards and remaining a great favourite with employers and nannies alike.

'Suddenly we are back in a world where there are more jobs than girls after the recession and we are really busy.'

The Nanny Service, 9 Paddington Street, London W1M 3LA Tel: 0171 935 3515
Fees: above average.
Paul Rendle owns this agency, which has been going since 1976. Corrina Slater has been there since 1995 and is in charge of nanny placements and maternity nurses, mother's helps and lots of reliable temps, a boon in emergencies. References are checked and girls are always interviewed. Australians and New Zealanders are available through them.

The Nanny Service (East Midlands), 10 Mill Road, Oundle, Peterborough, PE8 4BW Tel: 01832 274420
Fees: average.
This approachable grandmother makes an excellent agent. Carole Williams has been running this place for seven years after a lifetime of journalism, PR, full-time motherhood, a degree in psychology and a later career in admin in the health service. She has mostly daily nannies, many of whom are trained locally.

'The colleges don't tell the girls how to look for a job, but they do tell them not to accept a live-in one.'

Network Special Needs Agency, 154B Ewell Road, Surbiton, Surrey KT6 6HE Tel: 0181 390 5845
Fees: average.
Lucy O'Donnell has just married and re-started her excellent small agency, which acts as much as a help and advice line as a business. She has many years of experience with special needs children and their problems and is an incredibly helpful, idealistic agent who is also effective. The special needs world has been bereft of her wisdom and contacts in her absence – welcome back Lucy!

Newbury Nannies, Rye Cottage, Peasemore, Newbury, Berks RG16 0JN Tel: 01635 248091
Fees: average.
Rosemary Head, Nicola Walters and Anne Collins run this confident happy agency and provide nannies, maternity nurses, mother's helps, temps and babysitters. Norlanders are often available. They interview everyone and take up references.
'The wages remain exorbitant but employers expect really good value for money. It takes a lot of time and trouble to place people correctly.'

The Norland Registry, Norland Nursery Training College, Denford Park, Hungerford, Berks RG17 0PQ Tel: 01488 681164
Fees: There is a non-returnable deposit of £35 to engage a probationary nurse. Then she can be employed on payment of £800 plus VAT and a qualified nurse will cost you £900 plus VAT.
Mrs Ward runs the Norland Register and prospective employers are advised to write or telephone and will then be sent a registration form. They fill in their requirements and it is a good idea to send a detailed job description with a covering letter and some photographs too. The details are then circulated and the Registry seeks to match employers' requirements to nurses' capabilities and wishes. Norlanders contact the Register for many years after qualification for long-term and temporary situations, where they are often wanted for maternity work or as proxy mothers. Even those with school-age children often ring up requesting short-term posts.
Probationers are guided by the Principal and the Registrar in their choice of post but 'their learning is fresh in their minds and they are very keen to make a success of their first job in order to qualify for the full Diploma.' The College provides excellent back-up.

Norfolk Care Search Agency, 19 London Road, Downham Market, Norfolk P38 9BP Tel: 01366 384448
Fees: below average.
Mrs Parker is an SRN and health visitor who provides experienced and trained nannies, 'new' nannies and mother's helps. She enjoys a high reputation as does her agency, which has been going since 1985.
'I look for nannies who really love children and are safe, kind and caring.'

North London Nannies, 92 Creighton Avenue, London N10 1NT Tel: 0181 444 4911
Fees: average.
Jackie Lewis has run this agency since 1983 and has four children herself. She supplies trained nannies and mother's helps. She also deals in au pairs. Interviews and aftercare are good and there are lots of appreciative noises made by satisfied customers. She is currently keen on South Africans for nannies and trained Eastern bloc girls, who marry Englishmen, for au pairs.

Occasional and Permanent Nannies, 2 Cromwell Place, London SW7 2JE Tel: 0171 225 1555
Fees: above average.
This is an agency with a long-standing reputation for carefulness and thoroughness. They supply nannies, mother's helps, governesses and maternity nurses in the UK, Europe and abroad, and are renowned for good temps.
'It's extremely friendly in the new offices with lots of toys and all open plan with everyone chatting. Everything is going fine.'

Pembroke Maternity Service, P.O. Box 449, London W8 4RX Tel: 0171 727 5058
Fees: below average.
Patsy Smith has run this specialized agency, which provides maternity nurses of every kind, since 1986. She has exacting standards, befitting an ex-Great Ormond Street trained nurse, where she held responsible positions for many years before becoming a maternity nurse herself. She is reassuring, direct and kind. Interviews are excellent and advice and aftercare constantly available. Many agencies who find maternity work a nuisance hand on their clients' enquiries to her.
'All my business is by word of mouth and we have had no complaints at all. We deal with twins, triplets and quads sometimes and have excellent nurses on our books.'

Pre-Select Staff Agency, 924 Stratford Road, Springfield, Birmingham B11 4BT Tel: 0121 702 2100
Fees: above average.
Set up by Sue Wasmuth in 1983, this innovative agency now does domestic and estate staff, and only highly qualified nannies. Sue was one of the first to develop a contract for employers and is also a member of the Institute of Employment Consultants. She keeps a stable of career nanny pros and choosey wealthy employers. She runs a health check questionnaire which she reckons tells her a lot more than a police check – 'it's too general and the girl has to have gone to court for her to have a record, and even then anything minor is wiped off soon. Our health checks through doctors attest to mental and physical stability.'

The Princess Christian College Register, 26 Wilbraham Road, Fallowfield, Manchester M14 6JX Tel: 0161 224 4560
Fees: above average.
Mrs Rigby is still inundated with inquiries at her small college.
'It is quite impossible to meet demands.' Although people take it rather personally when they fail to make the top of the list, many go on trying.

Quick Help Agency, 307A Finchley Road, London NW3 6EH Tel: 0171 435 7671
Fees: just above average.
Mrs Norma Cutner, the proprietor of this agency since 1971, speaks French. Although Mrs Cutner has some English nannies, she specializes in Australians, New Zealanders and South Africans. They are always girls with previous nannying experience who are interviewed in their home countries and arrive to work in pre-selected jobs. Mrs Cutner reckons on an 85 per cent success rate.
'Most of my clients want the nanny/mother's help/housekeeper type and these young women have a practical approach to domestic life.'

Regency Nannies, 50 Hans Crescent, London SW1X 0NA Tel: 0171 225 1055. Another branch is dedicated to the overseas division: 2 Penta Court, Station Road, Elstree, Herts WD6 1SL Tel: 0181 905 2221
Fees: above average.
Eileen Wright has owned this big thriving agency since 1983. It supplies nannies, mother's helps, excellent temps, proxy mothers

and is particularly known for a large pool of maternity nurses both in the UK and abroad. This is a thoroughly professional outfit.

'We have set up a separate division for the international placements which will be my baby. We have had a very busy time lately, but we are always pleased to provide the exceptions, like a special nurse for a sick baby.'

Rockinghorse, 3 Oatlands Road, Oxford OX2 0EU Tel: 01865 246188
Fees: average.
James Cridland took over this agency in November 1996 and is now supplying nannies, mother's helps, maternity nurses and babysitters locally and throughout the southern counties from Wales to Southampton, and rather more than previously to London. He also runs a care agency called Camomile Care.

Swansons, 4 Brackley Road London W4 2HN 1QD Tel: 0181 994 5275
Fees: average.
Anne Babb has provided nannies and mother's helps since 1983. She is a delightful person to deal with and interviews everyone 'eventually' and issues weekly lists. She also rings up if a possible match appears between lists. References are always checked and good, reliable aftercare is offered. Clients are mostly local, though nannies come from all over the country. Employers recommend this agency highly.

'Smaller agencies often take greater care than big ones. They may have a larger selection of girls, but they don't often take as much trouble as they should.'

Tinies, Nexus House, Riverdene Industrial Estate, Molesey Road, Hersham, Surrey KT12 4RG Tel: 01932 254747.
Fees: above average.
Janet Trethewy started this agency in 1975 and has sold franchises. There are now seventeen branches, mostly round the M25, linked by their owners being trained by the franchisors, Janet Trethewy and Susan Boothroyd, and using a common operational manual. They all set aside one room as an office and work from home. They provide nannies, mother's helps, temps, maternity nurses and proxy mothers.

'One of our strengths is that girls are passed from office to office, so we can be very useful if a temp is needed desperately.'

Top Notch Nannies and Brilliant Au Pairs, 22a Campden Grove, London W8 4JG Tel: 0171 938 4742/2006
Fees: average.

Jean Birtles has been running this rather off beat agency for five years. She is chatty and approachable and worked in education previously. She has nannies, mother's helps, babysitters (at £4 an hour on weekdays) au pairs, maternity nurses, temps and part-timers.

'It's definitely a nanny's market nowadays. We are in touch with New Zealand colleges and bringing them over. We will wind up scouring China to find them!'

Universal Aunts, PO Box 304, London SW4 0NN Tel: 0171 738 8937
Fees: variable.

This agency was set up in 1921 as a personal service bureau. Now there are offices in different parts of London with a central switchboard. Mrs Sinclair and her staff provide nannies, mother's helps, daily child care babysitters and proxy mothers amongst a host of other services. They are famous for their proxy mothers – Universal Aunts originated the service. They are 'women of some experience' – ex-nannies, Montessori teachers, nurses or mothers who have brought up their own children. Another excellent service is meeting and dispatching prep and boarding school children at the beginning and end of school terms and putting them up for occasional nights when they need to catch their connections on flights or trains the following day.

'There is always a demand for the proxy mothers particularly. Our clients have used us for years.'

Universal Care, Chester House, 9 Windsor End, Beaconsfield, Bucks HP9 2JJ Tel: 014946 78811
Fees: below average.

Peter and Gillian Cullimore have been running this agency since 1987 and provide nannies, mother's helps, au pairs and proxy mothers. Their staff includes an SRN and they have close contacts with their local NNEB colleges where they hand out Universal Care awards to the best students.

'Our aim is to give a complete service from a professional office with excellent organization.'

Wallaroo, 3 Adam and Eve Mews, London W8 6UG Tel: 0171 937 7075
Fees: above average.

Clare Williams runs this Australasian-based business and says that male nannies are hard to place in the UK because British husbands can't cope. She is friendly and helpful and has all the usual variations of nannies and maternity nurses and an excellent babysitting service and weekend nanny register.

Wealden Nannies, Ringle Crouch, Sandhurst, Cranbrook, Kent TN18 5PA Tel: 01580 850585
Fees: below average.
Rosemary Broadbent, an SRN, set up in 1985 and provides mother's helps and nannies and a lot of temps. They come from excellent local colleges. She runs a personal and reliable service. She interviews, checks references and provides excellent aftercare.

'We interview every applicant for at least 45 minutes and after all these years I think I have a good idea of whether they'll be any good or not.'

Westminster Nannies, 16 The Croft, Clevedon, North Somerset BS21 6AT Tel: 01275 876082
Fees: above average.
Jill Bassett has run this admirable business since 1988 and knows just what she's about. She was a nanny, then mother of five and is now a granny. More than 80 per cent of her nannies go to jobs abroad in extremely prestigious families all over the world – she is particularly well established in the Middle East, though she sends girls to jobs everywhere – in one week recently to Egypt, Australia, Malaysia and India. Her clients want experienced nannies from their twenties to their sixties and Jill interviews them thoroughly 'often for at least a couple of hours' and takes several references from her overseas clients also.

'I think when I interview the nannies – would I like you to be working for me? And with my clients – would I like my daughter to be working for you? I am easy-going and don't force anybody to do anything they don't want to and I see both sides of any question. Recommendations come by word of mouth and things rarely go wrong.'

Woodford Nannies, Southview, Lower Woodford, Salisbury, Wiltshire SP4 6NQ Tel: 01722 782782
Fees: average.
This is a brand new agency with a very good boss called Clare Mutch, who deserves great success with it because she is so

knowledgeable, capable and conscientious. She was herself a nanny for 12 years, of which the last seven were in maternity work. She has excellent contacts, therefore, and provides maternity nurses, nannies and mother's helps. She meets both clients and nannies.

'I think nannying is a brilliant job which should be vocational. I am very fussy but I have placed some really good girls. I want to improve the nanny recruitment scene and I really care deeply about getting good nannies into the right jobs for them.'

Yorkshire Nannies and Nurses, 26/27 High Street, Doncaster DN1 1DW Tel: 01302 349393
Fees: 10 per cent of annual gross salary.
For 20 years Christine Braim has been running this solid agency, which provides qualified and experienced nannies in the UK and abroad, mother's helps and temps. Everyone is interviewed on the premises and girls must bring a photo and references from previous employers and a full career history. Employers appreciate her down-to-earth approach.

'I am very fussy. The girls are grilled and drilled and I don't accept everyone. Some NNEBs are like babies.'

Agencies Specializing in Au Pairs and Mother's Helps

Like the agencies that concentrate on nannies, when you ask an au pair agency how it places its au pairs, most put great emphasis on 'recommendation', i.e. one mother has used it and tells her best friend it is marvellous. But as often as not an employer rings six agencies on the trot and plumps for the one that has a suitable girl ready to start work immediately. An agency's success depends a lot on whether they are lucky enough to have the right girl at the right time.

Most agencies recruit girls from commercial agencies (and several state ones) in Europe. They may have as many as 20 or 30 such agents scattered about the continent who advertise for girls and organize their papers. The European agent receives a fee from the girl for getting her a job in the UK; it receives nothing from the UK agent.

Agents also talk about 'contacts', which can mean anybody – their aunt, a friend, school and university teachers, embassies, the British Council – or an au pair they have placed in the past does a bit of agency work herself and vets local girls. 'Contacts' are good news for the au pair employer. Many agencies zone in on two or three countries where they have a special link, and gather the majority of their September and December harvest there.

Some UK agencies also advertise in foreign papers and periodicals. In the UK a great many advertise in *The Lady* magazine and in local papers, but most of them favour the Yellow Pages.

Some are proud to say they never advertise. They say this is because they don't need to. Many of the one-woman bands that are au pair agencies are comfortably placing 100 to 200 au pairs a year and have built up the business to an extent that makes advertising superfluous. The bigger agencies recruit more girls – 400 to 600 plus – and are more likely to advertise. One big agent comments, 'I never believe these agents who say they don't need advertising – what they mean is they can't afford it.'

References

Most agencies say they ask for at least two written references from the au pairs recruited from abroad. The 'walk-in' au pair girls already in this country often don't have references from abroad with them. Most agencies don't check an au pair's references. They say flatly that they cannot afford the time or money given their fees, to make overseas phone calls, which is fair enough. Others say that references are checked 'where possible' by the European agency involved; some will have actually interviewed the girls in person. Others, often the smaller agencies, where the owner has direct links with the prospective au pair's homeland, are likely to have a brief chat with the girl concerned so that doubts and queries can be cleared up straight away.

A few agencies ask for a registration fee or deposit which has to be sent with the agency's completed questionnaire about the client's requirements and information about her family. This fee may be deducted from the final bill once an au pair has been found for the client, or it may be an unrecoverable, once-only fee. Most others work on a 'no au pair no fee' basis. Many agencies want their full fee, once you have agreed on a particular au pair, before divulging the girl's address and telephone number.

Most agencies say that they will replace a girl who doesn't work out after about two to three weeks. A lot won't refund; some have a sliding scale. It isn't a problem with many agencies as they give the employer two weeks' grace to make up her mind about the girl before expecting payment. If a girl leaves early, for example after four months, because of some crisis at home, good agencies will come to some arrangement to compensate for the lost months. A few replace completely free of charge if the girl lets the family down and leaves before she is meant to.

Cost

Rates of pay for an au pair are between £30-£45 for a week of five hours a day five days a week and the top end of that for London. Au pairs used to have a minimum of one full day off a week, but now the Home Office stipulates two days off. If you can afford it and/or you reckon she has a tougher job than other au pairs – like several small children to handle, plenty of housework, quite a lot of sole charge, or she has to walk miles to the nearest bus – then pay above the local rate. A litmus test is to say, 'Would I do this job for this pocket money if I was an au pair in a foreign country?' Otherwise pay her what you think is *reasonable* as the Home Office puts it, rather than exploitative, given her duties.

Many agencies, particularly around London, can arrange 'au pair plus' i.e. a longer working week for more pay. Girls from the European Union often want full-time work and they are not restricted by the 'au pair agreement' the Home Office monitors. Many girls from outside the EU want to spend the free half of their day doing an English language course and so don't want the extra hours' work.

Most of the agents interviewed for the following pages were helpful and gave the impression they were responsible, offering everything you would expect from a good agency, like an 'aftercare' service for employers and girls if they had problems, and some sort of replacement deal if things didn't jell. They all say they require two references, a medical certificate and two colour photographs.

Whatever they tell you when you ring them, it is wise to be sceptical and spell out to the agency the sort of au pair you don't want, e.g. minimal English or one who doesn't want to go to classes. Trying for a good match is a luxury, too often the host family has to take whatever is available. Girls have the same problem, because they need somewhere to live, they accept any family and only after the event do they become clear themselves about what sort of host family they'd prefer.

One London agency with a good reputation comments: 'I can't give you the names of the cowboy agents but, believe me, there are loads of them. The number of girls I get in here in tears because the job wasn't what she thought it would be. One au pair the other day was thrown out because she smoked 40 cigarettes a day. It seemed that the employer said she didn't want a smoker and the girl claims she said she smoked on her form. These agents aren't doing their homework.'

Summer au pairs

Summer au pairs are popular because they aren't around for long, but they can give working parents or a busy mother a break. Many agents place around 40 to 50 summer au pairs a year. For once there are usually more girls seeking summer jobs than families wanting them. Many families only learn about this type of au pair through friends, who have had a happy experience with a short-stay au pair. They are particularly useful to keep an eye on school age children in the long summer holidays

One agent comments: 'It's quite a different deal. There are no classes to go to so the girls spend a lot of time with the families and they are much more flexible about the number of paid hours they are prepared to be on duty. Because they stay only for the summer holidays I only take on girls with good English. A lot are teachers on holiday or girls who are about to go to college.

Living abroad

Many of the agents listed below also place British girls as au pairs, and would be delighted to help anyone planning to live abroad who wants part-time help. Within the EU there are no restrictions about taking a British mother's help either.

Nationality of agents

Where possible the au pair agency list below highlights the non-British origins of the agents and/or whether they have been au pairs or have ever hired them. Being of foreign extraction is a plus in the au pair business, not least because the agent probably speaks at least one other language fluently and is likely to have good contacts with agencies and girls back home. It is a good idea to ask the agent if she speaks any other language and to go for the girls that the agent knows most about, i.e. she speaks the same language or was born in the same country.

Choosing an au pair agency

Most employers have about three or four agents whom they ring and use regularly. Loyalty to an agent reaps dividends, in that the agent naturally makes great efforts for a tried and tested employer who pays her fee promptly and has a good track record as hostess to the girls she hires. It is very much pot luck whether the girl you are assigned to is going to be a success, as nobody, including her, can place much confidence in her child care skills, since this is likely to be her first and only au pair job.

Fees

Usually agencies either concentrate on nannies or au pairs. Mother's helps fall between the two and neither type of agency majors in them. It is usually cheaper to recruit a nanny or a British mother's help from a mainly au pair agency because the bulk of its overheads – and time and expertise – goes on its au pair business. The smaller number of mother's helps or nannies, who perhaps live locally, are windfall placements.

Fees listed below are rated 'below average' if under £120 for a six months or more placement, 'average' is £120 to £130 and 'above average' is anything between £130 to £180. Agents who work from home charge the least: £100–£120. Nanny and mother's helps' fees are rated as for the nanny agencies.

The Agencies

NB: MHS = MOTHER'S HELPS

The Adam Agency, 139 North Hill, London N6 4DP Tel: 0181 348 4004
Fees: below average.
Proprietor since 1982: Swedish-born Mrs Kerstin Adams. Medium-sized au pair agency, Swedish girls only. Mrs A comes to visit clients in their homes in London so she can get an idea of the sort of girl they will like.

Au Pair Agency Bournemouth, 45 Stroudon Road, Bournemouth BH9 1QL Tel: 01202 5326
Fees: below average, but high registration fee.
Proprietor since she founded it in 1977: Mrs Andrea Rose. A big, long established au pair only agency, which places girls all over the south west as far as Bristol and into West Sussex.

The Au Pair Company, 2 Welch Place, Pinner, Middlesex HA5 3TA Tel: 0181 429031
Fees: above average. Nannies = twice weekly net wage.

Founded 1987. Partners Annabel Wagner and Pamela Sinclair offer au pairs, MHs and some nannies. Do all nationalities all over UK but a preponderance of Turkish and Slovenian girls.

Au Pairs International, 59 Redland Street, Newport, Gwent NP9 5LZ Tel: 01633 859422
Fees: way above average.
This small au pair and mother's help agency, set up in 1991, is a subsidiary of Welsh firm Redland Human Resources, and is run by Wendy Frewin. It specializes in Dutch and Czech girls and also places British girls abroad.

Au Pairs of Surrey, England, 7 Highway, Edgecumbe Park, Crowthorne, Berks RG45 6HE Tel: 01344 778246
Fees: average. FRES member.
Wendy and Gordon Gibbings now run this well established, big au pair-only agency which took over well known Avalon and Linden agencies. Recruits from all countries and services the southern counties.

Bees Knees Agency (see also nanny agencies), 53 Church Avenue, East Sheen, London SW14 8NL Tel: 0181 876 7039/948 5134
Fees: expensive, way above average.
Proprietor since 1980: Mrs S Crane. She specializes in nannies, MHs, and UK and overseas au pairs. She is French and so does a lot of work with France. She also places British girls in nanny and MH jobs abroad.

The C.A.R.E. Agency, 71 Fellowes Road, London NW3 3JY Tel: 0171 916 0117
Fees: average.
This company has been going for 30 years and Julia Stebbing runs it now. Never advertises. Good after care service which gets girls in touch with their country's clubs, Julia concentrates on matching personalities: 'I very much enjoy it and we are as busy as ever.'

East-West Au Pairs, Squire House, Pickett's Hill, Headley, Hants GU35 8TD Tel/Fax: 01428 714814
Fees: below average.
Proprietor and founder since 1992: Sarah Coleby has Eastern European connections, so concentrates on Czech and Slovak Republics. But 'these countries have quite small populations so

after the post Communist initial flood, the supply of girls has
dropped and it's difficult to meet demand.'

Edgware Au Pair Agency, 19 Manor Park Crescent, Edgware,
Middlesex HA8 7NH Tel: 0181 952 5522 Fax 0181 951 1005
Fees: average.
Founder and proprietor since 1963: Lorraine Bass, who speaks five
languages. Big au pair, demi and au pair plus agency. Is a regional
organizer for Au Pair in America and has lots of East European
girls: 'They are flooding in and are really good,' says Mrs Bass. She
promotes boy au pairs but only takes high quality applicants: experience of children already, a driver, can stay a year. She also says
'Once a family has had one, after that they always want a boy.'

European Au Pair Agency, 89 Valance Road, Lewes, Sussex BN7
1SJ Tel/Fax 01273 474738
Fees: average.
Proprietor since 1990: Czech-born Alena Stone. A small agency
specializing in Czechs, though does other European countries too.

Euroyouth Ltd, Educational Holidays, Paying Guests and Au
Pairs, 301 Westborough Road, Westcliff-on-Sea SS0 9PT Tel:
01702 341434
Fees: below average.
Proprietor since 1961: Austrian-born Mrs Hancock. Au pairs only.
A well-established agency which never advertises.

Fiola Agency, 89 Fulford Grove, Watford, Herts WD1 6QJ Tel:
0181 428 5883
Fees: below average.
Judi Bayly runs a very much part-time business placing au pairs
only. 'I am fussy about the girls and the families. If I'm not sure
about either, I won't match them just to get business.'

The German Catholic Social Centre, Lioba House, 40 Exeter
Road, London NW2 4SB Tel: 0181 452 8566
Fees: way below average.
Run by Miss A von Oy since 1971. A non-profit making organization which organizes trips and outings for young German-speak-
ing women staying in London. German girls can stay at the hostel
for a few days on arrival and the Centre finds them a family. All
employers have to call *in person* and meet the manageress to help
successful matching.

The German YWCA/Verein fur Internationale Jugendarbeit, 39 Craven Road, London W2 3BX Tel: 0171 723 0216
Fees: the YWCA asks for a donation and pitches its suggested figure a bit lower than the cheapest agency.
Part of a worldwide non-commercial organization, which has been going in London since 1978. It is not a hostel and it recruits direct from Germany with excellent access to girls and boys wishing to be au pairs. It has a thorough aftercare service with organized trips and events.

Global Au Pairs and Nannies, St Bride's House, 32 High Street, Beckton, Kent BR3 1BD Tel: 0181 874 2324
Fees: above average plus VAT. Nannies: average plus VAT.
FRES member. Dates from l989, current proprietor: Mrs Skupien who speaks French and German. FRES member. Does more au pairs (good back up: organizes trips and socials) than Mhs and nannies, but the latter is being built up.

Handihelps Ltd, 484 Honeypot Lane, Stanmore, Middx HA7 1JR Tel: 0181 951 5827
Fees: below average for au pairs and for MHs and nannies.
Founded in 1981. Proprietors since 1989: Mrs Maureen Green, who does the live-out (which the company specializes in) and Mrs Joy Russell, who does the live-in. Both former employers of au pairs. The company majors in living-out care including babysitters. It also provides au pairs, mainly Spanish, Hungarian and Croatian.

Helping Hands Au Pair and Domestic Agency, 39 Rutland Avenue, Southend, Essex SS1 2XJ Tel: 01702 602067
Fees: bottom end of average.
Long-established agency now run by Sandra Clark, which provides MHs, au pairs, au-pair pluses and demi-pairs from EU countries .

Home from Home, Walnut Orchard, Chearsley, Aylesbury, Bucks HP18 09A Tel: 01844 208561
Fees: above average.
Proprietor since 1992: Carolyn Turner, who runs a small agency, personally recommended to the *Guide*. She was an au pair once, worked for the National Trust and speaks fluent French. Very good after-care service for her mainly French and Hungarian girls and a few boys.

Ianda Au Pair Agency, 3 Green Acres Drive, Stanmore Middlesex
HA7 3QJ Tel: 0181 954 9900
Fees: below average.
Proprietor since 1982: Mrs Suzanne Aarons. Fairly large au pair
and MH agency. Mrs Aarons says 'less girls now that EU girls can
get ordinary jobs. Clients ask for au pairs but what they mean is a
mother's help who can run the house while they're at work.'

Islington Au Pair, Box 358, Edgware, Middlesex HA8 8JA Tel:
0181 203 4243 Fax: 0181 203 3404
Fees: average.
Owned by Mrs Bass of Edgware Au Pairs. It is designed to suit
working parents: open from 5–9.30 pm weekdays and 9–5 pm Saturdays. Places in north London and neighbouring counties.

Janet White Employment Agency, 67 Jackson Avenue, Leeds LS8
1NS Tel: 0113 2666507
Fees: average but plus VAT. Registration fee is deducted.
FRES member. Proprietor of this medium sized nanny and au pair
agency since 1978 : Janet White does au pairs for the north of England (see also nanny agencies).

Jolaine Agency, 18 Escot Way, Barnet, Herts EN5 3AN Tel: 0181
449 1334
Fees: average.
Proprietor since 1975: Mrs Irene Rendlick. A big au pair agency
which also does all other domestic staff and paying guests.

Labe Au Pairs, Littlewood, Crossfield Place, Weybridge, Surrey
KT13 0RG Tel: 01932 820076
Fees: average.
Proprietor since 1992: Valdka Murphy. Mrs Murphy was once an
au pair herself and specializes in au pairs from her native Czechoslovakia, where she has plenty of contacts, and which she visits to
recruit each year. She says, 'Czech girls are popular because
they're not spoilt and they come over here for the right reason: to
learn English'.

Leeside Agency, 107 Leeside Crescent, London NW11 0JN Tel:
0181 455 8496
Fees : top end of average.
Swiss born Lea Ferney set up her agency in 1977. She speaks
French and German and has strong contacts in Switzerland and so
does mostly Swiss au pairs for all over the UK. Never advertises.

Lloyds Agency, 32 Kensington Place, Newport, South Wales NP9 8GP Tel: 01633 216710
Fees: above average.
Owner of this mainly nanny agency since 1989, Gaynor Lloyd. She has a special relationship with Turkey and places a lot of Turkish au pairs in Wales. She says 'Turkish girls seem actually to want to live in the country, unlike most other nationalities.' Impressive and rare policy of refusing to place an au pair with a child under two years old if the parents work, even if one or other of them works at home.

London Au Pair & Nanny Agency, 4 Sunnyside, Child's Hill, London NW3 5JY Tel: 0171 435 3891
Fees: Au pairs and nannies: average.
Maggie Dyer runs this small agency, which does mostly au pairs and some nannies. A caring, intelligent service. She won't place au pairs sole charge while mum's at work.

Metro Agency, 4 Yarrowside, Little Chalfont, Bucks HP7 9QL Tel: 01494 765173
Fees: above average.
Swiss born Susanne Singh set up her agency in 1979. She speaks Swiss, German, Italian and French. She has mostly Swiss girls and some Czech and places them all over the UK, but chiefly locally and in London. Almost uniquely, she talks to every girl by phone and won't take them if their English is too poor. She holds coffee mornings for locally placed girls.

Mondial Agency, 32 Links Road, West Wickham, Kent BR4 0QW Tel: 0181 777 6271
Fees: below average.
Mr Talbot set up this au pair and paying guest agency in 1949, now his widow, Mrs J Talbot, runs it. Places au pairs especially French, Austrian and Spanish. Does summer au pairs. Covers South East and Greater London.

The Montrose Au Pair Agency, 23 Bullescroft Road, Middlesex HA 8RN Tel: 0181 958 9209 Fax: 0181 905 4157
Fees: 4 times weekly wage + average for MHs, au pairs: just above average.
Proprietor since 1983: *Guide* reader-recommended Linda Taylor, who offers au pairs countrywide and especially MHs from the Antipodes and South Africa.

Mum's Army, 10 Hither Green Lane, Redditch, Worcs B98 9BW
Tel: 01527 61661
Fees: above average.
Proprietor: Marian Farr since 1987. Middle-sized au pair only agency placing a lot of German girls all over the UK, except London.

The Personal Au Pair Service, 273 Eversholt, London NW1 1BA
Tel: 0171 383 5581 Fax: 0171 387 9086
Fees: above average.
Proprietor since 1985: Ms Teresa Godbold, speaks several languages. Above-average sized au pair agency specializing in Swedish and Danish girls. Most of her au pairs and MHs are already in London and she interviews them all. The rest she brings over from abroad. 'I used to visit all the families, but it took so much time, I found it doesn't help particularly. My role model has been Sister Sheelah at St Patrick's. She is so caring. She taught me about matching family and girl; it's so important.'

Problems Unlimited Agency, 86 Alexandra Road, Windsor, Berks SL4 1HU Tel: 01753 830101
Fees: just above average.
Founder and proprietor of this fairly large agency since 1980: Mrs Hilli Matthews, who speaks French, Italian and some German. Recruits from these countries, also Spain, Yugoslavia, Turkey, Czechoslovakia and Hungary and some English MHs. Also places British girls abroad. Has a few boy placements. Has produced her own book 'Au Pairs Without Tears' and is thoroughly convinced of the need to match au pairs with families. She won't place girls with pre-school children where the mother is out at work full-time.

Putney Au Pairs, 32 Rusholme Road, London SW15 3LG Tel: 0181 785 0040
Fees: above average.
Set up in 1996 by Nicky Adams and Janie Stevens. Small personal au pair-only agency which recruits mainly Swiss girls. Good back up info pack, au pair coffee mornings. Nicky says 'We concentrate on Putney, so we're here and can see girls if they have a problem. Most agencies are miles away from their placements.'

Quick Help Agency, 307A Finchley Road, London NW3 6EH.
Tel: 0171 435 7671
Fees: just above average.

Proprietor since 1971: Mrs Norma Cutner, who speaks French. She places and receives girls from all over Europe. One of the biggest au pair agencies. (See also Nanny Agencies.)

St Patrick's International Centre, St Patrick's School, 24 Great Chapel Street, London W1V 3AF Tel: 0171 734 2156/439 0116
Fees: below average.
Manageress since 1984: Sister Sheelah Clarke. St Patrick's has a language school and houses the International Society for Catholic Girls (see Addresses) which has a social programme for young people. Mostly au pairs, some MHs.

Simply Domestics, 65 Coney Hatch Lane, London N10 1LR Tel: 0181 444 4304 Fax: 0181 444 4791
Fees: average for au pairs; below average for nannies and MHs.
Proprietor and founder since 1989: Judith Ivers, who concentrates on au pairs and every kind of domestic from Greater London, because of her poor experience trying to find help for her three children. She says: 'We're not out to place a girl and forget about her. We have proper aftercare with a friendship circle.'

Solihull Au Pair and Nanny Agency, 1565 Stratford Road, Hall Green, Birmingham B28 9JA Tel: 0121 7336444 Fax: 0121 7336565
Fees: average for all, but plus VAT.
A sister company of, and bigger than, Mrs Bass's Edgware Agency. It is run by Pat Ryall who organizes every kind of child care including maternity nurses and nannies anywhere in the UK.

Stepping Stones Christian Agency, Hunts Wood House, Harpsden, Henley on Thames, Oxon RG9 4HY Tel: 01491 577076
Fees: above average for au pairs, average for nannies.
Louise Vincent set up this Christian au pair, nanny and MH agency in 1994. She has mostly Swiss, German and Hungarian girls, also Antipodeans. 'Many employers like the idea of employing a Christian and whatever their denomination – Catholic, Baptist – nannies and au pairs seek me out, the others avoid me!'

Swan Au Pair, 47 Oakhill Road, London SW15 2QJ Tel: 0181 459 0692 Fax: 0181 877 3462
Fees: just above average.
Proprietor and founder since 1989: Joanna Tennant. Marks to this au pair-only agency for being a FRES member. Concentrates on

girls from Switzerland, Norway, Czechoslovakia, Turkey and
Yugoslavia. Mrs Tennant speaks French and Spanish and hires her
own au pairs for her three children. She looks after her au pairs
once placed (mainly in London SW postal districts); they receive a
list of other local au pairs and the *Foreign Students' and Au Pairs'
Magazine*.

Other useful places to contact: the local Catholic priest and/or
convents. Many convents in London put up foreign Catholic girls.
The best known is the Convent of Mary Immaculate, 16 Southwell
Gardens, London SW7 4NR Tel: 0171 373 7007, which often has
girls looking for a family. There is no fee but a donation is appreciated, as with all convents.

Resourceful employers also put notices up in the churches and
clubs of the various nationalities like the Swedish Church and the
Danish Club (see Useful Addresses). The Swiss Benevolent Society at 83 Marylebone High Street, London W1M 3DE, tel: 0171
935 1303 cares for Swiss girls and will help families to find au pairs
by putting them in contact with appropriate agencies.

Feedback?

The authors would welcome advice, information and opinion
to augment and update the next edition of *The Good Nanny
Guide*. If you use an agency, we would like to hear what you
thought of it, if you have a firm view about any aspect of the
profession we would be glad to receive it. Please write to us
c/o Vermilion, Random House, 20 Vauxhall Bridge Road,
London SW1V 2SA or fax 0171 840 8406.

Useful Addresses

Au Pair in America, 37 Queen's Gate, London SW7 5HR Tel: 0l71 581 2730

Business & Technician Education Council (BTEC), Central House, Upper Woburn Place, London WC1H OHH Tel: 0171 387 4141. (Nursery nurse qualifications).

The Campaign for Tax Relief and Childcare, 11-13 Charterhouse Buildings, London EC1M 7AN Tel: 0171 834 9619. Group of interested bodies (like Childcare Vouchers) which campaigns for all employer-funded child care to be tax-free for employees.

Childcare Vouchers, 50 Vauxhall Bridge Road, London SW1 2RS Tel: 0171 834 6666. (A subsidiary of Luncheon Vouchers, sells businesses childcare vouchers which their employees can use in lieu of pay to anyone legally entitled to look after their children including: childminders, nannies, shared nannies, day nurseries, mother's helps and grandparents.)

Chiltern College, Peppard Road, Caversham, Reading, Berks RG4 8JZ Tel: 01734 471847

Christine Hill, Strand End, 78 Grove Park Road, London W4 3QA Tel: 0181 994 4349 (excellent ante- and postnatal classes and professional support).

City & Guilds of London Institute, 46 Britannia Street, London WC1X 9RG Tel: 0171 278 2468

Council for Awards in Child Care and Education (CACHE), 8 Chequer Street, St Albans, Herts AL1 3XZ Tel: 01727 867333

The Danish Church, 5 St Katherine's Precinct, Regent's Park, London NW1 4HH Tel: 0171 935 7585

The Danish Club, 62 Knightsbridge, London SW1Y 7JX Tel: 0171 235 5121

The Dutch Church, 7 Austin Friars, London EC2N 2EJ Tel: 0171 588 1684

The Federation of Recruitment and Employment Services (FRES), 36–8 Mortimer Street, London W1N 7RB Tel: 0171 323 4300

The Kensington Committee of Friendship for Overseas Students, Basement, 13 Prince's Gardens, London SW7 1NE Tel: 0171 584 3989 between 10.30 am and 5.30 pm weekdays only. (Excellent social introductions for an au pair who may enjoy this charity's full programme of events for small membership fee. Once a month there's a large tea party where members can bring a friend.)

The International Catholic Society for Girls, 24 Great Chapel Street, London W1V 3AS Tel: 0171 734 2156

The Isle College, Ramneth Road, Wisbech, Cambs PE13 2JE Tel: 01945 582561

The Kids Club Network (until recently known as the National Out of School Alliance), Bellerive House, 3 Muirfield Crescent, London E14 9SZ Tel: 0171 512 2112

The Lady, 39-40 Bedford Street, London WC2 9ER Tel: 0171 379 4717. Copy date: Wednesday for the following week.

The London Montessori Centre, 18 Balderton Street, London W1Y 1TG Tel: 0171 493 0165

Maternity Alliance, 15 Britannia Street, London WC1X 9JP Tel: 0171 837 1265 (Provides information on maternity rights and services, send an s.a.e. with request.)

Nannies Friendship and Information Circle, Co-ordinator: Linda Downes, 3 Rosedale Road, Toronto, Ontario, Canada M4W 2P1 Tel: 001 416 920 3409

Nannytax: Tel: 01273 3626256, Taxing Nannies: Tel: 0181 361 3755, Kathy Kelly (Ilkley Yorkshire) Tel: 01943 609524. All three are payroll companies that run special child carer tax and NICs service.)

National Association of Nursery Nurses (NANN), c/o 28 Ravenswood, Crescent, Rayners Lane, Middlesex HA2 9JN No telephone number given out. Apply in writing.

The National Association for Maternal and Child Welfare (NAMCW) 40–42 Osnaburgh Street, London NW1 3ND Tel: 0171 383 4541

National Childbirth Trust (NCT) Alexandra House, Oldham Terrace, London W3 6NH Tel: 0191 992 8637

The National Childminding Association, 8 Mason's Hill, Bromley, Kent BR2 9EY Tel: 0181 464 6164. Information line: 0181 466 0200. Mon and Tues 2–4pm, Thurs 1–3pm.

The Norland Nursery Training College, Denford Park, Hungerford, Berks RG17 0PQ Tel: 01488 682252

The Norwegian Club, 21–24 Cockspur Street, London SW1Y 5BN Tel: 0171 930 3632 Secretary: 0171 930 4084

The Norwegian Seaman's Church, 1 Albion Street, London SE16 1JB Tel: 0171 237 5587/5588. Au pairs are welcome Sunday afternoons.

The Norwegian YWCA, 52 Holland Park, London W11 3RS Tel: 0171 727 9897/9346

Nursery World, Lector Court, 151–153 Farringdon Road, London EC1R 3AD Tel: 0171 837 7224 (Deadline for nanny ads: 4.30 Thurs for following Thurs publication.)

Parents at Work, 45 Beech Street, Barbican, London EC2Y 8AD Tel: 0171 628 3578. Set up in 1985, it seeks to help working parents find good childcare. It promotes 'good practice' guidelines in childcare, has a useful handbook and free guides on child care options, childminders, nannies and nurseries.

The Professional Association of Nursery Nurses (PANN), 2 St James's Court, Friar Gate, Derbyshire DE1 1BT Tel: 01332 343029

The Princess Christian College, 26 Wilbraham Road, Fallowfield, Manchester M14 6JX Tel: 0161 224 4560

Scottish Nursery Nurses Examination Board (SNNEB), 6 Kilnford Crescent, Dundonald, Kilmarnock M14 6JX Tel: 01563 850057

TNT Magazine (The News and Travel), 14–15 Childs Place, London SW5 9RX Tel: 0171 373 3377 Fax: 0171 244 0020. *The* place to advertise for Antipodeans. Deadline: noon on Thursday for Monday publication.

Working for Childcare, 77 Holloway Road, London N7 8JZ Tel: 0171 700 0281 (This charity evolved out of the Workplace Nurseries Campaign and promotes quality child care and the needs of working parents and their children. It has a consultancy business which advises companies and local councils on the logistics of setting up day nurseries.)

Bibliography

Baby Travel, St John's Wood Press, 1987

Beyfus, D., *Modern Manners*, Hamlyn, 1992

Binswanger, Barbara and Ryan, Betsy, *Live-in Child Care*, Dolphin, 1986

Birtles, Jean and Jasmine, *The Top Notch Nanny Guide*, Summersdale, l996

Brannen, J. and Moss, P., *New Mothers at Work*, Unwin, 1988

Conran, S., *Superwoman*, Sidgwick & Jackson, 1975

Cooper, Jilly, *Class*, Corgi, 1985

Coote, A. and Gill, T., *Women's Rights*, Penguin, 1974

Cullum, M., *Becoming a Nursery Nurse*, Batsford, 1986

Cuthbert, A. and Holford, A., *The Briefcase and the Baby – a Nanny and Mother's Handbook*, Mandarin, 1982

Gathorne-Hardy, J., *The Rise and Fall of the British Nanny*, Weidenfeld & Nicolson, 1972

Gostelow, M., *The Complete Woman's Handbook*, Penguin, 1986

Griffith, S. and Legg, S., *The Au Pair and Nanny's Guide to Working Abroad*, Vacation Work, 1989

Hodgkinson, L., *The Working Woman's Guide*, Thorsons Publishers, 1985

Mulder von, Marianne, H., *Das Au-Pair-Buch*, Athenaeum, 1986

Martin, J. and Roberts, C., *Women and Employment: A Lifelong Perspective*, HMSO, 1984

Metzroth, Jane P., *Picking the Perfect Nanny*, Pocket Books, 1984

Moss, P., *A Review of Childminding Research*, Thomas Coram Institute, 1987

The LEGO National Childcare Directory, CAMC Publications (ISBN 1872838-06-5. Very useful database directory on UK private day nurseries, nursery schools and nanny agencies. Your central library should have it; if not, ask them to order it.)

New, Caroline and David, Miriam, *For the Children's Sake*, Pelican, 1987

Purves, L., *How Not To Be a Perfect Mother*, Fontana, 1986

Rice, R., *The American Nanny*, TAN Press, 1985

Scarr, S. and Dunn, J., *Mother Care Other Care*, Pelican, 1987

Slaughter, A., ed., *The Working Woman's Handbook*, Century, 1986

Solomon, J., *Green Parenting*, Optima, 1990
Solomon, J., *Holding the Reins*, Fontana, 1987
Thompson, M., *A Handbook For Nannies*, Batsford, 1986
Travers, P. L., *Mary Poppins*, Puffin, 1962
Velmans, M. and Litvinoff, S.,*Working Mother*, Corgi, 1987
Whitehorn, Katharine, *How to Survive Children*, Methuen, 1975
Woodford, S. and De Zoysa, A., *The Good Nursery Guide*, Vermilion, 1993
The Working Parents Handbook, (constantly updated by WMA), 1981

Index